FREIBURG AND THE BREISGAU

FREIBURG AND THE BREISGAU

Town–Country Relations in the Age of Reformation and Peasants' War

TOM SCOTT

CLARENDON PRESS · OXFORD
1986

Oxford University Press, Walton Street, Oxford OX2 6DP
Oxford New York Toronto
Delhi Bombay Calcutta Madras Karachi
Petaling Jaya Singapore Hong Kong Tokyo
Nairobi Dar es Salaam Cape Town
Melbourne Auckland
and associated companies in
Beirut Berlin Ibadan Nicosia

Oxford is a trade mark of Oxford University Press

Published in the United States
by Oxford University Press, New York

© *Tom Scott 1986*

All rights reserved. No part of this publication may be reproduced,
stored in a retrieval system, or transmitted, in any form or by any means,
electronic, mechanical, photocopying, recording, or otherwise,
without the prior permission of Oxford University Press

British Library Cataloguing in Publication Data
Scott, Tom, 1947–
Freiburg and the Breisgau: t-c relations in the Age of
Reformation and Peasant's War.
1. Freiburg im Breisgau Region (Germany)—Social
conditions
i. Title
943'.46 HN458.F/
ISBN 0–19–821996–2

Set by Hope Services, Abingdon
Printed in Great Britain
at the Alden Press, Oxford

I gcuimhne Mhíchíl Uí Choileáin,
16 Deireadh Fómhair 1890–22 Lúnasa 1922,
fuair bás ar son na hÉireann.

Preface

IN the long gestation of this work I have incurred many debts. Without the financial support of the British Academy and the University of Liverpool, but above all the award of a fellowship by the Alexander von Humboldt Foundation in Bonn, the book could not have been completed. The directors and staff of the many archives and libraries visited have been unfailingly helpful in making available a wide range of documentary material. A special acknowledgement is due, however, to the directors past and present of the town archives of Freiburg im Breisgau, Prof. Berent Schwineköper, Dr Franz Laubenberger, and Dr Hans Schadek, for their unstinting encouragement and advice. In Freiburg many scholars have generously placed their time and expertise over the years at my disposal: Prof. Erich Hassinger, Prof. Klaus Deppermann, Herr Josef Steinhart, Frau Rosemarie Merkel, Herr Willy Schulze, Dr Christian Dietrich, Herr Paul Prießner, the late Dr Martin Wellmer and the late Dr Folkmar Thiele. Beyond Freiburg the author has benefited from numerous conversations with Hans-Joachim Hecker (Munich), Dr R. J. Geary (Lancaster), Dr H. J. Cohn (Coventry), and Prof. S. W. Rowan (St Louis). The continuing interest and support shown by Prof. Sir Geoffrey Elton (Cambridge), under whom my original doctoral research was conducted, has been invaluable throughout many adversities. These friends and colleagues have contributed immeasurably to my argument, but the responsibility for error rests with me alone.

Liverpool, T.S.
22 August 1985

Contents

List of Tables	x
List of Maps	xi
Abbreviations	xii
Note on Proper Names	xiii
Introduction	1

PART ONE: THE TERRITORIAL TOWN IN THE LATER MIDDLE AGES

I. Freiburg and its Relations with the Breisgau	15
II. The Anatomy of a Craft Town	47

PART TWO: CRISIS AND CHANGE

III. Conflict between Freiburg and the Breisgau	77
IV. The Decline and Recovery of Freiburg's Economy	114
V. Conclusion	155

PART THREE: THE AGE OF PEASANT REVOLT

VI. The Bundschuh Uprisings	165
VII. Freiburg and the Peasants' War	190
Conclusion	229
Bibliography	236
Index	257

List of Tables

A. Compulsory Auctions, 1444–59 and 1494–1520	122
B. Rent-charges on Houses Compulsorily Auctioned, 1444–59 and 1494–1520	122
C. Known Participants in the Communal Opposition of the 1490s, Listed by Gilds	143
D. Offices Held by Members of the Communal Opposition, 1487–96	144
E. Wealth of Mastercraftsmen who Took Part in the Communal Opposition of the 1490s	145
F. Total of Craftmasters in each Gild, 1481–1550	152
G. Wealth of Craftsmen by Tallage Groups, 1481–1550	153

List of Maps

1. The Outer Austrian Lands on the Upper Rhine in the Sixteenth Century — 21
2. The Breisgau in the Sixteenth Century — 22
3. Freiburg's Territorial Development to 1600 — 43
4. Routes over the Black Forest in the Fifteenth and Sixteenth Centuries — 60
5. Location of Freiburg's Outburghers in 1500 — 83
6. The Growth of Country Markets in the Breisgau, 1200–1500 — 117
7. Reforming Priests in the Breisgau to 1525 — 193

Abbreviations

AmtKrB	*Freiburg im Breisgau, Stadtkreis und Landkreis. Amtliche Kreisbeschreibung* (4 vols. in 2, Freiburg, 1965–74)
FDA	*Freiburger Diözesanarchiv*
MGH	*Monumenta Germaniae Historica*
NF	Neue Folge (new series)
UBStFr	Johann Heinrich Schreiber (ed.), *Urkundenbuch der Stadt Freiburg im Breisgau* (2 vols., Freiburg, 1828–9)
ZFrGV	*Zeitschrift des Freiburger Geschichtsvereins*
ZGGFr	*Zeitschrift der Gesellschaft für Beförderung der Geschichts-, Altertums- und Volkskunde von Freiburg, dem Breisgau und den angrenzenden Landschaften*
ZGO	*Zeitschrift für die Geschichte des Oberrheins*

Note on Proper Names

PLACE-names are rendered according to existing political frontiers, e.g. Strasbourg, not Straßburg, Mulhouse, not Mülhausen. Only the commonest English forms have been employed: Cologne, Munich, Brunswick, but Speyer and Mainz rather than the antiquated Spires and Mayence. Freiburg im Breisgau is abbreviated to Freiburg in all references to place of publication; for clarity, Fribourg is preferred to Freiburg im Üchtland. The names of nobles are given in the language which they spoke: e.g. Wilhelm von Rappoltstein, not Guillaume de Ribeaupierre; Kaspar von Mörsberg, not Gaspard de Morimont. The German style of family titles has been retained where proper, e.g. Georg von Frundsberg, not George of Frundsberg, but the English style is used for ruling houses, e.g. margrave Karl of Baden, not Karl von Baden; duke Anthony of Lorraine, not Antoine de Lorraine. German Christian names are retained in all cases barring the German emperors and some Austrian (arch) dukes. The sixteenth-century Alemannic spelling of all other proper names is retained; variants have been reconciled to one version of each name.

Introduction

IN both history and literature town and country have traditionally been regarded as contrasting, even opposing cultures.[1] This assumption underlies much of the historiography of pre-industrial Europe which has preferred to study either urban or rural society in isolation from the other. The dichotomy runs so deep that it has skewed the central issue of economic and social debate amongst historians of early modern Europe, the transition from feudalism to capitalism. On the origins of industrialization and manufacturing capitalism, as well as on the more nebulous question of modernization, great efforts have been expended to locate the roots of secular transformation in either town or country. For a long time two divergent and, indeed, apparently mutually exclusive views have held the field: one which sees the mainsprings of economic development in towns as centres of mercantile enterprise, to which the countryside could only react or adapt; the other which argues for the rural economy as the cradle of agrarian capitalism and proto-manufacturing which created the preconditions for a fully fledged industrial revolution.

Both interpretations have recently been subjected to thoroughgoing scrutiny by John Langton and Göran Hoppe, who take issue with the premiss that town and country are self-contained and self-explanatory categories which stand in apposition to or in conflict with each other.[2] The belief in urban dynamism over against rural inertia certainly has a longer pedigree and is still more widely shared than its counterpart which posits rural progress in the face of urban stagnation. A long tradition of historians from Pirenne to Postan has seen the medieval town as breaking the mould of a closed feudal-agrarian society, whilst primary capital accumulation, commodity production and the division of labour were, according to Marx, originally located in towns. Only the penetration of urban capital could invigorate a rural economy seen as 'incapable of autonomous transformation'.[3] This approach has come

---

[1] Cf. Raymond Williams, *The Country and the City* (London, 1973).
[2] John Langton and Göran Hoppe, *Town and Country in the Development of Early Modern Western Europe* (Historical Geography Research Series, xi) (Norwich, 1983).
[3] Ibid., p. 13.

under attack from several quarters. The external impact of the urban economy upon feudal society as a means of explaining its transition to capitalism is now recognized to be incompatible with the principles of dialectical materialism which require that feudalism must collapse as a consequence of its internal contradictions.[4]

Not only, therefore, are towns now commonly seen as integral parts of the feudal system,[5] the focus of enquiry has shifted to charting the channels of capitalist development within agrarian society itself. The development of an international market for grain in the sixteenth century gave a significant impetus to the growth of capitalist demesne agriculture, which in much of north-eastern Europe depended upon servile labour.[6] In western Europe, by contrast, where manumission was widespread in the later Middle Ages, rural society divaricated into areas of hereditary peasant tenure and revocable leasehold. The seeds of capitalist transformation inherent in the latter were, as Robert Brenner has suggested, supremely and perhaps uniquely evident in England, where the lords' long-standing practice of converting customary tenancies to commercial leases resulted by the seventeenth century in their owning three-quarters of the land and in the virtual disappearance of a traditional peasant class.[7] Despite its trenchancy, Brenner's argument has not yet carried the day; his denial of any capacity for decisive capitalist development in traditional peasant society has been criticized by continental European historians.[8]

Both models of rural capitalist development are in any case open to a more fundamental objection: the areas of agrarian capitalism seldom

[4] Ibid., p. 17.

[5] John Merrington, 'Town and Country in the Transition to Capitalism', in Rodney Hilton *et al.*, *The Transition from Feudalism to Capitalism* (London, 1976), 174–5; Rodney Hilton, 'Towns in Societies—Medieval England', *Urban History Yearbook*, 1982, 7.

[6] On the apparent contradiction of a feudal institution—serfdom—supporting a capitalist mode of production cf. Heide Wunder, 'Serfdom in Later Medieval and Early Modern Germany', in T. H. Aston, P. R. Coss, Christopher Dyer, and Joan Thirsk (eds.), *Social Relations and Ideas. Essays in Honour of R. H. Hilton* (Cambridge, 1983), 271–2.

[7] Robert Brenner, 'Agrarian Class Structure and Economic Development in Pre-Industrial Europe', *Past and Present*, lxx (1976), 30–75. The quite separate attempt by Alan Macfarlane in *The Origins of English Individualism* (Oxford, 1978) to deny the existence of a true peasantry in medieval England and to affirm the rise of capitalism in the countryside from the 13th c. onwards has been adequately disposed of by Rodney Hilton's review in *New Left Review*, cxx (1980), 109–11.

[8] Cf. the symposium discussion and related contributions in *Past and Present*, lxxviii (1978), 24–5; lxxix (1978), 55–69; lxxx (1978), 3–65; lxxxv (1979), 49–67; and Brenner's rejoinder, 'The Agrarian Roots of European Capitalism', ibid., xcvi (1982), 16–113.

Introduction 3

coincide with the regions of subsequent industrial revolution.[9] That has prompted historians to turn their attention instead to the forerunners of factory production itself, the various forms of proto-industrialization in early modern Europe.[10] Aside from the spread of rural textiles controlled by urban capitalists through the putting-out system in the densely populated hinterlands of the larger commercial cities, cottage industries also grew up in the more remote, less fertile upland districts given over to pastoral agriculture. In these areas partible inheritance was common, so that lords bent upon screwing up their incomes could subdivide holdings or rack-rent, thereby forcing the peasantry to raise cash through by-employments. The correlation between marginal agricultural areas and the location of rural industries is now widely accepted.[11] And yet such economic activity was highly precarious: a relatively small rise in population or shrinkage of available land could destroy the peasants' balance of subsistence within a lifetime.[12] To seek the origins of long-term economic transformation in regions such as these may therefore be unwise. At the same time, according to these arguments, the mass of towns in early modern Europe, apart from capital cities commanding emergent national economies, is held to have lagged behind a vital rural economy, either because they were controlled by protectionist gilds hostile towards early capitalist forms of production, or else because their mercantile élites had chosen to live off rentier income (usury capital) rather than the riskier return on entrepreneurial ventures.[13]

The shortcomings of these rival interpretations, Langton and Hoppe insist, point beyond the catalogue of exceptions and anomalies inherent in any general framework of explanation to an underlying conceptual fallacy. Economic development, they argue, cannot have been driven by a dialectical contradiction of town and country, since the diversity within these artificial categories is so great as to vitiate their use as analytic concepts.[14] The increasing specialization of

[9] Langton and Hoppe, *Town and Country*, p. 24.
[10] Peter Kriedte, Hans Medick, and Jürgen Schlumbohm, *Industrialization before Industrialization. Rural Industry in the Genesis of Capitalism* (Cambridge/Paris, 1981).
[11] Ibid., 14–15, 24. Sidney Pollard, *Peaceful Conquest. The Industrialization of Europe, 1760–1970* (Oxford, 1981), 74.
[12] Langton and Hoppe, *Town and Country*, pp. 28–9.
[13] Merrington, 'Town and Country', pp. 183–4.
[14] Langton and Hoppe, *Town and Country*, p. 38. It is precisely the mutually reinforcing interdependence of agriculture and industry which Brenner believes caused the English economy in the 17th and 18th c. to outstrip its continental rivals and achieve the first industrial revolution. Brenner, 'Agrarian Roots', pp. 112–13.

production which is the hallmark of early modern Europe presupposed a growing interdependence not only between diverse agricultural districts—pastoral regions, for instance, must have constituted a growing market for the cereal produce of other areas.[15]—but between town and country as well. Whilst proto-industrialization was essentially located in the countryside, large-scale production for distant markets, as Jan de Vries has observed, required the communications and coordination which only cities could provide.[16] The correct framework within which to understand the secular transformation of European economy and society, it is now suggested, should be the geographic region which treats cities and their hinterlands as complementary dimensions of an integrated system.[17]

The pioneering achievements of regional historical analysis have largely been the work of historical geographers. In a tradition stretching back to the theories of location advanced in the nineteenth century by von Thünen[18] and much refined by August Lösch[19] in the twentieth, they have developed a methodology which seeks to explain the distribution of towns according to economic function or importance, especially in marketing and distribution. The most famous example of this method was the publication in 1933 of Walter Christaller's *Central Places in Southern Germany*.[20] Christaller proposed a locational system based upon a rank-size distribution of settlements whose level of centrality is determined by the surplus of central economic functions which they perform relative to population size. Upon this principle he constructed a grid of central places whose complementary regions (or hinterlands) formed an interlocking hexagonal hierarchy. Although Christaller's chosen measure of centrality—the number of telephone connections—was shown at the time to be seriously flawed,[21] his theory nevertheless possessed several distinct advantages. On the one hand, he was able to show that a central place need not be a town,

[15] Langton and Hoppe, *Town and Country*, p. 31.
[16] Jan de Vries, *European Urbanization 1500–1800* (London, 1984), 8.
[17] Langton and Hoppe, *Town and Country*, p. 40.
[18] J. H. von Thünen, *Der isolierte Staat in Beziehung auf Landwirtschaft und Nationalökonomie* (Hamburg, 1826).
[19] August Lösch, *The Economics of Location* (New Haven/London, 1954).
[20] Walter Christaller, *Die zentralen Orte in Süddeutschland. Eine ökonomisch-geographische Untersuchung über die Gesetzmäßigkeit der Verbreitung und Entwicklung der Siedlungen mit städtischer Funktion* (Jena, 1933; repr. Darmstadt, 1968). Eng. transl. by Carlisle W. Baskin as *Central Places in Southern Germany* (Englewood Cliffs, NJ, 1966).
[21] Cf. Ernst Neef, 'Das Problem der zentralen Orte', in Peter Schöller (ed.), *Zentralitätsforschung* (Wege der Forschung, ccci) (Darmstadt, 1972), 199–200.

thereby overcoming the rigid separation of 'town' and 'country'; on the other, he demonstrated the regularity and predictability of the location of, and intervals between, central places. Yet the drawbacks of Christaller's highly schematic system cannot be overlooked. Although his theory admits of a dynamic element—the possible multiplication of central places within a pre-ordained dispersion—it is still essentially static and normative. In elaborating a perfect-mesh hierarchy of central places he seems to ignore or deny the possibility of competition or conflict between central places of differing rank-sizes. The hexagonal grid also presupposes the neutral influence of non-economic factors, even though its regular pattern must clearly be disturbed by topographical features (mountains, lakes) and by political boundaries. Despite these objections Christaller's fundamental insights have entered the canon of historical geographers and planners. As Peter Schöller remarks, 'centrality is therefore the relative importance of a settlement in relation to its surrounding area, or the degree to which that place exercises central functions',[22] though it is now generally accepted that centrality should be measured by more than simply the provision of goods and services; central functions extend in principle to all spheres of human society and culture.[23]

At the same time, it is intrinsic to central place theory that its principal and most successful application has been to the distribution and interrelation of marketing centres,[24] and the most recent methodologies of regionalism have usually taken the existence of a market system as their main starting-point. For pre-industrial Europe the most detailed and rigorous regional analysis has been that advanced by Gilbert Rozman, based upon urban networks.

An urban network is a hierarchy of settlements differentiated according to population or commercial and administrative functions. These settlements included in the urban network are called central places and can be distinguished from ordinary villages by the presence of an administrative seat or a periodic market.[25]

---

[22] Peter Schöller, 'Aufgaben und Probleme der Stadtgeographie', *Erdkunde*, vii (1953), 172.

[23] Hans Carol, 'Sozialräumliche Gliederung und planerische Gestaltung des Großstadtbereiches. Dargestellt am Beispiel Zürich (1956)', in Schöller, *Zentralitätsforschung*, p. 414.

[24] Most notably by G. William Skinner, 'Marketing and Social Structure in Rural China', *Journal of Asian Studies*, xxiv (1964–5), 3–43; 195–228; 363–99.

[25] Gilbert Rozman, *Urban Networks in Russia, 1750–1800, and Pre-Modern Periodization* (Princeton, NJ, 1976), 33.

Drawing upon his researches on China, Japan, and Russia, as well as on the work of other scholars in France and England, he has constructed a seven-stage model of pre-modern urban development, in which the emergence of the next higher stage reflects a further degree of administrative and market integration up to national level.[26] Rozman's model is remarkable in several respects. It offers a much more elaborately phased evolution of central places than previous typologies such as the five or three levels proposed for England by Hoskins[27] and then Everitt.[28] More importantly, it argues that a mature urban system, that is, one in which all seven levels of centrality are present, is a 'pre-modern' achievement, for it pre-dates the full emergence of capitalism in the industrial revolution. Indeed, the development of a comprehensive urban system Rozman regards as the pre-condition of modern industrial society. Although the description attached to his model may mislead—the earliest stages of his hierarchy do not involve towns, whilst market centres develop at a rather later stage than administrative centres—there is little doubt that Rozman's approach (in effect a socio-economic teleology of modernization) is predicated upon the leading function of cities, so that their hinterlands appear to be relegated to a subordinate or ancillary role. The wheel has come full circle: regional development depends upon the emergence of an urban system; it alone can generate the regional economy.[29]

An emphasis on urban systems as the true determinants of regional growth, however plausible for the centuries immediately preceding the industrial age, seems less fruitful in analyzing the later Middle Ages, when the absolute size of cities and the relative density of population were much lower. In a striking inversion of the customary phraseology J. C. Russell's study of *Medieval Regions and their Cities* casts doubt on whether even an area such as the Rhineland, often loosely described by historians as 'urbanized' in the Middle Ages, deserves the epithet, since its largest city, Cologne, never exceeded a population of 40,000 throughout the period.[30] In questioning both the dominance and the

---

[26] Cf. also idem, 'Urban Networks and Historical Stages', *Journal of Interdisciplinary History*, ix (1978), 65–91.

[27] W. G. Hoskins, 'An Elizabethan Provincial Town, Leicester', in J. H. Plumb (ed.), *Studies in Social History* (London, 1955), 35–9.

[28] Alan Everitt, 'The Marketing of Agricultural Produce', in Joan Thirsk (ed.), *The Agrarian History of England and Wales*, iv (Cambridge, 1967), 466–592.

[29] Cf. de Vries, *European Urbanization*, p. 10.

[30] J. C. Russell, *Medieval Regions and their Cities* (Studies in Historical Geography) (Newton Abbot, 1972), 78.

Introduction

centrality of medieval cities he points out that regions divided amongst several political leaders might contain no one metropolitan city of overriding importance,[31] whilst the largest cities might sometimes be located at the gateway to their regions (portal cities), rather than at the centre.[32] Although Russell's methodology is considerably less rigorous and his system less detailed than Rozman's, not least because he relies on population size alone to provide an adequate indicator of centrality, his approach nonetheless reveals an apparent shift from medieval regions, only loosely defined by an urban hierarchy, to early modern regions which are driven by a generative urban system.

That transition in town–country relations is the subject of the present study, which traces the fortunes of Freiburg im Breisgau from the late fourteenth to the early sixteenth century in the regional context of the Upper Rhine. In a threefold analysis it describes the structural interdependences between a middling craft town and its hinterland from the aftermath of the late medieval agrarian crisis to the advent of consolidated autarkic territories; it charts the changing pattern of cooperation and conflict between town and country as Freiburg struggled to attain political and economic stability; and it examines the repercussions of those changes on relations between townsfolk and peasantry in the age of religious and social upheaval in Germany which culminated in the Peasants' War, the greatest popular uprising in European history before the French Revolution.

The extensive literature on town–country relations in Germany draws upon the long and illustrious tradition of regional historical studies—*geschichtliche Landeskunde*, a term, significantly enough, without an exact equivalent in English. The decentralized political structure of the Federal Republic has undoubtedly lent a fresh impetus to regional studies in the West, though they receive great emphasis in East Germany as well. Historians have devoted much of this research to the later Middle Ages,[33] for they witnessed the rise of powerful international trading cities and commercial networks in Germany, together with embryonic forms of early capitalist production radiating from these centres into the countryside, most notably the putting-out system

[31] Ibid., p. 38.   [32] Ibid., p. 231.
[33] Cf. the bibliographical survey by Rolf Kießling, 'Stadt–Land–Beziehungen im Spätmittelalter. Überlegungen zur Problemstellung und Methode anhand neuerer Arbeiten vorwiegend zu süddeutschen Beispielen', *Zeitschrift für bayerische Landesgeschichte*, xl (1977), 829–67. Cf. also Rautgundis Machalka-Felser, 'Stadt und Umland im Herrschafts- und Wirtschaftsgefüge des Spätmittelalters', *Die Alte Stadt. Zeitschrift für Stadtgeschichte und Denkmalpflege*, vi (1979), 329–47.

8 *Introduction*

(*Verlagswesen*). The most distinguished and prolific of these scholars is Hektor Ammann, who in a series of brilliant case-studies,[34] culminating in his monograph on Nuremberg's late medieval commercial significance,[35] laid the foundations for a comparative typology of the relations between cities and their hinterlands. In order to gauge the centrality of urban settlements, he argued, the radius of diffusion of five variables must be established: the penetration of urban capital into rural property (estates and rents); the circulation of coinage; the use of dry weights and measures; and the area of supply of goods and services (the market area, together with the distance travelled by market visitors).[36] On the basis of Ammann's criteria a hexagonal grid of towns and cities may be constructed in which each is accorded its appropriate centrality in an interlocking hierarchy of central places.[37] The correct weighting of the variables, however, has not been fully resolved. Some historians give precedence to the acquisition of landed property,[38]

---

[34] Cf. esp. Hektor Ammann, *Wirtschaft und Lebensraum der mittelalterlichen Kleinstadt*, i: *Rheinfelden* (Frick, 1950); idem, *Schaffhauser Wirtschaft im Mittelalter* (Thayngen, 1948); idem, 'Vom Lebensraum der mittelalterlichen Stadt. Eine Untersuchung an schwäbischen Beispielen', in Karl Heinz Schröder (ed.), *Studien zur südwestdeutschen Landeskunde. Festschrift zu Ehren von Friedrich Huttenlocher anläßlich seines 70. Geburtstages* (Bad Godesberg, 1963), 284–316.
[35] Hektor Ammann, *Die wirtschaftliche Stellung der Reichsstadt Nürnberg im Spätmittelalter* (Nürnberger Forschungen, xiii) (Nuremberg, 1970).
[36] Cf. Peter Schöller, 'Stadt und Einzugsgebiet. Ein geographisches Forschungsproblem und seine Bedeutung für Landeskunde, Geschichte und Kulturraumforschung', in idem, *Zentralitätsforschung*, p. 285.
[37] Cf. the extrapolation from Ammann's data on Schaffhausen in Peter Schöller, 'Der Markt als Zentralisationsphänomen. Das Grundprinzip und seine Wandlungen in Zeit und Raum', *Westfälische Forschungen*, xv (1962), 85–95.
[38] Cf. Rolf Kießling, 'Bürgerlicher Besitz auf dem Land — ein Schlüssel zu den Stadt–Land–Beziehungen im Spätmittelalter, aufgezeigt am Beispiel Augsburgs und anderer oberschwäbischer Städte', *Augsburger Beiträge zur Landesgeschichte Bayerisch-Schwabens*, i (1979), 121–40; idem, 'Herrschaft — Markt — Landbesitz. Aspekte der Zentralität und der Stadt–Land–Beziehungen spätmittelalterlicher Städte an ostschwäbischen Beispielen', in Emil Meynen (ed.), *Zentralität als Problem der mittelalterlichen Stadtgeschichtsforschung* (Städteforschung. Veröffentlichungen des Instituts für vergleichende Städtegeschichte in Münster, Reihe A viii) (Cologne/Vienna, 1979), 180–218, esp. 206 ff. Nicolas Morard, 'Les investissements bourgeois dans le plat pays autour de Fribourg de 1250 à 1350', in Gaston Gaudard, Carl Pfaff, and Roland Ruffieux (eds.), *Fribourg, ville et territoire. Aspects politiques, sociaux et culturels de la relation ville–campagne depuis le bas Moyen Age* (Fribourg, 1981), 89–104; Jean-François Bergier, 'Les rapports économiques et sociaux entre les villes et la campagne en Suisse au cours du temps moderne', in ibid., pp. 42–59, esp. 52–3; Heinrich Rüthing, 'Bürgerlicher Landbesitz in Höxter um 1500', in Neithard Bulst, Jochen Hoock, and Franz Irsigler (eds.), *Bevölkerung, Wirtschaft und Gesellschaft. Stadt–Land–Beziehungen in Deutschland und Frankreich 14. bis 19. Jahrhundert* (Trier, 1983), 139–68.

Introduction 9

others to the radius of rural–urban migration,[39] but beyond the differences in emphasis lies a broad consensus that the overriding criterion of centrality by the later Middle Ages was economic function, influence, and interest. The primacy of economic variables mirrors the growing dominance of commercial centres and market areas as the determinants of centrality in contrast to the pull of administrative, cultural, or legal centres such as monasteries, castles, or courts of appeal in the High Middle Ages.[40] This change is summed up in Ammann's concept of the 'economic unit' (*Wirtschaftseinheit*), a regional entity predicated upon the interaction of a city and its hinterland.[41]

The intensification of commercial networks in the later Middle Ages has led many historians to concentrate their research into town–country relations upon the metropolitan centres of southern and western Germany[42]—Nuremberg, Augsburg, Cologne—or the overseas trading cities of the Hanseatic league.[43] Even the more detailed local studies have focused on areas such as Swabia whose many smaller cities, engaged in textile manufacture for an international market, were asserting increasing economic domination of their hinterlands through the putting-out system.[44] For the mass of German towns, however,

---

[39] Ammann, 'Lebensraum', p. 287; Urs Portmann, 'Die Datenbank "Freiburger Bürgerbuch 1341–1416" als Forschungsinstrument: Herkunft der Bewohner Freiburgs im XIV. Jahrhundert', in *Fribourg, ville et territoire*, pp. 105–23.

[40] Kießling, 'Herrschaft — Markt — Landbesitz', p. 183. For the High Middle Ages cf. Klaus Fehn, *Die zentralörtlichen Funktionen früher Zentren in Altbayern. Raumbindende Umlandbeziehungen im bayerisch-österreichischen Altsiedelland von der Spätlatènezeit bis zum Ende des Hochmittelalters* (Wiesbaden, 1970) and, 'Die Bedeutung der zentralörtlichen Funktionen für die früh- und hochmittelalterlichen Zentren Altbayerns', in *Stadt–Land–Beziehungen und Zentralität als Problem der historischen Raumforschung* (Forschungs- und Sitzungsberichte der Akademie für Raumforschung und Landesplanung, lxxxviii: Historische Raumforschung, xi) (Hanover, 1974), 77–90. On appellate courts (*Oberhöfe*) cf. Franz Irsigler, 'Stadt und Umland in der historischen Forschung: Theorien und Konzepte', in *Bevölkerung, Wirtschaft und Gesellschaft*, p. 22.

[41] Ammann, *Wirtschaftliche Stellung Nürnbergs*, pp. 194 ff.

[42] Cf. Franz Irsigler, 'Stadt und Umland im Spätmittelalter. Zur zentralitätsfördernden Kraft von Fernhandel und Exportgewerbe', in Meynen, *Zentralität*, p. 2.

[43] Konrad Fritze, *Bürger und Bauern zur Hansezeit. Studien zu den Stadt–Land–Beziehungen an der südwestlichen Ostseeküste vom 13. bis zum 16. Jahrhundert* (Abhandlungen zur Handels- und Sozialgeschichte, xvi) (Weimar, 1976); idem, 'Probleme der Stadt–Land–Beziehungen im Bereich der Wendischen Hansestädte nach 1370', *Hansische Geschichtsblätter*, lxxxv (1967), 38–57; Evamaria Engel, 'Zu einigen Aspekten spätmittelalterlicher Stadt–Land–Beziehungen vornehmlich im Bereich von Hansestädten', *Jahrbuch für Geschichte des Feudalismus*, iv (1980), 151–72.

[44] Ammann, 'Lebensraum', *passim*; Rolf Kießling, 'Stadt und Land im Textilgewerbe Ostschwabens vom 14. bis zur Mitte des 16. Jahrhunderts', in *Bevölkerung, Wirtschaft und*

employed in artisan production, governed by craft gilds and catering for their immediate market area (*Umland*) these findings simply do not apply. Without the commercial clout of the mercantile cities these lesser communities were often hard put to preserve their influence and authority over the surrounding countryside in the face of economic competition and territorial consolidation. Their experience is only intelligible, therefore, in the context of their wider region.

For Freiburg and the Breisgau lying at the foot of the Black Forest half-way between Basel and Strasbourg that region is the Upper Rhine. Alongside Saxony and parts of Franconia the Upper Rhine experienced some of the most rapid transformation of economy and society in late medieval Germany. For these were the areas of greatest economic diversification and specialization as well as social differentiation and stratification, characterized by the rise of commodity production, the growth of an internal market, the division of labour, and class formation, in short, by those features which mark the transition from feudalism to early capitalism. But whereas Saxony's economy was driven by the territorial mining industry and Franconia's by the pull of Nuremberg's international commerce, the Upper Rhine had neither the raw materials nor the capital resources to emulate its rivals. Its hallmark was neither the state enterprise of princes who exploited their regalian mining rights nor the entrepreneurialism of urban merchants engaged in manufacturing through the putting-out system, but rather the generative activity of the rural economy in an area of dense population, monocultures, and partible inheritance. The pattern of settlement and system of landholding, more Mediterranean than Germanic, encouraged at an early stage the commercialization of agriculture and its integration into an urban market system.[45] The key to the resilience of the rural economy lay in the specific nature of the Upper Rhine as a broad alluvial valley flanked by mountain ranges. As

---

Gesellschaft, pp. 115–37. Cf. Irsigler, 'Stadt und Umland im Spätmittelalter', p. 7 and the general survey by Hermann Kellenbenz, 'Rural Industries in the West from the End of the Middle Ages to the Eighteenth Century', in Peter Earle (ed.), *Essays in European Economic History 1500–1800* (Oxford, 1974), 45–88.

[45] Cf. Etienne Juillard, 'Paysans d'Alsace, paysans rhénans', in *Paysans d'Alsace* (Publications de la Société Savante d'Alsace et des Régions de l'Est, grandes publications vii) (Strasbourg, 1959), 624. For the 16th c. cf. Albrecht Strobel, *Agrarverfassung im Übergang. Studien zur Agrargeschichte des badischen Breisgaus vom Beginn des 16. bis zum Ausgang des 18. Jahrhunderts* (Forschungen zur oberrheinischen Landesgeschichte, xxiii) (Frieburg/Munich, 1972).

a region it comprised both valley and mountain, upland and plain, forest and clearing, pasture and arable, country crafts and industrial crops, nucleated villages and dispersed farmsteads. Within the primary sector, therefore, the interdependence of supply and demand gave rise to an unusually intense degree of market exchange and monetary circulation.

The Upper Rhine, moreover, was a region of notorious territorial fragmentation and political rivalry, exacerbated in the sixteenth century by confessional divisions. Neither the greater territorial princes—the Austrian Habsburgs and the margraves of Baden—nor the leading cities with their rural dependencies—Basel and Strasbourg —were powerful enough to dominate the economy of the region. The dispersion of economic and commercial power amongst a multiplicity of central places only accelerated the exchange of goods and diversification of production. Against this background the ordinary craft towns, accustomed to controlling resources and distribution within their immediate hinterlands, faced a severe challenge to their traditional function and autonomy. Nowhere were these difficulties more tellingly exemplified than in the shifting fortunes of the leading town on the right bank of the Rhine, the capital of the ancient duchy of Zähringen, Freiburg im Breisgau.

By the fifteenth century Freiburg was the principal town of Outer Austria, the collective designation for the Habsburg lands on the Upper Rhine. Lying at the foot of the Dreisam valley the town reckoned as its hinterland both the fertile Breisgau plain to the west and the Black Forest hills to the east. In the face of steep decline from the mid-fourteenth century onwards Freiburg's hopes of economic and demographic recovery depended to a large extent upon consolidating its legal and political influence over, and exploiting the human and material resources of, its variegated hinterland. But these efforts not only brought the town into frequent conflict with the surrounding lords and peasants, they were in any case hampered by the political fragmentation of the Breisgau, an Austrian possession heavily indented by several lordships belonging to the margraves of Baden, one indeed on Freiburg's own doorstep. Yet the price of its eventual success was the estrangement of that hinterland, with fateful consequences for the town amidst the gathering storm of rural unrest which was to discharge itself on the Upper Rhine with peculiar ferocity during the Peasants' War of 1525.

By using the methodology of town–country relations this case-study of one community and its hinterland on the Upper Rhine consequently challenges the prevailing interpretation of the Peasants' War as a 'revolution of the common man' which united town and country. In that sense it is more than an analysis of regional transformation: it is a contribution to the theory of revolution.

PART ONE

THE TERRITORIAL TOWN
IN THE
LATER MIDDLE AGES

I
Freiburg and its Relations with the Breisgau

I

WITH the death in 1218 of duke Bertold V the most powerful dynasty in South-West Germany, the house of Zähringen, became extinct. Its lands along the Upper Rhine to the foothills of the Alps, once governed as a coherent whole, devolved upon collateral lines and fell asunder. Out of the partitions and political entanglements which followed grew a maze of fragmented territories and overlapping jurisdictions which lay strewn across the map of South-West Germany until the Napoleonic Wars.[1] Yet one noble family contrived to turn this endemic instability so shrewdly to its advantage that it was able to exert decisive influence upon the fortunes of the Upper Rhine for the next six hundred years—the Zähringers' successors, the counts of Habsburg.

By the thirteenth century the Habsburgs held vast but scattered possessions in southern Germany, Switzerland, and Alsace. When Rudolf of Habsburg was elected to the German throne in 1273, he seized the chance of using imperial authority to forge these hereditary lands into a unified state. At first he sought to revive the old Hohenstaufen duchy of Swabia as a Habsburg principality, but his efforts were baulked by stern resistance from neighbouring territorial lords.[2] Even on the western frontiers of the Empire, where dynastic and imperial interests coincided, Rudolf found his attempts to extend Habsburg control beyond the confines of Upper Alsace thwarted by the vigilant opposition of the Imperial Free Cities, foremost among them Strasbourg.[3] With the Habsburgs' loss of the imperial title for

---

[1] On the Zähringers cf. Theodor Mayer, 'Die Zähringer und Freiburg im Breisgau', in idem, *Mittelalterliche Studien: Gesammelte Aufsätze* (Lindau/Constance, 1959), *passim*, esp. 375–6; idem, 'Der Staat der Herzöge von Zähringen', in ibid., pp. 350–64.

[2] Cf. Hans Erich Feine, 'Die Territorialbildung der Habsburger im deutschen Südwesten vornehmlich im späten Mittelalter', *Zeitschrift der Savigny-Stiftung für Rechtsgeschichte, Germanistische Abteilung*, lxvii (1950), 192–3; Karl Siegfried Bader, *Der deutsche Südwesten in seiner territorialstaatlichen Entwicklung* (Stuttgart, 1950), 68–9.

[3] Feine, 'Territorialbidung', p. 210; Theodor Mayer, 'Die Habsburger am Oberrhein im Mittelalter', in idem, *Mittelalterliche Studien*, p. 381.

more than one hundred years at the beginning of the fourteenth century any further hope of resurrecting the duchy of Swabia as the nucleus of a territorial state across the breadth of southern Germany was dashed. By then, in any case, growing involvement in the east, above all the task of administering the newly won Austrian lands, had deflected the Habsburgs' attention away from the Upper Rhine. The shift was symbolized in their change of title: the counts of Habsburg became the dukes of Austria.[4]

Although thereafter the Habsburgs had to trim their western ambitions to the more modest dimensions of other German princes, the strategic attraction of forging a territorial link between their Rhenish, Swabian and Swiss possessions still remained. Success depended ultimately upon gaining political control of the Breisgau on the right bank of the Rhine. Despite the slow and piecemeal accumulation of lands and jurisdictions the Habsburgs never lost sight of their original design, but since they were territorial intruders in the Breisgau their advance was constantly challenged by local lords who felt their power threatened.[5] The Habsburgs at least enjoyed the great advantage of having gained a foothold in the south of the Black Forest as early as the thirteenth century. There the lordship of Hauenstein and the stewardship of the abbey of St Blasien, one of the most powerful Benedictine foundations in Germany, formed a western bridgehead into the Breisgau.[6] On the upper reaches of the Rhine itself the Habsburgs were already lords of the so-called Forest Towns— Rheinfelden, Säckingen, Laufenburg, and Waldshut—which stood as bulwarks against the Swiss along the vital artery of trade between lake Constance and Alsace.[7] After 1300 skilful intervention in the struggles between burghers and their lords allowed the Habsburgs to establish their authority over the towns of Villingen and Bräunlingen,

---

[4] Feine, 'Territorialbildung', pp. 232; 215.

[5] For several centuries the Habsburgs had owned a few scattered estates in the Breisgau, but these were inadequate as a basis for state-building. By 1300, moreover, the most famous possession, castle Limburg on the Rhine, had passed from the Habsburgs to the counts of Freiburg. Martin Wellmer, 'Der vorderösterreichische Breisgau', in *Vorderösterreich. Eine geschichtliche Landeskunde*, ed. Friedrich Metz, 2nd edn. (Freiburg, 1967), 271.

[6] Ibid., p. 271. The abbey of St Blasien did not submit to Austrian territorial jurisdiction until 1361.

[7] The Habsburgs themselves had founded Laufenburg, Säckingen and Waldshut, the latter to protect their St Blasien subjects. Rheinfelden, originally a Free City of the Empire, was pawned to the Habsburgs in 1330, who retained it with short interruptions. Karl Schib, 'Die vier Waldstädte', in *Vorderösterreich*, pp. 377–81.

both important crossroads on the upland routes from Rhine to Danube. With the purchase in 1355 of the lordship of Triberg in the heart of the Black Forest the stage was set for a major penetration of the Breisgau from the east.⁸

Several lesser Breisgau lordships had already fallen under their control. During his reign the German king, Rudolf of Habsburg, had acquired the stewardship of St Trudpert, a Benedictine monastery in the Münster valley east of Staufen,⁹ but the real expansion came in the first half of the fourteenth century. Two imperial towns on the Rhine, Neuenburg and the strategic fortress Breisach, were mortgaged to the Austrian dukes in 1331; around that date too, Kastelberg and Schwarzenberg, two lordships in the north of the Breisgau which controlled routes over the Black Forest through the Simonswald and Glotter valleys, passed into the hands of the Habsburgs. And in 1365 after prolonged litigation with the margraves of Hachberg they upheld their claim to inherit the lordship of Kürnberg with the town of Kenzingen, though it was pawned to Strasbourg for much of the next century. By the 1360s, therefore, the Austrian dukes controlled important, but largely peripheral, territories throughout the Breisgau. With the acquisition of Freiburg in 1368 the situation changed dramatically.

At that time Freiburg was far and away the largest town in the Upper Rhine valley between Basel and Strasbourg. It had been founded in 1120 as the capital of their duchy by the Zähringers, and under their patronage the town had grown in wealth and size. Under their successors, the counts of Freiburg, the town continued to prosper, but several divided inheritances left its new overlords with strictly limited resources. Apart from Freiburg itself the counts owned a handful of nearby villages, held the stewardship of the abbey of St Peter in the Black Forest and wielded some useful mining and hunting rights.¹⁰ This modest patrimony was further dissipated by the counts' financial ineptitude. A chronic shortage of money forced them to concede important privileges to Freiburg—above all the right to form independent alliances—in return for borrowing large sums of silver coin. To compensate for the erosion of their authority the counts strove to tighten their military hold over the town. Its citizens certainly knew how precarious their liberties might be: they only had to glance

---

[8] Wellmer, 'Breisgau', p. 276; Feine, 'Territorialbildung', pp. 252–3.
[9] Wellmer, 'Breisgau', pp. 272–3.
[10] Mayer, 'Zähringer und Freiburg', p. 375.

upwards to see the counts' redoubtable castle perched menacingly on a crag above the walls.

In 1366 the latent tensions between Freiburg and its overlord, count Egon, broke into open hostilities. Though neighbouring cities, including Basel, hurried to Freiburg's aid, their strength of arms was not enough to withstand the forces of count Egon and his numerous noble allies, prominent among them margrave Otto of Hachberg. After its defeat at the battle of Endingen in 1367 Freiburg was obliged to come to terms. Austria seized the opportunity of turning the ensuing negotiations to its advantage by acting as one of the intermediaries. In the peace treaty which was concluded the following year count Egon agreed to relinquish his jurisdiction over Freiburg in return for financial compensation and the lordship of Badenweiler; the town in its turn was free to choose another lord. But the choice could not run very far: only the Habsburgs had the resources to give Freiburg the political protection and financial subvention which it urgently needed. In 1368, therefore, Freiburg submitted to Austrian territorial jurisdiction. With two brief interruptions it was to remain in Austrian hands until 1805 when the Breisgau was absorbed into the duchy of Baden.

For the Habsburgs the acquisition of Freiburg had a double significance. It meant that they now controlled the most important thoroughfare between Alsace and Swabia over the Black Forest. At the same time it enabled them to impose their jurisdiction on the secular and monastic lords who held burgher's rights in Freiburg. Furthermore, the Habsburgs succeeded in extending their control to two powerful Breisgau abbeys, Tennenbach and St Märgen, by being vested with their stewardships.[11] Over the next half-century several more Breisgau lordships succumbed to the political attraction of the Habsburgs. In this manner Austria at last was able to establish its authority in the centre of the Breisgau; a few steps more and the vision of a Habsburg state in the south-west of the empire would have become victorious reality.

The obstacles in its path did not seem so very formidable. Only the margraviate of Hachberg and the lordship of Badenweiler continued to elude their grasp. The margraves, however, had inherited from the Zähringers the legal title to the landgraviate of the Breisgau, that is, the rights which constituted territorial jurisdiction over the region.[12] Whilst the title no longer entailed any political authority (not least

[11] Wellmer, 'Breisgau', pp. 301–2.
[12] Mayer, 'Zähringer und Freiburg, p. 375.

because the frontiers of the landgraviate no longer coincided with actual territorial boundaries), it remained a useful weapon in the fight against Austria's expansionist ambitions. Part of the landgraviate had already been pawned to the counts of Freiburg in 1318,[13] and when count Egon relinquished Freiburg half a century later he expressly retained the title of landgrave and attached it to his remaining possessions, including the lordship of Badenweiler. In 1395 his son, count Konrad, was reconfirmed in the title by the margraves, a gesture patently intended to secure their protection and support. Unfortunately, this legal stockade was no defence against disintegration from within. A recurrence of the financial difficulties which had plagued the counts so often in the past compelled Konrad to pawn his lands to the highest bidder: in 1398 Austria took possession of the lordship of Badenweiler and promptly laid claim to the landgraviate.[14] What the Habsburgs could not gain by design they had achieved by accident.

Yet the triumph was in vain. On the threshold of supremacy political miscalculation destroyed the Habsburgs' grand ambition. During the Council of Constance in 1415 duke Frederick IV, the ruler of Tirol and the western Habsburg lands, cast his weight behind the antipope John XXIII, whereupon he was duly excommunicated, and placed under the imperial ban by emperor Sigismund. In the ensuing turmoil count Konrad of Freiburg seized his chance to redeem the lordship of Badenweiler. The Swiss, meanwhile, had struck at the heart of Habsburg power in northern Switzerland by occupying the Aargau. Despite Frederick's reconciliation with Sigismund in 1418 and the general restitution of 1425 whereby Frederick regained the Habsburg lands in Swabia, the Breisgau, and Alsace, the Aargau remained Swiss.[15] Without it, Austria's territorial ambitions lost much of their coherence. There remained at best the hope of strengthening the bridegehead between Rhine and Danube by establishing hegemony over the Breisgau as a whole. But with the death of count Konrad in 1444 and the reversion of his lands by inheritance to the margraves of Hachberg even that last hope was extinguished.[16] Thereafter the Habsburg possessions west of the Tirolean Alps—the 'outer lands', as they came to be known—remained a patchwork of fragmented

---

[13] The margraves retained the title for their own villages within the old landgraviate of the Breisgau. Later they fought a protracted legal battle with Austria over ownership of the title which was not resolved until the 18th c. Wellmer, 'Breisgau', pp. 283–4.
[14] Mayer, 'Habsburger am Oberrhein', p. 384.
[15] Feine, 'Territorialbildung', p. 273.
[16] Mayer, 'Habsburger am Oberrhein', p. 385.

jurisdictions which was never resolved into a unified territory. Instead, each region gradually developed its own identity. Separate administrations were instituted for each of the 'outer lands': Danubian Swabia was governed from Ehingen, the Vorarlberg from Bregenz, and the lands on the Upper Rhine—Outer Austria proper—from the little Alsatian town of Ensisheim.[17] This particularism, however, was never converted into constitutional independence; the 'outer lands' were destined to remain a peripheral part of a much larger territorial system under the control of the Upper Austrian government in Innsbruck, which acted as court of appeal and political overlord. Yet in their internal affairs the western lands displayed a striking degree of autonomy until the later sixteenth century. The reasons for this apparent neglect of the lands which they had struggled so long to control lay in the changed political constellation which confronted the Habsburgs in the early 1400s. Once they had failed to create a unitary state the task of reducing the variety of existing jurisdictions—lordships, counties, landgraviates—to some intelligible order lost much of its attraction.[18] After regaining the German crown in 1437, moreover, the Habsburgs were preoccupied with establishing their ascendancy in the face of opposition from two of the most powerful princes of the Empire, the Bavarian Wittelsbachs and the Luxemburgs in Bohemia. That, coupled with the growing Turkish threat, diverted their attentions eastwards. The western provinces as a result were left largely to their own devices.

On the Upper Rhine Outer Austria proper was simply a confederation of four separate and diverse regions. On the left bank of the Rhine lay the various scattered Alsatian lordships and the self-contained territory of the Sundgau extending westwards to the gates of Burgundy. On the right bank stood the Austrian Breisgau, heavily indented by lordships belonging to the margraves of Baden, and the Black Forest lands. The latter comprised the lordships of Triberg and St Blasien, the county of Hauenstein, the towns of Villingen and Bräunlingen with their rural dependencies, and lastly the four Forest Towns on the Rhine itself. At the outset each district had its own bailiff but by the early fifteenth century they owed allegiance to a single

---

[17] Of the remaining possessions, the territory of Nellenburg was administered from Stockach, the county of Hohenberg from Rottenburg am Neckar, and the margraviate of Burgau from Günzburg.

[18] Feine, 'Territorialbildung', p. 301.

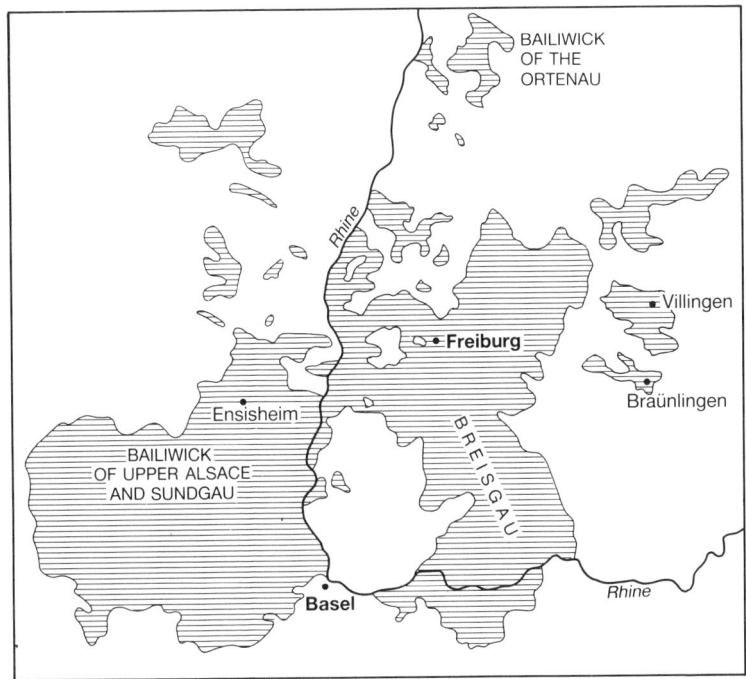

Map 1. The Outer Austrian Lands on the Upper Rhine in the Sixteenth Century

governor with his headquarters in Ensisheim.[19] A unitary administration for all four districts did not exist until 1463, and even then its organization and competence remained rudimentary and restricted.[20] It was staffed by members of the ducal household whose business was largely confined to conscripting troops and arbitrating in legal conflicts. A formal administration was unknown until the early sixteenth century, whilst a treasury was not established until 1570.[21]

---

[19] Wellmer, 'Breisgau', p. 290 dates the unitary governorship from 1416; Feine, 'Territorialbildung', p. 302 n. 290 argues for 1432, following Otto Stolz, *Geschichtliche Beschreibung der ober- und vorderösterreichischen Lande* (Quellen und Forschungen zur Siedlungs- und Volkstumsgeschichte der Oberrheinlande, iv) (Karlsruhe, 1943), 178. Between 1416 and 1425, whilst duke Frederick was divested of its sovereignty, Outer Austria was ruled by imperial governors.

[20] Cf. Wilhelm Beemelmans, 'Die Organisation der vorderösterreichischen Behörden in Ensisheim im 16. Jahrhundert', *ZGO* NF xxii (1907) 57–8; Wellmer, 'Breisgau' p. 297.

[21] Beemelmans, 'Organisation', p. 57–8; Stolz, *Beschreibung*, p. 66.

Map 2. The Breisgau in the Sixteenth Century

Freiburg's Relations with the Breisgau 23

The limited authority of the Ensisheim government rarely impinged upon the jurisdiction of local lords in town and country. They, in turn, showed little interest in the higher realms of Austrian politics. In the course of the fourteenth century, however, the political misfortunes of South-West Germany, for which the Habsburg dukes were as often as not to blame, forced both civic and rural lords to take a much more active part in government. Constant (and ineffectual) campaigns against the rebellious Swiss could only be mounted if the lords of Outer Austria were willing to provide not only men and arms, but also money. The prelates, nobles, and towns of Outer Austria, upon whom the contributions fell, began to seek consultation and debate with the governor and his councillors before granting further sums. As these gatherings became more regular, so their composition grew more formal, until those attending were summoned not as individuals but as members of the three estates of clergy, nobles, and burghers. This corporate identity was the outward sign that the estates of Outer Austria had assumed the function of representative assemblies.[22]

The significance of the local lords as upholders of public authority was pointedly revealed whenever the government in Ensisheim was suspended or dismantled in the wake of some political disaster. In 1415, after duke Frederick had fallen under the ban of the Empire, the western Habsburg lands were placed under the control of an imperial governor; ten years elapsed before they were finally restored to Austria. During that time the leading towns of Alsace and the Breisgau combined with the Elector Palatine to resist margrave Bernhard of Baden's efforts to extend his territorial authority at the expense of their liberties.[23] Then, in 1469, Frederick's son, Sigismund, in a desperate attempt to stop the Swiss advance, decided to pawn Alsace, the Sundgau, the Forest Towns, and Breisach to duke Charles the Bold of Burgundy.[24] The five years of harsh Burgundian rule which followed

---

[22] Cf. Franz Huter, 'Vorderösterreich und Österreich: Von ihren mittelalterlichen Beziehungen', in *Vorderösterreich*, p. 78. The origins and development of the Outer Austrian estates are traced by Hermann J. Schwarzweber, 'Die Landstände Vorderösterreichs im 15. Jahrhundert', *Forschungen und Mitteilungen zur Geschichte Tirols und Vorarlbergs*, v (1908), 145–57; 203–302. Cf. esp. 211–12.

[23] Cf. Richard Fester, 'Markgraf Bernhard I. und die Anfänge des badischen Territorialstaates', *Neujahrsblätter der Badischen Historischen Kommission*, vi (1896), 111–12; Berthold Sütterlin, *Geschichte Badens*, i, 2nd edn. (Karlsruhe, 1968), 299–300.

[24] Feine, 'Territorialbildung', p. 278. In general cf. Hildburg Brauer-Gramm, *Der Landvogt Peter von Hagenbach. Die burgundische Herrschaft am Oberrhein 1469–1474* (Göttinger Bausteine zur Geschichtswissenschaft, xxvii) (Göttingen, 1957).

left only the Breisgau in Austrian hands. Until 1471 it was administered by margrave Karl of Baden, who had been appointed governor of Outer Austria in 1468,[25] but after the events of 1469 he made no attempt to maintain a separate administration or summon assemblies for the Breisgau alone. Instead, he preferred to seek the direct co-operation of the local lords, particularly the Breisgau towns, in raising armed levies and organizing defence.[26]

Once Austrian rule was restored in 1474 the influence of the ecclesiastical and secular lords could scarcely be ignored, and the territorial diets of Outer Austria, to which they were summoned, became an intrinsic part of government. Nowhere was the role of the estates so evident as in Sigismund's last years. Chronic lack of money, which had already obliged him to raise a special excise, the so-called Evil Penny, from the estates in 1478,[27] strengthened the desire of a weary and disillusioned ruler to lay aside the burden of government. To that end Sigismund resolved in 1487 to pawn the bulk of the 'outer lands'—Alsace, the Breisgau, and Swabia—to the dukes of Bavaria. Forthwith his cousin, the later emperor Maximilian intervened to prevent the alienation of Habsburg patrimony by appealing directly to the Breisgau estates to put pressure on Sigismund to change his mind. In the face of further intervention by Maximilian's father, the Habsburg emperor, Frederick III, the hapless duke retreated and the pawn was cancelled.[28] At the subsequent general diet in Merano the combined estates of Inner and Outer Austria forced Sigismund to accept heavy cuts in expenditure and reforms in his administration. Furthermore, the twenty-four new councillors who were appointed to supervise the changes were made accountable not merely to the duke but also to the estates.[29] But by far the most radical concession which

[25] StAFr, A 1 v a 16, 2 June 1471; *UBStFr* ii. 519; *Regesten der Markgrafen von Baden und Hachberg 1050–1515*, iv (1453–1475), ed. Albert Krieger (Innsbruck, 1915), 240, no. 9641; Konrad Krimm, *Baden und Habsburg um die Mitte des 15. Jahrhunderts. Fürstlicher Dienst und Reichsgewalt im späten Mittelalter* (Veröffentlichungen der Kommission für geschichtliche Landeskunde in Baden-Württemberg, Reihe B lxxxix) (Stuttgart, 1976), 66.

[26] Cf. *UBStFr* ii. 526–7.

[27] Ibid., pp. 559–60. Though the excise was levied throughout Outer Austria the Breisgau received separate acknowledgement of its contribution, a sign of its special position among the estates. Ibid., pp. 562–4.

[28] Stiftsarchiv St Paul im Lavanttal, Handschriften 93/2 a 1. Leonard Leopold Maldoner, 'Brisgovia vetus et nova, das ist alt und neues Breysgau mit einer reichen folge von Sammlungen merkwürdiger und trefflicher Urkunden aus Archiven und gewahrsammen . . .' (1754). Allgemeiner Teil, fo. 102ᵛ. Cf. Wellmer, 'Breisgau' p. 304.

[29] *UBStFr* ii. 574; cf. Wellmer, 'Breisgau', p. 304.

the new territorial constitution wrung from Sigismund concerned the loyalty of his subjects. If he flouted its provisions or tried to dispose of his dominions, the estates could forswear their oaths of allegiance and choose instead as their ruler another member of the house of Austria.[30]

The occasion never arose, for in 1490 Sigismund handed over his entire dominions to Maximilian in return for a handsome annual pension of 52,000 fl. With that, however, the Outer Austrian lands suddenly regained their strategic significance, since Maximilian's marriage to Maria of Burgundy, the daughter of Charles the Bold, had brought a considerable inheritance on the western fringes of the Empire.[31] Between these Burgundian acquisitions in the west and the Habsburg heartlands in the east lay Outer Austria as the sole and indispensable connection.[32] For the first time, therefore, its administration became a matter of political importance, so that Maximilian had every reason for extending the authority of the Ensisheim government. That he confined himself to recasting its internal organization is a striking indication of the political counterweight which the Outer Austrian estates exerted. Within half a century they had acquired a degree of influence and initiative scarcely paralleled in any other German territory west of the Elbe.

The importance of the estates, however, cannot disguise the differences in cohesion and political effectiveness which were evident both within the three tiers of membership and between the separate estates for each of the four regions which together made up Outer Austria. Sometimes the estates of one region would meet independently; sometimes assemblies of one estate from several regions were summoned. In general, though, the third estate of towns and districts[33]

[30] *UBStFr* ii. 576.
[31] For the international background to these events cf. Hermann Wiesflecker, *Kaiser Maximilian I. Das Reich, Österreich und Europa an der Wende zur Neuzeit*, i (Munich, 1971), 258–9. His treatement of Outer Austria in general is cursory and unenlightening.
[32] Feine, 'Territorialbildung', p. 280. In 1493 it was implausibly rumoured that Maximilian intended to pawn several of the outer lands, among them the Breisgau, to margrave Christoph of Baden. HHSA, Maximiliana 2/I, fo. 14^{r-v}.
[33] The sources refer variously to the third estate as comprising *Städte und Landschaften, Städte und Ämter*, or *Städte, Märkte und Ämter*. This suggests that the terms *Amt* and *Landschaft* are interchangeable, and designate administrative districts. In the Breisgau and the Black Forest these districts were presumably those areas directly under the control of the Austrian dukes (such as the lordships of Hauenstein and Triberg) or else jurisdictions which comprised a town and its dependent hinterland (e.g. Burkheim am Kaiserstuhl and the *Talgang*). In Alsace and the Sundgau, however, *Landschaft* was used as a collective term to cover both towns and administrative districts. Cf. Peter Blickle, *Landschaften im Alten Reich. Die staatliche Funktion des gemeinen Mannes in Oberdeutschland* (Munich, 1973), 16–19.

could exert greater pressure than its more illustrious counterparts, the prelates and nobles, partly because the towns were better organized (they could look back on a tradition of co-operation from the days of urban defence leagues in the fourteenth century), partly because they alone could mobilize sufficient resources to bail the dukes out of their frequent military and financial extremities. Without huge contributions from the towns, for instance, it is unlikely that the Outer Austrian lands which Sigismund pawned to Burgundy could have been redeemed in 1474.[34]

As a consequence, the towns of Outer Austria came to enjoy greater autonomy than the run of German territorial towns which were firmly under the thumb of their princely rulers. Of course, they could not aspire to the self-contained independence of the Imperial Free Cities; and even within Outer Austria not all towns carried equal weight. The smaller communes, whose inhabitants were mostly wine-growers or farmers, had more in common with the surrounding villages than with the larger craft towns or merchant cities. In Alsace and the Sundgau, for instance, where the towns acted as centres of administrative districts, they often had little separate identity from their hinterland, just as in the neighbouring territories of Baden and Württemberg. But in the Breisgau, where the estates as a whole were recognized as distinct from, and superior to, the remaining regional estates,[35] the towns had greater standing and authority. Their effective responsibility for security and public order on the right bank of the Rhine, coupled with their defiant survival during the Burgundian occupation, helps to account for their peculiar influence. The strategic importance of Breisach or the Forest Towns, for example, certainly compensated for their otherwise modest size and resources. But none of these could hope to emulate the richest, largest, and most powerful city of Outer Austria: the capital of the old duchy of Zähringen, Freiburg im Breisgau.

II

Yet after its submission to Austria in 1368 Freiburg faced a period of contraction and decline. The war against count Egon and the huge

---

[34] Wellmer, 'Breisgau', p. 300. The distribution of regular taxation, however, was spread with great scruple equally between prelates and nobles on the one hand, and towns and districts on the other. Ibid., p. 307.
[35] Schwarzweber, 'Landstände', pp. 301–2.

ransom which he extracted cost the town dearly; as a result Freiburg was saddled throughout the fifteenth century with a considerable burden of public debt. More and more the town took on the aspect of a middling craft community as many patricians who had fought on the side of count Egon withdrew to their country estates.[36] Its new overlords were content to keep its internal administration on a loose rein, so that the town was able to preserve its constitution and privileges largely unaltered.[37] Nevertheless, the Habsburgs took care to leave Freiburg little scope for independent external action by depriving it of its earlier right to form alliances unless they were expressly sanctioned.[38] Moreover, after the gild revolution of 1388–92 they ordained that the annual election of the town council had to be ratified in the presence of the governor of Outer Austria and two of his councillors.[39]

To these constitutional constraints came the military insecurity and political turbulence of the early fifteenth century. Between 1415 and 1427, it is true, Freiburg had a short intermezzo as an Imperial Free City, but the opportunity for maintaining its independence was more apparent than real.[40] Already in 1408–9 and again from 1420–4 Freiburg and the other Breisgau towns were drawn into bitter conflict with the margraves of Baden.[41] Although in the end margrave Bernhard was forced to make concessions to his chief princely opponent, the Elector Palatine, the ensuing treaty of Mühlburg between Baden and the Breisgau towns stripped Freiburg and its neighbours of their right to hold burgher subjects in margravial territory.[42] By submitting to Austria once more in 1427 Freiburg was in effect acknowledging that it was too weak, even as an independent city

---

[36] Steven W. Rowan, 'The Guilds of Freiburg im Breisgau in the later Middle Ages as Social and Political Entities' (Ph.D. Diss., Harvard Univ., 1970), 47; Wolfgang Leiser, '*Sie dienen auch jetzt noch aber fremden Göttern.*' *Der Freiburger Herrschaftswechsel 1368* (Veröffentlichungen des Alemannischen Instituts, xxv) (Bühl, 1968), 28.

[37] Many scholars have noted the unusual degree of internal autonomy which Freiburg enjoyed. Cf. most recently Claudia Ulbrich, *Leibherrschaft am Oberrhein im Spätmittelalter* (Veröffentlichungen des Max-Planck-Instituts für Geschichte, lviii) (Göttingen, 1979), 192–3. These observations, however, underplay the obstacles to the pursuit of a genuinely independent foreign policy.

[38] *UBStFr* i. 545.   [39] *UBStFr* ii. 89.

[40] During the intermezzo, Ulbrich argues, Freiburg would at least have been better able to carve out a territory for itself. Ulbrich, *Leibherrschaft*, p. 192. This view is not altogether convincing since it ignores the threat from Baden. On Freiburg's policies as an Imperial Free City cf. in general the admirable study by Thea van Rossum, 'Studien zur Politik Freiburgs als Reichsstadt' (Diss. phil. Freiburg, 1950).

[41] Sütterlin, *Geschichte Badens*, pp. 299–300.

[42] *UBStFr* ii. 345. Cf. Fester, 'Markgraf Bernhard', pp. 111–12.

in a network of alliances, to protect its immediate interests over against the growing power of Baden. At that time Freiburg in fact pleaded to retain its short-lived freedom to conclude alliances, but the request was apparently rejected by the Habsburgs and never revived.[43] Although during the rest of the century the common need to keep the Swiss and the Burgundians at bay ensured that relations between the ruling houses of Baden and Habsburg remained generally cordial,[44] that did not preclude repeated litigation between the margraves and the Austrian Breisgau towns, above all Freiburg, over Baden's encroachment upon their political influence in the countryside.

Whilst in its external affairs Freiburg was reduced to the level of a territorial town, its importance within Outer Austria itself continued to grow throughout the fifteenth century. As long as the seat of government remained in the otherwise insignificant Alsatian town of Ensisheim, Freiburg's dominant role on the right bank of the Rhine was bound to lend it vicarious political authority. This was particularly evident after the administrative partition of the Austrian lands in 1444 which led the ruler of the western territories, archduke Albrecht, to choose Freiburg as his capital.[45] Although the impetuous Albrecht used his position to tamper injudiciously with the town's constitution, he nevertheless made Freiburg a major centre of learning by founding a university in 1457, at that time the only high school throughout Austria and southern Germany from Vienna to the Vosges.[46]

[43] Freiburg sought the right to enter into any alliance which did not prejudice Austria or the Empire. *UBStFr* ii, 373. The subsequent oath, however, merely repeated the traditional terms of submission. Ibid., pp. 378–9. In other words, alliances continued to depend on Austrian sanction. The view expressed by Friedrich Hefele, 'Freiburg als vorderösterreichische Stadt', in *Vorderösterreich*, p. 345 is therefore misleading.

[44] Krimm, *Baden und Habsburg*, pp. 49–50; 66–7. Many Austrian nobles entered margravial service as councillors, and the margraves sometimes acted as Outer Austrian governors. Ibid., pp. 32–3.

[45] The older view that Albrecht resided permanently in Freiburg during his reign is unlikely. Cf. Stolz, *Beschreibung*, p. 36. On his frequent visits to Freiburg the archduke is supposed to have resided in the Dominican convent, but recently it has been suggested that he took quarters in Freiburg castle, even though it has commonly been assumed that the castle remained in ruins after its destruction by the burghers in 1366. Berent Schwineköper, 'Das "Große Fest" zu Freiburg (3.–8. Juli 1454)', in Erich Hassinger, H. J. Müller and Hugo Ott (eds.), *Geschichte, Wirtschaft, Gesellschaft. Festschrift für Clemens Bauer* (Berlin, 1974), 86–7.

[46] *UBStFr* ii. 447–59. Cf. Friedrich Schaub, 'Die vorderösterreichische Universität Freiburg', in *Vorderösterreich*, p. 249. On the background to the founding of the university cf. ibid., *passim*, Albrecht omitted, however, to provide his new academic foundation with a sufficient endowment, so that in its early years the university was often in serious financial difficulties. Cf. Clemens Bauer, 'Die wirtschaftliche Ausstattung der

Nowhere was Freiburg's influence ultimately so visible, however, as in the territorial estates. Although during the fifteenth century the Outer Austrian diets met in Neuenburg or Ensisheim, the sixteenth century saw regular meetings in Freiburg, which gradually developed as the centre of the estates' constitutional activity.[47] It was also the headquarters of the separate and influential assemblies of the Breisgau regional estates. In 1487 Freiburg was referred to explicitly as the capital of the Breisgau,[48] and it represented the Breisgau towns at Austrian general diets and their committees.[49] That Freiburg was a driving force within the body of estates can be seen even before they reached full institutional identity. In 1469, on the eve of the Burgundian occupation, Freiburg called the Breisgau towns to a preliminary discussion of the business before the Outer Austrian diet which the governor, margrave Karl of Baden, had summoned to Neuenburg.[50] In 1487 Freiburg even planned to call an assembly of the entire third estate of Outer Austria to consider archduke Sigismund's demands for payment of the Evil Penny.[51] Although these efforts never succeeded in gaining for the estates the right to summon general territorial diets themselves, the practice of preliminary consultation to draw up grievances and agree on a common platform became firmly established, at least on the right bank of the Rhine, where under Freiburg's leadership regional assemblies were convened to debate matters of defence and public order.[52]

Freiburger Universität in ihrer Gründungsperiode', in idem, *Gesammelte Aufsätze zur Wirtschafts- und Sozialgeschichte* (Freiburg/Basel/Vienna, 1965), 148–85.

[47] Schwarzweber, 'Landstände', pp. 269–70.
[48] *UBStFr* ii. 571; Schwarzweber, 'Landstände', p. 302. Cf. Hefele, 'Freiburg', p. 346.
[49] e.g. on the estates' committee set up at the general diet of Merano in 1487 to punish those who had abetted the proposed mortgaging of the Austrian lands by archduke Sigismund. StAFr, C 1 Landstände 1. Relation über den Landtag zu Meran de anno 1487.
[50] StAFr, B 5 XI, iii. 10, fo. 29ᵛ. Freiburg to Neuenburg, Endingen, and Breisach, 7 Apr. 1469.
[51] *UBStFr* ii. 567–9. Though the plan was turned down by the governor, ibid., p. 569, it would be wrong to interpret the prohibition as a sign of growing princely power over against the estates, as does Schwarzweber, 'Landstände', p. 268. In 1487 Sigismund's greatest wish was to lay down the burden of government. Freiburg's proposal was presumably rejected because it encroached upon Sigismund's fiscal prerogatives.
[52] In 1490 the four Forest Towns and the Black Forest communities invited the Breisgau towns to Rheinfelden to discuss their various grievances in the wake of the transfer of Tirol and the 'outer lands' to Maximilian. *UBStFr* ii. 580–1. Schwarzweber, 'Landstände', p. 268 may well be right to argue that this was not a regional diet of towns. In 1522, however, Villingen expressly called upon Freiburg to summon an assembly of

Once Maximilian had taken over the government of Tirol and the 'outer lands' in 1490 from his cousin Sigismund, Freiburg's political importance and prestige were enhanced still further. The Habsburg ruler's strategic interest in the Upper Rhine as the link between Austria and Burgundy made him eager to bolster the economic and military strength of its leading town. He used his influence accordingly to promote much-needed reforms in the town's finances and administration,[53] whilst augmenting its wider political standing by choosing Freiburg as the setting in 1497–8 for the one and only imperial diet in its history.[54] He even planned to build an official residence in the town for future visits and assemblies.[55] Freiburg's sphere of influence stretched in any case well beyond the confines of Outer Austria proper. Many South-West German towns, including several imperial cities, looked to Freiburg as the arbiter of their legal codes and charters which were often derived from Freiburg's own

the Breisgau third estate to discuss grievances concerning the Jews in Bräunlingen. StAFr, A 1 XII c 32, 26 Nov. 1522. Villingen to Freiburg: 'ir wöllend furderlich und on allen verzug gemain stett und landschaft hie dishalb Rins (prelaten und ritterschaft ussgeschlossen) öüch die vier stett am Rin mit dem wald uff ain namlichen tag in ewer statt beschriben und uns by disem poten verkünden.'

[53] Maximilian's allegedly great affection for Freiburg, dating from his first visit as a child in 1473, has been much overdone by generations of local historians. Cf. Johann Heinrich Schreiber, *Geschichte der Stadt und Universität Freiburg im Breisgau*, iii (Freiburg, 1857), 183–4; Hefele, 'Freiburg', p. 347.

[54] It was planned to transfer a diet of 1511 from Strasbourg to Freiburg because of French military preparations. HHSA, Maximiliana 23, fos. 122^r–123^v, 16 Dec. 1510. A further diet was planned there in 1515 but was never summoned. HHSA, Maximiliana 33, fo. 27^r, 11 May 1515. There was opposition to Freiburg as a meeting-place on account of its poor amenities and limited accommodation. Cf. Steven W. Rowan, 'A Reichstag in the Reform Era: Freiburg im Breisgau, 1497–98', in idem and James A. Vann (eds.), *The Old Reich: Essays on German Political Institutions 1495–1806* (Studies presented to the International Commission for the History of Representative and Parliamentary Institutions, xlviii) (Brussels, 1974), 41, 43. However, during the Grand Festival at Freiburg in 1454 many princes and large retinues were apparently accommodated in the town. Schwineköper, 'Das "Große Fest"', p. 86.

[55] StAFr, B 5 XIIIa, viii, fo. 106^r, 28 Nov. 1498. Cf. B 5 VIII a 1, 2 fo. 2^r, n.d. (1498). Cramped conditions at the imperial diet just ended may well have prompted Maximilian to contemplate a permanent residence. The common notions that Maximilian intended to retire to Freiburg, or that the house 'Zum Walfisch', rented by Erasmus after his arrival in Freiburg, had been built by the imperial treasurer, Jakob Villinger, in 1516 on Maximilian's express instructions, rest upon very slender evidence. For critical remarks on this subject, cf. Clemens Bauer, 'Jakob Villinger, Großschatzmeister Kaiser Maximilians. Ein Umriß', in idem, *Gesammelte Aufsätze*, pp. 246–7 n. 16; and, more recently, Hans Schadek, 'Wurde das Haus "Zum Walfisch" in Freiburg als Stadtresidenz und Alterssitz Kaiser Maximilians I. erbaut?', *Zeitschrift des Breisgau-Geschichtsvereins* ('Schau-ins-Land'), xcviii (1979), 129–34.

constitution. The town council also acted on occasion as the court of appeal for those neighbouring communes which were entitled to seek external jurisdiction.[56]

III

Its power and pre-eminence within Outer Austria, nevertheless, could not shield Freiburg from the constant difficulties and dangers which beset the notoriously unsettled Upper Rhine during the later Middle Ages. The external threats—the constant struggle to contain the Swiss, the incursions of the so-called Armagnac mercenaries in mid-century,[57] the Burgundian occupation—served only to compound the grave internal problems which faced the town after 1368. It is therefore understandable that the mainspring of Freiburg's foreign policy up to and beyond the fifteenth century was the search for security and stability. Through liasons with the Breisgau nobility, the acquisition of burgher subjects in the countryside, and later the accumulation of a landed territory, Freiburg strove to construct a network of relationships which would serve its economic, political, and strategic interests and strengthen its position.

By the fourteenth century Freiburg had already established close connections with its Breisgau hinterland. Leading patricians of the town had bought extensive estates in the surrounding countryside which allowed them in due course to acquire titles of nobility whilst retaining their burgher's rights. The most striking example was the Snewlin family which dominated civic politics both before and after 1368, and whose many branches formed the backbone of the Breisgau aristocracy in the fifteenth century.[58] As a consequence, Freiburg's noble outburghers (as they were called) appear to have accepted the overlordship of Austria collectively in 1368 alongside the town. Two

[56] Johanna Bastian, *Der Freiburger Oberhof* (Veröffentlichungen des Alemannischen Instituts Freiburg im Breisgau, ii) (Freiburg, 1934), 21–2; Bader, *Deutscher Südwesten*, p. 83. Cf. *UBStFr* ii. 182–3.

[57] Cf. Heinrich Witte, *Die Armagnaken im Elsaß* (Beiträge zur Landes- und Volkskunde von Elsaß-Lothringen, iii. 11) (Strasbourg, 1892).

[58] Josef Fleckenstein, 'Bürgertum und Rittertum in der Geschichte des mittelalterlichen Breisgaus', in Wolfgang Müller (ed.), *Freiburg im Mittelalter. Vorträge zum Stadtjubiläum 1970* (Veröffentlichungen des Alemannischen Instituts, xxix) (Bühl, 1970), 91; Mayer, 'Zähringer und Freiburg', p. 374. Cf. Hermann Nehlsen, *Die Freiburger Familie Snewlin. Rechts- und sozialgeschichtliche Studien zur Entwicklung des mittelalterlichen Bürgertums* (Veröffentlichungen aus dem Archiv der Stadt Freiburg im Breisgau, ix) (Freiburg, 1967).

years later, at any rate, in the name of their common fealty to Austria sixty-two noble burghers, the Snewlins prominent amongst them, allied themselves for mutual aid and protection.[59] This common loyalty to Austria, however, could not disguise the tensions between town and nobility. In the war of independence many noble outburghers had fought on the side of count Egon, so that their defensive alliance in 1370 may represent a conscious closing of the ranks in response to a delicate political conjuncture. Into the fifteenth century, and not least after the gild revolution of 1388-92, many nobles in fact withdrew permanently to their country estates. According to the constitution, it is true, Freiburg's mayor had still to be of noble birth, but the nobles' reluctance to participate in civic affairs can be adjudged from an amendment to that constitution in 1435 which permitted merchants and burghers to make up the shortfall of council seats left vacant by the nobility.[60] Insofar as the nobles kept their burgher's rights, it was largely to enjoy the social and recreational advantages which the town could offer. Many kept town houses which, together with the nobles' fraternity in the minster square, the *Gesellschaft zum Ritter*, doubtless made a welcome change from their draughty, rat-infested castles in the Breisgau.[61]

But the nobility's gradual detachment from civic affairs did not destroy its usefulness to the town. As noble outburghers they contributed to the town's revenues through their annual taxes and the excise on wine; their military skills were placed at the town's disposal; and the basic allegiance to the town which their burgher's oaths entailed was a political asset in Freiburg's relations with the countryside. Moreover, by the early fifteenth century most of the remaining Breisgau and Black Forest lords, both ecclesiastical and secular, had been obliged to recognize Austrian territorial jurisdiction,[62] even those, such as the lords of Staufen, who had continued to uphold their allegiance to the counts of Freiburg.[63] Only the two princes with serious territorial ambitions, the counts of Fürstenberg and the margraves of Baden, stood aside. With their submission to Austria

---

[59] *UBStFr* ii. 4-10; Wolfgang Stülpnagel, 'Herrschaft und Stadt', in *AmtKrB* i. 1 (Freiburg, 1965), 242; Leiser, *Herrschaftswechsel*, p. 28; Rowan, 'Guilds', p. 37.
[60] *UBStFr* ii. 389-90.
[61] Cf. Schreiber, *Geschichte Freiburgs*, ii (Freiburg, 1857), 259-60.
[62] Leiser, *Herrschaftswechsel*, p. 20.
[63] Wolfgang Stülpnagel, 'Die Herren von Staufen im Breisgau', *Schau-ins-Land*, lxxvi (1958), 53.

several of the lesser lords in turn took out citizenship in Freiburg,[64] so that the town was able to build up an extensive system of political clientage throughout the Breisgau.

The common loyalty to Austria overcame the need for more formal alliances between the town and the surrounding nobility. The few recorded initiatives towards a closer association came, it appears, from the nobles' desire for greater protection in time of war. In 1460, possibly under the threat of a renewed Swiss attack, they concluded an agreement for mutual assistance and defence which they encouraged the Breisgau towns to join.[65] Because the latter had to look urgently to their own defences, it was left to Freiburg to negotiate terms.[66] But the negotiations were hampered by the lords' reluctance to abandon appeals to the much resented ecclesiastical and imperial courts in cases where they sought to press claims against subjects of the towns living under their jurisdictions.[67] Only if the lords were prepared to extend their pact to forgo such lawsuits between each other to the towns and their rural dependents as well was Freiburg willing to participate.[68] In the end it is doubtful whether the towns did join the nobles' association.[69] Eight years later, in the hectic summer of 1468, when duke Sigismund's feeble attempts to mount effective resistance against the Swiss in the Mulhouse War had led to another emergency on the Upper Rhine, the Breisgau nobility once again took the lead in seeking a joint defensive alliance with the towns and margrave Karl of Baden.[70]

[64] Though not the lords of Staufen. Cf. Rudolf Hugard, 'Die Beziehungen der Herren von Staufen zur Stadt Freiburg', *Schau-ins-Land*, xiv (1887), 90, who wrongly believed that they actually took up residence in Freiburg.

[65] StAFr, B 5 XI, iii. 1, fo. 27^r. Freiburg to Breisach (and Neuenburg and Endingen), 6 Sept. 1460. Wellmer, 'Breisgau', p. 295, following Maldoner's compilation, declared that an alliance between the nobility and the Breisgau towns (though without the prelates) was in fact sealed on 26 Sept. Cf. Stiftsarchiv St Paul im Lavanttal, Handschriften 93/2, a 1, Maldoner, 'Brisgovia vetus et nova', fos. 74^v ff. (summarized by Wellmer, 'Breisgau', pp. 295–6). Cf. Krimm, *Baden und Habsburg*, p. 42. The evidence of the Freiburg letterbooks makes this reading quite impossible.

[66] StAFr B 5 XI, iii. 1 fo. 30^v. Freiburg to Neuenburg, 26 Sept. 1460; ibid., fo. 32^r. Freiburg to Breisach, 1 Oct. 1460; cf. also ibid., fos. 33^r, 34^{r-v}.

[67] Freiburg at first demurred on the less than ingenuous grounds that it had no liberty to enter into alliances. Ibid., fo. 32^r. Freiburg to Breisach, 1 Oct. 1460.

[68] Ibid., fo. 33^r. Freiburg to Neuenburg and Endingen, 10 Oct. 1460.

[69] The correspondence between the nobility and the Breisgau towns continued at least until 17 Dec. StAFr, B 5 XI, iii. 2, fo. 25^r. Freiburg to Jakob von Staufen, apologizing for delay in the negotiations. Whether they went on into 1461 cannot be determined since the Freiburg letterbooks, the only surviving contemporary source, are missing for that year.

[70] *Regesten der Markgrafen von Baden*, iv. 236–7, no. 9609; cf. *UBStFr* ii. 500; Krimm, *Baden und Habsburg*, p. 42.

The terms of the proposed treaty, however, made plain that it was only for the duration of the war and had no wider purpose,[71] but since its ratification depended upon Sigismund's consent, it, too, seems never to have got off the ground.[72] The obstacles in the path of formal alliances, therefore, were considerable; above all, the need to close ranks to ward off external dangers could not conceal the division between towns and nobles over their immediate domestic interests.

Between Freiburg and the other Breisgau towns relations were naturally much closer. With Breisach, Neuenburg, and Endingen Freiburg had the most frequent contact, since they were fellow-members of the third estate, though it was not until the aftermath of the Burgundian occupation that they saw the need to form a more solemn and binding association. In 1475 the four towns signed a ten-year treaty for mutual defence and arbitration in disputes between members.[73] Clearly the treaty satisfied a need, if only psychological, for it was twice renewed up to the turn of the century.[74] Towards the remaining lesser towns of the Austrian Breisgau, which lacked a direct political voice,[75] Freiburg's attitude, by contrast, was more tutelary and even, during the stormy years of the Reformation and Peasants' War, openly dictatorial.

Freiburg also sought to extend its influence in the Breisgau by developing strong seigneurial ties with the surrounding countryside through the acquisition of peasant outburghers. Long before 1368, in common with Breisach and other towns in the region, Freiburg had granted burgher's rights to many rural subjects of the counts of Freiburg and other local lords with the latter's knowledge and consent.

---

[71] *UBStFr* ii. 500–1.

[72] Margrave Karl of Baden, who was then on the best of terms with duke Sigismund, and shortly to become Outer Austrian governor, insisted upon this condition. Krimm, *Baden und Habsburg*, pp. 42–3. Cf. Henny Grüneisen, 'Herzog Sigmund von Tirol, der Kaiser und die Achtung der Eidgenossen 1469', in *Aus Reichstagen des 15. und 16. Jahrhunderts* (Schriftenreihe der Historischen Kommission bei der Bayerischen Akademie der Wissenschaften, v) (Göttingen, 1958), 184–5, who points out that the Outer Austrian governor, Thüring von Hallwil, and certain representatives of the Outer Austrian estates had already tried unsuccessfully in June 1468 to withdraw their allegiance from Sigismund and attach themselves instead to the Elector Palatine.

[73] *UBStFr* ii. 553–6.

[74] At first for fourteen and then for another ten years. Ibid., ii. 556–7. Cf. Schreiber, *Geschichte Freiburgs*, iii. 174–5.

[75] These towns—Staufen, Burkheim, Kenzingen, Waldkirch, Elzach—were excluded from political participation by the fact that they were under the control of, or else mortgaged to, intermediate lords. On occasion, however, they were summoned to the territorial diets in their own right.

The existence of these peasant outburghers—commonly called paleburghers—became a source of mounting friction between the German towns and the emerging territorial lords, who were concerned to halt the flight of serfs from the land into the freedom of the urban communes.[76] The gradual ascendancy of the territorial princes at the expense of the towns was pointedly reflected in emperor Charles IV's Golden Bull of 1356, the constitutional foundation of the Empire until its dissolution, which forbad the acquisition of paleburghers.[77] Such prohibitions by a weakened imperial authority admittedly had little impact at a local level,[78] and Freiburg was later to argue—rather boldly for a town whose Habsburg overlords in the mean time had made the Empire their dynastic fief—that imperial decrees had no force to override long-established local law and custom. The town in any case invariably referred to all its rural burghers—nobles and peasants alike—without distinction as outburghers, a tactic obviously calculated to get round the imperial edicts against, and the pejorative connotations of, paleburghers.[79]

Among the political concessions which Freiburg had to accept alongside its huge financial sacrifice as the price of its freedom from the counts of Freiburg was the abandonment of its peasant outburghers.

[76] In 1220 emperor Frederick II in his *Confoederatio cum principibus ecclesiasticis* had forbidden towns to accept the serfs of ecclesiastical or seculuar lords as burghers. *MGH, Legum Sectio IV: Constitutiones et acta publica imperatorum et regum*, ii, ed. Ludwig Weiland (Hanover, 1896), 86–91. In 1231 his son, king Henry, in his *Statutum in favorem principum* repeated this provision and added a further clause condemning paleburghers. Ibid., pp. 418–20. Cf. Ulbrich, *Leibherrschaft*, p. 223 n. 45.

[77] Karl Zeumer (ed.), *Die Goldene Bulle Kaiser Karls IV. Text der Goldenen Bulle und Urkunden zu ihrer Geschichte und Erläuterung* (Quellen und Studien zur Verfassungsgeschichte des Deutschen Reiches in Mittelalter und Neuzeit, ii, 2) (Weimar, 1908), 31–2. At that time the prohibition was directed particularly against Strasbourg which was undermining the territorial power of its bishop by accepting scores of his subjects as paleburghers. Cf. idem, *Die Goldene Bulle Kaiser Karls IV. Entstehung und Bedeutung der Goldenen Bulle* (Quellen und Studien zur Verfassungsgeschichte des Deutschen Reiches in Mittelalter und Neuzeit, ii. 1) (Weimar, 1908), 76–7.

[78] The prohibition had to be repeated in a separate statute by emperor Sigismund in 1431, which alluded to the continuing and notorious dissensions between lords and towns. Its rather curious wording states that not only the towns, but also the princes, counts, and nobles must not accept paleburghers. *Deutsche Reichstagsakten*, ix, ed. Dietrich Kerler (Gotha, 1887), 568. This must presumably refer to those lords who themselves controlled towns.

[79] Cf. Henri Dubled, 'La bourgeoisie foraine en Alsace, principalement à Strasbourg: "Pfalburger" et "Ausburger"', *Cahiers d'Archéologie et d'Histoire d'Alsace*, cxxxiii (1953), 141. He points out that originally the distinction between *Ausbürger* (the ecclesiastical and secular lords) and *Pfahlbürger* (inhabitants of suburbs and villagers) was social, not legal: each, at least in theory, enjoyed the same protection from the towns. Ibid., pp. 139–41.

In the various peace treaties of 1368 Freiburg and its urban allies in the war of independence, Breisach and Neuenburg, agreed to give up their outburghers in the Breisgau villages, whilst count Egon and the Breisgau nobles who had fought with him undertook in return to allow existing outburghers to move to the towns within two months. In future the towns were to acquire no more outburghers without the lords' permission, whilst burghers who wished to emigrate to the countryside must submit to seigneurial jurisdiction and obligations, in return for which they would receive full communal rights of woodland and pasture.[80]

Despite these manifold undertakings, Freiburg, and to a lesser extent Breisach, contrived to keep many of their peasant outburghers, which suggests that their value to the towns—political, military, and financial—was great enough to outweigh the risk of antagonizing the local nobility. The secret of their success lay undoubtedly in the loose wording of the treaties. On the one hand, the ban on accepting outburghers applied essentially to the lords' servile subjects, not their freemen, who were still entitled to take out burgher's rights.[81] On the other, the treaties did not exclude the possibility of peasants becoming outburghers with their lords' consent. Freiburg subsequently maintained that that was exactly what had happened.[82] The readiness of sovereign princes, however, such as the margraves of Baden, to tolerate outburghers visibly diminished once they set about consolidating their various lordships into a unitary territory with exclusive jurisdiction in the early fifteenth century. When the treaty of Mühlburg between margrave Bernhard I and the towns of Freiburg, Breisach, and Endingen[83] was signed after the four-year war in 1424, it reiterated the prohibition on the Breisgau towns' holding outburghers in margravial

---

[80] *UBStFr* i. 516–7; 526–7; GLA 67/206, fos. 9ʳ–10ᵛ (cf. Ulbrich, *Leibherrschaft*, p. 223); StAFr, A 1 XIV Staufen 13, 1368–1562, 30 Mar. 1368. Treaty between Breisach and Neuenburg and the lords of Staufen (copy); ibid., 6 Apr. 1368. Treaty between Freiburg and the lords of Staufen (copy).

[81] On the assumption that they moved to the towns; whether they could stay as burghers in the villages was one of the grey areas of the treaties which gave rise to frequent disputes.

[82] StAFr, A 1 XII d 5, 15/16th c. Heft C, n.d. (1452), fo. 1ʳ. 'Item das grof Egens brief wiset, man habe im die sinen, die usburger woren, ledig gezalt, das ist zů merken, die sin eigen woren. Item das man der sinen deheinen me zů usburger enpfolhen sol denn mit der herren willen. doby ist zů merken, dz die burger, so also bliben, nit die sinen woren, und ob su yemans weren gewesen, das su mit der herren willen weren burger bliben, als ouch sithar etwie maniger burger worden ist mit sins herren willen.'

[83] Whether Endingen had many outburghers can no longer be determined.

territory.⁸⁴ The terms of the treaty essentially echoed the settlement of 1368, with the all-important proviso that the margraves had the right to claim within a year any of their subjects who had fled their jurisdiction to the freedom of the towns.⁸⁵

Although Freiburg managed to retain some outburghers in margravial territory after 1424,⁸⁶ they were increasingly confined to its own territories and the villages of the Breisgau lords under Austrian territorial sovereignty, many of whom were themselves noble outburghers of the town. The survival of the outburghers, therefore, depended upon coming to terms with the Breisgau nobility.⁸⁷ But the latter, after mid-century, was also concerned to establish exclusive authority over its villages by making residence within them the sole criterion of seigneurial dependence. As a result, the outburghers, whose allegiance to Freiburg was bound to cut across such ambitions, became the victims of growing harassment by the local lords. Nevertheless, by the end of the fifteenth century Freiburg had not only succeeded in retaining most of its outburghers, but even persuaded Maximilian in 1510 to issue a proclamation recognizing their existence and affording them protection.⁸⁸ This victory, however, as the edict itself made plain, had only been achieved at the cost of reducing the outburghers' status to the equivalent of the lords' own serfs.⁸⁹ In any case, the edict was

[84] *UBStFr* ii. 345.

[85] Ibid., pp. 342–3. Cf. Ulbrich, *Leibherrschaft*, p. 197. Whether this right applied to all subjects, or only to serfs, is not clear. In 1415 emperor Sigismund had granted the margraves the right to pursue not only their own serfs but other dependent subjects within their lands as well. GLA 36/69, 4 Feb. 1415. Later, however, the right was restricted largely to margravial serfs. GLA 36/73, 24 Oct. 1475 (contained in a confirmation of 27 July 1504). Cf. Ulbrich, *Leibherrschaft*, p. 224.

[86] StAFr A I XII d 13, 18 Apr. 1442. Apart from a handful of outburghers in margravial territory recorded in the earliest surviving outburgher tallage list of 1453 (E I A II a 4, 1453: in Haslach, Leutersberg, and Wolfenweiler), Freiburg retained a sizeable community of outburghers in Gallenweiler, which was an exclave of the margravial lordship of Badenweiler, throughout the fifteenth century and beyond without incurring any undue friction with Baden. Cf. A I XII d 44, 1502–56, no. 2 (1504); no. 11 (1535), with Freiburg's reply, B 5 XI, xiv, fos. 212ᵛ–213ʳ, 12 Nov. 1535.

[87] That Austria itself had no objection to the existence of outburghers in its territories can be seen from archduke Albrecht's attempts to raise a war-levy in 1454. In his demand to Freiburg he enquired whether the town had any villages, burghers, or subjects beyond its walls, in order that they might be included in the town's assessment. *UBStFr* ii. 441. Cf. Wellmer, 'Breisgau', pp. 294–5.

[88] In an instruction to the Outer Austrian governor. StAFr, A I XII d 49, 13 Mar. 1510.

[89] Ibid., 'wiewol sy von alter her . . . etlich aigen lewt, die man nennet awspurger, auf dem landt allenthalben under den von prelaten und adlen im preysgew . . . sitzen gehept.' Cf. Ulbrich, *Leibherrschaft*, p. 191 n. 290.

unable to prevent the daily war of attrition waged by certain Breisgau nobles against the outburghers, so that in the early decades of the sixteenth century Freiburg finally agreed to sell several of its larger outburgher communities to their respective village lords. Even so, the number of outburghers remained quite large, though often they lived in the safety of the town's own rural territories, until, in the 1570s Freiburg at last decided to dispose of the remainder of its peasant burghers.[90] Their usefulness to the town by then had all but gone, for the thrust of Freiburg's external policy had long since shifted to the construction of a landed territory which would provide political and strategic security as well as an economic reservoir.

The beginnings of Freiburg's expansion from the thirteenth century onwards, however, were piecemeal and contingent, a direct response to the town's increasing size and need of resources rather than the outflow of a deliberate territorial policy. As the population outgrew the confines of the Old Town, faubourgs sprang up beyond the city walls: some planned settlements such as the Neuburg to the north, others haphazard extensions of existing hamlets to the west, or gradual enlargements of older communities on the south bank of the Dreisam. By 1368 the suburbs north and south of the Dreisam had in their turn been circumvallated and constitutionally incorporated into the town,[91] though the village of Adelhausen south of the river took much longer to absorb, since Freiburg's leading patrician family, the Snewlins, exploited a protracted dispute over the village's boundaries to uphold and extend certain seigneurial rights which they held there.[92] Not until

[90] StAFr, A 1 XII d 63, 1573/6; cf. A 1 XII d 5, 15/16th c. Heft D, n.d. (c.1570); Ulbrich, *Leibherrschaft*, p. 201.

[91] *UBStFr* i. 513–4, 534, 540. Cf. Emil Notheisen, 'Die Vororte', in *AmtKrB* i. 2 (Freiburg, 1965), 1035. On the origins and development of Freiburg's suburbs cf. Berent Schwineköper, 'Die vorstädte von Freiburg im Breisgau während des Mittelalters', in Erich Maschke and Jürgen Sydow (eds.), *Stadterweiterung und Vorstadt* (Veröffentlichungen der Kommission für geschichtliche Landeskunde in Baden-Württemberg, Reihe B li) (Stuttgart, 1969), 39–58.

[92] In 1412 part of Adelhausen which lay outside the town's march-stones was mortgaged to Freiburg by Austria. *UBStFr* ii. 247. In 1456 archduke Albrecht transferred 'outer' Adelhausen to two of his councillors, ibid., pp. 443–4, but it was restored to Freiburg by duke Sigismund in 1459, ibid., pp. 462–5, and thereafter remained in the town's possession. Cf. Tom Scott, 'Zum Problem der Rechts- und Besitzverhältnisse eines Freiburger Vorortes: Das Dorf Adelhausen im 15. Jahrhundert', *Zeitschrift des Breisgau-Geschichtsvereins ('Schau-ins-Land')*, ci (1982), 97–106. In Old Adelhausen the Freiburg patrician family of Snewlin held the *Burgrecht*, a hearth-tax originally connected with the castle, which they tried to extend to 'outer' Adelhausen. StAFr, A 1 VIII a α 24, 1465–1510, 3 Oct. 1399; 9 Nov. 1444. After much wrangling the claim to 'outer' Adelhausen was abandoned in 1478, when Sigismund cancelled the

Freiburg's Relations with the Breisgau 39

the Snewlins surrendered their remaining claims in 1510 was Freiburg able to bring Adelhausen fully under its control.[93] Thereafter the physical extent of Freiburg's settlement barely altered until the nineteenth century. Meanwhile, as the demand for timber and grazing land began to outstrip its resources, Freiburg had to go further afield into the Breisgau to find fresh woodlands and pasture. Sometimes the town was able to annex virgin land, but usually it had to buy up land in the surrounding villages who were offered grazing and forest rights thereon at a nominal rent.[94] Over the years the town acquired an extensive hinterland up into the Black Forest and across into the valley of the Rhine which forms Freiburg's municipal boundary to the present day.

Freiburg's extension of its civic domain yielded only gradually to a more conscious policy of building up a landed territory separate from and subordinate to the town. Previously the counts of Freiburg had stood in the way of any territorial designs, so that the town concentrated instead on acquiring outburghers, but after 1368 the Habsburgs' benign tolerance of its local ambitions allowed Freiburg to contemplate carving out a rural lordship for itself.[95] Even so, it was only in the mid-fifteenth century, under the impact of a severe financial crisis and economic recession together with the continuing military emergencies on the Upper Rhine, that the town actively set about buying villages and lordships in the Breisgau. Until then it had only acquired the nearby village of Betzenhausen in 1381 for the paltry sum of eighteen silver marks.[96] But Betzenhausen was too small and insignificant to be of much use to Freiburg, and it never became the stepping-stone towards the creation of a wider landed territory west of the town.[97] Its purchase was more a matter of chance, since the village

---

original enfeoffment and issued a new privilege for Old Adelhausen alone. At the same time Freiburg warned the villagers of Old Adelhausen that they must by right continue to pay Bartholme Snewlin the *Burgrecht* to which he was still entitled there. B 5 XIIIa, iv, fo. 40ʳ, n.d. (Sept. 1478).

[93] StAFr, A 1 VIII a α 43, 1 Oct. 1510.

[94] Helmut Brandl, *Der Stadtwald von Freiburg. Eine forst- und wirtschaftsgeschichtliche Untersuchung über die Beziehung zwischen Waldnutzung und wirtschaftlicher Entwicklung der Stadt Freiburg vom Mittelalter bis zur Gegenwart* (Veröffentlichungen aus dem Archiv der Stadt Freiburg im Breisgau, xii) (Freiburg, 1970), 35, 38, 111–12. Cf. StAFr, B 3 11, 1432–1658, fos. 30ʳ–31ʳ, 2 Sept. 1432.

[95] Cf. Ulbrich, *Leibherrschaft*, pp. 191–2.

[96] *UBStFr* ii. 28–9.

[97] Despite Emil Notheisen, 'Stadtgemeinde: Außenbesitzungen', in *AmtKrB*, i. 2, 873.

had been owned by burghers of Freiburg from the early fourteenth century and in 1381 had already been on the market once that year.[98] The town subsequently made no move to incorporate the village: its inhabitants were treated simply as rural subjects; they were not granted burgher's rights or allowed entry to the gilds.[99]

For three-quarters of a century Betzenhausen remained Freiburg's only rural possession until, in 1457, it bought the manor and village of Herdern beyond its northern gates from the Teutonic Order of Knights for 2,550 fl.[100] The latter had only held Herdern on a lease from the counts of Fürstenberg and the town could not incorporate the village unless it acquired full rights of ownership so that it would pass under Austrian sovereignty. That was only achieved in 1538;[101] until then Herdern remained a rural dependency just as Betzenhausen, though the two villages were far from similar. Unlike Betzenhausen Herdern was more prosperous and market-oriented—witness the huge difference in the purchase price. Its 130 or so inhabitants[102] grew vines and corn as cash crops, as well as the much rarer and more valuable commodity of saffron.[103] That the town's reasons for buying Herdern were primarily economic is evident from the administrative changes which Freiburg forthwith introduced. It recast the previous weights and measures, levied tolls at the full rate and appropriated all the court fines, as well as interfering in the villagers' customary rights.[104] Until the late sixteenth century Freiburg bought no more villages outright, though in 1496 on Maximilian's instructions it took over the administration of three margravial villages, Opfingen, Wolfenweiler, and Haslach, which had previously been mortgaged to a Breisgau nobleman, whilst a dispute over his inheritance was settled.[105]

---

[98] *UBStFr* ii. 27–8; cf. Notheisen, 'Außenbesitzungen', p. 873.

[99] Ibid., p. 873. The villagers also had to pay tolls at the full rate. Karl Vogel, *Geschichte des Zollwesens der Stadt Freiburg i. Br. bis zum Ende des 16. Jahrhunderts* (Abhandlungen zur mittleren und neueren Geschichte, xxxiv) (Berlin/Leipzig, 1911), 88.

[100] StAFr, A I VIII a γ 42, 4 July 1457; *UBStFr* ii. 445–6.

[101] StAFr, A I VIII a γ 63, 29 July 1538. The cost was 575 fl. Cf. Franz Ludwig Baumann and Georg Tumbült (eds.), *Mitteilungen aus dem fürstlich fürstenbergischen Archive*, i (Tübingen, 1894), 6 n. 2. Cf. StAFr, B 5 XIIIa, xi, fo. 17ᵛ, 26 June 1538.

[102] Notheisen, 'Vororte', p. 1058. Herdern had approximately 26 hearths.

[103] Cf. *UBStFr* ii. 446.

[104] StAFr, A I VIII a γ 43, c.1460. Grievances of the village of Herdern, n.d. (c.1463).

[105] GLA 229/80590, 27 Feb. 1463; cf. StAFr, B 2 12, fos. 103ʳ–105ʳ. A I XIX Wolfenweiler 3, 5 Dec. 1495–5 Mar. 1496. Maximilian to Freiburg, 5 Dec. 1495. For the quarrel over inheritance, cf. the testimonies of 1494 in the surviving parchment fragment M 53/1 (to B 2 16).

Freiburg's Relations with the Breisgau

The council was chary of undertaking the responsibility; apart from the cost, the authorities were worried that Maximilian would gain a false impression of the town's economic strength,[106] whilst the implications of taking over foreign territory from Baden were much more ominous than acquiring lordships already under Austrian jurisdiction. Within four years, however, the mortgage was redeemed and in 1503 the villages restored to Baden.[107]

The accumulation of scattered villages in the Breisgau plain could not compete, however, with the bolder and much more extensive acquisition of land in the second half of the fifteenth century which the council undertook to the east of the town in the valley of the Dreisam and its tributaries flowing down from the Black Forest. Economically and strategically control of the Dreisam valley was of major significance for Freiburg. Lying at the foot of the mountains, Freiburg commanded a vantage-point on the main trade route from the Rhine across the Black Forest to the Upper Swabian merchant cities where the road left the broad plain to wind along the narrowing valley, up the Wagensteig pass and across the uplands by way of Urach to Villingen, or else took the steeper path along the Falkenstein valley up the Höllental gorge to Neustadt, Donaueschingen, and Schaffhausen.[108] But to make these routes safe for travellers and to ensure steady collection of the toll dues was no easy matter. During the fourteenth century brigandage by robber knights who sortied from their castles strung along the Dreisam and its offshoots posed a constant menace to the town's interests, and

---

[106] StAFr, B 5 XIIIa, iva, fo. 34ᵛ, 13 Feb. 1496. Eventually the town took over the mortgage for 2,900 fl. (GLA 229/80590, 20 Feb. 1496), but it was unable (or unwilling) to raise the full sum at once, and agreed instead to pay an annuity of 60 fl. on the outstanding 1,200 fl. StAFr, A 1 VII f 442, 25 Feb. 1496. Thereupon the villagers became sworn subjects of Freiburg, liable for civic taxes and military service. Cf. A 1 XIX Wolfenweiler 4, 18 Apr. 1496; B 5 X 1, fos. 4ʳ, 10ʳ; E 1 A II b 4, 'Reiss in Hoch Burgund, Anno domini 1498'.

[107] The mortgage was redeemed by Rudolf von Blumeneck, bailiff of the margravial lordship of Badenweiler. GLA 21/5816. Negotiations had been under way since 1498, cf. GLA 21/5814–15. This may also be inferred from the disappearance in 1500 from the list of councillors of the names of the overseers of the three villages. StAFr, B 5 I a, 2, fos. 74ᵛ, 76ʳ. Cf. also Rolf Süss, *Heimat am Tuniberg: Opfingen gestern und heute, 1006–1976* (Opfingen, 1976), 21.

[108] That the Falkenstein-Höllental was older, and throughout much of the Middle Ages more frequented, than the Wagensteig road, which was only built by Villingen in the early 14th c., has recently been demonstrated by Alfons Schäfer, 'Die Höllentalstraße. Ihre Erschließung und ihre Bedeutung für den Handelsverkehr vom Mittelalter bis ins 19. Jahrhundert', in *Festschrift Bauer*, 111–51. What is more arguable, however, is whether the Höllental retained its importance in the 15th c., when both Freiburg and Villingen had a vested interest in diverting traffic through the Wagensteig valley.

the council mounted several expeditions to attack and destroy their strongholds.[109] But instead of taking over the knights' estates and castles as the nucleus of a rural territory,[110] Freiburg preferred to make allies of the nobles by granting them the rights and privileges of outburghers. Once the brigandage declined, the council took no further steps during the first half of the fifteenth century to consolidate its authority over the Dreisam valley.

Yet in 1462 Freiburg decided to buy the entire estates of the abbey of St Märgen from the crest of the Wagensteig down into the Dreisam valley for 4,800 fl.,[111] and rounded off its jurisdiction the next year by buying the stewardship of the lands from Hans Snewlin von Landeck for another 1,000 fl.[112] The council's action certainly comes as a surprise, the more so since it followed hard upon the purchase of Herdern which had dealt a serious blow to the town's already rickety finances. In fact, it looks as if the council was not so much carrying out a calculated policy as reacting to a uniquely favourable opportunity. In 1462 St Märgen had come close to bankruptcy and the abbey was desperate to raise cash by selling its landed possessions. Freiburg seized the chance of acquiring a landed territory which would allow it to control a vital artery of trade at a price well below the true market value. In buying the stewardship the following year, moreover, the town may well have been driven by immediate political considerations, since the steward, Hans von Landeck, perhaps in order to counter Freiburg's intentions, had enlisted in a campaign by the Elector Palatine which threatened to engulf the Breisgau. In buying off Landeck, who controlled the important fortress of Wiesneck castle by Kirchzarten, the council may have hoped to avert a strategic danger at the centre of its new territorial interests.[113]

---

[109] Cf. *UBStFr* ii. 16–22, 59–83; Fritz Armbruster, 'Die Freiburger Talvogtei im Dreisamtal', in *Vorderösterreich*, 367.

[110] As, for instance, in Brunswick. Cf. Heinz Germer, *Die Landgebietspolitik der Stadt Braunschweig bis zum Ausgang des 15. Jahrhunderts* (Studien und Vorarbeiten zum historischen Atlas Niedersachsens, xvi) (Göttingen, 1937), 14, 18.

[111] StAFr, A 1 VIII a ζ 36, 29 Apr. 1462; *UBStFr* ii. 473–8.

[112] Ibid., pp. 479–84.

[113] Wolfgang Müller, 'Studien zur Geschichte der Klöster St Märgen und Allerheiligen, Freiburg im Breisgau', *Freiburger Diözesanarchiv*, lxxxix (1969), 53–4. Müller argues that Freiburg may have bought the St Märgen estates in order to thwart Landeck. However, they were acquired at the end of Apr. 1462—more than a month before Landeck placed himself in the service of palgrave Frederick in his campaign against count Ulrich of Württemberg, the bishop of Speyer and margrave Karl of Baden. If anything, the reverse was true (as Müller concedes).

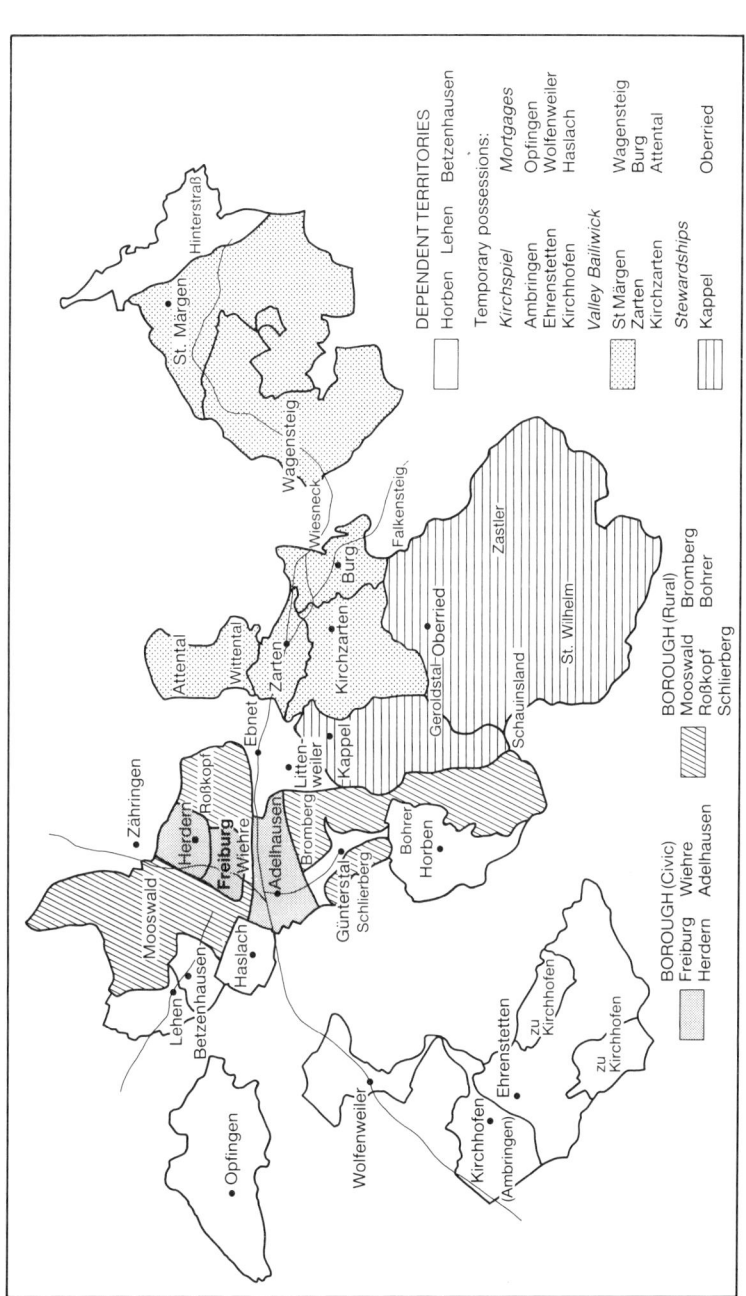

Map 3. Freiburg's Territorial Development to 1600

But even if the purchase was unpremeditated, Freiburg's interest in acquiring a landed territory had become acute by mid-century. Chronic economic difficulties coupled with frequent military emergencies brought home forcibly to the council how far the town's recovery and survival depended upon resources and support beyond its own walls. Even so, it is unlikely that Freiburg from the outset deliberately envisaged the creation of an extensive rural dependency along the Dreisam, since it took another thirty years before the town began to expand upon its St Märgen estates.[114] To bridge the gap between them and the town the council undertook a string of purchases throughout the 1490s. First it acquired the village and castle of Kirchzarten from Dietrich von Blumeneck and Konrad von Halfingen between 1491 and 1496;[115] in 1493 the jurisdiction over Himmelreich at the foot of the Höllental gorge from Martin von Blumeneck;[116] and in 1499 the Atten valley north of Kirchzarten as an Austrian mortgage from the abbey of St Peter.[117] Lastly, in 1502, Freiburg bought three farms east of Himmelreich and the toll at Zarten from the counts of Fürstenberg.[118] Together these territories, though never rounded off into a self-contained whole, comprised what Freiburg subsequently called its Valley Bailiwick (*Talvogtei*), a rural bastion with a unitary administration which the town retained until the nineteenth century.

Furthermore, in 1495–6 Freiburg acquired the stewardship of the monastery of Oberried, a Wilhelmite foundation with two priories, one in the town itself, the other at St Wilhelm above Oberried east of the town.[119] The former had the lordship of the Kappel valley which

[114] Though in 1462 Freiburg had begun negotiations to buy the nether manor of Birkenreute, south of Kirchzarten, the deal was not finally completed until 1556 when the town bought the manor and castle from Georg von Schneider. Max Weber, 'Die Kirchzartner Geschichte', in Günther Haselier (ed.), *Kirchzarten. Geographie — Geschichte — Gegenwart* (Kirchzarten, 1966), 245; cf. Armbruster, 'Talvogtei', p. 367.

[115] StAFr, A I VIII a ζ 92, 1 Aug. 1491; ibid., 93, n.d. (Sept. 1492); ibid., 96, 23 Apr. 1493; ibid., 111, 7 Dec. 1496. Cf. Fritz Armbruster, 'Die Freiburger Talvogtei im Dreisamtal. Studien zur Entwicklung und zur Verfassungsgeschichte bis zum Jahre 1661' (Diss. jur. Freiburg, 1950), 90–1, 96.

[116] StAFr, A I VIII a ζ 98, 12 June 1493; cf. Armbruster, 'Freiburger Talvogtei', p. 74.

[117] StAFr, A I VIII a ζ 118, 119, 20 Sept. 1499; cf. Armbruster, 'Freiburger Talvogtei', pp. 81–2.

[118] StAFr, A I VI d 94, 28 June 1502.

[119] For their foundation cf. Kaspar Elm, *Beiträge zur Geschichte des Wilhelmiterordens* (Münstersche Forschungen, xiv) (Cologne/Graz, 1962), 83–5. Originally the stewardship of both priories, the town claimed, had been entrusted on its behalf to local noblemen. Their alleged abuse of office led to town to reassume control. The town priory appears voluntarily to have transferred the stewardship to the council, as well as criminal jurisdiction over the Kappel valley. The stewardship of the 'forest' priory was given to

Freiburg's Relations with the Breisgau 45

adjoined the estates of the so-called 'forest' priory stretching from Geroldstal to the head of the Oberried valley in Hofsgrund.[120] Together they comprised a sizeable block of lands above Kirchzarten which, though never incorporated into the Valley Bailiwick, formed a southern buffer for Freiburg's Dreisam territory.[121]

This burst of acquisitions at the end of the fifteenth century clearly stemmed from a conscious effort to consolidate its landed territory, but why the council took so long to act is not easy to explain. There can be no doubt that the council was always determined to hang on to its St Märgen estates, since it firmly rebuffed repeated attempts by the abbey from the 1470s onwards to buy them back.[122] The delay in adding to its original purchase may simply have been the result of financial incapacity; Freiburg's economy was not really on the road to recovery until the 1490s, and even then the new acquisitions amounted to a considerable drain on the town's reserves.[123] By then, however, the council was obviously convinced that it had to take its chance, since it went ahead with the purchase of Kirchzarten despite Maximilian's

Freiburg on Maximilian's instructions after a bitter wrangle between the two previous priors and their steward. StAFr, A 1 XVI A o 34, 4 Sept. 1495 (cf. C 1 Kirchensachen 129, Oberried, 16th c.–1740); A 1 XVI A o 35, 31 Oct. 1495; B 1 2, fos. 60ʳ–62ᵛ; B 2 4, p. 236, c. 21 Feb. 1496; cf. B 5 XIIIa, iva, fo. 32ʳ⁻ᵛ; B 2 4; p. 242, 18 July 1496.

[120] StAFr, B 1 2, fo. 60ᵛ; Wolfgang Stülpnagel, 'Oberried: Frühere Herrschafts- und Besitzverhältnisse', in *AmtKrB* ii. 2 (Freiburg, 1974), 771.

[121] As the town clerk, Ulrich Zasius, explicitly recognized: 'das sölichs der stat (die sunst vil herlicheit im tal haben) nit unfruchtbar sin möcht.' StAFr, B 1 2, fo. 60ᵛ. In 1507 long-standing differences between the two priories were resolved by amalgamating them. The lands of the St Wilhelm foundation were incorporated into the town priory, though some monks remained at St Wilhelm to provide church services. Ferdinand Gießler, *Die Geschichte des Wilhelmitenklosters in Oberried bei Freiburg im Breisgau* (Freiburg, 1911), 38–9. Geißler errs, however, in believing that the stewardship of the two priories was not given to Freiburg until 1507. Ibid., p. 34.

[122] Armbruster, 'Freiburger Talvogtei', pp. 93–4. In 1490, after protracted litigation before the Outer Austrian government in Ensisheim, St Märgen finally gave up its attempts to repossess its estates and signed a treaty with Freiburg. GLA 13/8, 10 Feb. 1490. The settlement had been reached through the arbitration of a commission of Freiburg gildsmen. StAFr, A 1 VIII a ζ 89, 31 Mar. 1490. The purchase was finally confirmed by Maximilian in 1495. Ibid., 105, 15 Apr. 1495.

[123] Kirchzarten cost a total of 2,575 fl., Himmelreich 110 fl. (ibid., 99, 12 June 1493), the Atten valley 150 fl., and the three farms and the Zarten toll 450 fl. gold (in fact 489 fl. in current coin: cf. E 1 A 1 a 1, no. 2, 1503, fo. 5ʳ). That the town had difficulty in raising the money can be seen from its acknowledgement in 1492 that it still owed Konrad von Halfingen his 1,650 fl. (StAFr, A 1 VIII a ζ 93, n.d. (Sept. 1492)), and his willingness to defer payment once again the following year (ibid., 96, 23 Apr. 1493). Birkenreute cost 4,050 fl. in 1556, admittedly at a time when the town's finances had largely recovered (and when inflation had further reduced the real worth of the Rhenish gulden). Cf. Weber, 'Kirchzarten', p. 245.

avowed reservations.[124] In the face of continuing instability on the Upper Rhine, a convalescent economy, and the deteriorating fortunes of its outburghers Freiburg clearly believed that the acquisition of a landed territory was the only way of safeguarding and strengthening its position at the very time when its influence and responsibilities within Outer Austria were steadily mounting. Freiburg might lack the prestige of an Imperial Free City, but by 1500 its political powers in the Breisgau and its effective voice in Outer Austrian affairs lent it an aura of independence far greater than other territorial towns of late medieval Germany.[125]

---

[124] Maximilian's objection was twofold. The sale of Kirchzarten led to a dispute between Blumeneck and Halfingen over their share of the land, and the king was anxious to uphold Blumeneck's claim, as he was a royal councillor. The king also took exception to Freiburg's purchase of Kirchzarten castle, since the town had no right to acquire fortresses without the knowledge of its territorial ruler. StAFr, A 1 VIII a ζ 92, 1 Aug. 1491 and 9 Sept. 1491. The quarrel with Blumeneck was resolved two years later (ibid., 95, 12 Mar. 1493; ibid., 97, 24 May 1493). In 1495, after the town had sent a deputation to him at the imperial diet at Worms, Maximilian not only confirmed the purchase of Kirchzarten (and St Märgen), but conferred a series of privileges upon Freiburg as well. B 1 2, fos. 18ᵛ–24ʳ; cp. B 2 3, pp. 127–30, 15 Apr. 1495. These details considerably modify Armbruster's view, 'Freiburger Talvogtei', pp. 90–1, and idem, 'Talvogtei', p. 368, that Maximilian strongly objected in principle to the purchase. Cf. also *Deutsche Reichstagsakten*, mittlere Reihe, ed. Heinz Angermeier (Göttingen, 1981), 1048, nos. 1407, 1408.

[125] For a wider analysis of Freiburg's territorial policy, cf. Tom Scott, 'Die Territorialpolitik der Stadt Freiburg im Breisgau im ausgehenden Mittelalter', *Zeitschrift des Breisgau-Geschichtsvereins ('Schau-ins-Land')*, cii (1983), 7–24.

II

The Anatomy of a Craft Town

I

BY the mid-fourteenth century when Freiburg came under Austrian control the town was already characterized by a well-developed gild organization engaged chiefly in craft manufactures alongside the commercial, financial, and mining interests of the original merchant class. Formal craft corporations are first recorded in 1293,[1] but they certainly existed well before that. Even in a town founded explicitly as a merchant community craftsmen had always been able to acquire burgher's rights by buying property to the value of only one mark of silver.[2] By the end of the thirteenth century, moreover, it is clear that the gilds enjoyed some measure of autonomy for the master of each gild could draft its constitution in consultation with the mayor and magistrate, as well as lead his men on military campaigns.[3]

The function of the gilds as more than simply craft organizations received further recognition during the fourteenth century. In 1316 the gilds were given the right to elect their own masters,[4] and in 1338 it was decreed that everyone who resided in Freiburg for more than three months must join a gild.[5] This provision, it seems, was intended to strengthen the town's military organization which was already drawn up by gilds. Indeed, much of the gilds' political muscle derived from their role as backbone of the civic militia, a role underlined in 1416 when the council determined that only craftsmen who actually lived in Freiburg or its territories might join a gild: it wanted men who would be readily available in an emergency.[6] By 1293 the gilds had also been

---

[1] *UBStFr* i. 140–3.
[2] Hermann Flamm, *Der wirtschaftliche Niedergang Freiburgs im Breisgau* (Volkswirtschaftliche Abhandlungen der badischen Hochschulen, viii, supplementary vol. 3) (Karlsruhe, 1905), 41.
[3] *UBStFr* i. 140–1.
[4] Ibid., pp. 208–10.   [5] Ibid., pp. 336–7.
[6] Cf. Gustav Hinderschiedt, 'Die Freiburger Zunftordnungen des 15. und des 16. Jahrhunderts' (Diss. phil. Freiburg, 1953), 10. Hinderschiedt rightly rejects Flamm's view that the council's intention was to counteract the growing number of

granted some say in fiscal and economic matters. The council, then dominated by a permanent body of non-elected patricians to which the inclusion of an elected group of craftsmen from the commons made little practical difference, was, nevertheless, required to consult the gilds before levying taxes or disposing of public property.[7]

The source of the gilds' growing power stemmed from the compulsion to join a gild from 1338 onwards, though the provision was not always strictly enforced during the fourteenth century. The only gild not to carry through a closed shop was the humble fraternity of wine-growers, a motley assortment of peasant burghers, day-labourers, servants, and carters as well as the vintagers themselves.[8] Even if the gilds came to exercise some autonomy within their own corporations, however, their political power within the city as a whole—on the council and in municipal administration—remained subordinate to that of the patriciate well after Freiburg's submission to Austria. But after 1368 vastly changed circumstances led the craft gilds to stage what has been called a gild revolution in 1388. The financial legacy of 1368 made Freiburg less attractive a domicile for richer residents. Frequent involvement in Austrian campaigns against the Swiss gave the patriciate an opportunity to display chivalric prowess, but led in 1386 to the crushing defeat of the Habsburg forces at the battle of Sempach near Lucerne. Many scions of Freiburg's noble families fell in the battle with the result that the council was shorn of its most illustrious and powerful members. The serious shortfall of councillors to fill the main civic offices appears to have brought severe disarray to the town government, and in January 1388 the commons mounted a successful and bloodless coup. The new government which was formed gave a majority of seats to representatives of the eighteen gilds and relegated the rump of the patriciate to the sidelines. Although the gild-dominated administration does not appear to have pursued any particularly novel or radical policies, except to take energetic action against robber barons in the Dreisam valley, the coup incurred the

artisans in the countryside. Concern about footloose soldiery was reflected in a letter to the council that year. *UBStFr* ii. 267–8.

[7] *UBStFr* i. 142.

[8] In 1417 the vintagers petitioned the council for the right of compulsory membership but were refused because the council wished to preserve the right of all inhabitants to employ native or foreign labour according to their needs. Cf. Joseph Ehrler, 'Stadtverfassung und Zünfte Freiburgs im Breisgau. Ein Beitrag zur oberrheinischen Wirtschaftsgeschichte', part II, *Jahrbücher für Nationalökonomie und Statistik*, xliv (1912), 457.

wrath of the Austrian ruler, duke Leopold, whose prerogative to sanction constitutional change had clearly been slighted. After considerable negotiations Leopold gave his consent to a new constitution in 1392 which, whilst restoring pre-eminence to the particiate, recognized for the first time the *de facto* political influence which the gilds had acquired and formally altered the composition and appointment of the council and its administrative boards to take account of gild demands.[9]

The constitution of 1392 remained, with one brief interruption in the mid-fifteenth century, the foundation of Freiburg's municipal government for the next century and a half. Even when the gilds had effectively seized complete power in the second half of the fifteenth century, the organization and scope of civic government remained much the same: the gilds had simply hollowed out the constitution from within. The reforms of 1392 swept away the old two-tier council structure of a non-elective patrician body alongside an elected body of patricians and craftsmen in favour of a single body, all of whose members were subject to annual election, which provided for parity between patriciate and gilds. Henceforth twelve nobles and twelve merchants were to sit alongside the eighteen gildmasters (who were ex officio councillors) and six further gildsmen drawn from the ranks of the master craftsmen. Moreover, the town magistrate, whose office remained pawned to the town by Austria, now had to be drawn from the council members rather than being arbitrarily installed by the Habsburgs. Because the council in its turn controlled all aspects of civic administration, the reforms of 1392 were bound to have an impact on the gilds' participation in the day to day running of the town's affairs. The supervision of the town's economic and financial business was entrusted to a Board of the Exchange whose six members were drawn equally from the three groups of nobles, merchants, and gildsmen. This division applied likewise to the two chief organs of justice, the higher criminal court and the civil and lesser criminal court, over both of which the magistrate presided. These were the essential branches of municipal government defined by the constitution, whose composition could only be altered with the sanction of the territorial ruler. But in the remaining boards of administration, whose staffing was at the council's sole discretion,[10] the gilds, by virtue of the

[9] *UBStFr* ii. 88–93.
[10] The nine main boards throughout the fifteenth century were: Public Works; Forests; Bread and Meat Inspectors; the Minster; the Lazaret; the Church of

new constitution, were at last given the opportunity of proper representation. These boards were staffed by councillors, and from 1392 onwards until the mid-fifteenth century all the main boards usually had three members, two patricians and one gildsman.

Though the transition to a more democratic—or, rather, a more accountable—civic government was accomplished without main force, the constitution of 1392 certainly fell well short of the gilds' full aspirations, and quickly revealed several shortcomings in the early decades of the next century. In the first place, the formal parity between patriciate and gilds on a council of 48 members barely disguised the fact that in reality nobles and merchants retained the upper hand. Already the provision that each year twelve members of the outgoing council should be reselected onto the new council to furnish continuity and experience shifted the political balance of the council in favour of the patriciate, for these twelve old councillors were not to be drawn equally from patriciate and gilds but rather four each from nobles, merchants, and gildsmen, thereby leaving the latter in a minority. This division of political representation into thirds was carried right through the municipal administration, so that nobles and merchants together could always outvote or outmanœuvre the gilds on the boards.

The effective restoration of power to the patriciate after the upheavals of 1388 reveals, however, the essential paradox at the heart of the 1392 constitution. The constitution sanctioned by duke Leopold had at the same time to recognize the right of the nobility to leave the town more or less at will—a concession of great significance since permission to leave was dependent upon the payment of a large discharge-fine in lieu of lost tax revenues.[11] A constitution, therefore, designed to ensure the continued dominance of the patriciate in public office simultaneously permitted it to quit the town and slough off its civic responsibilities. Between 1393 and 1397, it has been reckoned, at least twenty substantial residents used the provisions of 1392/3 to dissolve their households and withdraw, and of these at least eight

St Nicholas; Orphans; the Hospital. Until the end of the 14th c. there was a Board of Jewish Affairs. Other boards were added after 1454, notably to administer the affairs of the outburghers and the new territories. Altogether, there were generally 12–15 boards, much the same as in the preceding century. Cf. Rowan, 'Guilds', pp. 106–7.

[11] *UBStFr* ii. 92. Within ten years the nobles might depart without paying a quittance. The decree was repeated the following year, when the nobility were required to declare within a fortnight whether they would stay or go. Ibid., pp. 93–4.

were patrician members of the council.[12] As a result, in every subsequent year there was a shortfall of council members from the patriciate, particularly from the merchants whose livelihood was threatened by the decline of the silver-mines and who saw little opportunity in a town increasingly attuned to craft rather than commercial interests. That inevitably placed a heavy burden of responsibility on those who remained, who had to take on several posts at once on the boards of administration.[13] The holding of a string of offices by one councillor, so frequently recorded in the council lists of the early fifteenth century, should not be seen so much as a sign of oligarchic tendencies within the town government as of sheer necessity.

By the early 1400s the constitution of 1392 was becoming increasingly unworkable, or unrealizable. At last in 1413, after long and loud protests from the citizenry at the delay in bringing cases to court, duke Frederick was obliged to allow the busiest board of justice, the civil and lesser criminal court, to be staffed by four members of each rank—nobles, merchants, and gildsmen—rather than three, and to decree that its members need not always be councillors, but could be drawn from the community at large.[14] The pressure of business was greatest there, since all public litigation and the bulk of felonies which could be redeemed by a fine passed through this court, and it was regarded as a public scandal that the council was unable to staff it adequately.

The shortfall of patricians was not confined to the administrative boards alone. By 1435 it had emerged that the council itself could not make up its quota of patrician members, as a result of which the conduct and regularity of meetings was apparently suffering. To remedy the situation duke Frederick had to step in once again to ordain that the council should make up the complement of membership by filling vacant patrician seats through the co-option of common gildsmen.[15] These, however, were *ad hoc* arrangements sanctioned by Austria: the constitution itself remained in its fundamentals unaltered. It was perhaps this characteristic reluctance to envisage far-reaching

[12] Steven W. Rowan, 'Community Survival. Freiburg im Breisgau from the Black Death to the Reformation' (unpublished MS), 116.
[13] The Board of the Exchange likewise appears to have suffered from understaffing. Around mid-century the council considered reducing its membership from six to four, with the rule that its officers should hold no other civic post except a council seat. StAFr, ungeordnete Bestände (to B 5 XIIIa, iia), Ratsbeschlüsse, n.d. (*c*.1450), fos. 1^r, 2^r.
[14] *UBStFr* ii. 250–1.   [15] Ibid., pp. 389–90.

changes which discouraged the gilds during the first half of the fifteenth century from trying to take the council by storm; instead they sought to bring popular pressure to bear on it from outside. This can be seen from the growth of an extra-conciliar body, the so-called Eight, a committee of elders drawn from each gild who were not already council members. Their advice was sought, at first informally, and then obligatorily, on major issues: sensitive matters of internal policy and overriding decisions of war and peace. The first recorded instance of consultation with the Eight comes in 1428 when they, and the gilds as a whole, were sounded out on their attitude towards levying an excise on corn sent for milling, a highly charged issue since it involved raising money from the staple diet of the population, bread.[16]

The upshot of these developments was that by mid-century the council had become estranged from political reality. By the terms of its constitutional composition it was unable to govern effectively, and by the same token its membership failed to reflect the vast shift in social structure amongst Freiburg's population, since its submission to Austria, away from a merchant community towards a craft town of middling artisans, organized into gilds, who bore the brunt of the town's public requirements—in defence, in taxation—without a corresponding political voice. But the remedy which archduke Albrecht prescribed in 1454 during his rule of the western Habsburg lands was drastic, inappropriate and reactionary. He recognized that the town was still suffering the crippling effects of the debts it had incurred in 1368, but the way he chose to help it out of its plight placed the blame for the continuing crisis squarely on the behaviour of the gildsmen within the council who, he alleged, had sown discord and disruption which had militated against smooth and efficient administration. Moreover, he contended that a number of gild councillors were not fitted to hold public office, either because they were disreputable and dishonest, or else because they were too poor to afford to serve in government.[17] Some craftsmen on the council, it was stated, had no more than what they earned by their daily labour. Albrecht's solution to this sorry state of affairs was to abolish the gilds as corporations altogether, thereby necessitating an entire recasting of

---

[16] Rowan, 'Guilds', p. 305.

[17] In view of the subsequent reduction from 18 gilds to 12 by 1459 this charge may well have been correct. Cf. Ute Keßner, 'Albrecht VI. von Österreich und das Freiburger Zunftverbot 1454' (Wissenschaftliche Prüfungsarbeit, Univ. of Freiburg, 1976), 43.

the town's administration.[18] The size of the council was halved to twenty-four members, parity of a sort being retained by balancing six nobles and six merchants against twelve men chosen from the commons. Of these, six represented the wards into which Albrecht had decided to divide the town as a surrogate for the abandoned gild organization, and the remainder were drawn from craftsmen or other commoners. Half the councillors, drawn equally from the four groups, were to serve on the subsequent council as guarantors of stability and continuity. The new constitution did preserve a balance between patriciate and commons, but it was a balance which, as in the case of the Board of the Exchange, excluded commoners and left ward-masters in a minority over against the nobles and merchants. In what may be seen as a conscious resurrection of the old administration before 1388, the function of the higher criminal court was transferred to the council sitting as a whole,[19] whilst the lesser court was to be staffed by three nobles, three merchants, and three others taken from the ward-masters, craftsmen, or other commoners, though it appears that the court was in fact reduced to only seven members,[20] with the mayor present ex officio. The latter was to receive two advisers, one a merchant, the other a ward-master, to act as spokesmen for his office before the community.

Albrecht's constitutional innovations contained the seeds of their own collapse. The constitution, which was designed to shore up the power of the patriciate, implicitly acknowledged that its numbers were dwindling, inasmuch as it halved the size of the council and legislated from the outset for a possible shortfall of members. But unlike the provisions of 1435, the shortfall in the patriciate could only be compensated by juggling the number of nobles and merchants: total numbers could not be made up by fresh blood from the commons. Moreover, the role of the two advisers to the mayor, who remained a nobleman, was a tacit admission that the mayor could not be relied upon to keep properly informed about the internal affairs of the town or give a coherent account of the council's motives and policies; he was, in other words, a figure-head rather than a chief executive. More

---

[18] *UBStFr* ii. 434–41.

[19] Cf. Hermann Joachim, 'Gilde und Stadtgemeinde in Freiburg i. Br. Zugleich ein Beitrag zur Rechts- und Verfassungsgeschichte dieser Stadt', in *Festgabe zum 21. Juli 1905 Anton Hagedorn . . . gewidmet* (Hamburg/Leipzig, 1906), 92–3.

[20] StAFr, B 5 I a, 2. Between 1454 and 1458 the council lists contain no lists of the nine lesser court members but instead 'die VII'. The balance of nobles and merchants varied slightly from year to year.

generally, it was apparent that the wards were entirely artificial divisions which could not hope to become the focus of communal loyalties and activity in the way that the gilds as living corporations and social entities had been.[21] The abolition of the gilds may not have been economically deleterious, for the crafts themselves remained, but the framework of the town's military organization had been destroyed. Not only was the abolition of the gilds a crude manœuvre which created resentment and unrest, it was an act of state which entirely evaded the real problems facing the town which the archduke in his own words was so eager to alleviate.[22]

Within five years, by 1459, the gilds were restored and Freiburg's administration recast once more.[23] In 1464 Albrecht's successor, Sigismund, granted the gilds a general restitution which was endorsed by the Outer Austrian governor.[24] Although no formal constitution after the restoration of the gilds has survived, we can reconstruct the shape of the new town government from the surviving council-lists. The pattern of 1392 was reaffirmed, except that the gilds were at last given genuine parity, or even a preponderance, in public office. The council was expanded to thirty, twelve members coming from the patriciate and the gildmasters respectively, and another six supplementary councillors from patriciate and commons alike, though within a year the additional councillors were being drawn exclusively from the gilds, and after 1465 the pretence that they represented patricians and commons was quietly dropped. Half the outgoing council was taken up into the new council, and here too the gild members soon came to predominate. The gilds' growing influence was reflected equally in the structure of municipal administration. The higher criminal court was restored with a notional parity of twelve patricians and twelve gildsmen;[25] the lower court appears to have had four each, with the mayor present ex officio. Although he was again accorded two

---

[21] The authorities recognized that the new wards could not acquire parlours unless the gilds' assets were sequestered and redistributed throughout the whole community. This they resolved to do, though whether the plan was carried out is not certain. StAFr, A 1 vi d 69, n.d. (1454).

[22] Keßner correctly observes that the abolition of the gilds did not destroy the influence of the leading craft patricians, who continued to serve as individuals on the council; the measure was really directed against the lesser gildsmen in an attempt to forestall a genuine 'democratization' of civic government. Keßner, 'Zunftverbot', p. 44.

[23] StAFr, B 5 I a, 2 fo. 9ʳ. Albrecht apparently contemplated reintroducing the gilds before 1459. B 2 2, fo. 4ʳ. Keßner, 'Zunftverbot', p. 55.

[24] StAFr, A 1 I e 27, 18 Sept. 1464; UBStFr ii. 484–5.

[25] StAFr, B 5 I a, 2, fo. 9ᵛ.

spokesmen, as in 1454, they disappear from the record after 1464. Nor surprisingly, perhaps, the Board of the Exchange, as the arbiter of the town's economy, proved more resistant to gild influence. It was reconstituted with two nobles, two merchants, and two gildsmen, but this balance was rapidly overturned by the absence of sufficient patricians to do duty on it.[26] Nevertheless, the Exchange appears to have remained under the control of the richer and more powerful gildsmen, and accusations of malpractice (or lack of accountability) led to a chain of popularly inspired reforms of the Board during the 1490s. On the remaining boards which the council staffed a new pattern was immediately visible. Instead of two patricians and one gildsman, the main public offices were henceforth staffed in the ratio of one patrician to two gildsmen, and by the end of the century some boards were composed entirely of gildsmen.

Over against 1454 the events of 1459/64 represented a decisive political restoration, but compared with 1392 no startling shift of power had taken place, except that a few checks and balances intended to moderate the effects of gild rule were retained, though these were then quickly discarded. The gilds' domination of Freiburg's affairs was the work of the following decades, as the continuing disappearance of nobles and merchants more or less forced the gilds to assume greater responsibility. The erosion of the power of the patriciate from within, as it were, can most vividly be observed in the actual composition of the council and its boards over the succeeding decades when set alongside its notional composition. By 1490 the thirty members of the full council comprised six nobles, and twelve gildmasters, and twelve additional councillors from the gilds,[27] who by the early sixteenth century had become such an established feature of the administration that their appointment was formalized to ensure that they were drawn from each of the twelve gilds, rather than being recruited haphazard from the more powerful corporations. As Rowan has remarked, the holding of these additional seats is a truer test of the gilds' political influence than the seats of the gildmasters; the latter were ex officio members by virtue of their gild nomination, whereas the supplementary councillors were elected by the whole of the outgoing council, and were therefore relatively immune from the vagaries of popular favour.

[26] StAFr, B 5 I a, 2, *passim*. From 1477 numbers varied between five and six; from 1493 five only.

[27] By the early 16th c. there were 14 or even 15 supplementary councillors. In 1502 for the first time they were listed alongside their respective gildmasters.

Year in, year out certain powerful gildsmen continued to sit on the council for long stretches by alternating between gildmastership and supplementary co-option.[28]

The real distribution of power on the council highlights the most significant aspect of the triumph of gild rule in Freiburg: the gilds' domination of civic affairs after 1464 by no means led to more accountable or open (let alone democratic) government. Power within the gilds was confined to the wealthy; throughout the fifteenth century councillors were drawn almost exclusively from the wealthiest third of gild membership. To temper this exclusivity the council had to agree to the Eight as the leading body of non-councillors having a say in the running of public affairs, particularly the finances. In 1467, for instance, it was formally agreed that the council could not raise any further loans and so increase the already considerable public debt without the express consent of the Eight.[29] Even the scrutiny of the Eight, however, could not prevent the growth of oligarchic tendencies on the part of the small group of long-serving gildmasters who dominated the council, especially since in 1481 the character of the Eight was substantially altered by a council decision that the custom of a few gilds, in which candidates were appointed each year by their predecessors in office, should henceforth apply to all the gilds.[30] The upshot was that the gilds, and eventually the town government itself, fell into the hands of cliques. By 1489/90 popular disquiet at the conduct of civic affairs led king Maximilian to intervene, but even his sanctioned reforms of the town's financial administration could not prevent Freiburg falling victim to a decade of upheaval and unrest. Gild government, as Naujoks has observed, was bound by the nature of its function and composition to estrange itself from the commons from which it was ultimately recruited.[31] Its ostensibly 'democratic' character was no guarantee of good relations between council and craft gilds.

II

By the end of the fifteenth century the gilds had set their stamp as firmly on the organization and scope of Freiburg's economy as they

[28] Rowan, 'Guilds', p. 255. [29] StAFr, B 5 XIIIa, iv, fo. 5ᵛ; cf. B 2 4, p. 165.
[30] StAFr, B 5 XIIIa, iv, fo. 48ʳ.
[31] Cf. Eberhard Naujoks, 'Obrigkeit und Zunftverfassung in den süddeutschen Reichsstädten', *Zeitschrift für württembergische Landesgeschichte*, xxxiii (1974), 61–2.

The Anatomy of a Craft Town

had upon its government and politics. Freiburg, the city which had been founded expressly for merchants, sank back into a community of small artisan producers. The merchants gradually withdrew until by the mid-fifteenth century they were no longer entered separately in the list of council members. More and more Freiburg became a craft town whose economy depended upon organized gilds who were often hostile towards entrepreneurs and merchant capitalists.

How the gilds had developed as public corporations during the fourteenth century up to their coup in 1388 is by no means clear, but their number certainly did not tally with the total of crafts in manufacturing and services that existed. A good half-dozen gilds comprised several independent crafts, not always related to each other. The builders' gild, for example, comprised not only masons, but also carpenters, joiners, cartwrights, and potters, whilst the painters' gild was even more disparate since it embraced within one organization glaziers, saddlers, ropemakers, bath-house-keepers and cuppers, and the leech-doctors.[32] It has already been stressed that the *raison d'être* of the gild structure was military rather than economic, so that within each gild the various crafts retained their own identity, with separate ordinances and statutes, even though they had no individual political voice.

Freiburg's gild organization, however, was not as all-embracing as it appeared. For one thing, the largest gild of all, the wine-growers', had no proper structure and was unable to enforce a closed shop. The reason lay in its function as a refuge for the lower and semi-skilled elements in the population, day-labourers and servants as well as vintagers. In 1412 the council in fact declared that all immigrants who derived their livelihood from unskilled manual labour should join the wine-growers' gild.[33] In contrast to other gilds the wine-growers lacked any effective say in their own affairs, not least because the responsibility for fixing labourers' wage-rates lay with the council, not the gild. When the latter unsuccessfully petitioned the council in 1417 to grant a closed shop, it was hoping not only to regulate its membership but also to acquire the administrative authority and

---

[32] Cf. Ernst Theodor Nauck, *Aus der Geschichte der Freiburger Wundärzte und verwandter Berufe* (Veröffentlichungen aus dem Archiv der Stadt Freiburg im Breisgau, viii) (Freiburg, 1965), 11. In 1378 the ropemakers were mentioned as a separate gild but no longer in the gild lists of 1390. StAFr, A 1 vi e v 1, 2 Jan. 1378. Cf. Schreiber, *Geschichte*, i. 2 (Freiburg, 1857), 203.

[33] Eberhard Gothein, *Wirtschaftsgeschichte des Schwarzwaldes und der angrenzenden Landschaften*, i (Strasbourg, 1892), 367.

privileges which the other gilds already enjoyed.[34] For another, even during the era of gild ascendancy some economic activity took place outwith the gild framework. The fraternity of cutters and polishers, founded in 1451, had no separate gild organization; its members joined the existing gilds. The craft had grown up in Freiburg and Waldkirch during the fifteenth century after semiprecious stones had been found in the same areas as the earlier silver-mines.[35] That the working of semiprecious stones occupied an important place in Freiburg's economy at the turn of the century[36] is underlined by a council letter of 1520 which recorded the town's leading trades as cutting and polishing, mining, and the cultivation of saffron,[37] although, as it conceded, the silver-mines were greatly in decline.[38] It is worth noting that all three were luxury trades, which suggests that the preponderance of purely craft manufactures was not considered to provide the real impetus of Freiburg's economy.

That the economic decline of the fifteenth century dealt a severe blow to the viability of several crafts can be seen in the reduction of the number of gilds from eighteen to twelve sometime before 1459, a change reflected in the composition of the council after the gild restoration that year. The six gilds which disappeared were the fishers, carters, victuallers, millers, furriers, and taverners. These trades were in fact merged with the remaining gilds, losing their gild autonomy but retaining their craft identity.[39] For that reason the amalgamation has been interpreted as a deliberate attempt to weaken the gild structure in the wake of archduke Albrecht's reversion to a patrician constitution. However, the reduction occurred when the gilds were already suspended,[40] and it seems more likely that the council had administrative and military reasons for supplementing the numbers of some gilds by allocating to them others which had been seriously weakened as a

[34] Ehrler, 'Stadtverfassung', part II, p. 457.

[35] The trade received a further impetus from the use of the water-driven grinding-wheel, which was probably pioneered in Freiburg in the early 15th c. Rudolf Metz, 'Bergbau und Hüttenwesen in den Vorlanden', in *Vorderösterreich*, p. 179.

[36] Freiburg's crystal had a high enough reputation for emperor Charles V to order some. Gothein, *Wirtschaftsgeschichte*, p. 569.

[37] Saffron was used as a perfume, a spice, and a dye. It was listed amongst the toll goods in 1494, but otherwise is rarely mentioned in the sources.

[38] StAFr, B 5 XI, x, fos. 253ʳ–254ᵛ.

[39] Fishers and carters joined the butchers; victuallers joined the bakers; millers the builders; furriers the haberdashers; and taverners the coopers.

[40] The council lists record 18 gilds in 1454, the year in which they were abolished; by 1459, when they reappear, their number was 12.

result of the town's economic and demographic decline. The disregard for craft affinities suggests that economic criteria were not paramount. Indeed, the somewhat artificial colligation later gave rise to complaints during the years of unrest after 1490. The haberdashers argued that the victuallers had suffered by having to join the bakers' gild instead of their own; the bakers themselves, it transpired, were equally unhappy about the liaison.[41]

The reduction in the number of gilds must not be interpreted as a sign of weakening in their collective influence over civic affairs as a whole. If anything, it was a prelude to its growth, for after 1459/64 the gilds, reorganized and revitalized, began to press the council to carry through economic and financial reforms in their interest. This can be seen from the spate of new gild constitutions which the council sanctioned in 1477. These, it has been commonly argued, mark a caesura in the economic and political life of Freiburg for the ordinances embraced openly for the first time—against the background of a convalescent economy and shrinking market—the principle of small-scale artisan production by independent masters, which was intended to guarantee a reasonable living for all by fixing limits on production and employment, so that the richer gildsmen should not corner the market or be able to exercise their capital reserves or entrepreneurial skill to bring some mastercraftsmen into dependence upon them.[42] As the corporations grew more exclusive, so the compulsion to join was more rigorously enforced.

These developments throw into sharper relief the isolation of the wine-growers, which became increasingly apparent after 1464. By 1468 the gilds had succeeded in requiring the cutters and polishers, as well as richer gentlemen and rentiers who did not ply a trade, to join a gild; which they chose was immaterial, but the wine-growers' gild was barred to them: it was evidently too mean and lowly for persons of quality.[43] At the same time, the council was concerned to encompass even the humblest workers within the gild framework, but its task was not easy amongst so shifting a population. Council decrees of 1479[44] and 1481[45] reiterated earlier legislation on compulsory gild membership; in 1477 manual labourers—diggers and ditchers—and carriers of salt

---

[41] StAFr, A 1 VI e α 3, 21 Feb. 1472; 14 Apr. 1497; 30 Oct. 1499. 'Reformierung der zunfft', n.d. (1495), p. 25.
[42] Cf. Hinderschiedt, 'Zunftordnungen', pp. 22–3, 56.
[43] StAFr, A 1 VI e α 2, 23 Sept. 1468; cf. B 2 4, p. 158.
[44] StAFr, B 5 XI, iv, 11, fo. 142^v.   [45] StAFr, B 5 XIIIa, iv, fo. 47^r.

and iron were compelled to join a gild,[46] as were domestic servants in 1497.[47] The only exceptions remained the so-called dishonourable professions—knacker, hangman, brothel-keeper, whores—along with shiftless spinning-girls; they were gathered into a separate tax system based on streets of residence rather than gild membership.

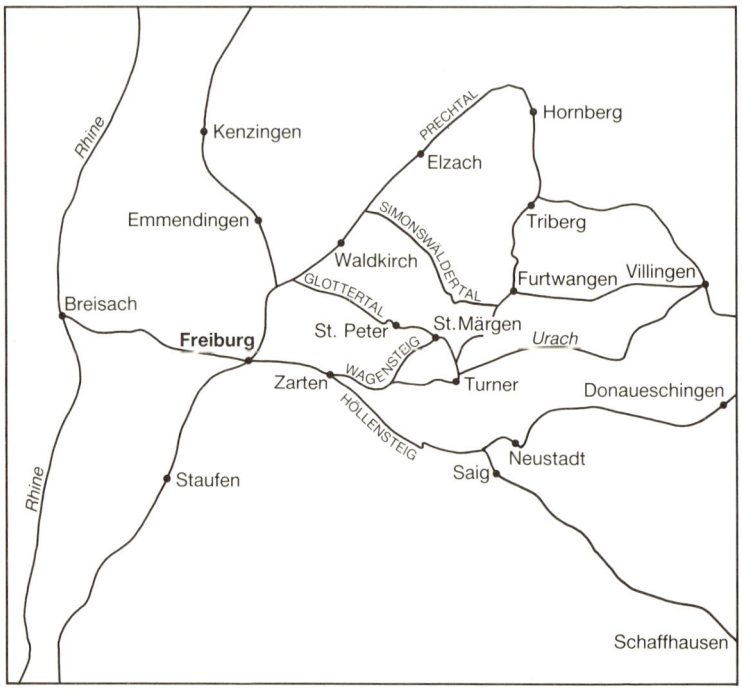

Map 4. Routes over the Black Forest in the Fifteenth and Sixteenth Centuries

The character of the gild economy was also affected by Freiburg's geographical location, its resources and supply, trade routes, and market area. Once the silver-mines had ceased to yield a lucrative income, the town was thrown back upon its own resources. Although precious stones were latterly found locally, Freiburg's economic strength came to rest essentially upon its strategic market situation

[46] Ibid., fo. 36ᵛ; cf. B 5 XIIIa, iva, fo. 5ʳ; B 2 4, p. 213.
[47] StAFr, B 5 XIIIa, vi, fo. 16ʳ; cf. B 5 XIIIa, iva, fo. 42ʳ⁻ᵛ; B 5 XIIIa, vii, fo. 2ᵛ. The edict was repeated eleven years later. B 5 XIIIa, x, fo. 98ʳ.

rather than on any natural resources of great significance. Commanding a vantage-point on the east–west trade route over the Black Forest to the Breisgau and Alsace, where the Dreisam valley broadens into the fertile plain of the Upper Rhine, Freiburg was a natural entrepôt both for goods travelling over longer distances to Swabia and beyond and for the local exchange of produce between the pastoral uplands and arable lowlands of the South-West. Once, as a merchant community, Freiburg had relied upon entrepreneurial flair to manufacture fine cloths which were traded over a considerable distance, but in the economic recession of the late Middle Ages that market contracted and was lost. Thereafter the cloth gild was generally too poor, even if it had retained its enterprise and skill, to raise the capital necessary to overcome previous disinvestment. By the 1390s Freiburg had all but ceased to manufacture for a wider market and was forced to live largely on trade with its immediate hinterland.

How far the town was at the mercy of its economic relations with the surrounding countryside can be gauged by examining whether Freiburg depended for its raw materials and other goods on local supplies or imports from afar. Its own resources within municipal territory were confined to woodland and water. As the town had expanded in the thirteenth and fourteenth century, the council had sought to extend its ownership of the nearby forests which provided essential building material and heating fuel. That involved taking land from the surrounding villages,[48] who were granted grazing rights thereon as compensation.[49] The acquisition of the Valley Bailiwick in the fifteenth century greatly augmented its reserves of woodland, but the town never became an important centre for rafting unlike several communities at the foot of the Black Forest. The council was content to lease rafting rights to its burghers,[50] but most of the timber felled was required by the town itself; indeed, there are signs that supplies were dwindling throughout the fifteenth century due to lack of systematic clearing and replanting. Freiburg's watercourse, on the other hand, was a vital element in the town's economy which markedly affected the nature and scope of craft production. The Dreisam had been dammed early, as the name Wiehre for the southern faubourg indicates. The weir supplied water to the town culverts—an important and unusual measure of medieval public hygiene—and to the moat.

[48] Brandl, *Stadtwald*, p. 38.
[49] Ibid., pp. 111–12. Cf. StAFr, B 3 11, pp. 30–1.
[50] Cf. StAFr, A 1 VIII d 18, 27 Apr. 1491; ibid., 20, 2 Sept. 1513.

The sluices also channelled water through conduits, known as *Runze*, fast-flowing watercourses which supplied energy for the various craft installations along their banks. Their owners formed themselves into riparian associations to supervise and maintain the sluices, water-meadows, and installations, and to tax craftsmen—such as tanners—who drew upon the water supply for their trade.[51] Along these conduits were strung out the fourteen or so flour-mills, as well as oil-presses, the two fulling-mills, forge-hammers, and the several grinding-wheels of the cutters and polishers.

These were the needs which Freiburg could supply itself. What it lacked was any extent of common land for grazing or cultivation. The expansion of the suburbs and Freiburg's geographical restriction by mountain and forest left little clear ground. What there was—the upper and lower holms between the conduits—was customarily let out to individual burghers,[52] though the butchers fattened stock for market on the common outside the town limits,[53] such as the Bohrer, the valley stretching from Günterstal to the foot of the Schauinsland. Supplies of meat came mostly from the Breisgau, though in times of shortage cattle were imported from as far afield as Swabia and Burgundy.[54] In general, the surrounding peasantry supplied the town with food and animal products—skins, tallow, lard—which were in turn vital raw materials for several of the town's crafts. Wool came from the Breisgau, especially from the vast flocks of sheep kept by the Knights of St John on their estates at Heitersheim.[55] Equally, the town imported much of its cloth ready-made from centres such as Liège, Malines, or even London:[56] much of it was bought at international fairs such as Frankfurt. The town was acutely aware of its dependence on its hinterland, and was held back from imposing higher taxes on the outburgher nobility by the thought that they might retaliate by ordering their subjects to boycott the market.[57]

Certain essential commodities, however, lay entirely beyond the council's ambit; they could only be obtained through long-distance

---

[51] Gothein, *Wirtschaftsgeschichte*, pp. 101, 494.
[52] Often to councillors: StAFr, B 5 XI, iv, 11, fo. 75^r; ibid., fo. 76^r; ibid., fo. 77^r.
[53] Cf. StAFr, B 1 2, fo. 101^r.
[54] Cf. Flamm, *Niedergang*, p. 65. The cattle market at Cernay in Upper Alsace served as the entrepôt between Burgundy and the territories on the Upper Rhine.
[55] Theophil Frank, 'Das Textilgewerbe der Stadt Freiburg i. Br. bis zum Ausgang des 16. Jahrhunderts' (Diss. phil. Freiburg, 1912), 16–17.
[56] Gothein, *Wirtschaftsgeschichte*, p. 540.
[57] Cf. StAFr, B 5 XIIIa, iv, fo. 30^{r-v}.

commerce. Steel had to be imported from Lombardy, iron from industrial centres such as Nuremberg.[58] The toll-charge lists give a wide range of other imports: salt, spices, furs, paint, tin, copper, lead, and latterly precious stones (not merely from the Black Forest but also from the Westrich in the Rhineland Palatinate, Switzerland, and later even Bohemia).[59] In other words, except for wood and water Freiburg was nowhere near self-sufficient. For food and many of its basic raw materials it was dependent on the Breisgau, which by the fifteenth century constituted its chief market area. But certain goods had to be imported from much further afield, so that even in the age of craft production Freiburg's economy was never entirely divorced from regional and international trade.

That is further underlined by the role of Freiburg's market which not only supplied the town's immediate needs but also functioned as an entrepôt for merchants. The daily market served the basic needs of the populace by selling craft goods in exchange for agrarian produce. The town in fact had several separate market-places for the sale of produce, of which the front of the minster square was the most important.[60] These stood under the authority of the Board of the Exchange which supervised not only the conduct of business and the exchange of coin, but also the payment of tolls and excises. During the era of gild ascendancy the council was increasingly tempted to intervene in the conduct of business by controlling the quality and type of goods, by fixing the price of basic commodities, and by staggering the toll rates in favour of residents rather than outsiders. Unfortunately, we know very little about the radius of visitors to the daily market, except that by the end of the fifteenth century the council was at pains to exclude foreign merchants and pedlars, particularly wandering Savoyards (the ubiquitous *welsche Krämer*), who were accused of driving up prices, particularly of foodstuffs, by regrating and forestalling.[61]

---

[58] Vogel, *Zollwesen*, p. 75. Freiburg had its own foundry, however.

[59] Metz, 'Bergbau', p. 179. Cf. Elsbeth Schragmüller, *Die Bruderschaft der Borer und Balierer von Freiburg und Waldkirch. Beitrag zur Gewerbegeschichte des Oberrheins* (Volkswirtschaftliche Abhandlungen der badischen Hochschulen, NF xxx) (Karlsruhe, 1914), 10–11.

[60] Cf. Adalbert Poinsignon, *Geschichtliche Ortsbeschreibung der Stadt Freiburg i. Br.*, i (Veröffentlichungen aus dem Archiv der Stadt Freiburg im Breisgau, ii) (Freiburg, 1891), 114–16. The original market-place stood on the site of the present town hall square.

[61] Cf. Karl Martin, 'Die Einwanderung aus Savoyen nach Südbaden. Ein Beitrag zur Erforschung der blutmäßigen Zusammensetzung unserer Bevölkerung', *Schau-ins-Land*, lxv/lxvi (1938–9), 7–8.

Equally, the council was perfectly willing to trade corn with its neighbours such as Basel whenever it had a surplus.[62]

Commodity exchange, however, was the hallmark of Freiburg's annual fairs, which were openly designated as free markets. During the fifteenth century there were two: a summer fair after midsummer and an autumn fair at Martinmas after the wine-harvest.[63] To these Maximilian added a third in 1516, to be held in the early spring, after the council had complained that its summer fair was losing business to its rival in Strasbourg.[64] Visits to the fairs in the sixteenth century show that Freiburg acted as a point of interchange for merchants throughout the Upper Rhine and beyond, though never on the scale of Basel or Strasbourg. Amongst regular patrons of the Freiburg fairs were merchants from as far afield as Cologne, Geneva, and northern Italy.[65] Moreover, although Freiburg had long ceased to be predominantly a merchant community, some gildsmen still engaged in middle-distance trade: Marx Hoff, a relatively modest haberdasher who dealt primarily in wine-stone, regularly travelled to the Frankfurt fairs at the end of the fifteenth century.[66] These observations should make one pause before asserting that Freiburg's craft economy had altogether turned its back on commerce and was content to subsist in simple symbiosis with its immediate hinterland.

The character of the craft economy becomes clearer if we examine economic policies and the organization of craft production in Freiburg

[62] Karl Friedrich Müller, *Geschichte der Getreidehandelspolitik, des Bäcker- und Müllergewerbes der Stadt Freiburg i. Br. im. 14., 15. und 16. Jahrhundert*. ZGGFr Beiheft II (Freiburg, 1926), 6–9.

[63] In 1465 emperor Frederick III added a third, to be held on the Fri. and Sat. after Corpus Christi. *UBStFr* ii. 489–90. This appears no longer to have existed in 1516.

[64] StAFr, A 1 1 d 52, 20 Apr. 1516. The market was to be held on the Tues. after Invocavit. For the negotiations cf. C 1 Landstände 1. Freiburg to Ulrich Württner, 19 Mar. 1516. Cf. B 5 XI, ix, fos. 272ʳ–274ʳ. The summer fair was subsequently abandoned; by mid-century only the Lent and Martinmas fairs remained. Cf. E 1 A III 1, 1 (1547 ff.).

[65] Cf. Berent Schwineköper, 'Beobachtungen zum Lebensraum südwestdeutscher Städte im Mittelalter, insbesondere zum engeren und weiteren Einzugsbereich der Freiburger Jahrmärkte in der zweiten Hälfte des 16. Jahrhunderts', in Erich Maschke and Jürgen Sydow (eds.), *Stadt und Umland* (Veröffentlichungen der Kommission für geschichtliche Landeskunde in Baden-Württemberg, Reihe B lxxxii) (Stuttgart, 1974), 44–5; map, p. 50. Cf. Berent Schwineköper, 'Bonn, Köln und Freiburg im Breisgau. Bemerkungen zu den mittelalterlichen Beziehungen der Städte', in Werner Besch, Klaus Fehn, Dietrich Höroldt, Franz Irsigler, Matthias Zender (eds.), *Die Stadt in der europäischen Geschichte. Festschrift Edith Ennen* (Bonn, 1972), 483–4.

[66] Cf. Steven W. Rowan (ed.), 'Die Jahresrechnungen eines Freiburger Kaufmanns 1487/88. Ein Beitrag zur Handelsgeschichte des Oberrheins', in Maschke/Sydow, *Stadt und Umland*, 227–77.

in the era of gild ascendancy. The principle of compulsory gild membership which had prevailed since the fourteenth century was certainly more strenuously (if not always successfully) enforced. Moreover, because craft producers were by then the mainstay of the town's economy, the gilds were able to press the council to use closed membership as an instrument of protectionism. Non-gildsmen were forbidden to ply their particular craft; the first such regulation came in 1472 when the tailors' gild banned independent tailors outside the gild from working in their own shops or at customers' houses.[67] It took well on another quarter-century, though, before the council yielded fully to such demands.

Indeed, not only was the council reluctant to press ahead too fast, it specifically tolerated certain forms of capitalist activity. Regrating and forestalling were commonly used until the 1480s as a means of building up stocks of foodstuffs, particularly grain, to cope with shortages and sudden price increases when they arose. Moreover, except for one brief interruption, one of Freiburg's leading gilds, the clothmakers', was run by competitive and unrestricted manufacture. Originally the right to make cloth was open to anyone who purchased the necessary weaving and fulling licence without being required to join the gild.[68] In 1472, however, the council tried to counteract the decline of the town's textile industry by restricting competition. Independent producers were only allowed to employ gild journeymen, and newcomers had to take out gild membership. Four years later this policy was abandoned, and the council reverted to open competition. Fees for the manufacturing concession were reduced, compulsory gild membership was suspended, and several new types of cloth were promoted. Thereafter clothmaking remained an unfettered trade in which capitalist methods prevailed; the richer gildsmen often farmed out work beyond the capacity of their own looms to the poorer weavers by the putting-out system, the most characteristic form of early capitalist production.[69]

In any case, it would be quite wrong to imagine that all Freiburg's craftsmen were independent producers. Quite apart from those engaged in the service trades, many artisans had no independent standing at all. The progressive division of labour was most noticeable, predictably enough, in the clothmakers' gild. There the linen-weavers

[67] Hinderschiedt, 'Zunftordnungen', pp. 11–12.
[68] Gothein, *Wirtschaftsgeschichte*, pp. 536–7.
[69] Ibid., pp. 539–40; Frank, 'Textilgewerbe', pp. 92–3.

were exclusively wage-workers who wove to order, and customers were encouraged to pay less than the tariffs fixed in 1464 and the weavers forbidden to demand more.[70] The woollen-weavers, too, were mostly job-workers; though they were allowed to manufacture independently as well, as early as 1425 it had been necessary to prevent the clothiers from installing looms in their own homes, thereby further depriving the weavers of a livelihood.[71] The teasers and carders, meanwhile, had sunk to the level of journeymen; they worked on weekly hire with no security of employment and their wages were fixed by the council. For their part, the hatters and serge-makers were not allowed to make cloth at all, lest they adulterate it with hairs and dyed wool used in their own craft.[72] A division of labour is also evident in the bakers' gild, where the house bakers worked for customers in their own homes, whilst the trading bakers sold at the market. When the council tried to divide the gild in 1483, the latter objected that the house bakers should at least be allowed to bake some bread for the market, but in 1493 they were stripped of that right.[73]

The description of Freiburg as a craft town should not, therefore, disguise the complexity of its socio-economic structure.[74] Alongside the independent craftmasters were ranged dependent, hired, and unskilled workers, quite apart from journeymen and apprentices. Direct production for the market was not the hallmark of all crafts. Some traded competitively with the world at large, and some gildsmen clearly engaged in regional commerce. Direct selling to the consumer predominated, but the activity of middlemen was recognized and accepted in certain circumstances. Above all, the enforcement of a policy of fully fledged protectionism came up against the bare facts of economic life. Freiburg was not self-sufficient: it needed to trade, and, whatever the ordinary gildsmen might think, it needed the profits from commerce as well, so long as the foundations of a craft-gild economy were neither shaken nor destroyed. Internally that meant promoting the new commercial venture of cutting and polishing, as well as deregulating the manufacture of textiles; externally it meant allowing all restrictions to fall on access, trading, and prices at the annual fairs.

---

[70] Gothein, *Wirtschaftsgeschichte*, p. 525.   [71] Ibid., p. 537.

[72] Ibid., pp. 536–7. They also leased the two fulling-mills owned by the gild, and their prices were strictly controlled by the council. Ibid., p. 538.

[73] Ibid., p. 506 n. 4.

[74] Nor can it disguise that Freiburg still possessed a remarkably bucolic character in the 15th c., witness a council decree of 1477 forbidding bakers from keeping pigs in the Old Town for fattening without special permission. StAFr, B 5 XIIIa, iv, fo. 32ᵛ.

III

By the fifteenth century the gilds had also firmly established themselves as the arbiters of Freiburg's society and culture. The failure of archduke Albrecht's reforms in 1454 can indeed ultimately be traced to the fact that the gilds were no longer mere interest groups, or even political and military corporations: they had become the forum and focus of Freiburg's civic life. The gilds—unlike the wards—were living communities caring for, representing, and ordering the aspirations of their individual members. Each gild had its own hall, where the disciplinary court was held, and the master and Eight elected each year.[75] The halls were above all clubs for conviviality and concourse; there the craftsmen celebrated christenings, marriages, and wakes. Nor was the gilds' cohesiveness confined to internal affairs; their solidarity was outwardly demonstrated by parading through the town at popular festivals, decked with banners, fifes, and drums, and by acting together in the Corpus Christi Passion plays. These manifestations highlight another important feature of gild life: the masters who taught their journeymen and apprentices a skill also, in an age of little formal education, helped instil a sense of good conduct, neighbourliness, piety, and moderation through the communal life of the gild hall.

This picture of social cohesiveness built upon paternalism should not, however, be taken at face value. Although the constitution granted equal political representation to the twelve gilds, their social standing and influence varied considerably. The gradations of prestige are graphically illustrated by the scale of entry fees to the gilds, ranging from £6 for the goldsmiths and butchers to a mere £1 for the winegrowers.[76] The wealthiest and mightiest gilds were the tailors,[77] haberdashers, smiths, and butchers. Thanks to vigorous and persistent defence of their privileges the butchers enjoyed a powerful standing, yet the nature of their trade left them rather outside the mainstream of civic society, as became particularly apparent during the troubles of the 1490s.[78] The prestige of these gilds contrasted with the far humbler

---

[75] The gilds also owned other property, whose income helped support their various responsibilities. Cf. Rowan, 'Guilds', p. 194, who cites the example of the butchers.

[76] StAFr, B 2 4, p. 169.

[77] The cutters and polishers tended to join either the tailors' or the bakers' gild.

[78] The knacker (*Wasenmetzger*) by virtue of his 'dishonourable' trade was not admitted to the gild.

standing of the masons, carpenters, and wine-growers, who were all noticeably poorer than the other gilds. The wine-growers in particular, as a plebeian corporation, had an average wealth assessment at the end of the fifteenth century so low that it fell below the first rung of the municipal tallage rates. Nearly one-tenth of its membership was dependent on charity;[79] the notables and rentiers were forbidden to join it; and, at £1, its entry fee was nominal compared with the customary £3 or £4 for the other gilds.[80]

The distinctiveness of the separate gilds was reinforced by their pattern of residence, for the tendency of certain gilds to congregate in specific areas, often on account of their craft, upheld social barriers. The lowlier gilds dwelt predominantly in the suburbs, in itself a mark of inferiority. In the first planned faubourg, the Neuburg, lived wine-growers, smallholders, labourers, and tanners; there, too, the lazaret, almshouse, and municipal brothel were situated.[81] The Prediger and Lehen suburbs likewise housed smallholders and vintagers alongside barbers and cuppers. The millers to be found there also appear in the Schneckcn suburb along the upper and lower holms of the Dreisam, where fishers, furriers, and more tanners lived and worked, whilst by the waterside stood the town shambles.[82] These social divisions underscore the widely varying political influence exerted by the gilds. The wine-growers, for instance, far and away the largest gild, never held any of the high civic offices such as the magistracy or gild commandership, and were grossly underrepresented on the boards of administration. Nevertheless, differences in status within the individual gilds were often sufficiently marked to countervail the distinctions between them. Quite apart from the journeymen and apprentices who had no standing, there were clear differences between masters and others: day-labourers working for fixed wages could not hope to compete for influence with independent craftmasters. Moreover, most gilds contained many impoverished members, and some embraced

[79] Berent Schwineköper, 'Bemerkungen zum Problem der städtischen Unterschichten aus Freiburger Sicht', in Erich Maschke and Jürgen Sydow (eds.), *Gesellschaftliche Unterschichten in den südwestdeutschen Städten* (Veröffentlichungen der Kommission für geschichtliche Landeskunde in Baden-Württemberg, Reihe B xli) (Stuttgart, 1967), 142.

[80] Cf. StAFr, A 1 VI e α 2, 23 Sept. 1468; B 2 4, p. 158. In 1497 the fee was raised to £2, no doubt because the council wished to limit the numbers of poorer workers who might become destitute and politically restive. B 5 XIIIa, iva, fo. 42^{r-v}; ibid., vii, fo. 8^r; ibid., vi, fos. 19^v, 20^r. The edict was repeated 5 years later. Ibid., iva, fo. 49^v; cf. B 2 4, p. 258.

[81] Schwineköper, 'Vorstädte', pp. 42–3.   [82] Ibid., p. 46.

known beggars. An accurate assessment of the gilds' social structure is further complicated by the amalgamation of 1459, when several of the lowlier craft gilds were affiliated to more prestigious corporations. The variations in employment and status within the clothmakers', bakers', or haberdashers' gilds, for example, are particularly striking.

The disconformity between gilds and crafts makes it equally hard to arrive at accurate figures for the individual artisan branches. The surviving craft lists before and after the 1459 amalgamation show how enfeebled the six gilds which disappeared had become. Most gilds numbered between sixty and eighty masters, with the notable exceptions of the small number of tanners (tawers belonged to the haberdashers' gild), and the vast reservoir of menials in the winegrower's gild. By the later fifteenth century there were around one thousand mastercraftsmen in Freiburg, a significant reduction from the peak of the mid-fourteenth century. Even harder to gauge are the numbers of journeymen and apprentices, since the sources are so sparse. Whilst their position within the gilds was obviously inferior to the masters, the real distinction lay between natives of Freiburg—sons who could expect to succeed to their fathers' workshops—and the wandering journeymen from beyond the town who enjoyed better terms of employment. The proportion of one to the other is not easy to establish, but a surviving list of journeymen coopers from 1475 to 1552 shows three-quarters to have been immigrants, mostly from Württemberg, Swabia, and the area around lake Constance.[83] During the fifteenth century several fraternities of journeymen were founded, essentially for social and charitable purposes, but which could act as guardians of the journeymen's interests as a whole. The journeymen retailers' constitution of 1415, for instance, laid down that no market retailer employ a journeyman from outside the fraternity.[84] Regional associations of journeymen—such as the Alsatian and Breisgau bakers—also developed alongside existing craft leagues throughout southern Germany which embraced masters and journeymen alike.[85]

It would be misleading to infer any great increase, however, in the journeymen's corporate identity or influence during the fifteenth century. The growth of brotherhoods was altogether haphazard; some crafts only formed associations much later—the journeymen tailors in 1525, the weavers in 1591.[86] In one vital respect, nevertheless, they

---

[83] Hermann Flamm, 'Das Bruderschaftsbuch der Küfergesellen in Freiburg im Breisgau, 1475–1552 bzw. 1584', *Freiburger Adresskalender*, 1907, 17–31.
[84] Gothein, *Wirtschaftsgeschichte*, p. 369.   [85] Ibid., p. 373.   [86] Ibid., p. 371.

had a lever: by the end of the fifteenth century journeymen had taken over many of the gilds' military duties, which gave rise to complaints that the craftmasters were taking their ease while the journeymen fought in campaigns or stood watch along the town walls. For Maximilian's campaign against the Swiss in 1499 Freiburg raised a contingent of 113 men from the gilds, of whom all but fourteen were journeymen paid to stand in for their masters.[87] One such muster from 1519 provides, in fact, the best surviving evidence for the number of journeymen in Freiburg. It lists 404 journeymen and apprentices from the gilds, together with a further 56, including carters, who belonged to no gild.[88] Remarkably enough, only ten journeymen were recruited from the wine-growers, which strongly suggests that the gild for the most part comprised unskilled labourers who never went through a craft apprenticeship. The much higher figure—seventy-four—for the builders reflects, in contrast, the preponderance of hired masons and carpenters who moved like the journeymen from job to job without setting up their own workshops. Beyond the total of 460 come those journeymen and apprentices too young to bear arms. By comparison, the Common Penny lists of 1497, which included all those over fifteen, give a total of 475. On the basis of these figures, which are certainly too low, Schwineköper has posited a true total of around five hundred journeymen and apprentices at the turn of the century.[89] To these must be added the many unmarried servant girls in the town—388 according to the Common Penny lists—as well as some of the single women also recorded. Thus the grand total of journeymen, apprentices, and maids on Freiburg can safely be put at around one thousand in 1500, nearly one-sixth of the entire population. Between dependent workers and masters, therefore, there was an exact balance: each master had, on average, either a maid or a journeyman.[90]

Within Freiburg, however, there were many inhabitants who escaped the net of obligatory gild membership: the nobles, the regular and secular clergy, and the civic officials. After 1457 they were joined by members of the university, professors and students, who stood entirely outside municipal jurisdiction. The notables congregated in two exclusive societies. One was the *Gesellschaft zum Ritter*, which in the fourteenth century had comprised nobles and merchants but which in the wake of Sempach in 1386 became the preserve of Freiburg's noble outburghers. By 1500 it contained seventeen scions of the

[87] StAFr, B 5 X 1, fos. 13ʳ–16ʳ.   [88] StAFr, C 1 Militaria 180 (1519–1620).
[89] Schwineköper, 'Unterschichten', p. 146.   [90] Ibid.

The Anatomy of a Craft Town

town's oldest patrician families. The other was the *Gesellschaft zum Gauch*, once a club for merchants[91] but which latterly opened its doors to the town's salaried officials, the higher clergy, and the gild commanders.[92] These various groups made up a sizeable segment of the population. The tax lists record over thirty nobles (though not all were permanent residents); twenty-three religious houses and six lay orders; and at least thirty miscellaneous notables and their families in civic employ;[93] whilst well over 150 students and more than a dozen professors, along with their servants and dependents, gave a university population of at least 200. Though it is impossible to gain reliable estimates of the number of inmates of the convents or the size of nobles' households, the total of honourable non-gildsmen and their dependents in Freiburg must easily have exceeded five hundred.

Yet far beneath the illustrious patricians and nobles was ranged another group of non-gildsmen, those who were either debarred from gild membership or else gathered into a separate tax category called the street tallage (*Gassengewerft*). The street tallage was originally intended as an administrative concession to the very poor which allowed those who could not afford gild membership still to earn a living in Freiburg. It overwhelmingly comprised women: spinning-girls, seamstresses, and the like. At the end of the fifteenth century, according to a surviving war-levy register,[94] there were as many as 240, a figure far in excess of any previous estimate of the town's plebeian population.[95] The list is almost certainly reliable, since the tax inspectors apparently went from house to house enquiring who was lodging within. Not surprisingly, many of the these girls were to be found in the suburbs. Some were recorded as servants, despite the council decree of 1497 requiring all domestics to join a gild; some as laundresses or bath-house attendants. Many had come from beyond

[91] *UBStFr* i. 483–6. Cf. Fritz Geiges, *Der mittelalterliche Fensterschmuck des Freiburger Münsters* (Freiburg, 1931), 228.

[92] *UBStFr* ii. 426–7. The gild commanders only appear after 1451, which may indicate that in spite of their responsibilities as military captains of the town contingents and keepers of one of the town seals they encountered some social antagonism from the patricians.

[93] Cf. StAFr, E 1 A II b 4. Levy for the campaigns against France and Switzerland, 1498–9; and the tallage lists. E 1 A II a 1.

[94] StAFr, E 1 A II b 4. 'Reisgelt fur xx wochen von den unzunftigen uff der gassen uff Quasimod im lxxxxviiii iar wider die schwitzer uffgehept.'

[95] Flamm, *Niedergang*, pp. 34–5 reckoned no more than 150 such non-gildsmen all told, including wives and children. Schwineköper's figure of 40, 'Unterschichten', p. 148, refers to a quite separate list of those specifically excluded from gild membership, which is discussed below.

the Breisgau, shiftless vagabonds.[96] Most paid no more than 3d. a week towards the war levy, half the rate set for the 'poor'. But the street tallage certainly did not comprehend all those on the lowest rungs of Freiburg's society. Separate registers were drawn up for those exempted or excluded from the gilds.[97] At one end these lists took in the honourable non-gildsmen or their widows, but at the other they recorded over forty persons, the majority men, of divers sorts and conditions. Sixteen were named as beggars, who appear to have moved freely in and out of gild membership (predominantly the winegrowers') as their circumstances dictated.[98] Of the remainder, by no means all were on the verge of poverty. Some had been expelled from their gilds for having taken part in the attempted coup of 1492, notably the butchers. Others may well have been convicted criminals beyond the pale of respectable society, as were the so-called dishonourable professions. A comparison of these latter lists with the street tallage is highly revealing. Because the lists of those excluded from the gilds were not drawn up by streets and contain no one who was demonstrably an immigrant, they must have recorded those who were already notorious to the council, whereas the street tallage was clearly intended to provide surveillance of a shifting and unknown population just as much as to collect revenue. In the latter, significantly, one-fifth of the women were identified solely by their place of origin. Taken together, however, these groups made up a rump of plebeians beyond gild control over whom the authorities kept constant watch.[99]

As the council strove unsuccessfully to staunch the swelling ranks of beggars and vagrants, the threat of violent unrest was lessened only by the fact that the women labourers in the street tallage far outnumbered the volatile and dangerous core of criminals and outcasts.[100] Even in a

[96] Cf. also Thomas Fischer, *Städtische Armut und Armenfürsorge im 15. und 16. Jahrhundert. Sozialgeschichtliche Untersuchungen am Beispiel der Städte Basel, Freiburg i. Br. und Straßburg* (Göttinger Beiträge zur Wirtschafts- und Sozialgeschichte, iv) (Göttingen, 1979), 77.
[97] StAFr, E 1 A II b 4. 'Deren man sich in zunften nit an nimpt.'
[98] Ibid. 'Betler, die in zunften vergriffen werdent und doch nit das spenglin antragen.' Cf. Fischer, *Armut*, p. 71.
[99] For an extensive analysis of Freiburg's *Unterschichten* cf. Tom Scott, 'Relations between Freiburg im Breisgau and the surrounding countryside in the age of South-West German agrarian unrest before the Peasants' War, circa 1450–1520' (Ph.D. diss., Univ. of Cambridge, 1973), 46–61.
[100] In 1520 the town's new law code banned the *Gassengewerft*, doubtless in order to stem the flow of indigent persons into Freiburg. Ulrich Zasius, *Nüwe Stattrechten und Statuten der löblichen Statt Fryburg im Pryszgow gelegen* (Basel, 1520), fo. 91ᵛ. Yet the tallage must have continued, for it was abolished once more in 1541. StAFr, A 1 X a 30,

community dominated by its craft gilds, therefore, there remained many who were never encompassed within the framework of the gilds. By the late fifteenth century, nevertheless, the values and mentalities of the craftsmen increasingly held sway, as the council struggled to arrest the process of social and economic differentiation and the growth of a proletarian class, in order that, in the words of a later ordinance of the journeymen goldsmiths, 'the poor man alongside the rich and each next the other may the better prosper and survive'.[101] The only group missing from this picture of Freiburg's society was the Jews, who had been banished in the early fifteenth century, and thereafter retained no more than the right of free passage and overnight lodging in the Wiehre.[102] Freiburg was to remain a notoriously anti-Semitic city well into the sixteenth century.[103]

11 July 1541, fos. 3^v-4^r; B 5 XIIIa, xi, fo. 132^v. The attempt was not very successful, for further measures had to be taken four years later. B 5 XIIIa, xii, fo. 322^r. Cf. Fischer, *Armut*, p. 78.

[101] Karl Hartfelder, *Die alten Zunftordnungen der Stadt Freiburg im Breisgau*, part I (Beilage zum Programm des Gymnasiums zu Freiburg im Breisgau) (Freiburg, 1879), 35.

[102] They were first expelled in 1401, *UBStFr* ii. 167–75; and again in 1424. StAFr, A 1 XII c, 22 Feb. 1424. However, in 1453 'Mosse der jud, unser burger' was mentioned. B 5 XI, ii, 4, fo. 88^v.

[103] Cf. in general Berent Schwineköper and Franz Laubenberger, *Geschichte und Schicksal der Freiburger Juden. Aus Anlaß des 100jährigen Bestehens der israelitischen Gemeinde in Freiburg* (Freiburger Stadthefte, vi) (Freiburg, 1963).

PART TWO

CRISIS AND CHANGE

III
Conflict between Freiburg and the Breisgau

I

THE ambivalence which characterized Freiburg's situation in the fifteenth century—increasing weight in external affairs set against a background of internal decline and uncertainty—was nowhere more visible than in Freiburg's relations with the Breisgau. The defence of its rights and privileges and the extension of its influence and authority over its hinterland may well have been vital to the town's survival and recovery, but they involved Freiburg in frequent conflict with its neighbours, from the prelates, nobility, and gentry downwards through its own rural dependencies to the Breisgau villages themselves.

The network of clientage and protection through which Freiburg sought to secure the nobles' allegiance not only proved incapable of sustaining their involvement in civic government, it also offered no guarantee of co-operation when their essential interests were at stake. Within the town the council might come up against the privileges and immunities of the many religious houses and the nobility's resistance to increases in its composition tax, but it was in the countryside that Freiburg clashed most violently with the ecclesiastical and secular lords. Many were engaged in an often desperate struggle of their own to survive in the face of mounting debts and shrinking real income, as Freiburg's persistent attempts to bring in municipal tax arrears and interest-payments to its burghers from a number of notorious defaulters testify.[1] Disputes over the major sources of revenue, such as tolls and highway dues, were therefore not uncommon, especially once Freiburg set about constructing a landed territory along the Dreisam.

---

[1] Two examples: 1. Balthasar von Blumeneck in 1506. StAFr, B 5 XI, viii, 1, fos. 62ʳ, 68ᵛ–69ʳ; B 5 XIIIa, ix, fo. 110ʳ. In 1511: ibid., x, fos. 173ᵛ, 193ᵛ. He was finally twice placed under the ban of the imperial court of justice in Rottweil. A 1 1 k 151, 16 Sept. 1511; A 1 XIV Blumeneck 296, 4 May 1514. He faced many other claims for debt between 1510 and 1518. 2. Anton von Landeck in 1502–6. B 5 XI, vii, 1, fos. 5ᵛ, 156ᵛ; ibid., viii, 1, fo. 64ᵛ. In 1516: ibid., x, fo. 15ʳ. There are numerous further instances involving other lords.

The town's failure to link its lordships into a continuous jurisdiction through the valley left certain key toll-stages and fortresses, particularly the village of Ebnet and the castles of Wiesneck and Falkenstein, in the hands of a powerful and refractory outburgher dynasty, the Snewlin-Landeck. Throughout the later fifteenth and much of the sixteenth century there was repeated friction between Freiburg and the Landecks over toll privileges and highway rights in the Falkenstein valley,[2] but that was merely the prelude to a much wider-ranging conflict with the local lords and peasants over the construction of a rival turnpike across the Black Forest in the years following 1467.[3]

By far and away the most contentious issue between Freiburg and the Breisgau nobility throughout the fifteenth and early sixteenth century, however, remained the existence of its peasant outburghers. By the terms of the 1368 treaties Freiburg had, of course, been forced to abandon its outburghers amongst the unfree subjects of count Egon and other Breisgau lords, but the provisions clearly implied that the town had also acquired peasant burghers who were free men, whom it might therefore retain, as a later council memorandum indeed confirmed.[4] The source of the conflict lay in the outburghers' legal status which conferred upon them a special position within the villages. During court cases it was sometimes asserted that the custom of the landgraviate of the Breisgau provided that peasants of whatever lords should sit mingled in the villages and all enjoy freedom of movement and marriage. But during the fifteenth century these traditional rights were being eroded at the expense of foreign subjects of urban or noble lords, as village seigneurs not only began to intensify the obligations already laid upon such peasants in respect of the usufruct of common land, but increasingly sought to extract from such residents (known as *Hintersassen*) the payment of a tax as a mark of servile dependence by virtue of their residence within the lord's jurisdiction (*Zwing und*

---

[2] StAFr, A 1 VI d 33, 15–16th c.; including the dispute with Hans von Landeck, 1451 ff. Cf. *UBStFr* ii. 32–4. Landeck's rebuilding of castle Falkenstein commanding the entrance to the valley, which the town had destroyed in 1388 as a robber baron's nest, provoked a serious clash with Freiburg in 1451/2, for the council claimed that Landeck had no right to restore a fortress which had been deliberately and lastingly razed. Ibid., pp. 59–83; StAFr, A 1 XII d 18, 1451–72. A further dispute with David von Landeck occurred in 1492. B 5 XI, v, 4, fo. 7ʳ. Before it acquired Burg, another important toll-stage, as part of the St Märgen estates in 1462, Freiburg had quarrelled with Engelhart von Blumeneck over highway dues and maintenance. A 1 VI b 7, 20 Oct.–24 Nov. 1447.

[3] See below, pp. 103 ff.

[4] StAFr, A 1 XII d 5, 15/16th c. Heft C, n.d. (1452), fo. 1ʳ.

Bann). In that way, as one outburgher seigneur, Gabriel von Bollschweil, acknowledged in 1511, two kinds of bondage had developed in the Breisgau.⁵ The first was personal servitude, attaching by inheritance from mother to child from one generation to the next; the second was serfdom seen as an impersonal condition imposed upon any subject resident under a given lord, which was automatically discharged upon emigration beyond the frontiers of the old landgraviate.⁶

In that sense, the difficulties which Freiburg's outburghers encountered were no different from those facing any other *Hintersassen* in the villages. In practice, however, their situation was more exposed, inasmuch as their liberties and privileges as urban citizens were more tangible and extensive than those of other lords' subjects. Even though by the late fourteenth century Freiburg regarded its rural subjects as serfs in all but name, in formal constitutional terms they remained burghers. That is to say, they took the burgher's oath,⁷ had the right of recourse to the civic courts in which they were answerable, paid the municipal tallage, and discharged their military service with the town's troop rather than the village levies.⁸ In addition to their civic taxes, however, the outburghers had to pay an annual fine (a purely nominal sum) in recognition of the town's servile jurisdiction over them.⁹ Yet unlike rural serfs they were free to move—indeed, as Ulbrich has pointed out, freedom of movement seems to have been the principal (if not the only) distinction between free and unfree peasants in South-West Germany by the end of the fourteenth century.¹⁰ In common with the rest of Freiburg's citizens, the outburghers were subject to the departure-fine which had been levied on all inhabitants after 1368 in order to reduce the civic debt, but when the fine was abolished in 1446 the outburghers continued to have to pay. By then it amounted to ten times their annual tallage and, as a former mayor, Hans von Landeck, himself a noble outburgher, bitterly declared, the sum was so high that

---

⁵ GLA 229/8577. Submission of Gabriel von Bollschweil, n.d. (1511).
⁶ The frontiers of the old landgraviate stretched well beyond the modern district of the Breisgau. They took in the ancient lands of the dukes of Zähringen, the margraves of Hachberg, and the counts of Freiburg, but excluded subsequent Austrian acquisitions on the right bank of the Rhine such as the lordship of Triberg, Villingen, Bräunlingen, the Forest Towns, and the march of Ettenheim. Cf. Franz Kreutter, *Geschichte der k. k. Vorderösterreichischen Staaten*, i (St Blasien, 1790), xi–xiv.
⁷ Cf. StAFr, B 5 XIIIa, x, fo. 193ʳ.
⁸ Cf. StAFr, E 1 A II b 4, no. 10 (1499) (formerly E 1 A II a 4).
⁹ Outburghers also paid reduced tolls. Cf. StAFr, B 3 18, fo. 11ʳ. This right appears to have been whittled away by the late 16th c. Cf. A 1 XII d 63, 1573/6: 18 Jan. 1576.
¹⁰ Ulbrich, *Leibherrschaft*, p. 257.

the outburghers were often forced to remain in servile allegiance to the town because they could not afford the fine.[11] In effect, therefore, their freedom of movement was curtailed, though they were always at liberty to take refuge within the city walls, a privilege denied the subjects of rural lords.

In theory the outburghers were able to marry and inherit freely, though they rapidly fell victim to the intensification of seigneurial authority, as lords attempted to prevent their subjects marrying outside their jurisdiction on pain of stiff fines. Given the widespread fragmentation of lordship on the Upper Rhine, some form of working arrangement became necessary. By the early fifteenth century the practice of exchanging bondmen between lords (known as *Gegenwechsel*) grew up, either by direct exchange, or else through the release of a subject on promise of a future exchange, during which interval the first lord might continue to demand his recognition tax of servile allegiance. In such exchanges Freiburg was obliged to treat its outburghers on a par with the country lords' servile peasantry.[12] Inheritance, by contrast, was freed from servile dues. Instead of paying a personal heriot, the children of a deceased outburgher simply remained in that status, unless they wished to buy themselves free, in which case they paid the departure-fine.[13]

In their relations with the country lords and fellow-villagers the outburghers had to accept some share of communal obligations. They might be required to serve as jurors in the village court, or help to maintain roads, paths, hedges, and ditches. By the late fifteenth century they commonly rendered an annual Shrovetide fowl and one day's labour-service to the village lord in recognition of their usufruct of wood and pasture.[14] Only when the lords tried to extend these dues by demanding the servile tax as recognition of residence within and acceptance of their exclusive village jurisdiction did the real conflict begin. As tenants, rather than as serfs, the outburghers were subject to the prevailing manorial law of the Breisgau, whereby they rendered

---

[11] StAFr, A I XII d 18, 1451–72. Heft A, fo. 3^{r-v}.

[12] Scott, 'Relations', pp. 237–8. In such treaties of exchange, however, Freiburg took care not to describe its outburghers as *Eigenleute*, a term it reserved for rural serfs. Cf. GLA 67/124, fos. 282^r–285^v (1497).

[13] Scott, 'Relations', p. 240.

[14] Cf. StAFr, B 5 XIIIa, iv, fo. 37^r (1478). The council tried to resist the introduction of these obligations on learning that Breisach's outburghers were exempt, but by the end of the century, it seems, they were well established. A I XII d 34, 11 Feb. 1495. Cf. Ulbrich, *Leibherrschaft*, p. 199.

service only where they lived, regardless of the lands they might hold in other places. In civil cases, too, they were required to accept jurisdiction wherever the dispute had arisen, in conformity with the long-standing custom of the Breisgau.[15] Over criminal jurisdiction, on the other hand, friction regularly ensued, for here Freiburg insisted that their burgher's rights entitled the outburghers to be heard before the civic criminal court. Not only did this slight the lords' village jurisdiction, it further deprived them of the penalties, distraints, and fines arising from such cases.

It was this legal exemption rather than any specific aspect of their personal status which ultimately distinguished the outburghers from the remainder of the village population. Moreover, since they were often drawn from the wealthier families, their privileged position might be assumed to have aroused resentment on the part of the ordinary villagers as much as the lords themselves. In that respect the position of the outburghers within their communities was certainly ambivalent, yet it was precisely their access to civic jurisdiction which allowed the outburghers in turn to lend support to their fellow-villagers—notably in one notorious dispute from the 1470s onwards between Wilhelm von Lichtenfels, another former mayor, and his villagers in Neuershausen[16]—by enlisting Freiburg's protection vicariously on behalf of the village as a whole.

By their very situation, therefore, the outburghers were bound to form the focus of discontent as Freiburg's system of rural clientage began to break down. Conflict became endemic with the lords of the Austrian Breisgau, many of whom were themselves noble outburghers of the town. Not only were these petty lords hard pressed to shore up their finances; it was above all in their own villages that the outburghers had survived after independence and Freiburg's subsequent hostilities with the margraves of Baden in 1424. In the course of the second half of the fifteenth century—when reliable records begin—the number of Freiburg's outburghers remained remarkably constant despite the lords' harassment, yet their distribution throughout the Breisgau changed appreciably. The many pockets of outburghers scattered over a wide area gradually disappeared, as the town concentrated upon retaining and consolidating several sizeable outburgher communities closer at hand. Their distinct identity derived from dynasties of peasant burghers who had dwelt in certain villages

[15] Cf. *UBStFr* ii. 342–5.
[16] StAFr, A 1 XII d 25, 1477–1549.

for generations, and was reflected in the organization of Freiburg's outburgher administration. By the end of the fifteenth century outburghers were located in no more than 25 villages, whereas at mid-century they had been spread across 41 communities; by 1525, indeed, only twelve villages sheltering outburghers remained, three of which were situated in the Valley Bailiwick.[17] The outburghers were concentrated in the Breisgau plain and the Dreisam valley, many in the wine-growing villages on the edge of the Kaiserstuhl. There several large outburgher communities were located—Merdingen, Waltershofen, and Oberschaffhausen, with others in the march of Buchheim and Neuershausen; in the *Kirchspiel* south of Freiburg at Ambringen, Ehrenstetten, and Kirchhofen; and in the margravial exclave of Gallenweiler. In the Valley Bailiwick, where the outburghers sat cheek by jowl with the town's dependent peasantry, a separate community survived at Zarten. After mid-century the council appointed a special overseer for the outburghers,[18] whilst the larger communities chose stewards from within their ranks to act as spokesmen in dealings with the town, for which they received a modest fee.[19]

The surviving figures for heads of households—around 120 to the end of the fifteenth century, rising to nearly 150 in 1503, then falling back to near 100 after the sale of certain communities, before stabilizing at around 90 by 1525[20]—suggest that the population of outburgher families fluctuated between 500 in the early period and up to 600 by the turn of the century, only to settle back at 350 or more thereafter. On these figures the holding of outburghers added as much as one-tenth to Freiburg's urban population in 1500. That is no mean total, especially in view of the amount of tallage and other taxes which they contributed annually to the municipal exchequer. There was a significant decline, however, in the outburghers' assessed wealth (calculated upon immoveable and moveable property) after mid-century. In 1481 42 per cent of heads of households paid tallage at the lowest 'pauper' rates, but by 1525 that figure had increased to 75 per cent. In the same period the number of middling outburghers with

[17] Cf. Scott, 'Relations', p. 244, Table A.
[18] The post of overseer was first recorded in 1462, and continued without a break until 1542, and probably beyond. Cf. StAFr, B 5 I a, 2 fo. 16ʳ.
[19] They are recorded in the outburgher tallage lists from 1481 onwards. In that year 5s. was paid to each of the seven stewards from Kirchhofen, Krozingen, Merdingen, Waltershofen, Oberschaffhausen, Neuershausen, and Zarten. In 1503 and 1506 a further steward was mentioned in Tunsel. StAFr, E 1 A II b 4.
[20] Figures extrapolated from Scott, 'Relations', p. 224, Table A.

Freiburg's Conflict with the Breisgau 83

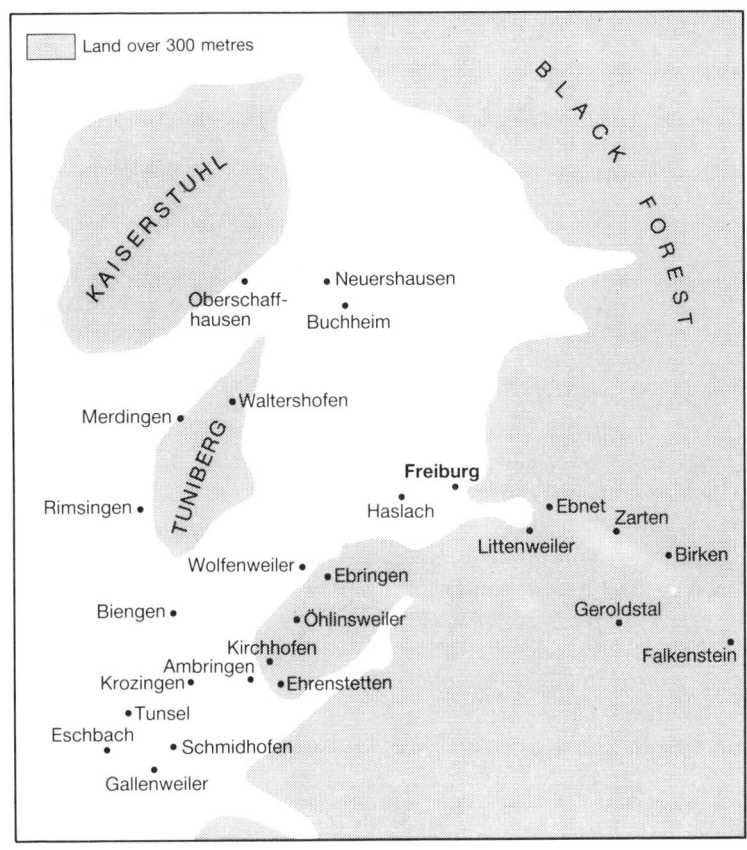

Map 5. Location of Freiburg's Outburghers in 1500

assessed wealth up to 100 fl. declined from 44 per cent to a mere 23 per cent.[21] Several reasons may be conjectured for the decline—military campaigns on the Upper Rhine, pestilence and crop failure, renewed population pressure on land resources—but it is more than likely that the fiscal exactions and encroachments of the village lords were chiefly to blame.[22]

---

[21] Figures extrapolated from ibid., p. 243, Table B.
[22] The amount of tax arrears after 1500 suggests that outburgher indebtedness was rising. StAFr, E 1 A II b 4. 'usszug der schulden, so an ussburgern verloren, ouch was aber in siner restantz halb schuldig ist zû ersetzen,' n.d. (c.1510).

This is borne out by the first major conflict which arose between Freiburg and the Breisgau nobility after mid-century. From 1451 onwards Hans von Landeck and then his son, lords of several villages, principally in the march of Buchheim north-west of Freiburg, conducted an embittered struggle to extend and entrench their village jurisdiction at the expense of their *Hintersassen* and outburghers, in which they challenged the latter's very right to exist, even though it had in practice come to be tacitly accepted on account of the close links between Freiburg and its outburgher nobility. Hans von Landeck paraded a formidable array of imperial and other precedents—the Golden Bull of Charles IV, which had prohibited paleburghers; emperor Sigismund's statute against paleburghers of 1431; as well as the Breisgau settlement of 1368—as evidence that the town should hold no country burghers.[23] During an extensive court hearing in 1452 Landeck presented eleven heads of grievance against the town ranging widely over alleged infringements of his jurisdiction but concentrating upon the outburghers. In his attempts to draw the noose of dependence more tightly around the totality of his village subjects Landeck readily conceded that the earlier custom of the Breisgau had recognized a far greater measure of peasant freedom, but he denied Freiburg's right to invoke such custom on the grounds that those legal arrangements had been concluded amongst the rural lords alone, both ecclesiastical and secular, and not by the town which had no right in any case to own peasant burghers.

In protest at the town's alleged interference in his jurisdiction Landeck gave up his noble outburgher rights and quit the town.[24] Whatever the outcome of the case, whose judgment does not survive, friction continued between the Landecks and Freiburg for two decades.[25] For the rest of the century, indeed, the Snewlin-Landecks, once so prominent in the ranks of Freiburg's aristocracy, took no

---

[23] StAFr, A 1 XII d 18, 1451–72. Heft A, fos. 2ᵛ, 3ᵛ, 24ᵛ, 36ᵛ. Scott, 'Relations', p. 211. At the end of his submission Landeck confused Sigismund's statute of 1431 with the *Reformatio Sigismundi*, although this famous reform tract in fact defended the freedom of imperial cities to accept extramural burghers. For the 1431 statute cf. *Deutsche Reichstagsakten*, ix, ed. Dietrich Kerler (Gotha, 1887), 566–88, no. 429. For the provisions of the *Reformatio Sigismundi* cf. Heinrich Koller (ed.), *Reformation Kaiser Siegmunds* (*MGH, Staatsschriften des späteren Mittelalters*, vi) (Stuttgart, 1964), 322.

[24] StAFr, A 1 XII d 18, 1451–72. Heft B, fo. 12ʳ. Cf. A 1 VII d 12, 20 June 1446–17 Apr. 1452.

[25] In 1462 Hans von Landeck junior pawned—temporarily, it would appear—the March villages to Freiburg, a sure sign of financial embarrassment. StAFr, A 1 XIX Marchdörfer 2, 21 June 1462.

further part in civic affairs.²⁶ The Landeck dispute is of double significance. On the one hand it highlights the local lords' inchoate efforts to buttress their fragile jurisdictions, a process in which the outburghers were bound to become the target of mounting resentment. On the other, it gave Freiburg the opportunity to iterate and justify in painstaking detail how the outburghers had managed to survive after the settlements of 1368 and 1424. Essentially, the council argued, it had kept its peasant outburghers as burghers under the terms of its ancient constitution; thereby they had sworn fealty to Austria as well as the town, in return for which the privileges and liberties of Freiburg's burghers had been confirmed by successive Habsburg dukes up to that day. Landeck might deny the town's right to accept serfs as burghers or, having once acquired country burghers, to treat them as serfs, but, Freiburg riposted, he was seizing upon a mere rhetorical device: they were to all intents and purposes treated as bondmen, but the council still called them burghers and allowed them the freedom of movement to which citizens not serfs were entitled. The objections to paleburghers in the Golden Bull and thereafter the council serenely dismissed by declaring that it held no subjects of that description, and recurred to the customary usage of the Breisgau, under which it was not uncommon to have *Hintersassen* from as many as six different lordships resident within one jurisdiction at any given time, each of whose foreign allegiance was ultimately acknowledged by financial and legal accountability to his original lord.²⁷

As long as intermingled lordship remained common in the Breisgau, the outburghers presented no real problem. With the rise of local bondage, however, the struggle began. As Freiburg remarked, Landeck himself was only able to mount his specious attack upon its outburghers because he had already forced many other *Hintersassen* in his villages into servile subjection. Although no very clear record survives,²⁸ it can be inferred that relations between Freiburg and the Breisgau nobility continued to deteriorate after the Landeck affair.²⁹

---

[26] Hans von Landeck junior sat once as a councillor in 1464, but that was all. StAFr, B 5 I a, 1, fo. 19ʳ.

[27] StAFr, A I XII d 18, 1451–72, Heft A, fo. 11ʳ.

[28] The proposed association of 1460 touched upon the issue of outburghers, but it was stillborn. See p. 33.

[29] A quite separate conflict arose in 1476/7 over the nobles' rights as outburghers paying a composition tax. Cf. Tom Scott (ed.), *Die Freiburger Enquete von 1476. Quellen zur Wirtschafts- und Verwaltungsgeschichte der Stadt Freiburg im Breisgau im fünfzehnten Jahrhundert* (Veröffentlichungen aus dem Archiv der Stadt Freiburg im Breisgau, xx) (Freiburg, 1986).

Not until 1483, though, did formal negotiations get under way between Freiburg and Breisach (the only towns to retain outburghers in any number) and the nobility of the Austrian Breisgau. The latter hoped to secure a comprehensive agreement covering all aspects of the rights of both foreign subjects and of town-dwellers in the countryside which would take the treaty of Mühlburg in 1424 as its starting-point.[30] The nobles demanded the abolition of all peasant outburghers (whilst reserving their own right as prelates and secular lords to acquire citizenship), but offered in return not to force any more peasants within their jurisdictions into serfdom, and to guarantee freedom of movement to those peasants who were not serfs or who had immigrated into the Breisgau. In both civil and criminal cases they proposed that disputes should be heard at the place of incident, whether over debts, rents, tithes, inheritance, or disposal of property. At the same time the nobility gave an assurance not to increase dues on tenancies, and to allow town-dwellers free access to their rural holdings in spring and autumn. Lastly, no restrictions were to be placed upon marriage, but children should follow their mother's status, free or unfree.[31]

The effect of these proposals would have been to reaffirm the ancient custom of the Breisgau and to halt the encroachment of residential bondage, whilst prohibiting one category of *Hintersassen*, namely outburghers. Not surprisingly, therefore, these proposals were unacceptable to Freiburg and Breisach. Instead, a compromise solution was put forward by two of Freiburg's leading aristocratic outburghers, the abbot of St Peter and Kaspar von Falkenstein, its burgomaster in 1483.[32] It suggested a truce of two to three years, during which time neither side should accept any new serfs: the

[30] The treaty of Mühlburg was first cited as a precedent in a quarrel between Werner von Staufen and Freiburg and Breisach's outburghers in his villages of Öhlinsweiler and Pfaffenweiler in 1435. The judgment did not, however, question the outburghers' right to live in peace in those places. StAFr, A 1 XII d 11, 26 Sept. 1435. Scott, 'Relations', pp. 264–5.

[31] StAFr, A 1 XII d 5, 15/16th c. Heft A, n.d. (1483). 'Vermerkt artikel zwischend den hern, rittern und knechten im Brisgaw.' The dating of this and companion documents can be established from the edicts and letters of 1483 which do survive. Cf. StAFr, B 5 XI, v, 1, fo. 31ʳ. In its original form the draft had envisaged complete freedom of marriage (fo. 2ᵛ), but this clause was deleted and replaced by another with the significant proviso concerning the status of offspring (fo. 3ʳ). The draft went on to propose that the ecclesiastical courts and the imperial court of justice at Rottweil were not to be used in purely secular matters such as debt, unless the claimant was left without any other redress or was the victim of undue delay (fo. 3ᵛ).

[32] Ibid., Heft B, n.d. (1483).

nobility should accept immigrants only as *Hintersassen* with freedom of movement, whilst the two towns were to accept only civic burghers, not outburghers. In other words, those outburghers already in the Breisgau villages were permitted to stay, and the compromise went on to elaborate their rights and duties. As before, tallage and military service should belong to the towns, whilst the local lords were to receive the habitual Shrovetide fowl and certain boon-services in recognition of usufruct of the common. In legal affairs, crimes, and inheritance disputes were to be heard where they arose, and the outburghers must allow any claims they pressed against other rural subjects to be challenged in the latter's court instead of only in the civic courts. Any unfree subjects, including outburghers, who married outside their lords' jurisdictions without permission would be liable to a fine.[33]

These compromise proposals were intended to resolve the specific issue of the outburghers, and accordingly ignored the wider issues raised in the nobility's original draft.[34] They amounted, in effect, to a restatement and confirmation of the outburghers' basic rights, but at the same time acknowledged the restrictions upon unfree peasants' becoming outburghers which the treaty of 1368 had imposed. Yet their survival, as the clause concerning marriage made plain, could only be bought at the price of Freiburg's treating its outburghers on exactly the same footing as the lords' own serfs by accepting an automatic exchange of subjects (*Gegenwechsel*) as the precondition of permission to marry.[35] Moreover, the towns were being obliged to abandon their insistence that outburghers be free to invoke municipal jurisdiction in all civil and criminal cases, excepting debt.

The result of these negotiations, the most significant of the fifteenth century, does not survive in any formal document, but we can readily infer its implications from the subsequent course of events. The village

---

[33] Ibid., fo. 2ᵛ.

[34] Ibid., fo. 3ʳ. The question of foreign courts was made harder to resolve by the fact that duke Sigismund had recently issued an edict specifically enjoining their use on the grounds of swiftness and competence. This provoked grave opposition from Freiburg and Breisach who complained that such courts were chiefly employed by the country lords against the towns and their subjects. Sigismund was reluctant to revoke his edict so soon, and proposed instead that the Outer Austrian governor summon representatives of the prelates, nobles, and towns before him to reach an agreement which should then be sent to Sigismund for ratification. StAFr, L 1 (Stadtarchiv Breisach), Urkunden I 143, 6 Mar. 1483. Cf. TLA, Kanzleibücher, ältere Reihe, Lit. D, fo. 135ʳ.

[35] The town had already acknowledged as much in the Landeck dispute. Cf. StAFr, A 1 XII d 18, 1451–72. Heft A, fo. 8ʳ.

lords continued to consolidate their authority by imposing residential bondage, but at the same time they effectively abandoned any further attempts to challenge the outburghers' right to exist. Instead, the lords chose to harass the towns' country subjects on a massive scale using every trick at their disposal, but chiefly by trying to lure them into residential bondage like the other *Hintersassen*. Harassment had, of course, occurred before 1483, or else there would have been no need for a settlement, but after that date its scope and intensity markedly increased. That is evident from a series of protracted disputes between various outburgher lords and Freiburg at the turn of the century: Wilhelm von Lichtenfels in Neuershausen after 1495; Rudolf von Blumeneck in Waltershofen in 1505; and again with his brother Kaspar in Merdingen in 1515. In these instances for the first time entire communities of outburghers were attacked collectively, instead of the piecemeal harassment of individuals which had been common before then.

The pattern of intimidation and violence was rich and varied. Direct attempts to force the outburghers into servitude by demanding abjuration of their old and the swearing of new oaths of fealty to the village lords were comparatively rare, doubtless because such flagrant breaches of the law would have been rapidly apprehended by the Freiburg authorities. None the less, the outburghers in Waltershofen protested in 1505 that Rudolf von Blumeneck had tried to make them swear fealty as his serfs, whereas they were only prepared to acknowledge him as *Hintersassen*.[36] Much more common were attempts to impose servile taxes and obligations. The hallmark of bondage was the payment of a recognition due until the completion of a marriage exchange, the so-called *Eigenschilling*, and the general servile tax, known as the *Steuer*. In 1495 Wilhelm von Lichtenfels, a noble outburgher, mayor and councillor of many years' standing, imposed a host of innovations upon the peasants of Neuershausen and neighbouring March villages, both upon his own subjects and on *Hintersassen* who were margravial serfs and outburghers. Lichtenfels was seeking to curtail not only the peasants' rights of common, but above all to reduce the *Hintersassen* to his own serfs by extracting payment of the *Steuer*. Complex and protracted litigation ensued, in which Freiburg, by defending the rights of its outburghers, found itself drawn into the wider struggle to protect the villagers' rights as a whole.[37] As

[36] StAFr, A 1 XII d 45, 1504–5, fo. 20ʳ.
[37] StAFr, A 1 XII d 25, 1477–1549.

Ulrich Zasius, the town clerk, drawing upon his vast legal expertise, explained in a memorandum, the council could not possibly concede Lichtenfels's claims, since payment of the *Steuer* formally implied servile obedience to the recipient: the liberty of its burghers was therefore at stake.[38] Nevertheless, since Lichtenfels was a noble outburgher, the town was reluctant to allow the dispute to sour relations entirely,[39] but its efforts to find a compromise were frustrated by Lichtenfels's intransigence, and the case dragged on for many years.[40] Similar claims were advanced by the commandery of the Hospitallers in Heitersheim, who tried to levy the *Steuer* upon Freiburg's outburghers in their village of Wendlingen in 1504.[41] Despite the council's intervention the demand was repeated the following year.[42] Individual burghers, too, were the victims of such claims, as in 1514 and the following year when the council had to intercede repeatedly with Christoph von Neuenfels to prevent him from taxing its outburgher, Hans Wildenstein from Krozingen, as his serf.[43]

These frontal assaults were unlikely to succeed since they contravened the outburghers' sworn oath of loyalty to Freiburg and to Austria. For that reason indirect attempts to enforce servile subjection by stealth were much more frequent. Since the chief anomaly of the outburghers' status was their freedom of movement, the village lords were eager to

---

[38] StAFr, B 1 2, fos. 26ᵛ–27ʳ. Cf. A 1 XII d 25, 1477–1549. Freiburg's memorandum, n.d. (1495). The villagers of Neuershausen themselves stated that it was not the custom of the village that foreign subjects should pay a servile tax to the jurisdictional lord, but simply a Shrovetide fowl and one day's boon-work. Ibid., 'Dero von nuwershüsen altharkomen', n.d. (Copy, 1495).

[39] The council considered instructing its outburghers to pay the tax, not because it was legal but in order to put an end to the unrest which the dispute as a whole was causing. Ibid., Freiburg's memorandum. 'So achten doch min herren, wenn zů disem artikel geschriben, das die pfunden us keinem rechten, sonder um frids willen und sich von unruw ze entledigen, geben, das dann an disem artikel nit span werd.'

[40] Lichtenfels's exactions may have been less the product of financial exigency than the means to further his political ambitions by raising revenue to acquire the stewardship of the lordship of Triberg from king Maximilian. In 1495 he was successful, but the cost of the mortgage by the end of his period in office had reached 2300 fl. Cf. Claudia Ulbrich, 'Bäuerlicher Widerstand in Triberg', in Peter Blickle (ed.), *Aufruhr und Empörung? Studien zum bäuerlichen Widerstand im Alten Reich* (Munich, 1980), 166–7.

[41] StAFr, B 5 XIIIa, ix, fo. 32ʳ; B 5 XI, vii, fo. 38ʳ.

[42] StAFr, B 5 XIIIa, ix, fo. 68ʳ. Here too, when faced with a corporate ecclesiastical outburgher, the council was chary of pressing more than the general principle. One peasant who had already sworn to obey the Order's jurisdiction should be allowed to seek legal redress, the council urged, but it did not intend to intervene on his behalf itself.

[43] StAFr, B 5 XI, ix, fos. 187ʳ, 190ʳ, 194ʳ.

restrict that right or else demand permanent residence in their jurisdictions. In 1485 Ludwig von Blumeneck was threatening to curtail the future right to move of an outburgher in Merdingen who wished to stay in the village whilst his wife was pregnant.[44] The pressure to tie outburghers to their dwelling-place can also be seen from the Waltershofen list of grievances in 1504/5, in which the outburgher community there asserted its traditional freedom of movement against Rudolf von Blumeneck's encroachments.[45]

Almost as contentious was the outburghers' freedom to marry. In 1476 Freiburg had to intervene to defend the wife of an outburgher from Tunsel, a former margravial bondwoman, from continuing claims against her by the margravial bailiff of Badenweiler, Hansmichael von Neuenfels.[46] The council accepted that the margraves were entitled to levy the *Eigenschilling* until an exchange had been agreed, as was the custom between Freiburg and Baden, the Blumenecks and the lords zum Wyger,[47] and to which Neuenfels had referred at the time of the marriage, but it could not tolerate further demands after the exchange had been completed.[48] Freiburg was faced with a similar attempt by the margravial bailiff of Ihringen over one of its outburghers in Merdingen in 1512,[49] whilst two years later the widow of an outburgher in Tiengen was ordered to pay a servile tax by Ludwig von Pfirt who claimed lordship over her after her husband's death.[50] Despite the *Gegenwechsel* agreement the lords zum Wyger sought to extract merchets from the outburghers in their jurisdiction in 1484,[51] and twenty years later Rudolf von Blumeneck was accused of interfering in its right to marry by the outburgher community in Waltershofen.[52] A decade later Rudolf and his brother Kaspar voiced the novel complaint that the outburghers in Merdingen were forcing the female subjects of religious houses into serfdom by marrying them, since according to the custom of the Breisgau such women were traditionally free to move.[53]

---

[44] StAFr, B 5 XI, v, 3, fo. 10ʳ.   [45] StAFr, A 1 XII d 45, 1504–5, fo. 20ʳ.
[46] StAFr, B 5 XI, iv, 8, fo. 26ʳ.
[47] Cf. Freiburg's letter to the new bailiff, Henmann, Truchsess of Rheinfelden, in 1479. StAFr, B 5 XI, iv, 11, fo. 137ʳ.
[48] This emerges from a much later attempt in 1487 by Hansmichael von Neuenfels to levy a tax upon Husler's wife. StAFr, B 5 XI, v, 3, fo. 92ᵛ.
[49] StAFr, B 5 XI, ix, fo. 24ᵛ.   [50] Ibid., fo. 140ʳ.
[51] StAFr, B 5 XI, v, 1, fo. 53ʳ.   [52] StAFr, A 1 XII d 45, 1504–5.
[53] StAFr, A 1 XII d 51, 23 Nov. 1515. The Blumenecks were stewards of the Teutonic Order in Freiburg's seigneurial rights in Merdingen, hence the reference to the subjects of religious houses. Cf. Wolfgang Stülpnagel, 'Merdingen: Frühere Herrschafts- und Besitzverhältnisse', in *AmtKrB* ii. 2. 675.

The lords also strove to establish their servile authority over the outburghers at the time of death, either by levying a heriot on the heirs or by distraining the deceased's goods until his heirs had acknowledged allegiance. The margravial castellan of Badenweiler demanded such a heriot in 1474 from the widow of an outburgher,[54] whilst the next year Freiburg had to plead with the abbot of St Trudpert, another corporate outburgher, to return a horse to the widow of an outburgher in Tunsel which he had seized as a heriot.[55] By 1505, however, another quarrel with St Trudpert showed how far the council had begun to accommodate the claims of outburgher lords. The abbey had claimed as heriotable the daughter of an outburgher from Staufen, since her mother had been the monastery's serf.[56] When the case came before Freiburg for arbitration, the outburgher vigorously denied the claim. In its judgement the council accepted that the girl was not liable for the time being, but conceded that the abbey might press its claim against her at the appropriate time.[57] Whatever her original status, the mother's marriage to an outburgher should have released her from any servile ties to the abbey, so that her daughter by rights should also have enjoyed the protection of burgher status.[58] Distraint of property in order to assert servile rights was much rarer, though in 1503 the Order of St John refused to allow an outburgher in Ambringen to inherit his estate until he had paid a bondage fine.[59] Since the outburgher's mother had been formally exchanged with one of the Order's serfs, the council argued, the Knights Hospitaller could no longer uphold any claims against her children. Such harassment by its nature, however, was directed against individuals rather than against the outburgher communities at large.

The lords' attitude stiffened noticeably when it came to recognizing the outburghers' loyalty and obligations towards Freiburg, for these extraneous commitments cut straight across their village authority. That applied especially to the general levies and territorial taxes which

[54] StAFr, A 1 XII d 24, 15 Nov. 1474.

[55] StAFr, B 5 XI, iv, 7, fo. 9^v.

[56] As the court record makes plain, this serfdom was the older personal serfdom inherited matrilineally, not residential bondage. According to Breisgau custom such monastery serfs were indeed free to move, but continued to render servile allegiance to their religious seigneurs.

[57] StAFr, B 5 III c 12 δ ßß, iii, 16, fos. 5^v–7^r.

[58] Since the abbey claimed the mother as a hereditary, not a residential, bondwoman, its claim upon the daughter may still have held, but in that case a conflict of laws between that right and the custom of *Gegenwechsel* clearly arose.

[59] StAFr, B 5 XI, vii, 1, fo. 118^r.

the outburghers, as sworn subjects of Freiburg and Austria, rendered with the town, not with the villages. The hearth-tax of 1487, for instance, which archduke Sigismund imposed on his lands in a desperate attempt to escape enveloping bankruptcy, led Rudolf von Blumeneck to try to raise the tax directly from the outburghers in Waltershofen, which gave rise to considerable correspondence with the Upper Austrian government in Innsbruck over the correct apportionment of the levy.[60] Although it was the outburghers' privilege to pay war-levies and carry out military service with the municipal contingent, several lords did not shy from incorporating them in their village assessments, either as communities, as in the case of Hansmichael von Neuenfels and the Krozingen outburghers in 1480,[61] or as individuals, as in the case of the Order of St John against two outburghers of Uffhausen in 1509.[62] Often the outburgher communities were pressed to bear arms with their fellow-villagers in the many campaigns which Outer Austria witnessed during the fifteenth and sixteenth century. In 1504 Konrad von Kranznau, the victor in an earlier skirmish with the town, threatened the outburghers in Oberschaffhausen with a collective fine of £3 unless they followed him to war,[63] and in 1498 Rudolf von Blumeneck had tried to force the Waltershofen community to muster with the rest of the village.[64] As joint lords of Merdingen, too, the Blumenecks protested that the outburghers would not serve with the village contingent, even though they enjoyed usufruct of the common land.[65]

That grievance highlights in turn the degree of friction which the outburghers' immunity generated over the issue of their contribution to the communal responsibilities of the village. On numerous occasions lords sought to curtail the outburghers' right of common, or else made them share in the burden of village taxation. In 1510 the Merdingen outburghers petitioned the council that their local rights, unlike those of the other *Hintersassen*, were being infringed by Rudolf von Blumeneck.[66] The year before the Knights of St John had

---

[60] StAFr, B 5 XI, v, 3, fo. 101ᵛ.   [61] StAFr, B 5 XI, iv, 11, fo. 155ᵛ.
[62] StAFr, B 5 XI, viii, 2, fo. 46ᵛ. Ten years earlier, significantly enough, Breisach had made similar demands upon a Freiburg outburgher in its own village of Niederrimsingen. StAFr, B 5 XI, v, 9, fo. 24ʳ. Defence of local jurisdictions was not the sole prerogative of the nobility, and Breisach was evidently not prepared to sacrifice its own interests for the sake of a country subject of a neighbour and ally, even though it held outburghers itself.
[63] StAFr, B 5 XI, vii, 2, fo. 25ᵛ.
[64] StAFr, B 5 XIIIa, vii, fo. 87ʳ.
[65] StAFr, A 1 XII d 51, 23 Nov. 1515.   [66] StAFr, B 5 XI, viii, 2, fo. 78ᵛ.

tried to ban the two outburghers from whom they had demanded a war-levy from the common in Uffhausen.[67] Such restrictions could be extended on occasion into a form of economic boycott, whereby the lords forbad their own subjects from selling property to the outburghers. Ludwig von Blumeneck and Ulrich von Lindau banned such sales in Merdingen in 1495, though repeated intercession by the town council succeeded in upholding the outburghers' rights, and confined their fiscal liability within the village to that of other *Hintersassen*.[68] The quarrel with Rudolf von Blumeneck over the Waltershofen community, by contrast, lasted much longer. In 1495 he had banned them from buying property,[69] but despite the council's intervention the outburghers appeared before it four years later to complain of fresh chicanery.[70] Their grievances persisted until 1504, when Freiburg embarked upon a final reckoning with the Blumenecks.[71] Much of the impetus behind these bans and exclusions derived from economic circumstance. When outburghers—and other *Hintersassen*—bought land, it was henceforth exempt from assessment for the main territorial tax, the *Bede*, which was commonly levied as a lump sum on the village as a whole.[72] That meant the more exempt *Hintersassen*, the fewer villagers to bear the lump sum.[73] It is no surprise, therefore, to find village lords distraining outburghers' property in lieu of village taxes. In 1496 Rudolf von Blumeneck seized the corn of an outburgher in Tunsel for that very reason.[74] The shortfall in communal revenue was to form one of his main grievances brought against the Waltershofen outburghers in 1504.[75]

Sometimes, however, the lords resorted to straightforward intimidation without benefit of legal pretext. In 1488, for instance, the Order of St John, despite its corporate outburgher rights, threatened to expel the outburgher communities in Uffhausen and Wendlingen at one fell swoop on pain of a £10 penalty.[76] Freiburg responded by threatening

---

[67] Ibid., fo. 46ᵛ.
[68] StAFr, A I XII d 34, 11 Feb. 1495.
[69] StAFr, B 5 III c 10, fos. 3ᵛ–4ʳ.
[70] StAFr, B 5 XI, v, 9, fo. 6ʳ.
[71] StAFr, A I XII d 45, 1504–5. Rudolf von Blumeneck's grievances, fo. 1ʳ; cf. grievances of the outburghers, fo. 20ʳ.
[72] Often the *Bede* was converted into a real levy attaching to the villagers' lands. Cf. Karl Siegfried Bader, *Studien zur Rechtsgeschichte des mittelalterlichen Dorfes*, i: *Das mittelalterliche Dorf als Friedens- und Rechtsbereich* (Weimar, 1957), 58.
[73] Cf. Max Georg Schmidt, 'Die Pfalbürger', *Zeitschrift für Kulturgeschichte*, ix (1902), 274.
[74] StAFr, B 5 XI, v, 7, fos. 49ᵛ–50ʳ.
[75] StAFr, A I XII d 45, 1504–5. Rudolf von Blumeneck's grievances, fo. 1ʳ.
[76] StAFr, B 5 XI, v, 3, fo. 114ʳ.

the Knights with suspension of their privileges, and no more, it seems, was heard of the matter. Less comprehensive, but equally serious, were acts of violence directed at individual outburghers, though many of these doubtless arose from disputes within the village, rather than from the outburghers' position as such. That was probably the case in 1479 when Hansmichael von Neuenfels destroyed an outburgher's weir at Krozingen, allegedly because of its incursion upon his fishing rights,[77] and again in 1516 when Gabriel von Bollschweil cut off the water to the miller of Wendlingen's mill-wheel.[78] The strangest case of all, however, concerned Konrad von Kranznau, seigneur of Oberschaffhausen, who in 1494 imprisoned the wife of the outburgher steward of the village, Hans von Elzach, for reasons not known.[79] The Freiburg council reacted with uncharacteristic fury by despatching a posse of horsemen without delay to capture several of Kranznau's peasants as a reprisal.[80] The incident came before the Ensisheim government, and even to the attention of Maximilian,[81] largely because the Outer Austrian governor, Kaspar von Mörsberg, who was already at loggerheads with the town, took Kranznau's part. Although the latter at last set the woman free, he extracted from her such large fines and seized so much of her property that she and her husband were forced to leave Oberschaffhausen and roam the countryside in misery and destitution.[82] Moreover, in the end Freiburg had to pay Kranznau damages for seizing his peasants.

These manifold incidents demonstrate beyond question that the negotiations of 1483 had failed to secure any form of peaceful coexistence for Freiburg's outburghers in the Breisgau villages. No sooner had the negotiations ended than Freiburg was casting around for a solution to its dilemma.[83] It approached Cologne to enquire how that mighty city handled its rural burghers but received the laconic reply that Cologne had no peasant outburghers.[84] As the century drew

---

[77] StAFr, B 5 XI, iv, 11, fo. 141ᵛ.   [78] StAFr, B 5 XI, x, fo. 7ᵛ.
[79] StAFr, B 5 XI, v, 5, fo. 18ᵛ.
[80] StAFr, B 1 2. 'Conradts von Crancznow handel, anfang und end', fo. 14ʳ.
[81] StAFr, B 5 XI, v, 6, fos. 1ᵛ–2ʳ, 2ᵛ, 5ᵛ.
[82] StAFr, B 1 2, fos. 18ʳ, 23ᵛ; B 5 III c 9, fo. 3ʳ.
[83] The negotiations continued throughout 1483 and were still in progress, it appears, in 1485. TLA, Kanzleibücher, ältere Reihe, Lit. D., fos. 134ᵛ–135ʳ, 167ʳ; Lit. H., n.d. (1485).
[84] StAFr, B 5 XI, v, 3, fo. 70ʳ, (Draft). In the margin it was noted: 'haben kein ussburger'. Cologne had preferred to conclude alliances with many of the Rhenish and Palatine nobility rather than build up a landed territory, but its network of noble outburghers never led to the acquisition of peasant burgher subjects. Cf. Hans J. Domsta,

to a close, the conflict grew more intense. Freiburg used the unique assembly of the imperial diet within its walls in 1498 to petition Maximilian on behalf of itself and Breisach, but the hearing before his councillors achieved no positive result.[85] Not until 1510 did Maximilian issue an edict affording imperial protection to the outburghers, in which they were described for the first time explicitly as serfs.[86] In any case, such edicts from on high were powerless to prevent the daily war of attrition waged by the local nobility against the towns' intrusive subjects. For over half a century Freiburg had struggled manfully to preserve and protect its rural subjects, but in the first two decades of the sixteenth century the council suddenly and drastically reversed its policy.[87] It abandoned three of the outburgher communities which had suffered the most persistent harassment—Waltershofen, Merdingen, and Neuershausen—to the village lords. The reason for the sale, as Freiburg readily admitted, was the unremitting friction with the Breisgau nobility, especially with those who were themselves noble allies of the town. But that immediate motive concealed much broader strategic and political considerations. By 1500 Freiburg had shifted its attention to the construction of a landed territory which offered a much more secure rural bulwark than the outburghers. Moreover, the beginnings of peasant revolt on the Upper Rhine—the Bundschuh conspiracies of 1493 in Alsace and 1502 in the bishopric of Speyer—obliged the town to reassess where its true interests lay. As a pillar of Outer Austria Freiburg sold its contentious outburgher communities, for to have retained them in the face of mounting rural discontent would only have increased the hostility of those with whom the town must in the last resort ally if the established order were attacked.

By February 1504 negotiations had been opened with Rudolf von Blumeneck over the sale of the outburghers in Waltershofen. Under the terms finally ratified by the Ensisheim government the purchase price was set at twenty-sixfold Freiburg's annual income from the

Die Kölner Außenbürger. Untersuchungen zur Politik und Verfassung der Stadt Köln von der Mitte des 13. bis zur Mitte des 16. Jahrhunderts (Rheinisches Archiv, lxxxiv) (Bonn, 1973).

[85] TLA, Maximiliana, XIV/44, fo. 269ʳ. To these events an undated supplication by Freiburg to Maximilian setting forth its grievances and requesting a royal edict protecting the outburghers can most properly be assigned. StAFr, A 1 XIV a 19, n.d. (*c*.1490).

[86] See p. 37, n. 89.

[87] That the change was indeed abrupt and deliberate emerges from Ulrich Zasius's comments in the *Geschichtbuch* and elsewhere.

outburghers. The outburghers were given the right of emigrating to the town, or whither they pleased after a further year's residence there. On death their heirs were to pay only one-third of the usual heriot. As a reciprocal gesture, Blumeneck's serfs were to be allowed to move to the town, but should they wish to move again, they had to return to Waltershofen and render the normal heriot.[88] The settlement itself caused acrimony because Blumeneck was reluctant to pay so steep a purchase price. The negotiations dragged on for over a year,[89] until on 1st April, 1505 a treaty between the parties confirmed the price and the sale.[90] Even then that did not prevent Blumeneck trying to force those outburghers who had emigrated to swear him allegiance.[91] In the wake of the planned Bundschuh revolt at Lehen on its very doorstep in 1513 Freiburg earnestly debated whether to sell all the remaining outburghers.[92] Because of their oaths to Austria the council had to consult the Ensisheim government, which granted permission on condition that the outburghers were allowed to move to Freiburg or any other Austrian territory.[93] In 1515, therefore, the council sold the outburghers in Merdingen to Rudolf and Kaspar von Blumeneck on the same terms and conditions and for the same price as had been agreed in Waltershofen.[94] In the same year, however, the two Blumenecks concluded a treaty with Breisach which explicitly recognized the continued presence of its outburghers in Merdingen and their right to render taxes, levies, and military service with the town, though they were required to swear loyal allegiance to the Blumenecks as other *Hintersassen*.[95] The reasons for this preferential treatment can only be conjectured, except that the relatively small number of Breisach's outburghers constituted a far less disruptive presence in the Breisgau villages than Freiburg's sizeable communities. Four years later, after a lengthy quarrel over their rights, Freiburg sold

---

[88] StAFr, A 1 XII d 45, 1504–5. Judgment of the deputy governor of Outer Austria, 6 Feb. 1504.

[89] Cf. ibid., fos. 9^r–12^v; StAFr, A 1 XII d 46, 17 June 1504; B 5 XIIIa, ix, fos. 44^r, 49^v.

[90] StAFr, A 1 XII d 45, 1504–5, fo. 15^r. The annual revenue amounted to £6.13s., therefore Blumeneck had to pay the considerable sum of £172.18s.

[91] StAFr, B 5 XI, viii, 1, fo. 60^v.   [92] StAFr, B 5 XIIIa, xa, p. 86.

[93] StAFr, A 1 XII d 50, 12 Aug. 1514.

[94] StAFr, A 1 XII d 51, 23 Nov. 1515. The document filed under A 1 XII d (outburghers) is a copy. The original is located, quite bizarrely, under Adelhausen: A 1 XVI A a 739, 23 Nov. 1515. The agreement departed from the government's stipulations only in curtailing the option on the lords' claiming the outburghers from ten years to one.

[95] StAFr, A 1 XVI A a 738, 17 Aug. 1515. The location of this document under Adelhausen is perplexing.

Freiburg's Conflict with the Breisgau 97

the community in Neuershausen to Wilhelm von Lichtenfels's son, Hans, under the same provisions as the earlier treaties.[96] The sale fell through, however,[97] and was not properly completed until 1545, when Hans von Lichtenfels paid 80 fl. for full seigneurial rights over the Neuershausen outburghers.[98]

Despite shedding three of the largest outburgher communities, Freiburg still managed to retain many of the smaller communities, including that in the margravial exclave of Gallenweiler, until the decision in principle to sell off the remaining outburghers was finally taken by the council in the 1570s. Throughout the first half of the sixteenth century the number of outburghers remained sizeable and remarkably constant despite the sales. Harassment certainly did not cease altogether[99]—there was trouble in 1544 with the villages of the *Kirchspiel* (Ambringen, Ehrenstetten, and Kirchhofen)[100]—but peace with the most obstreperous of the local nobility took the sting out of the conflict between Freiburg and the country lords.

If their legal status had been reduced to that of the rural serfs as a consequence of the sales, the outburghers would have had good cause to protest. In fact, their liberties were largely guaranteed if they were prepared to leave their native villages. Nevertheless, the petition which the Waltershofen outburghers addressed to Maximilian in 1505 reveals the deep sense of betrayal and abandonment which they felt. They declared that Freiburg had shown no just cause for selling those who had loyally served the town in fulfilment of their burgher's oaths.[101] Maximilian's response was highly revealing: if the outburghers were subjects of the territorial ruler (as their oaths indeed implied), then they should not be sold; but if they belonged to the town alone, or if Freiburg was merely proposing to sell its outburgher revenues, then

---

[96] StAFr, A 1 XII d 25, 1477–1549. Copy of treaty, n.d. (1519), datable from entries in the outburgher tallage lists for 1518 and 1520.

[97] From 1520 to 1524 the Neuershausen outburghers were grouped together with their neighbours in Buchheim under the rubric 'Bûcher stur'. Thereafter the Neuershauseners appeared once again as a separate entry.

[98] StAFr, A 1 XII d 60, 5 June 1545; B 5 XIIIa, xii, fo. 286^r. It is worth noting that the dispute over the villagers' rights in which the outburghers had become involved continued unabated until 1549, and a final settlement was not reached until 1810, three centuries later! Cf. Wellmer, 'Breisgau', p. 309.

[99] At the Austrian territorial diet in Innsbruck in 1518 the Breisgau towns submitted articles of grievance which included harassment of their outburghers. StAFr, C 1 Landstände 3, 4 May 1518.

[100] StAFr, B 5 XIIIa, xii, fos. 205^v, 244^r.

[101] StAFr, A 1 XII d 45, 1504–5, fo. 18^{r-v}.

the outburghers had no grounds for objection.[102] When it came to the point, in other words, the outburghers' oath of loyalty, which Freiburg always vaunted in any conflict with the Breisgau nobility, could not save them from their fate. No other record of the outburghers' reaction survives, but it is hardly likely that the other communities felt any happier at being abandoned to the village lords who had striven for so long by fair means or foul to make their existence intolerable. In the Bundschuh revolts and the Peasants' War the outburghers never rallied to the town's assistance: the solidarity which Freiburg once displayed towards its outburghers and with entire villages on occasion counted for nothing when the battle-lines were drawn.

II

If the defence of its outburghers during the fifteenth century enabled the town to pose as a champion of the peasants in certain instances, then the acquisition of villages and latterly a landed territory revealed Freiburg from quite another angle: as a civic lord bent upon extracting maximum economic and political advantage from its rural dependencies. Freiburg's high-handedness in dealing with its subject peasantry provoked reaction and disaffection which culminated in the ready response of the Dreisam peasants to the clarion of rebellion in 1525.

No sooner had Freiburg bought the village of Herdern in 1457 than its inhabitants were driven to seek redress from an array of innovations which the council had imposed. The articles of grievance submitted by Herdern to its liege lord, count Heinrich of Fürstenberg, demonstrate Freiburg's determination to use the village as a valuable source of revenue by exploiting its rights of lordship to the full. The council, it was alleged, had abolished the old weights and measures in favour of the lesser civic ones; it was appropriating the total of court fines instead of the customary one-third; it insisted that the villagers paid tolls at the foreign, rather than the domestic, rate; and it had levied a new toll on corn sold at the church-ale, which had been previously exempt. To these complaints were added various innovations and restrictions. Herdern's own field-watches had been replaced by members of the wine-growers' gild; the criminal court in the village had been suspended; a march-stone had been erected on their common without

[102] Ibid., fo. 20ʳ. In June 1505 a court-hearing was arranged between Freiburg and Blumeneck, but there is no doubt that the outburghers were finally sold. StAFr, A 1 XIV Blumeneck 207, 13 June 1505.

the villagers' sanction. Furthermore, those who had raised their voices in protest were arbitrarily arrested and flung into the municipal goal.[103] None of these measures ought to be construed as a covert attempt to integrate Herdern into the civic community; on the contrary, the villagers were excluded from burgher's rights and treated as peasant subjects who rendered ground-rents[104] and labour-services to the town.[105]

Freiburg's treatment of Herdern was constantly masterful, not least because the village remained a Fürstenberg enclave within Outer Austria until its final incorporation into the town in 1538.[106] Despite two decades of calm after the troubles of 1463, the villagers were once more roused to anger in 1481 by the reiterated demands of Freiburg's newly appointed feoffee (*Lehensträger*), Melchior von Falkenstein. On behalf of the villagers, Konrad Rapp, son of Peter Rapp who had led the opposition to Freiburg a generation earlier, informed Fürstenberg of renewed encroachments upon their customary rights.[107] As a result Falkenstein was threatened with legal action unless he desisted.[108] The town council tried to maintain that the dispute was an internal matter of no concern to Herdern's overlord,[109] but the case came before a Fürstenberg court the same year, though its outcome is unknown.[110] Thereafter Freiburg appears to have exercised unrestrained authority over Herdern through its nominated *Lehensträger*.

At first glance Freiburg's sweeping claims upon Herdern find no parallel in the town's handling of its Dreisam territories. The council appeared content to set up a seigneurial administration which would not interfere with or override the local custom of the separate

---

[103] StAFr, A 1 VIII a γ 43, c.1460. Herdern's articles of grievance, n.d. (1463). The document is a redaction probably drawn up in the Füstenberg chancery.

[104] Cf. StAFr, E 1 A v b 5, no. 2 (1528–44). Between these years the council received £30 annually in ground-rents.

[105] StAFr, B 5 XIIIa, iva, fo 36ʳ.

[106] A late 15 c. manorial roll suggests that the custom of Herdern afforded the villagers much greater liberties—e.g. complete freedom to marry and to move—than pertained in the villages of the Austrian Breisgau. Cf. Josef Kartels, *Herdern bei Freiburg i. Br.* (Freiburg, 1905), 110–12. It appears that attempts to adjust these rights to the prevailing Breisgau custom did not succeed before the mid-16th c. Ulbrich, *Leibherrschaft*, p. 197.

[107] Cf. Siegmund Riezler (ed.), *Fürstenbergisches Urkundenbuch*, iii (Tübingen, 1878), 363. Idem, *Geschichte des fürstlichen Hauses Fürstenberg und seiner Ahnen bis zum Jahre 1509* (Tübingen, 1883), 380.

[108] StAFr, A 1 VIII a γ 56, 1481–2.

[109] StAFr, B 5 XI, v, 1, fo. 6ᵛ. After 1457, Freiburg argued, Fürstenberg's rights had been confined to enfeoffments.

[110] Riezler, *Fürstenberg*, p. 380.

communities. The various village dooms—such as Kirchzarten's[111] and Zarten's[112]—still embodied local law. No attempt was made to establish a uniform jurisdiction to match the unitary administration of the Valley Bailiwick. This apparent restraint can be explained by the very different motives which lay behind the creation of the Valley Bailiwick. The gild-dominated middling craft towns which depended upon their immediate hinterland were more interested, as Raiser has convincingly argued, in the political, commercial, and strategic security that control of a landed territory was designed to achieve than in the direct economic and fiscal benefits of such estates.[113] All that Freiburg did was to carve out four administrative districts—St Märgen, Wagensteig, Zarten, and Kirchzarten—each with its own steward who was accountable to the Valley Bailiff with his seat in Kirchzarten.[114] Yet this division of responsibilities left little real power in the hands of the bailiff, for he in turn was accountable to two overseers chosen from the ranks of the council, and had in fact no legal authority whatsoever. Petty jurisdiction was vested in the four stewards[115] whilst capital jurisdiction remained firmly with the council. The bailiff's function was essentially that of factor: to see to the repair of the turnpikes, especially the Wagensteig road; to collect taxes and outstanding debts; to pay the wages of the bailiwick employees; and to present annual accounts to the two overseers sitting in the Exchange.[116]

Freiburg's income from feudal dues in the Dreisam valley remained comparatively modest. The bulk of revenues derived in any case from toll charges, which the bailiwick was designed to protect. The returns from the former St Märgen estates show that between 1484 (when records begin) and 1526 Freiburg received around £150 annually in ground-rents.[117] Other revenues from court fines, heriots, and the like

---

[111] Cf. *UBStFr* ii. 97–105.   [112] Cf. ibid., pp. 111–25.

[113] Cf. Elisabeth Raiser, *Städtische Territorialpolitik im Mittelalter. Eine vergleichende Untersuchung über verschiedene Formen am Beispiel Lübecks und Zürichs* (Historische Studien, cdvi) (Lübeck/Hamburg, 1969), 30. This point gains added weight from the fact that Freiburg was content to hold the stewardships of the Oberried estates which controlled a vast area of strategic importance, rather than convert its authority into full ownership. Armbruster's view that weight of tradition and a fear of innovation characteristic of medieval man inhibited the council from upsetting existing patterns of jurisdiction may be discounted. 'Freiburger Talvogtei', p. 105.

[114] Armbruster, 'Talvogtei', p. 369. Plans to separate the bailiff's authority into two vice-bailiwicks were abandoned at an early stage.   [115] Ibid., p. 372.

[116] Armbruster, 'Freiburger Talvogtei', pp. 143–4. Idem, 'Talvogtei', p. 369. His task was no sinecure, for he had to make up any deficit out of his own pocket. Ibid., p. 370.

[117] The peasants were also required to pay for the usufruct of forest land which belonged to the town. StAFr, B 5 XIIIa, iva, fo. 29ʳ.

Freiburg's Conflict with the Breisgau 101

naturally varied a good deal, but normally ranged between £25 and £45.[118] Approximately one-third of the bailiwick revenues went towards the wages of employees and general purposes. Yet the absence of fiscal pressure upon the peasants of the Dreisam territories must not be allowed to disguise the authoritarian and punctilious character of Freiburg's administration, or the ultimate aim of its seigneurial policy. In the first two decades of the sixteenth century Freiburg discussed shortcomings in its tax-gathering and debt-collection on several occasions, to the point of sending two emissaries to investigate matters and call the bailiff and stewards to account for their negligence.[119] The town might have been spared this embarrassment if the two council overseers had not shirked their duties by foisting the running of the Dreisam territories upon an inexperienced and doubtless overworked bailiff drawn from the local peasantry. At last, in 1513 the overseers themselves were ordered to ride round the bailiwick to drive in unpaid debts.[120] Such behaviour was unlikely to endear the town to its dependent peasantry.

Equally ominous was Freiburg's attempt to extinguish St Märgen's residual rights over those of its serfs beyond the bailiwick who had not been sold to Freiburg. What was at stake was less the revenue from heriots which the council was claiming than its determination to round off its seigneurial rights over against St Märgen as a step towards establishing exclusive jurisdiction within the Valley Bailiwick. In 1489 the Ensisheim government in fact recognized the council's right to pursue anyone who emigrated from its Dreisam territories, whether they were its own subjects or *Hintersassen*.[121] In practice, all inhabitants of the bailiwick, excepting the town's own outburghers,[122] had been reduced to the uniform status of rural serfs by the beginning of the sixteenth century.[123] Over the following decades Freiburg began systematically to exclude the rights of foreign lords over their *Hintersassen* in the Dreisam valley in order to establish a closed territory. In a series of legal battles Freiburg fought to abolish these

---

[118] StAFr, E 1 A v b 9, no. 1 (1484–1531). The peasants also made payments in kind. In 1502, for instance, the town received 698 eggs and 123 hens. B 4 10, 1502.
[119] StAFr, B 5 XIIIa, x, fos. 12ʳ, 12ᵛ–13ʳ, 14ʳ, 24ʳ.
[120] StAFr, B 5 XIIIa, xa, fo. 51ʳ.   [121] Ulbrich, *Leibherrschaft*, p. 209.
[122] The outburghers remained legally distinct from the mass of rural serfs. In 1542, for instance, an outburgher from the bailiwick was recognized by the council as exempt from paying taxes to the valley bailiff by virtue of his burgher status. StAFr, B 5 XIIIa, xii, fo. 9ʳ.
[123] Ulbrich, *Leibherrschaft*, p. 210.

rights until at last in 1570, no doubt as a deliberate counterpart to its decision to sell the remaining outburghers, it ordered all *Hintersassen* to renounce their allegiance to outside lords or else emigrate.[124] With that, Freiburg's landlordship over the Dreisam peasants became securely anchored in exclusive jurisdiction. The peasants' status and freedoms had been whittled down, even though their economic burdens had not been significantly increased. With the acquisition of the Dreisam territories Freiburg's era of expansion all but ceased. The occasional purchases of the sixteenth century did not alter fundamentally the balance of Freiburg's territorial influence which stretched eastwards to the Black Forest rather than westwards into the valley of the Upper Rhine.[125]

III

The scale of conflict between town and country at the close of the Middle Ages was nowhere more evident, however, than in Freiburg's rapidly deteriorating relations with the mass of peasantry beyond its outburgher and territorial jurisdiction. Whatever flexibility the town might display within its sphere of influence vanished altogether when confronted by a welter of challenges to its economic interests and political supremacy by the Breisgau villagers themselves. Towards those to whom it had no obligations the council's actions were unyielding, brusque, and often violent.

The construction of the Dreisam territory, for instance, was chiefly intended to safeguard Freiburg's commercial control over the main trade route through the Wagensteig and Höllental passes, so that the town reacted sharply when the peasantry evaded the route or, worse, began to build rival turnpikes over the Black Forest.[126] Already on the construction of a new road through the Falkenstein valley in 1379, a joint venture between Freiburg and Villingen, the local peasants refused to pay the new tolls, apparently at the instigation of the lords of Falkenstein.[127] Freiburg responded on occasion by imprisoning

---

[124] Ibid., p. 211.   [125] Cf. Scott, 'Territorialpolitik'.

[126] In the 14th c. Freiburg had concluded treaties with the lords of Schwarzenberg and the town of Villingen to protect its revenues from the Wagensteig road and to suppress the building of another through the Simonswald valley, so that the Black Forest peasants would buy their corn at Freiburg rather than in Waldkirch or Malterdingen. Otto Gönnenwein, 'Marktrecht und Städtewesen im alemannischen Gebiet', *ZGO* NF lix (1950), 375. Cf. Josef Rösch, 'Die Straßenanlagen und Zollrechte der Städte Freiburg and Villingen', *Freiburger Adresskalender*, 1853, iv.

[127] *UBStFr* ii. 31–2.

peasants, such as the Falkensteiners in 1420, who were caught bypassing the toll-stages.[128] The more serious threat, however, undoubtedly came from the proliferation of rival trade routes in the later fifteenth and early sixteenth century.[129] In 1467 the Simonswald peasants in the valley north of Waldkirch built a new road linking the latter with Furtwangen and Villingen, thereby reducing traffic through the Dreisam considerably.[130] Faced with this hazard to its toll revenues the council first sought a legal injunction to prevent its use, but when that failed it finally sent a raiding party to trap and bar the road in 1473.[131] Much to Freiburg's chagrin, the road was immediately cleared and restored, so that after due warning to the communities concerned the council was driven to destroy it a second time in November 1475,[132] whereupon the Simonswälders were instructed to leave well alone on pain of further direct action.[133] Despite the backing of the Ensisheim government, however,[134] Freiburg was unable to secure adequate safeguards about the road's future,[135] and in 1484 there were fresh incidents, culminating in the despatch of an armed contingent to capture the peasants' cattle as a reprisal.[136] For that the council incurred the wrath of the governor, who recommended referring the seemingly intractable dispute to archduke Sigismund.[137] After calling the parties to a hearing in Innsbruck,[138] he confirmed Freiburg's and Villingen's exclusive right to maintain a Black Forest turnpike,[139] but allowed the Simonswälders a track through their valley suitable for cattle and pack-horses, on which they might levy tolls providing that they undertook no carrying trade themselves.[140] Perhaps encouraged by this success, their neighbours to the north in the Prech valley set

---

[128] StAFr, A I VI d 46, 5 Sept. 1420.   [129] See above, Map 4, p. 60.

[130] In 1316 Freiburg had paid Heinrich von Schwarzenberg the considerable sum of 50 silver marks to ensure that no road was constructed through the Simonswald valley, after which there was no further trouble until 1467. StAFr, A I VI b 1, 25 May 1316. Cf. *Freiburger Urkundenbuch*, ed. Friedrich Hefele, iii (Freiburg, 1957), 305–6, no. 408.

[131] StAFr, A I VI b 9, 1473–84. Heft A. Freiburg's account, 1473.

[132] StAFr, B 5 XI, iv, 8, fo. 12^{r-v}. Freiburg sent warnings to Triberg, Elzach, and Neustadt, and tried to enlist active support from Villingen.

[133] Ibid., fo. 15^r.   [134] StAFr, A I VI b 15, 2 June 1477.

[135] There were several court-hearings in Ensisheim between Freiburg and the Simonswälders, and a flurry of correspondence, from 1473 to 1483. StAFr, A I VI b 10, 6 May 1473; 11, 1475–6; 17, 23 Oct. 1483.

[136] StAFr, A I VI b 18, 18 Aug. 1484.   [137] StAFr, A I VI b 19, 31 Aug. 1484.

[138] StAFr, A I VI b 20, 29 Sept. 1484.

[139] StAFr, A I VI b 23, 19 Jan. 1485. The privilege was renewed by Maximilian in 1493. A I VI b 25, 8 Apr. 1493.

[140] StAFr, A I VI b 24, 24 Jan. 1485.

about clearing a road over the pass to Hornberg in 1496, giving direct access from the head of the Elz valley to the Gutach and Kinzig rivers which formed a northern bridgehead to the central Black Forest from Wolfach down to Villingen.[141]

A chance encounter in 1505 reveals how long the memory of Freiburg's high-handedness towards the Simonswälders was kept alive by the Forest peasantry. The council, as a member of the Breisgau regional water association, had sent two of its employees to Waldkirch to inspect the rivers and streams. As they were taking a meal in an inn, several Forest peasants, chiefly from Furtwangen, broached the subject of the Simonswald road. Among them was the mayor of Triberg, who enquired what Freiburg proposed to do if the road were ever reopened. Seizing upon this cue to be truculent, the innkeeper exclaimed: 'Man schiss uff die von friburg. Sy sint nit mer herren im land—die von rotwil sint yetz herren.'[142] This sentiment was echoed by a peasant from the Simonswald, whereupon a chorus of voices threatened that the Freiburgers would end up with bloody heads if they attempted to destroy the road again. The last time Freiburg had sent horsemen to bar the road, declared the innkeeper, they fired their muskets so bloodthirstily that the corpses in the hospital cemetery awoke in fright and leapt from their graves. One of the Freiburg servants was so enraged by this wild talk that his companion, fearing an affray, had to hold his hand over the other's mouth to prevent him shouting back and so incensing the peasants even further.[143]

That was by no means the end of the matter. In 1520 the Simonswälders again set about building a proper road, which threatened Freiburg's monopoly on the route to Villingen and Rottweil.[144] Following a petition to the emperor Charles V, the Ensisheim government was ordered the next year to have the road destroyed,[145] despite protests that the cart-track was merely intended to fetch stone down the valley for a new church.[146] Through the road

[141] StAFr, A 1 VI b 29, 2 Aug. 1496.
[142] The scathing comment that Rottweil had ostensibly superseded Freiburg as a political force refers to the imperial city's having joined the Swiss Confederacy as an associate member in 1463, a particularly pointed shaft of abuse since the Swiss were widely regarded by the rural population of South-West Germany as champions of peasant freedom.
[143] StAFr, B 5 XIIIa, ix, fos. 51^{r-v}, 83^r.
[144] StAFr, C 1 Straßenbau 23. Villingen to Freiburg, 12 Dec. 1520.
[145] Ibid., Emperor Charles V to the Outer Austrian government, 10 Jan. 1521.
[146] Ibid., The provost of St Margaret's, Waldkirch to Freiburg, 17 Jan. 1521; the Outer Austrian government to Freiburg, 23 Jan. 1521; the community of the

probably then fell out of use, fresh efforts were made to revive it later in the century.[147]

A few years later Freiburg faced the same difficulty from a new quarter, as peasants from the Glotter valley half-way to Waldkirch joined hands with subjects of the abbey of St Peter in the hills above Freiburg to construct a road which formed a northern loop round the Dreisam to the Black Forest uplands.[148] Stiffened by earlier episodes, the council lost no time in destroying the road despite loud opposition from the margrave of Baden and the abbot (a noble outburgher) who stood to gain most from the new route.[149] All the same, two fresh attempts were made to replace the road in 1544[150] and 1560;[151] Freiburg's frequent expeditions to make these rival routes impassable, it seems, never had more than temporary success.

Freiburg's economic interests were likewise affected by disputes over grazing rights in those pastures once belonging to the surrounding villages which the town had acquired in the course of its fourteenth-century expansion and then relet to the peasants on an annual lease. In two notorious battles with margravial villages which broke out at regular intervals in the later fifteenth century the peasants claimed still to own the pastures and repudiated their leases. In 1443 Zähringen tried to regain possession of lands allegedly seized by the town, saying that it had enjoyed both ownership and usufruct since time immemorial. The villagers appealed for help to their lord, Peter zum Wyger, who as margravial bailiff of Hochberg brought the matter to the notice of margrave Jakob.[152] Freiburg countered by stressing that it, not the villagers, had owned the pasture as long as memory reached, but that it had rented part to the villagers marked off by boundary stones. Because the Zähringers had refused to sign a new lease, the council

---

Simonswald to Freiburg, 23 Jan. 1521; Leo von Staufen, lord of Kastelberg and Schwarzenberg, to Freiburg and Villingen, n.d. (1521).

[147] StAFr, B 5 XI, xix, fos. 640ʳ–644ʳ, 649ᵛ–654ʳ (1567). At the same time the road through the Prech valley seems to have been revived. Ibid., fos. 682ᵛ–686ʳ (1568).

[148] StAFr, B 5 XI, xii, fos. 100ᵛ–101ʳ (1523).   [149] Ibid., fo. 104ʳ⁻ᵛ.

[150] StAFr, B 5 XIIIa, xii, fos. 205ʳ, 206ʳ, 207ᵛ. Cf. Vogel, *Zollwesen*, p. 31. In 1545 Freiburg concluded a treaty with St Peter which prohibited the use of the Glotter valley road for commercial purposes, but which allowed the abbey's subjects in the Rohr valley between St Peter and Glottertal to use the track for better access to their farms. GLA 102/316. Cf. StAFr, B 2 3, fos. 157ᵛ–158ᵛ.

[151] StAFr, B 5 XI, xix, fos. 2ᵛ–3ʳ, 3ᵛ; StAVl, N 16 (no. 2014), 20 Sept. 1552–21 Feb. 1571; Freiburg to Villingen, 31 Jan. 1560.

[152] StAFr, A 1 VIII a θ 1, 22 July–9 Aug. 1443: Margrave Jakob of Baden to Freiburg, 22 July 1443.

had forbidden them to drive their cattle on to the pasture; then, on account of their continued stubbornness, it had seized the cattle, though they had later been returned.[153] This did nothing to mollify the margrave,[154] but for the time being the council appeared to have prevailed.[155]

In 1477, however, the villagers renewed their claims and, according to Freiburg, were grazing their beasts on the town's part of the pasture.[156] Zähringen must have remained adamant, for that September the council decided to arrest all its cowherds.[157] Though the Ensisheim government ordered their release, it stayed judgment on the substance of the dispute until the pastures, paths, and ditches in question had been inspected.[158] Several court-days followed without a settlement up to 1481,[159] when the record breaks off. Yet a generation later in 1507 Freiburg again had to instruct its foresters to expel the villagers from its pasture.[160]

A similar pattern unfolded with Zähringen's next-door neighbour, Gundelfingen, which in 1451 had rejected a new lease spelling out Freiburg's ownership of its village pastures.[161] The town promptly seized two of the villagers' cattle and told the aggrieved margravial bailiff that it intended to sell the five beasts as compensation for the breach of its privileges.[162] Despite the margrave's intervention the town would not relent until it finally accepted arbitration in Ensisheim the next year.[163] The council agreed to return the distrained cattle but threatened that it would round them up again if the villagers failed to renew their lease on 1 May.[164] Freiburg apparently won its case, for in

---

[153] Ibid., Freiburg to margrave Jakob, 24 July 1443.

[154] Ibid., Margrave Jakob to Freiburg, 2 Aug. 1443.

[155] Ibid., Freiburg to margrave Jakob, 9 Aug. 1443. Cf. the report to the council on the subsequent proceedings in Ensisheim in 1481. StAFr, A I VIII a θ 4, 1477–81.

[156] Ibid., The deputy governor of Outer Austria to Freiburg, 31 Aug. 1477. StAFr, B 5 IX, iv, 11, fo. 33^(r–v).

[157] Ibid., fo. 34^v.

[158] StAFr, A I VIII a θ 4, 1477–81. Judgment of the Outer Austrian government, 2 Mar. 1479.

[159] Ibid., The Outer Austrian governor to Freiburg, 27 Apr. 1480, 9 May 1480, 18 June 1480. In May 1481 a detailed report of the proceedings was sent to Freiburg, Ibid., 18 May 1481.

[160] StAFr, B 5 XIIIa, x, fo. 40^v.

[161] StAFr, C I Waidgang 4. Ludwig von Landeck, margravial bailiff of Hochberg, to Freiburg, 8 July 1451.

[162] Ibid., Freiburg to Ludwig von Landeck, 10 July 1451.

[163] Ibid., Margrave Karl of Baden to Freiburg, 16 Sept. 1451; Freiburg to margrave Karl, 25 Sept. 1451.

[164] Ibid., Freiburg to the Outer Austrian government, 21 Jan. 1452.

later years Gundelfingen still paid rent for usufruct of the pasture, but the price of victory here and in Zähringen was lasting disaffection, as the events of 1525 were to show.[165]

Nor was the assertion of the liberties and interests of the community as a whole the only source of conflict between Freiburg and the countryside. The council's defence of the rights of individual burghers led to bitter confrontations with the Breisgau peasantry. Rather than chronicle the many lesser instances, let us examine the quite extraordinary legal vendetta which Freiburg pursued against the village of Köndringen just north of Emmendingen in the early 1480s. The case arose from a private quarrel between two small-time merchants, Hans Dryhod from Freiburg,[166] and Paule Allgower from Breisach. The latter was apparently pressing claims against the former—presumably for debt. In 1479 Dryhod was passing through Köndringen on business and stopped for a friendly drink with the magistrate. As he was leaving, Hans Allgower, Paule's brother, chased after him, struck him with his sword, dragged him back to the village and forced him to swear to appear before its court to answer charges brought by the Breisach merchant. On his return home Dryhod naturally reported the incident to the council, which immediately refused to recognize the court's jurisdiction and cited its civic charters to demand that any charges be heard in Freiburg. Dryhod nevertheless was willing to go to Köndringen (perhaps to have the matter settled quickly), providing he was given due notice of the hearings. At the first three hearings, however, Dryhod was escorted by the Freiburg beadle who requested that the case be transferred to the civic courts. After the third hearing Margaret von Landeck, the wife of the village lord, agreed that the village jurors should be given a fortnight in which to decide to drop the case and let Dryhod know. When he heard nothing, he assumed the case had been referred, and went about his business to the Frankfurt fair, but on his return discovered that the Köndringen court had found against him by default in his absence, and that Hans Allgower was denouncing him to all and sundry as a perjurer.[167] The town council appealed to Breisach to persuade Paule Allgower either to drop the charges or else to lodge them in Freiburg, but in reply it received a very

---

[165] Freiburg took frequent action against individual peasants as well. In 1473, for instance, it imprisoned two peasants from Lehen and Betzenhausen for poaching fish from the town's water. StAFr, A 1 XI f 288, 23 July 1473; cf. A 1 XI f 291, 13 Aug. 1474.
[166] Dryhod paid the modest sum of 7s. tallage in 1481–2. StAFr, E 1 A II a 1.
[167] StAFr, B 5 XI, iv, 11, fos. 147^v–148^r.

different story. According to Allgower, Dryhod had forced him to swear to appear before the Köndringen court, and at five successive court-hearings the village jurors had compelled him to renew his pledge. Since the case had now been decided in his favour, he had no intention of seeing a judgment quashed to which he had submitted only on account of Dryhod's importunity.[168]

In the mean time, Paule Allgower had lodged an appeal in Ensisheim, which confirmed the legality of the original proceedings,[169] though there was clearly some doubt about the decision, since Freiburg was asked whether it or Dryhod had been informed of the fifth court-day, which it denied.[170] Finding itself under attack from two sides, the council decided that it was time to take matters into its own hands. Since there was no hope of redress from Ensisheim, it seemed, Freiburg cited the magistrate and dempsters of Köndringen before the imperial court of justice at Rottweil. Anton von Landeck regarded this as an infringement of his jurisdictional lordship and promptly complained to the Outer Austrian governor, Wilhelm von Rappoltstein, who ordered the town to desist and accept arbitration at Ensisheim instead.[171] After studying a copy of Freiburg's constitution, however, the Rottweil judges turned down the governor's application for referral,[172] and the town proceeded with its action[173] undeterred by Rappoltstein's warnings of the grave displeasure which archduke Sigismund would express at this slight upon his authority.[174] Yet the court found for Freiburg, quashed Dryhod's sentence and awarded the town compensation. If the sum was not paid before the next court-session the Köndringers would be placed under the ban of the empire.[175] Rappolstein tried once more to soften the council's intransigence[176] by inviting it to send an emissary to Ensisheim with full powers to negotiate,[177] but in vain: in June 1480 Köndringen was duly banned.[178]

From that point onwards the conflict increasingly assumed the character of a clash of political wills between the government and

[168] StAFr, A 1 1 k 106, 9 Oct. 1479.
[169] StAFr, A 1 1 k 107, 14 Oct. 1479.
[170] StAFr, B 5 XI, iv, 11, fo. 149ʳ.
[171] StAFr, A 1 1 k 109, 30 Oct. 1479.
[172] StAFr, A 1 1 k 111, 9 Nov. 1479.
[173] StAFr, B 5 XI, iv, 11, fo. 150ʳ.
[174] StAFr, A 1 1 k 112, 25 Nov. 1479.
[175] StAFr, A 1 1 k 114, 11 Apr. 1480.
[176] Freiburg ordered Köndringen to comply unless it wished to incur further expense and inconvenience StAFr, B 5 XI, iv, 11, fo. 158ʳ.
[177] StAFr, A 1 XIV Schnewlin-Landeck 46, 20 Apr. 1480.
[178] StAFr, A 1 1 k 115, 8 June 1480.

Freiburg. In 1481 Rappoltstein tried unsuccessfully to have the ban lifted and a fresh judgment issued in favour of Köndringen,[179] but a second Rottweil decision in the autumn granted Freiburg distraint of the villagers' property.[180] Moreover, the imperial court enjoined all other lords to assist Freiburg in taking possession of the village,[181] and in 1482 it urged the bishop of Constance to complete the outlawry by placing Köndringen under the spiritual ban of excommunication.[182] Under these circumstances, there seemed little the villagers could do except come to terms, until in June that year Margaret von Landeck tried to enlist the aid of the margrave of Baden, who had rights in the village.[183] This can have availed nothing, for a month later Köndringen finally gave in. In its settlement with Freiburg it agreed to pay 30 fl. within a week for breach of privilege.[184] Twice, however, the Landecks had to plead with Freiburg on behalf of the village for a stay of payment.[185] By the end of February 1483 the town had still to receive compensation, so it gave Köndringen seven more days in which to settle, or else the magistrate and jurors would face indefinite imprisonment in Freiburg.[186] There the evidence ceases.

Freiburg was not, of course, the only lord in the fifteenth century to wield the blunt instrument of the imperial court of justice against hapless villagers,[187] but its grim pursuit of Köndringen and its stern refusal to accept any form of arbitration even at the risk of antagonizing its Austrian overlord seem out of all proportion to the gravity of the offence. By the terms of its constitution Freiburg had right on its side, but the council's rigid adherence to the letter of the law placed it in a ridiculous position over against the village, its neighbour Breisach, and

[179] StAFr, A 1 1 k 118, 28 Apr. 1481.
[180] StAFr, A 1 1 k 120, 20 Nov. 1481.
[181] StAFr, A 1 1 k 121, 20 Nov. 1481.
[182] StAFr, A 1 1 k 122, 25 Feb. 1482.
[183] StAFr, A 1 1 k 123, 28 June 1482. At that time Köndringen was Austrian, but in 1488 the village was divided between the two sons of Ludwig von Landeck, Anton and Sebastian, which gave Baden a foothold to expand its influence. Chronic indebtedness forced Sebastian to sell his half of the village to Baden in 1511, and in 1538 Baden took over the accumulated Landeck debts in return for full territorial sovereignty over Köndringen. Martin Wellmer, *Zur Entstehungsgeschichte der Markgenossenschaften. Der Vierdörferwald bei Emmendingen* (Veröffentlichungen des Oberrheinischen Instituts für geschichtliche Landeskunde Freiburg im Breisgau, iv) (Freiburg, 1938), 60–1, 72–3.
[184] StAFr, A 1 1 k 124, 9 Aug. 1482–7 Feb. 1483. Settlement with Freiburg, 9 Aug. 1482.
[185] Ibid., Anton von Landeck to Freiburg, 28 Dec. 1482, 7 Feb. 1483.
[186] StAFr, B 5 XI, v, 1, fo. 21^v.
[187] It should be added that Köndringen was banned again by the abbey of St Margaret in Waldkirch in 1510. StAFr. A 1 XI g 83, 29 Jan. 1510.

the Ensisheim government itself. This was the reaction of a community on the defensive, determined to ride upon its principles even though its burgher, Hans Dryhod, whom it was supposedly defending, had been willing to settle the affair amicably. In its struggle for survival throughout the fifteenth century Freiburg had undoubtedly acquired something of a siege mentality, which helps to account for the council's overwrought reaction to any perceived external threat. Yet the bloodiest encounter between the town and the Breisgau villages before the Peasants' War was ultimately of its own making and sprang directly from that struggle to survive. During 1494 as part of a wider review of the tolls designed to raise more revenue the council had markedly increased the toll-charges on produce brought to market. The new charges caused considerable resentment, and in the spring of 1495 a peasant from Waltershofen 'had been dragged before the council for abusing a customs official at the town gates.[188] But the real trouble did not come until summer, when a party of Freiburg journeymen visited the church-ale in Ebringen, three miles south-west of the town. The bloodshed which ensued (in what soon came to be known as the 'Ebringen outrage') was more than a drunken brawl between villagers and townsfolk: it was a premeditated and vicious act of vengeance for the new toll by peasants whose pent-up anger at the council's overbearing behaviour discharged itself against the community at large.[189]

On the day of the church-ale, 16 August, a large group of Freiburg journeymen set off for Ebringen in the company of one of the town's former gild commanders, Pauly Briswerch. As tradition prescribed, they were carrying their weapons, flying banners, and beating drums. On hearing them approach, one old peasant exclaimed: 'Here come the Freiburgers—they should turn round and go home: that's best for them.'[190] As the journeymen were drinking in the tavern garden, about one hundred Ebringers, also armed with a savage array of weapons, passed deliberately close by and took up position in a nearby barn.[191] In the inn itself, meanwhile, a slanging-match had developed between the

[188] StAFr, A 1 VI d 88, 9–13 Apr. 1495.
[189] A party of Ebringers had beaten up the brother of a Freiburg burgher several days before the church-ale. StAFr, A 1 XIX Ebringen 5, 26 Aug. 1495. Heft A. Testimonies of the tailors' gild.
[190] *UBStFr* ii. 605.
[191] StAFr, A 1 XIX Ebringen 5, 26 Aug. 1495. Heft A. Testimonies of the tailors' gild. At first the Freiburgers thought that they were peasants from another village, come like themselves in full array to revel at the church-ale. *UBStFr* ii. 608–9, 612.

landlady and a journeyman girdler over a glass which the latter had inadvertently smashed,[192] but in the barn no one stirred: the Ebringers were biding their time. As evening drew on, the Freiburgers made to head home. As their drummer rounded up the journeymen, the standard-bearer went inside to settle up for the day's drinking.[193] A handful of Ebringers used this moment to steal into the tavern and remove the Freiburgers' crossbows, for outside scuffles had already begun. As the journeymen were fetching their muskets, a pewterer's apprentice knocked over a beehive, allowing the bees to swarm out.[194] Many of the journeymen were stung, but as they fled they found their path blocked by the Ebringers who had at last emerged from the barn, weapons in hand.[195] Though the apprentice wanted to pay for the damage, over which the bee-keeper himself was reluctant to make a great fuss, the Ebringers were in no mood to parley.[196] They began to fire on the Freiburgers, and two of them fell upon the standard, slashing it to ribbons. In vain the standard-bearer begged for peace, but the peasants only shouted: 'You buggers, you blasphemers, we'll pay you for the fruit toll.'[197] The gild commander tried to restore calm by offering to pay compensation out of his own pocket up to any sum they cared to name, but the village magistrate, eager to display the authority of his office, brushed Briswerch's offer aside, saying he would settle the matter himself.[198] The villagers paid no heed whatever, but closed upon the Freiburgers, firing their muskets and crossbows, brandishing halberds, and pelting them with stones. Clutching the tattered standard, the journeymen took to their heels, pursued by arrows, stones, and insults; they limped home to Freiburg bleeding, scared, and footsore.[199] In the mêlée one journeyman had been stabbed to death; many others had been severely injured.[200]

When word spread of the Ebringen violence, most inhabitants wished to wreak vengeance upon the villagers that same evening, but the council was unwilling to concede the prerogative of decision to the commons. When the old and new councils convened in joint session the next morning, some of the more experienced members argued that any reprisals should have been taken immediately, if at all, and that it

---

[192] StAFr, A 1 XIX Ebringen 5, 26 Aug. 1495. Heft A. Testimonies of the tailors' gild.
[193] *UBStFr* ii. 608, 611.   [194] Ibid., pp. 606, 608.
[195] StAFr, A 1 XIX Ebringen 5, 26 Aug. 1495. Heft A. Testimonies of the tailors' gild.
[196] Ibid.; *UBStFr* ii. 609–10.
[197] Ibid., p. 606.   [198] Ibid., pp. 604–6.
[199] Ibid., pp. 609, 611.   [200] StAFr, B 1 2, fo. 58^{r-v}.

would now be wrong to squander the town's entirely justified demand for legal redress by hasty and ill-considered countermeasures. A majority, however, was not prepared to take the outrage lying down, and its call for swift retribution finally carried the day. When it was announced that an armed troop would be despatched to round up a dozen or so villagers and take them hostage, more than seven hundred citizens responded to the call to arms and marched on Ebringen under the command of the mayor. Finding the village deserted, the troop paused for refreshment, but the mayor had great difficulty in keeping the men in order, since some plainly wanted to pillage and sack the place. Denied immediate revenge, the council decided to ban the Ebringers from the municipal market[201] and to hold hostage two peasants who had been sent to Freiburg as envoys.[202] All those in town and country under Freiburg's jurisdiction present at the church-ale were summoned to testify before the public prosecutors. From their statements other Breisgau villages clearly shared Ebringen's deep antagonism towards the town. A journeyman from Kirchhofen boasted that his lord had openly threatened that he would have sent sixty armed men to help the villagers, had he known that the Freiburgers were coming.[203] Still more ominously, several outburghers from Merdingen who had attended the church-ale voiced support for the Ebringers. Apparently smarting from a fine which the council had recently imposed, they rushed out of the tavern to the villagers' cause as soon as the affray began, despite the efforts of one outburgher to bar the door with his halberd.[204]

The affair was referred to Ensisheim for arbitration, where Freiburg insisted on appearing as plaintiff, despite the villagers' insistence that they had originally appealed to the government for redress. The town's advocates made much play with the fact that those who had gone to Ebringen were simple journeymen on a convivial outing, without armour and whose muskets were stuffed with paper to show they meant no harm.[205] The peasants, for their part, contended that the Freiburgers had attacked first, and denied all knowledge of the journeyman's death. But in the end they were obliged to adopt a more conciliatory tone and apologize for whatever wrongs they had

---

[201] Ibid., fos. 58ᵛ–59ᵛ.
[202] *UBStFr* ii. 614. Cf. StAFr, A 1 XIX Ebringen 4, 18 Aug. 1495.
[203] *UBStFr* ii. 606.   [204] Ibid., pp. 607–8.
[205] Ibid., pp. 612–17. The council also objected that the villagers were refusing to collected ground-rents and interest-payments owed to Freiburg burghers in retaliation for the council's refusal to grant them access to the market.

Freiburg's Conflict with the Breisgau 113

committed. Though the governor was perturbed by Freiburg's utter disregard for the lord of Ebringen's jurisdictional authority and its readiness to resort to force, he decided to annul all claims between the parties except for private suits by relatives of the dead and wounded. The villagers, however, were bound over to appear before the Freiburg council in a humble request for pardon.[206]

So ended a violent episode which mercilessly revealed how low relations between Freiburg and the Bresigau villages had sunk by the end of the fifteenth century. The town had won its case, but at the cost of leaving the peasants cowed and surly.[207] Not without reason has one local historican spoken of the Ebringen outrage as a harbinger of the Peasants' War.[208] What is so remarkable, nevertheless, are the sharp contours of conflict. The Ebringers' bitterness at the council's policies vented itself against young and powerless journeymen who had no part in the making of those measures. Freiburg as an entity was the target of attack, not simply the ruling elite, and it was the community as a whole—seven hundred male citizens!—which retaliated. The division was between town and economically dependent hinterland, between oppidans and villagers, not between rulers and ruled, exploiters and exploited, privileged and oppressed. Class solidarity which transcended legal and political frontiers was signally lacking, although the behaviour of the Merdingen outburghers suggests that disenchantment with their council overlord was capable of creating an embryonic awareness of class interests. To understand why it is necessary to analyse the intensifying economic competition between town and country during the fifteenth century, as each strove to recover from financial and social crisis. Who were the victors in that struggle remains a matter for debate.

---

[206] Ibid., pp. 617–19.
[207] At least Ulrich Zasius, the town clerk, realized how foolish the town's precipitate aggression was, since the town had a perfectly sound claim against the peasantry which did not require a blustering display of force to succeed. StAFr, B 1 2 fo. 60^{r-v}.
[208] Cf. Joseph Ludolph Wohleb, 'Bauernkriegsluft um Freiburg. Die Ebringer Kirchweihe von 1495', *Badische Heimat*, (1959), 163–5.

IV

The Decline and Recovery of Freiburg's Economy

I

BY 1368 when Freiburg submitted to Austria the town had already passed the peak of its commercial prosperity. That prosperity had largely been based upon revenues from the extraction and distribution of silver and other metals from the Black Forest mines around the Schauinsland. The town's merchants not only traded extensively in silver; by the mid-fourteenth century they owned most of the mines as well.[1] But during the next fifty years Freiburg's silver trade began to decline. In the face of fairly scanty evidence it was for a long time assumed that the mines simply petered out, forcing the merchants to withdraw from mining activity, a process allegedly hastened by the aftermath of the gild revolution of 1388. More recently it has been shown that with the exhaustion of the shallower mines near the surface the excavation of deeper shafts threw up severe technical problems. Pumping out water from the tunnels in the notoriously wet slopes of the Schauinsland around Hofsgrund involved huge capital outlay. Once an easy road to fortune, mining became a dangerous gamble. A few Black Forest mines continued to yield a good return, notably those around Todtnau and in the Kinzig valley above Offenburg. Even so, the few foreign entrepreneurs—one a wealthy burgher of Eßlingen, another a large-scale mining speculator from Basel who belonged to the Diesbach-Watt merchant company of St Gallen—following in the steps of the Freiburg merchants never, it seems, entirely recouped their investment.[2]

Without the receipts from silver Freiburg's administration was faced with declining revenues at a time of vastly increased expenditure. As

---

[1] Metz, 'Bergbau', p. 140.
[2] Albrecht Schlageter, 'Der mittelalterliche Bergbau im Schauinslandrevier', *Schau-ins-Land*, lxxxviii (1970), 157–61.

the price of independence count Egon demanded a quittance of 15,000 silver marks, another 5,000 marks' ransom for the release of prisoners, and the lordship of Badenweiler as compensation for loss of territory, which Freiburg first had to purchase for 25,000 fl.[3] For the standards of the time these were staggering sums, quite apart from the costs which the town had to carry from the foregoing campaigns.[4] In return Freiburg was promised no more than 32,000 fl. by the Habsburgs for accepting Austrian sovereignty, a sum which had still not been paid in full by 1377.[5] As a result the town had to resort to borrowing on a massive scale, with the bulk of loans coming from citizens of Basel, Freiburg's erstwhile ally. In the five years from 1365 to 1370 the town ran up a debt of 120,000 fl., a total which continued to creep upwards throughout succeeding decades.[6] Whether Freiburg could have brought its finances back on to an even keel, had it enjoyed a long period of peace and recuperation after 1368, must remain doubtful. In fact, its resources were further strained by the wars which afflicted the unsettled frontier area of South-West Germany intermittently for the rest of the fourteenth and throughout the fifteenth century. The cost of equipping, feeding, and paying the town's contingents which served in Austrian and imperial campaigns against the Swiss, French, and Burgundians greatly exceeded normal peacetime expenditure, not to mention the loans and subsidies which Freiburg and other Austrian subjects were required to provide in order to redeem possessions wantonly mortgaged by the spendthrift dukes.[7] Short of imposing swingeing taxes upon its citizens, who in any case had to shoulder the recurrent burden of Austrian and imperial levies—from the 1470s the Evil Penny and in 1497 the Common Penny—the town had no choice but to raise further loans. The upshot was a considerable public debt whose management brought Freiburg into serious financial difficulties, even to the point of bankruptcy, during the fifteenth century. Time and again the council lamented that the campaigns were disrupting and exhausting Freiburg's economy.

[3] Johannes Lahusen, 'Die Urkunden über Freiburgs i. Br. Übergang an Österreich 1368', *Mitteilungen des Instituts für österreichische Geschichtsforschung*, xxxiv (1913), 120; Feine, 'Territorialbildung', p. 258; Leiser, *Herrschaftswechsel*, p. 19.

[4] It was to cover the cost of the war that the council introduced the departure-tax in 1368. *UBStFr* i. 511–12.

[5] TLA, Schatzarchiv, Urk. I 2340, 13 Aug. 1375; 2342, 7 Dec. 1377. The information in Wellmer, 'Breisgau', p. 280 is not entirely accurate.

[6] StAFr, B 1 255. Hermann Flamm, 'Skizze einer Geschichte der Anleihepolitik der Stadt Freiburg im Breisgau bis zum Ausgang des Mittelalters', pp. 1a–2a.

[7] See pp. 24–6, 29.

What made the situation so precarious was that the town's financial viability was simultaneously being eroded by constant emigration—not merely of patricians but equally of craftsmen, thereby constricting the town's fiscal supply both in terms of direct revenues and of indirect consumption taxes. Freiburg was thereby caught in a spiral of decline, for any attempt to meet rising costs by increasing taxation was largely self-defeating. The richer burghers who could afford the departure-tax left, while the poorer craftsmen remained. Those wealthy institutions such as convents which remained often escaped their full share of taxes by compounding for a lump sum, and in any case enjoyed a variety of fiscal immunities which they jealously protected. Worst of all, new immigrants were deterred from settling in the town. These fundamental adversities were compounded by further set-backs during the fifteenth century. Not only were the town's finances at risk: its very economic function as a craft town and market centre became increasingly precarious. Freiburg's market was declining, the council lamented, in the face of competition from newly-founded rival markets in the Breisgau, whilst the rise of village crafts and cottage industries robbed the town of its immediate market area. In 1476 the council anxiously recorded the growing threat from country craftsmen;[8] ten years later it repeated its apprehensions.[9] Moreover, with the establishment of local markets in the Breisgau the peasantry no longer needed to rely on Freiburg as the outlet for its produce, but could visit nearer, more convenient markets in the countryside.

How damaging such competition was may properly be questioned. There was no new market within a seven-mile radius of Freiburg;[10] with heavy carts on rough tracks it was difficult in any case to travel much longer distances to market. Most of the newer markets lay closer to one another than to Freiburg, so that competition between themselves ought to have been much fiercer than against Freiburg. Towns such as Endingen and Waldkirch certainly suffered most directly from the rise of nearby rivals. But proximity alone was not decisive: periodicity mattered even more. Freiburg's market was hit by a deliberate clash of weekly market-days and by the growth of informal markets in the villages on Sundays after service, at church-ales, and at

[8] StAFr, A 1 VII b 14, 1443? Heft D (1476).
[9] StAFr, B 5 XI, v, 3, fo. 71^r.
[10] Cf. Tom Scott, 'Economic Conflict and Co-operation on the Upper Rhine, 1450–1600', in idem and E. I. Kouri (eds.), *Politics and Society in Reformation Europe* (London/Munich, 1987).

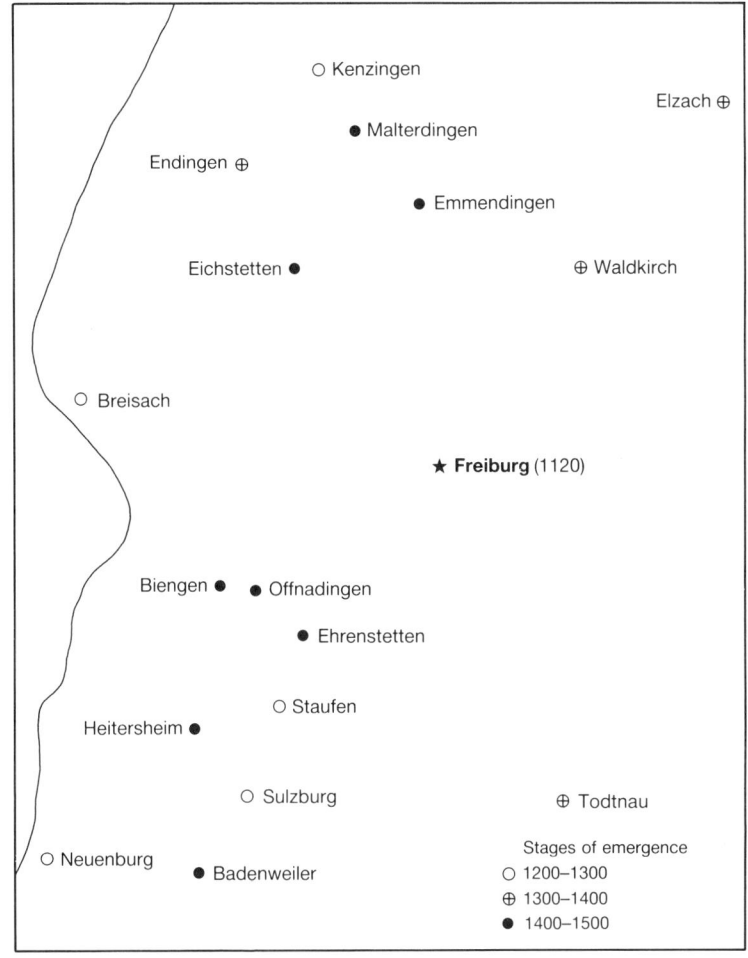

Map 6. The Growth of Country Markets in the Breisgau, 1200–1500

weddings. These problems, it is true, affected Freiburg less severely than neighbours such as Waldkirch because its market was held daily whereas none of its rivals had more than a weekly market and two annual fairs. Nevertheless, over the years, the number of small and occasional competitors simply grew so large that they could not help but take away some trade from the town, not least by forcing Freiburg's own craftsmen out into the villages if they wished to sell their goods. A series of pinpricks gradually tore an open wound. Before 1250 Freiburg had vied only with Breisach for the trade of the northern Breisgau, but by 1500 sixteen markets were founded within fifteen miles of Freiburg, eight of them after 1400.[11] The threat from rural competition was aggravated, furthermore, by the building of new roads through the Black Forest which evaded the town's market and tollbooths. The Simonswald road after 1467 gave peasants from Triberg, Furtwangen, and beyond easy access to markets in the Elz valley and the Breisgau plain such as Waldkirch, Emmendingen, and Malterdingen, instead of Freiburg which was further and more awkward to reach.[12] All the Outer Austrian towns, moreover, were placed at a special disadvantage after 1471, when the margraves of Baden forbad their subjects to sell produce at foreign markets,[13] the economic counterpart of residential bondage as a step towards the creation of an exclusive territory.

These structural problems which threatened to undermine the traditional autonomy of the craft town were not easy to resolve, as persistent complaints at the Outer Austrian diets during the sixteenth century attest.[14] But in the second half of the fifteenth century Freiburg sustained further blows to its economic stability from a series of natural catastrophes which it was quite powerless to arrest. Plague, which had remained quiescent in the Breisgau since the Black Death, struck again eight times between 1474 and 1527.[15] In 1480 the town was badly flooded; many buildings and the town walls were damaged, crops destroyed.[16] Many people died and food prices soared. The impoverishment of the inhabitants shore the council of its revenues, whilst the repair of houses, weirs, and bridges added to its necessary expenditure.

[11] Cf. Flamm, *Niedergang*, p. 15. Biengen is mentioned in idem, 'Die Geschichte des Metzgergewerbes in Freiburg im Breisgau seit Gründung der Stadt bis zur Gegenwart', in *Festschrift zum 28. Deutschen Fleischerverbandstag in Freiburg* (Freiburg, 1905), 25.

[12] See pp. 103–4.

[13] Eduard Christian Martini, 'Sulzburg: Eine Stadt-, Bergwerks- und Waldgeschichte', *ZGGFr* v (1879–82), 93–4.

[14] Cf. *UBStFr* ii. 677; StAFr, C 1 Landstände 1, n.d. (*c.*1510), fo. 1ᵛ; C 1 Landstände 3, 5 Dec. 1517, 14 Mar. 1518; GLA 79/1657 (*c.*1524); BNUS MS 845, fo. 10ʳ (22 May 1524).

[15] Hermann Mayer, 'Zur Geschichte der Pest im 15. und 16. Jahrhundert', *Schau-ins-Land*, xxviii (1901), 21–2. The evidence ultimately derives from Stiftsarchiv St Paul im Lavanttal, 93/2 b 1, Maldoner, 'Brisgovia vetus et nova', fo. 123ᵛ.

[16] StAFr, B 5 XI, iv, 11, fo. 165ᵛ. In 1484 the council was still preoccupied with the consequences of flooding and harvest failure. B 5 XIIIa, iv, fo. 63a (extra leaf).

Although the council stood helpless in the face of natural calamities, the policies designed to reverse the financial and economic decline of the city may in themselves have contributed yet further to its problems. When in 1446 the council at last abolished the departure-tax introduced in 1368, it openly admitted that its size, by then tenfold the annual tallage, had discouraged new immigrants and done nothing to maintain the existing population.[17] Instead of raising internal taxation, the council exploited market tolls as an easy source of revenue. But even here frequent increases brought their own revenge: trade patronizing the market languished, and it is small wonder that the peasantry flocked to local markets in the countryside. In 1476 the council in effect admitted the error of its ways by lowering the tolls on animals brought for sale in Freiburg or afterwards exported in order to stimulate the sluggish livestock market.[18] Raising transit tolls on the highways brought the council similar problems. After Freiburg and Villingen had constructed their new turnpike through the Falkenstein valley in the late fourteenth century, the Dreisam peasants refused to pay the tolls,[19] and Freiburg was not slow to imprison anyone caught bypassing the toll-stages.[20] Yet any attempt to restore Freiburg's competitiveness as a market by lowering tolls and allowing unrestricted access brought fresh problems in its wake, for by so doing the council at the same time attracted foreign traders to the town, who often undercut the prices of the native craftsmen. In trying to cure one evil the council had created another. In 1495 the haberdashers vigorously protested that visiting merchants were threatening to swamp the daily market with their wares.[21] Despite a decision to restrict them to the annual fairs the complaints continued, for foreigners still managed to give the authorities the slip at the daily market.[22] The council's frequent edicts against forestalling highlight its dilemma.[23] They made good sense as a means of keeping consumer prices down, but could just as easily deter merchants from visiting Freiburg at all, so that its craftsmen were deprived of essential raw materials.[24] Its essential dilemma lay, in fact, in trying to reconcile economic and financial

[17] StAFr, A I VII d 12, 20 June 1446; *UBStFr* ii. 421–3.
[18] StAFr, B 5 XIIIa, iv, fo. 86ʳ. [19] *UBStFr* ii. 31–2.
[20] StAFr, A I VI d 46, 5 Sept. 1420.
[21] Gothein, *Wirtschaftsgeschichte*, p. 466.
[22] Adolf Birkenmeier, 'Die fremden Krämer zu Freiburg im Breisgau und Zürich im Mittelalter bis zum Ausgang des 16. Jahrhunderts', *ZGGFr* xxix (1913), 96–7. Cf. StAFr, B 5 XIIIa, vii, fo. 154ʳ.
[23] Scott, 'Relations', pp. 147 ff. [24] Ibid., pp. 150–1.

objectives. Low tolls helped stimulate imports but reduced the flow of revenue needed to serve the debt-charge; high tolls might be necessary to balance the budget but on the council's own admission had brought about a decline in the cattle market. Because there was no easy or straightforward answer to Freiburg's difficulties the council cannot simply be accused of adopting policies which were misguided in themselves. Rather, it would be true to say that the council was confronted throughout the fifteenth century with a welter of financial and economic problems whose complexities and interrelations it neither fully understood nor mastered.

II

Evidence of a crisis in Freiburg's economy is not hard to come by: the outward signs of decay could scarcely be overlooked. Already by 1385 104 houses in the lower part of the Old Town and in the Lehen, Prediger, and Neuburg suburbs stood empty. These districts covered a little over half the town, so that for the whole of Freiburg something over 200 houses were probably unoccupied towards the end of the fourteenth century.[25] Moreover, a further decline in occupancy took place between 1450 and 1500, when the number of houses in the Old Town fell by a quarter from 1072 to around 800.[26] Some smaller houses and shacks were no doubt demolished to make way for bigger and more permanent buildings, and frequently neighbouring houses were knocked into one,[27] neither of which was necessarily a symptom of decline, but in the main the joining of houses was simply a prelude to their being knocked down and the land given over to sheds, styes, and orchards, particularly in the suburbs.

One reason was that the burden of rent-charges upon houses in Freiburg was mounting during the fifteenth century. When house-owners fell into arrears and defaulted, the rentiers usually resorted to a compulsory auction. If there was no bid, the property passed to the creditor, who was naturally tempted to demolish it rather than maintain it in good repair (as the council insisted) without an occupant. The figures for compulsory auctions are by no means the most satisfactory guide to the state of housing in Freiburg, but they provide such graphic illustration of low house-values and the weight of rent-

[25] Flamm, *Niedergang*, pp. 140–1. [26] Ibid., pp. 142–3.
[27] The residence of the abbot of St Peter took up land previously occupied by nineteen houses, and ten houses were pulled down to make way for the mansion of Maximilian's chancellor, Konrad Stürtzel. Ibid., pp. 126, 143.

charges that a decline in Freiburg's stock of housing cannot be denied. From the figures in Table A it emerges that in mid-century only 20 per cent of houses under compulsory auction were valued at more than the sum of outstanding rent-charges and their capital; by the end of the century the figure was only 6 per cent. Artificially low valuations can be ruled out because in the first period 50 per cent of the estimates attracted no bid at all, and in the second 71 per cent found no takers on the upset price. Overbidding was rare.[28] At first sight it appears quite astonishing that houses could be sold by rentiers simply on an undertaking to pay off the outstanding charges, or even to maintain the property, but they presumably had no alternative in hard times. Meanwhile, the volume of rent-charges themselves was rising towards the end of the fifteenth century. As Table B shows, the number of such charges increased by 20 per cent. These figures give substance to the council's frequent complaints that rent-charges were deleterious to property. They also suggest that demand for housing was itself weak; the low valuation of houses compulsorily auctioned is borne out by a general fall in house prices during the fifteenth century.[29] In 1417 the council was forced to issue an edict preventing houses from being pulled down and given over to gardens instead of being repaired as the quickest remedy for unsafe or untenanted buildings.[30]

The previous year the council had tried to outlaw the chief cause of the mounting burden of rent-charges, namely the practice of mortgaging houses to ecclesiastical foundations as mortuary payments.[31] The ultimate solution lay in securing redemption of the rent-charges, but when the council at last succeeded in persuading the Ensisheim government to order redemption in 1479, the convents still refused to give way.[32] Seven years later, therefore, when it was pleading with archduke Sigismund for a reduction in the war-levy, the council could point with some justice to the economic deterioration to which the dilapidated buildings attested.[33] As the century wore on, more and more property passed by default into the hands of religious corporations. Between 1450 and 1500 their estate in the Old Town increased from ten to thirteen acres out of a total of fifty-five built-on acres.[34] These additional three acres, moreover, consisted entirely of private houses.[35]

[28] Ibid., p. 118. [29] Ibid., pp. 127–30.
[30] Ibid., pp. 150–1. [31] Ibid., pp. 156–7.
[32] StAFr, B 5 XIIIa, iv, fo. 42ʳ; B 5 XI, iv, 11, fo. 142ʳ; *UBStFr* ii. 560–1; Flamm, *Niedergang*, pp. 146, 155.
[33] StAFr, B 5 XI, v, 3, fo. 71ʳ.
[34] Flamm, *Niedergang*, p. 119. [35] Ibid., p. 120.

Table A. Compulsory Auctions, 1444–59 and 1494–1520

Year-span	Compulsory Auctions	Houses	Starting price of A	B	C	No bid on A	B	C	Bid on A	B	C	Overbid on A	B	C
1444–1459	105	132	55	45	5	29	23	—	26	22	5	26	20	4
1494–1520	184	196	109	57	18	75	46	8	34	11	10	31	7	8

Note: A: Current and outstanding rent-charges; B: Current and outstanding rent-charges and capital; C: Repair of building.

Source: Flamm, *Niedergang*, pp. 106–7.

Table B. Rent-charges on Houses Compulsorily Auctioned, 1444–59 and 1494–1520

Year-span	Houses	Rent-charges	Owing to Benefices and convents	Holy-Ghost-Hospital	Nobles	Other Burghers	Unknown
1444–1459	132	179	74	9	6	79	11
1494–1520	192	321	127	11	36	143	4

Source: Flamm, *Niedergang*, pp. 121–2.

The more such properties fell into the hands of institutions which contributed very little to the town's prosperity, the fewer there remained for the craftsmen who by then were the backbone of the economy. As a result, their chances of earning a living were diminished by a shortage of unencumbered housing at the same time as buildings were standing empty because no one could afford the rent-charges. It is no wonder that in the 1510s the council was still arguing that the convents' recalcitrance was a grave economic and demographic handicap.[36] Only much later, by the late 1540s, was there much sign of improvement: a single house stood empty and only eleven needed repair.[37] By then the convents had lost some of their estate into the bargain.

The 200 unoccupied houses in 1385 and falling house prices during the fifteenth century point to slackening demand which in turn indicates a decline in population. The available statistics confirm this view. There is general agreement that between 1385 and 1450 the town lost just under a third of its population, only to recover to within 10 per cent of the 1385 population by the end of the century, but there is argument about the absolute figures on account of differing methods of calculation. According to the most recent analysis, Freiburg's population declined from 7,100 in 1385 to 4,800 in 1450, and climbed again to around 6,300 by 1500.[38] These figures require some comment. In the first place it is likely that Freiburg's population was already in decline before 1385 if 200 houses were by then uninhabited. Equally, the decline must have been fairly recent, for the houses cannot have stood empty for more than ten years. But to arrive at a reliable estimate of Freiburg's peak population is wellnigh impossible, since extrapolations based on isolated years are virtually meaningless, given that the size of urban populations and especially households

---

[36] StAFr, B 5 XI, viii, 2, fo. 120^{r-v}; ix, fos. 273^v–274^r; C 1 Landstände 3, 14 Mar.–4 May 1518. Cf. also the provisions in Freiburg's new law code of 1520. Zasius, *Nüwe Stattrechte*, fos. 87^v–89^r.

[37] Flamm, *Niedergang*, p. 141.

[38] Peter Johannes Schuler, 'Die Bevölkerungsstruktur der Stadt Freiburg im Breisgau im Spätmittelalter—Möglichkeiten und Grenzen einer quantitativen Quellenanalyse', in Wilfried Ehbrecht (ed.), *Voraussetzungen und Methoden geschichtlicher Städteforschung* (Städteforschung: Veröffentlichungen des Instituts für vergleichende Städtegeschichte in Münster, Reihe A vii) (Cologne/Vienna, 1979), 139–76. I regard the figures for the end of the century as too low. Schuler applies the multiplier only to gildsmen's households, not to the establishments of the resident artistocracy, notability, rentiers ('Müßiggänger'), clerics, and university members. He gives a total of 286 for university and clergy in Table 4, p. 154, but this seems to exclude domestics.

fluctuated a great deal.³⁹ Nevertheless, it is doubtful whether the population in the fourteenth century ever exceeded 10,000,⁴⁰ and, in view of the dislocations caused by the war of independence, the peak must surely have lain just before 1368. How rapidly the population declined between 1385 and 1450 is, again, not easy to assess, though the tallage list of 1406 discovered by Rowan would suggest a 10 per cent decline in twenty years.

For the end of the fifteenth century, however, we are on much firmer ground. Tax-lists survive (with some gaps) from 1481 onwards, and they can be set against the figures for adults over fifteen contained in the Common Penny lists of 1497.⁴¹ Provided one can agree on a rather lower multiplier for calculating household size from the total of heads of households than used to be supposed,⁴² then the two sources tally reasonably well. It is also clear that to speak of a population recovery after 1450 is somewhat artificial, since it includes the staff and students of the university (founded in 1457), together with their domestic servants. We are not entirely dependent on quantitative evidence, however, for signs of a demographic decline. The reduction

---

³⁹ The main sources before 1481 are an incomplete tallage list of 1385 used by Flamm, *Niedergang*, pp. 17–31; a list of craftmasters in 1390 given by Schreiber, *Geschichte*, i. 2. 203; a tallage list of 1406 discovered by Rowan, 'Guilds', p. 76; and another list of masters in the 18 gilds, datable to *c*.1450, unearthed by Flamm after the publication of *Niedergang*. There he had first argued that the population decline continued steadily until around 1500, but he revised his views in the light of the 1450 list. Idem, 'Die Einwohnerzahl Freiburgs im Jahre 1450', *Schau-ins-Land*, xxxix (1912), 37–9.

⁴⁰ The registers of pope Innocent IV contain an entry which gives the population of the parish of Freiburg as 40,000 in 1247. This figure can be discounted. Aloys Schulte, 'Die Einwohnerzahl von Freiburg im Jahre 1247', *ZGO* NF i (1886), 115–16.

⁴¹ StAFr, E I A II b 4, nos. 1–5. They have been analyzed by Schwineköper, 'Unterschichten', p. 146, and most recently by Rowan, 'The Common Penny (1495–99) as a Source of German Social and Demographic History', *Central European History*, x (1977), 148–64; Schuler, 'Bevölkerungsstruktur', pp. 151 ff.; Friedrich Schaub, 'Die Freiburger Universität und der Gemeine Pfennig von 1497', in Johannes Vincke (ed.), *Zur Geschichte der Universität Freiburg i. Br.* (Beiträge zur Freiburger Wissenschafts- und Universitätsgeschichte, xxxiii) (Freiburg, 1966), 17–52.

⁴² Flamm employed a higher multiplier of six and a lower of 4.68 (borrowed from studies of Nuremberg). Idem, *Niedergang*, p. 26. Recently Schuler has suggested that even the commonly accepted multiplier of five may be too high: four is more likely to be accurate. Idem, 'Bevölkerungsstruktur', p. 173. Schuler's estimates, however, disregard the question of fluctuations in household size, which he believes not to have occurred to any significant degree. Thereby he ignores altogether Rowan's important discovery that household size, which had shrunk by mid-century as fewer maids and journeymen were employed, had recovered to its 1385 levels by the end of the century as menials and apprentices were taken back into employment once more in considerable numbers. Idem, 'Common Penny', p. 162.

of the eighteen gilds to twelve in 1459 suggests that the numbers of craftsmen had dwindled so far that the weakest trades had to be affiliated in order to maintain the strength of the town's military units.[43]

The burden of the civic debt is much harder to gauge correctly, not least because for the fifteenth century we are at the mercy of partial and inadequate statistics. Lists of interest-payments (or, more properly, annual rentes paid to those who had bought them by advancing a capital sum) only survive for isolated years until around 1520, but on the whole they support the figures mentioned by the council in its frequent submissions to the Outer Austrian government. Taking the period 1438 to 1550 for which scattered records from various accounts survive,[44] it appears that the debt-charge declined gradually from a peak of around 9,500 fl. to around 7,000 fl. in 1550, but, more importantly, the proportion of the debt-charge as a percentage of annual civic expenditure fell dramatically after 1540 from a fairly constant 75 per cent to no more than 40 per cent.[45] This suggests that the town was able to reduce its interest-payments only gradually over many years.[46]

There can be no reasonable doubt that the debt-charge was a heavy burden upon Freiburg's finances for much of the fifteenth century. In the late 1440s the council complained that it swallowed up three-quarters of all expenditure in a time of war: 9,000 fl. to 3,000 fl.,[47] a claim which the surviving evidence seems to bear out. In real terms the debt declined thereafter, and by 1520 other expenditure had greatly increased, as indeed had income, so that even with relatively high

[43] See pp. 58–9.
[44] StAFr, A 1 VII f 281, 1443; E 1 A IV i, 1445, 1479, 1550; E 1 A I a 1, no. 2 (1503); E 1 A 1 b 1, no. 1 (1520).
[45] Norbert Ohler, 'Freiburg i. Br. im. 16. und 17. Jahrhundert. Kreditaufnahme und Geldanlage der Stadt', in Hans Fenske, Wolfgang Reinhard, Ernst Schulin (eds.), *Historia Integra. Festschrift für Erich Hassinger zum 70. Geburtstag* (Berlin, 1977), 159 ff.; Norbert Ohler, 'Strukturen des Finanzhaushalts der Stadt Freiburg i. Br. in der frühen Neuzeit', *ZGO* (1977), 111–2.
[46] The 1503 accounts, however, contain a number of extraordinary items which remind one that the annual balance sheet could be temporarily distorted by special provisions. An outstanding loan of 4,000 fl. by the town and the Breisgau nobility to Maximilian (presumably part of the money raised to pension off archduke Sigismund) was still being carried forward from 1488, though by 1520 the total of such provisions had fallen back to just over 1,000 fl. E 1 A 1 a 1, no. 2 (1503), fo. 8ᵛ. In 1514 the town tried to secure repayment (HHSA, Maximiliana 32, 23 July 1514), but some of the loan was still outstanding in 1523. StAFr, ungeordnete Bestände (to C 1 Gemeindevermögen 12, 10–16 Aug. 1523).
[47] StAFr, A 1 VII b 14, 1443? Heft C (*c*.1449), fo. 1ʳ.

interest-payments the council was able to discharge some of its larger loans. Probably the debt-charge would have declined more rapidly if Freiburg had not resorted to borrowing in order to buy land and villages in the Breisgau, an investment which yielded a steady, if modest, return on capital through feudal dues, court fines, and the like. Nor, of course, should the debt-charge be seen in isolation: municipal annuities offered the small investor a safe and attractive deposit at a time when private credit institutions were not well developed, though it is noticeable that by the mid-sixteenth century, when Freiburg's finances were restored and the annual budget regularly showed a surplus, the town was apparently reluctant to invest its money in capital projects.[48] The debt-charge was fateful for Freiburg in the fifteenth century not so much because of its volume but because Freiburg, unlike Basel,[49] never enjoyed the considerable periods of peace necessary to recuperate from its financial *malaise*, and because the extraordinary taxes to which Basel resorted to keep its debt-charge within manageable size could in Freiburg's case only drive away more inhabitants at a time when its population was already dwindling and public income on the wane.

That the town faced severe economic and financial difficulties is clear, but how far its decline continued throughout the fifteenth century is less clear. Between 1440 and 1460 Freiburg undoubtedly went through a political and economic crisis. By 1445 the deterioration of Freiburg's finances and the sluggishness of its economy had reached such a pass that the town drew up an extensive petition to the Austrian authorities which reviewed its manifold problems and made suggestions for reform. By then the fall in population had left the smaller gilds on the verge of extinction and, because they could no longer adequately fulfil their public duties, the government of the town

---

[48] Cf. Norbert Ohler, 'Zum Haushalt der Stadt Freiburg im Breisgau im 16. und 17. Jahrhundert', *Zeitschrift des Breisgau-Geschichtsvereins ('Schau-ins-Land')*, xciv/xcv (1976/7), 253–89.

[49] With a population similar to Freiburg's Basel's interest-payments in the 15th c. varied between £6,000 and £8,000 per annum, with an exceptional peak during the conciliar years of £12,290 (1425) to £14,255 (1429). The amount the city borrowed annually fluctuated wildly from 3.5% to 30% of total expenditure. Cf. Josef Rosen, 'Der Staatshaushalt Basels von 1360 bis 1535', in Hermann Kellenbenz (ed.), *Öffentliche Finanzen und privates Kapital im späten Mittelalter und in der ersten Hälfte des 19. Jahrhunderts* (Forschungen zur Sozial- und Wirtschaftsgeschichte, xvi) (Stuttgart, 1971), 33–4. For the 16th c. cf. also Martin H. Körner, *Solidarités financières suisses au XVIᵉ siècle* (Bibliothèque Historique Vaudoise, lxvi) (Lausanne, 1980), 297 ff.

had fallen into disorder, the pretext used by archduke Albrecht to abolish gild rule in 1454.

Even after mid-century there is every sign that the troubles persisted once gild rule was restored. The debt-charge remained high; competition from the countryside continued; military campaigns, especially the Burgundian War of 1474–6, ensured that demands upon Freiburg's resources remained great. Shortages in the wake of war and crop failure sent food prices up whilst fresh outbreaks of plague made for further agony. These adversities culminated in a crisis of political authority which discharged itself in a decade of disturbances and demonstrations between 1490 and 1500.

The troubles of the 1490s, none the less, were not born of the same economic difficulties as those of half a century earlier. The crisis of 1440–60 was the culmination of nearly a century's decline. During those years the town was more enfeebled, its finances more precarious, the chances of earning a decent living more remote, and the conduct of public affairs more irregular than at any time since the town's foundation. By the end of the century, on the other hand, the underlying structure of Freiburg's economy was much sounder. Indeed, the recovery was largely determined by the need for drastic action to shore up the economy after the afflictions of mid-century. But the council's efforts would have availed little, had not the most debilitating symptom of decline vanished: around 1450 the population ceased to fall, probably because by then it had at last reached the steady state at which the town's shrunken economy could support it. The craft economy produced too little surplus wealth to maintain and employ the same number of artisans as the merchant economy, especiallly in the face of added competition from its hinterland. It is in fact very difficult to think of any predominantly craft town in Germany which had more than 6,000 inhabitants in the fifteenth century or afterwards. Freiburg's population may have recovered to around 10,000 by 1600, but the town by then had become a centre of administration and learning, as well as regaining important export manufactures. A sign that Freiburg had begun to turn the corner after the mid-fifteenth century was the setting up in 1451 of the new luxury craft of cutting and polishing, which the council rightly believed would do more to restore the town's economic fortunes than the revival of more mundane trades.

A stable population implied that those who remained had at last the chance to earn an adequate living, so that the inducement to emigrate was lessened. Fresh immigrants appear to have compensated for those who left, though the turnover in population always remained quite large. The university after 1457 brought new inhabitants and consumers into the town (though not, of course, direct taxpayers). As a consequence the annual yield from taxation became more assured and predictable. Warily the council began to raise taxes to lower the debt. In 1467 the debt was pegged at the existing level and could not be increased without the consent of the gild Eights.[50] Although the temptation to raise loans in order to cover budget deficits remained, the debt held relatively steady and then decreased as the century wore on. Upon this foundation the council pursued its policies of economic retrenchment after the gild restoration of 1464. Notwithstanding the several misfortunes which befell the town in the 1470s and 1480s, Freiburg entered the sixteenth century with a much healthier economy. The crisis of the 1490s, therefore, cannot have sprung from further symptoms of decline. Even though both gilds and council agreed on the need for stable finances and a secure livelihood for all craftsmen, discontent welled up because the reforms were bound to demand sacrifices by the mass of the population—the poorer artisans—as long as the self-interest of Freiburg's governing class precluded radical measures such as the abandonment of a highly regressive tax system. At the same time, the burden which the population had to shoulder seemed out of all proportion to the eventual achievement of economic stability. In other words, measures of retrenchment might in the short run bring more hardship than relief to the populace at large. The economic situation of Freiburg's inhabitants in the later fifteenth century certainly gave little cause for comfort. But although the restoration of the town's economy was both arduous and slow, frequently encountered fresh set-backs, and sometimes gave rise to conflicts of policy which the council found hard to resolve, the decline had already reached its trough in mid-century. What came after was not malignant disease but delicate convalescence.

III

After the restoration of gild rule in 1464 the way was open for the council to set about a concerted programme of financial and economic retrenchment. The council's policies have indeed traditionally been

[50] StAFr, B 5 XIIIa, iv, fo. 5ʳ; cf. B 2 4, p. 165.

interpreted as the direct and deliberate expression of the demands and interests of the gilds themselves, which their dominant position on the council at last enabled them to pursue without interference or contradiction. The purpose of such policies, according to Flamm, was first to restrict and then to exclude any competition from foreigners[51] and as a corollary to curtail any middleman activity within the town itself.[52] This form of economic protectionism Flamm called the 'closed urban economy';[53] it was the means by which the gilds, who by nature were supposedly hostile towards entrepreneurial and capitalist methods, attempted to safeguard their livelihood. The core of this interpretation is certainly correct: from a prosperous trading town of merchants in the fourteenth century Freiburg was reduced by the sixteenth to a restrictive community of artisans, intolerant of competition in the sale of craft goods to its hinterland. In his eagerness to interpret all the major economic developments within the town between 1368 and 1500 as the outflow of a comprehensive programme of protectionism, however, Flamm wildly overstated his case. He argued that a gild caucus had advocated and indeed partially succeeded in enforcing protectionism before 1388,[54] which the gilds had afterwards deliberately and whole-heartedly espoused.[55] Flamm's arguments are seriously misleading, largely because he asked the wrong questions,[56] and they misconstrue the nature of retrenchment after 1464. If the establishment of a protectionist economy had been the chief aim of a council which was no more than the mouthpiece of the gilds then the troubles of the 1490s would be very hard to understand. But if retrenchment is seen in terms of the problems which the town faced instead of the

[51] Flamm, *Niedergang*, p. 53.   [52] Ibid., p. 80.
[53] 'Sie ist das Mittel, die Arbeitsgelegenheit der Stadt und ihrer nächsten Umgebung den Handwerkern durch Konkurrenzregulierung in auskömmlicher, gleicher und durch Zwischenhandel ungeschmälerter Weise zugänglich zu machen.' Ibid., p. 81.
[54] Flamm supposed that the gilds' opposition to freedom of movement led to the imposition of the departure-tax in 1368. Ibid., p. 13. In fact, it had been introduced to cover the cost of the war of independence.
[55] Flamm's evidence is critically assessed in Scott, 'Relations', pp. 127–8 n. 1.
[56] The subtitle of Flamm's work—*Ein Beitrag zur Geschichte der geschlossenen Stadtwirtschaft*—gives the clue to its purpose. He was not interested in Freiburg's economic decline for its own sake, but was rather concerned to investigate the accuracy of certain economic theories, such as Bücher's on the closed urban economy and Sombart's on land-rents, using Freiburg as a test case. For that reason he not only assessed events as epiphenomena of a fixed general theory, but also saw connections where none existed and consistent policy making where as often as not the council was coping with economic problems it did not fully comprehend and to which it responded with temporary expedients.

methods used to solve them, the divergence of interests between gilds and council becomes readily intelligible.

The council had to attack two fundamental evils: unsound finances and a contracting economy. Of these the first, not the second, was the council's constant and most pressing concern because it had to balance the yearly budget. If the debt-charge could not be covered by annual income then the town would be forced to lean more heavily on (mostly foreign) creditors for further loans, or else find new sources of income. An excessive increase in the accumulated debt clearly involved the risk of straining municipal revenues to the point of bankruptcy,[57] or else of unleashing a political revolt.[58] The council's financial measures, therefore, always ran the risk of antagonizing those who bore the brunt—the ordinary gildsmen. Its chief economic responsibility, meanwhile, was to restore the welfare and livelihood of the community as a whole in the face of hardship and impoverishment. That entailed not only reviving craft manufacturing and helping the gilds as producers, but also protecting the gildsmen as consumers in the face of food shortages, rising prices, and market evasion. However, what benefited the consumer might well hamper the producer. The council had to balance the interests of both at the danger of disaffecting one. Control of wages and prices was unlikely to be popular with the craftsmen concerned, such as teasers, carders, linen-weavers, or fullers. Even more tricky was the situation if outsiders could supply the townsfolk with goods cheaper than a native gild could sell. Even the supervision of methods of production, quality of goods, and standards of hygiene, whilst clearly essential for the reputation and well-being of the crafts both as consumers and producers, could arouse resentment because the council's detailed and paternalistic control of the drafting of such provisions in the gild charters was seen to detract from their authority and autonomy.

In combating these evils the council did indeed resort to protectionism, but such measures were only part of its policy. Much less of what the council did can be interpreted as protectionism than Flamm imagined, and when it did embrace restrictive economic policies its reasons were pragmatic not dogmatic. That is why council and gilds clashed over a strategy which Flamm believed united them, for until 1495 the council

---

[57] As in Mainz in 1462. Cf. E. B. and M. M. Fryde, 'Public Credit, with Special Reference to North-Western Europe', in *Cambridge Economic History of Europe*, iii, ed. M. M. Postan, E. E. Rich, and Edward Miller (Cambridge, 1963), 543.

[58] As in Cologne in 1481. Ibid., pp. 547–8.

refused to move far, fast, or furiously enough for the gilds' liking towards economic protectionism. The council's policies of retrenchment must, in fact, be set in a much wider context than simply an effort to shore up the home economy and protect the gilds. The council appreciated the importance of the town's network of relations with the surrounding countryside, how dependent it was on its hinterland, which provided economic and political support for a vulnerable and languishing community. The acquisition of villages and the Dreisam bailiwick after mid-century is as much a part of the council's strategy of recovery as its internal reforms. The purchases helped to offset the decline in population, revenues, and military strength without causing a vast rise in the number of inhabitants within the town which the craft economy could not readily have employed. Similarly, the attempted accommodation with the Breisgau nobility in 1483 over the outburghers was an obvious device to rescue subjects who served in the town contingent, paid civic taxes, visited the market, and formed a bond of loyalty with the town outside its walls.

In its financial policies, however, the council had very little room for manœuvre. Once it had agreed not to add to the accumulated debt in 1467, the only other means of raising income was by imposing higher internal taxes or else larger dues on outsiders.[59] It speaks for the council's lukewarm attitude towards protectionism that it was reluctant to resort to discriminatory tolls, despite the risks involved in stepping up municipal levies. Instead the council at first tried, logically enough, to shift the fiscal burden more equitably on to those who could best afford to pay, the nobility and above all the higher clergy and monastic institutions. The same ordinance of 1467 which pegged the debt devoted most of its text to doubling the composition fee which they paid in lieu of civic taxes.[60] There, if anywhere, is evidence of gild bias after 1464, rather than in any sweeping adoption of protectionism. But here the council had to tread warily, at least with the nobles. When there were plans in the wake of the general fiscal reforms of 1476 to raise the composition tax once more, the nobles protested vigorously and threatened to withdraw from the community altogether, so that the Outer Austrian governor acting a go-between tried to discourage the council by pointing out that if it antagonized the local lords they might be tempted to retaliate by preventing their village subjects from

---

[59] Flamm was, however, aware that protectionist policies could be introduced for solely fiscal purposes. Cf. Scott, 'Relations', p. 132 n. 2.
[60] StAFr, B 5 XIIIa, iv, fo. 5ᵛ; cf. B 2 4, p. 165.

supplying Freiburg with produce.⁶¹ As a result it was thought prudent to demand a larger fee only from those nobles actually resident in the town as a quid pro quo for their usufruct of the common land. Only three years later, moreover, the council decided to exempt nobles from the inheritance tax on any property lying within civic jurisdiction as a means of inducing them to remain as residents.⁶²

These efforts were overshadowed by a thoroughgoing reform of municipal taxation which the council undertook in the summer of 1476, as part of a much wider inquiry into the town's internal administration and its problems. The reform was preceded by an extensive commission of inquiry, in which the town clerk was despatched on a five-week fact-finding mission to South German, Swiss, and even South Tirolean cities in order to ascertain their practice with regard to fiscal affairs, council elections, gild administration, country competition, and the immunities of ecclesiastical foundations.⁶³ The upshot was the working-out of a new fiscal structure for the town which laid down the procedures for collecting taxes, categories of tax exemption, assessment of property, and the treatment of defaulters.⁶⁴ These proposals were put before the community at large and finally adopted. Although it has been questioned how far the new tax codes represent in reality a fundamental departure either in assessment or in the actual sums raised over against the practice which had prevailed since the late fourteenth century,⁶⁵ at the very least the reforms of 1476 suggest that the council was determined to ensure that the administration and collection of taxes were tightened up and more efficiently handled than had previously been the case.⁶⁶

⁶¹ StAFr, B 5 XIIIa, iv, fo. 30ʳ⁻ᵛ. The issue even reached archduke Sigismund, who ordered the governor the following year to act as arbitrator. A I XIV a 17, 4 Feb. 1477.

⁶² StAFr, B 5 XIIIa, iv, fo. 42ʳ. How fragile the loyalty of the nobility and notables had become in the face of mounting fiscal demands was tellingly revealed in 1484 when four learned doctors threatened to use the country lords to help press their grievances over assessment for the weekly special levy, which the council had introduced to cover the depredations of war, plague, and flooding. One, Dr Konrad Obernheim, who paid 12d. weekly, said in exasperation to a simple wine-grower: 'You are rich; you only give 1d. a week and the mayor likewise.' Ibid., fo. 63a (loose leaf) verso. Further attempts were undertaken around that time to reform the composition-tax. Cf. ungeordnete Bestände (to B 5 XIIIa, iv), n.d. (c.1484).

⁶³ StAFr, A I VII b 19a, 1476–82. Cf. Scott, *Enquete*, Introduction, *passim*.

⁶⁴ StAFr, B 5 XIIIa, iv, fos. 77ʳ⁻ᵛ, 71ᵛ–72ᵛ.

⁶⁵ Hubert Weißer, 'Verteilung und politischer Einfluß des Vermögens bei den Freiburger Zünften in der ersten Hälfte des 16. Jahrhunderts' (Staatsexamensarbeit, Univ. of Freiburg, 1972), 14–15.

⁶⁶ The collection of taxes was a perpetual headache. In 1472 the gilds had been bound on oath to declare all dutiable goods passing through their hands. StAFr, B 5

The new tax structure was still strongly weighted in favour of the wealthy, as was only to be expected, since the councillors themselves were recruited from the wealthiest third of gildsmen. Yet it would be wrong to imagine that the town thereby squandered a fine opportunity of raising greater revenue. Throughout the Middle Ages and beyond the town's main income came not from direct taxes such as the tallage, but from indirect consumption taxes such as the wine and corn excise to which the rich, by virtue of their larger households and more sumptuous life-style, contributed proportionately more than the mass of ordinary craftsmen.

The one real opportunity to screw more direct revenue out of the inhabitants was to make the ecclesiastical corporations pay for their residential privileges. But this was a notoriously thorny issue. On the one hand, the convents enjoyed a variety of legal and fiscal immunities which the town could not unilaterally override; on the other, they were the chief recipients of perpetual annuities which the council had to redeem if it was to succeed in reducing the debt-charge of rente-payments on the annuities. The legal obstacles made the council reluctant to tackle the problem head-on,[67] but in the 1490s it at last mounted a broad assault on the zareba of clerical privileges, backed by Maximilian himself. Its first priority was to get the convents to pay an extraordinary aid to help reduce the civic debt. This was the least controversial step since it did not directly infringe their immunities. But the Dominicans (and subsequently the Carthusians)[68] refused to comply. Thereupon the town resorted to drastic measures. It rescinded the convent's burgher's rights, denied it access to pasture and woodland, diverted water from its well, and boarded up the convent walls leaving only a narrow entrance to the convent church and the cloisters.[69] For that the town was cited before the papal court for grievously infringing the Dominicans' liberties. Maximilian came to the council's aid by issuing two edicts in 1491 encouraging the

XIIIa, iv, fo. 9ᵛ. In 1505 stern measures were announced against persistent tax-dodgers. B 5 XIIIa, ix, fos. 45ᵛ, 49ᵛ, 61ᵛ.

[67] As part of the reform of Freiburg's ecclesiastical institutions which archduke Sigismund and the council drew up around 1468, the convents agreed to pay the town all their taxes as before. These were not specified, but it appears that the convents paid only the excise duties and the composition-tax. StAFr, A 1 VII b 15, n.d. (1470; correct: c.1468; 16, n.d. (1470; correct: c.1468).

[68] StAFr, A 1 VII b 21, 2 June 1491; C 1 Kirchensachen 80, 2 May 1491; 10 Aug. 1491.

[69] Augustin Dold, 'Zur Wirtschaftsgeschichte des ehemaligen Dominikanerklosters zu Freiburg i. Br.', *ZGGFr* xxvi (1910), 255–6.

redemption of annuities,[70] and the following year issued a series of instructions to the Dominicans to pay the subsidy.[71] All to no avail, for the king had to convene a court of arbitration which found against the town in October 1492 by ordering it to restitute the subsidy, and awarded costs against the council. In return the hearing in Rome was abandoned and the Dominicans agreed to redeem a couple of annuities.[72] Having made some headway, the town decided to press its case further. In 1495 the council imposed a general military levy on the town, which the convents and clergy were ordered to pay on Maximilian's instructions.[73] The Austin canons,[74] the Franciscans,[75] Carthusians,[76] and the minster priests[77] in particular resisted payment, so that the council sent some of its members to negotiate. All this had no effect until the magistrate, Hans Han, went in person to petition king Maximilian at the imperial diet in Worms. The king hastily ordered the clerics to pay[78]—the levy had after all been imposed to finance his campaigns—and repeated an earlier prohibition on mortmain.[79] It is not clear how far this pressure was successful, for the following year the council once again had recourse to drastic action by cutting off the Franciscans' water supply.[80] The endless legal proceedings and protracted negotiations demonstrate both how difficult it was to bring the clergy to heel and also how much the council was resolved to restore civic finances and prevent further alienation of property.[81] Even so, such disputes continued at intervals

---

[70] *UBStFr* ii. 585–6, 586–8. The second edict explicitly encouraged the discharge of debts contracted in silver marks in current coin, a considerable advantage to the municipal treasury.

[71] StAFr, A I XVI A p 28, 8 May 1492.

[72] StAFr, B 2 2, fos. 131ʳ–132ʳ; Dold, 'Wirtschaftsgeschichte', p. 256.

[73] Cf. StAFr, A I VII b 24, 6 Aug. 1495. Tax-register for the subsidy. The amounts varied considerably: the lay orders were notably impoverished.

[74] StAFr, A I XVI A e 22, 1495. The issue was referred to the prior-general of the order, then to the ecclesiastical courts, and even threatened to reach Rome, as with the Dominicans five years earlier. A I VII b 24, 6 Aug. 1495; TLA, Maximiliana XIV/55, Concepte Streitsachen ohne Jahr, fos. 182ʳ–183ᵛ. Cf. StAFr, B I 2, fo. 42ʳ⁻ᵛ.

[75] Ibid., fo. 107ʳ.

[76] StAFr, A I XVI A k 115, 9 Aug. 1495; B I 2, fos. 39ʳ–40ᵛ.

[77] Ibid., fos. 21ᵛ–22ʳ.

[78] StAFr, A I VII b 26, 8–9 Aug. 1495; B I 2, fos. 43ʳ–45ʳ.

[79] Ibid., fo. 21ʳ.   [80] Ibid., fo. 107ʳ.

[81] With his legal expertise and contacts Ulrich Zasius played a key role in securing the redemption of debts and the suspension of clerical immunities. Cf. *UBStFr* ii. 596–9; StAFr, C I Kirchensachen 1, n.d. (*c.*1495). Draft of petition to king Maximilian; ungeordnete Bestände (to C I Gemeindevermögen 14). 'Dr Knappen Ratschlag' (Zasius's hand). The history of Freiburg's complex and drawn out litigation with the convents and secular clergy in the 1490s remains to be written.

well into the sixteenth century, involving not only the ecclesiastical foundations but the university as well as a privileged corporation.

These efforts to create a sounder financial basis by means of direct taxation were accompanied by isolated attempts to raise more money through indirect excises. As part of the 1476 reforms the council imposed a duty on flour despite the ill feeling it was likely to arouse amongst the inhabitants at large.[82] The unpopularity of levies upon basic foodstuffs, however, deterred the council from further measures until the 1490s, when the civic budget again fell into disarray. It therefore tried a new tack by reforming the toll rates. In 1494 middlemen trading in salt were to pay higher tolls, whilst the council itself began to act as a salt-broker. To the same end it reduced the *Saum* (the basic dry weight and liquid measure) by one-eighth, though it left the larger weights and measures unchanged. Lastly, a general toll review was carried out which introduced differential customs duties between foreigners and residents.[83]

These latter measures may seem direct evidence that the council had at last fully embraced a new economic strategy of protectionism. By the 1490s it must be asked, however, whether there was any practicable alternative to discriminatory tolls, given the political hostility which higher domestic excises and tolls so easily unleashed, especially, it remains to be seen, from the butchers, who had enjoyed considerable tax exemptions until the 1494 toll revision.[84] But the new tolls need to be interpreted with caution. Flamm believed that the council used the new tolls deliberately to exclude foreign traders from the market and to prevent the import of manufactures which were already produced in the town. In fact, the most that can be said is that the council was concerned to guarantee stocks of raw materials and produce by imposing higher, even double, export tolls on wool, butter, meat, and timber in order to protect the craftsmen whose livelihood depended upon the regular supply of these commodities.[85] Certainly the council was beginning to exclude foreign merchants and recognized the need to safeguard Freiburg's market area (as the measures against rival turnpikes testify), but it did not use toll-charges as the instrument of those policies.[86] What unintentional effects the 1494 tolls may have

[82] StAFr, B 5 XI, iv, 11, fo. 46^v.
[83] StAFr, B 5 XIIIa, iva, fos. 12^v–13^v; cf. B 2 4, pp. 218–19. In 1496 the sale of salt was confined entirely to the Exchange. Ibid., p. 235. Vogel, *Zollwesen*, p. 47.
[84] See pp. 149–50.   [85] Vogel, *Zollwesen*, p. 85.
[86] Significantly, the new tolls barely restricted foreigners trading in cloth, the one enterprise which was organized along the lines of open competition. Ibid., pp. 84–5.

had is hard to assess, though twenty years earlier the council had acknowledged that high import duties on cattle had sent the livestock market into decline.

It is equally misleading to regard the council's economic policies for reviving Freiburg's languishing crafts in the later fifteenth century as the outflow of a general strategy of autarkic and anti-entrepreneurial protectionism. The council only gave way gradually and reluctantly to the gilds' bolder demands. Its edicts against middlemen and forestalling were largely makeshift expedients to contain a severe price rise after the Burgundian campaigns; moreover, it re-established clothmaking in 1472 along explicitly competitive and commercial lines, whilst the new and lucrative enterprise of cutting and polishing, though subject after 1451 to restrictions on each master's production and prices, was free to negotiate contracts permitting foreign entrepreneurs to put up capital to employ fraternity members on piece-work.[87]

All the same, after 1464 the council was quick to fulfil one of the craftsmen's main wishes: it regulated the conditions and price of entry to the gilds, and compelled all those wishing to ply a trade in Freiburg to join their appropriate craft.[88] The general obligation to join a gild had, of course, existed in the fourteenth century, but from 1468 it was used for the first time to enforce rigid and restrictive divisions between the crafts which prevented the commercially minded from engaging in subsidiary trades.[89] Throughout the latter half of the century the boundaries between crafts were more sharply drawn and the closed shop extended to include menial workers and servants, though the number of edicts suggests that they were frequently evaded. The closed shop certainly accommodated the gilds' aversion towards unrestricted employment and production—in short, as Flamm argued, it protected the gilds from the competition of an open labour market. All the same, the council was prepared to adjust its policies to the needs of a particular situation, for instance, when the failure of protectionist reforms to revive clothmaking encouraged the council to revert in 1476 to an open market, abolish the closed shop, and reduce the price of the manufacturing concession.[90] Yet even the closed shop did not necessarily preclude entrepreneurial methods within the gilds

---

[87] Schragmüller, *Borer und Balierer*, pp. 75 ff.
[88] StAFr, A 1 VI e α 2, 23 Sept. 1468, fo. 1ᵛ.
[89] Hinderschiedt, 'Zunftordnungen', p. 11.
[90] Gothein, *Wirtschaftsgeschichte*, p. 540.

Economic Decline and Recovery 137

themselves: the putting-out system was never entirely prohibited.[91] Nor was any direct attempt made to thwart competition from country craftsmen despite the manifold complaints at their existence. Unlike many Swiss cities, Freiburg was unable to compel them to join a gild or conform to urban craft regulations, largely because the territorial fragmentation of the Breisgau made strict control of its hinterland quite impossible.[92] Against margravial village markets and country crafts the Austrian city was essentially powerless.[93] The most Freiburg could hope to achieve was the exclusion of middlemen from the radius of its privileged market area (*Bannmeile*).[94]

Once the gilds had turned their back upon a mercantile economy they pressed the council to limit production within each craft, so that the smaller and poorer artisans should not be driven out of business by their richer and more powerful fellows. It took over ten years, however, for the council to put their demands into practice. In 1466 the butchers' charter still allowed each member to slaughter and sell as much as he wished, and the decision to limit production the following year was only taken by a private vote within the gild itself in defiance of the council.[95] Not until 1477 in the wake of the council inquiry was the majority of gild charters revised so that they contained provisions enforcing quotas on production.[96] Certainly the reform of the gild constitutions in 1477 marks a turning-point in the council's attitude towards protectionism, but it is less than certain that the council was yielding to a gild campaign for protectionism, rather than choosing the only sensible course in the face of a contracting market area. In any

---

[91] For instance, although the butchers' charters of 1482 and 1538 both prohibited gild members from advancing money to their poorer fellows, the council still retained the right to suspend such provisions whenever there was a meat shortage. Ibid., p. 502.

[92] In 1470 Zürich banned all country crafts and compelled their practitioners to join a gild in the city; Lucerne did likewise the following year. In Fribourg master craftsmen in the countryside were required in 1505 to join one of the urban gilds. Hellmut Gutzwiller, 'Die Zünfte in Freiburg im Üchtland, 1460–1650', *Freiburger Geschichtsblätter*, xli/xlii (1949), 28–9; Hans Conrad Peyer, 'Wollgewerbe, Viehzucht, Solddienst und Bevölkerungsentwicklung in Stadt und Landschaft Freiburg i. Ue. vom 14. bis 16. Jahrhundert', in Hermann Kellenbenz (ed.), *Agrarisches Nebengewerbe und Formen der Reagrarisierung im Spätmittelalter und 19./20. Jahrhundert* (Forschungen zur Sozial- und Wirtschaftsgeschichte, xxi) (Stuttgart, 1975), 86–7.

[93] Within its own territories, of course, Freiburg's writ ran, just as in the Swiss city cantons. The butchers of the Valley Bailiwick, for instance, had to join the urban gild. Cf. StAFr, A 1 VI e ε 54, 1588; F A VI 15/1, 6 Feb. 1579.

[94] This was part of the measures adopted by the council in 1476 to regulate the corn market. Gothein, *Wirtschaftsgeschichte*, pp. 478–90.

[95] Rowan, 'Guilds', pp. 197–9.

[96] Hinderschiedt, 'Zunftordnungen', pp. 22, 56.

case, even after the allegedly sweeping introduction of protectionism the gilds were unable altogether to get their own way. In 1495, the very year in which the council accepted far-reaching plans for protectionism, it fobbed off the clothmakers' demands for a municipal monopoly on the purchase of wool, the establishment of a wool-staple, and the exclusion of forestallers with the promise of a more rigorous inspection of the quality of wool,[97] and blankly refused to grant the shoemakers' request for a limit on their production.[98]

One wonders, indeed, to what extent the gilds' protests really sprang from an unwavering ideological aversion to mercantile methods and activity. Hostility towards middlemen was a regular feature of late medieval and early modern society, not merely confined to gildsmen. Nothing was done to ban forestalling in Freiburg, after all, until the cost of the Burgundian campaigns and the calamities of the early 1480s caused disruptions and shortages of supply. In 1476 no one was allowed to buy corn at the market who had already laid in a year's supply,[99] whilst those who were entitled might not resell within a month. Six years later the ban was extended to all foodstuffs regardless—poultry and meat as well as produce—with stiff fines for violation.[100] As a corollary the council forbad traders from buying corn within two miles of the town if it was intended for the market; it enforced a staple by refusing to allow corn to pass through the town; and tried to hold prices down by compelling forestallers to offer corn to one purchaser at a time in order to avoid counterbids by third parties.[101] The suppression of forestalling—designed to protect consumers[102]—went hand in hand with measures against regrating (the stockpiling of raw materials)—which catered for the interests of producers. Edicts against regrating were, again, nothing new: they had been issued long before the gilds came to power. By the end of the fifteenth century provisions against regrating and forestalling over a whole range of goods from vines to timber and even shoes were extremely common.[103]

---

[97] Gothein, *Wirtschaftsgeschichte*, p. 543.
[98] Rowan, 'Guilds', p. 326.
[99] StAFr, B 5 XIIIa, iv, fo. 29ᵛ.
[100] Ibid., fo. 61ʳ.
[101] Gothein, *Wirtschaftsgeschichte*, pp. 478–90.
[102] The craft which suffered most from this legislation was the victuallers, whose gild had been amalgamated with the bakers' in 1459. A new charter of 1523 reduced the victuallers in effect to public servants who paid a trading concession of 10s. per annum, in return for which they were granted a monopoly on the retailing of fish, poultry, fruit, and butter. Ibid., pp. 480–1.
[103] Hinderschiedt, 'Zunftordnungen', p. 80.

The gilds' protectionist stance found its crassest expression, Flamm argued, in outright hostility towards foreign merchants; nothing united gilds and council after 1464 more than endeavours to exclude them. And it is perfectly true that as early as 1473 foreigners trading in any commodity were forbidden to sell retail in the market except during the annual fairs.[104] Foreign forestallers and regraters were bound to be just as unpopular as any native gildsman who engaged in cornering the market. However, the council's attitude was not as consistently rigorous as might appear. The clothmakers' petition to eliminate a notorious wool forestaller in Heitersheim in 1495 elicited, after all, no more than a promise to control the quality of wool more carefully: the authorities clearly had no intention of overturning the capitalist reorganization of 1476. Granted, the situation of cloth-manufacturing was exceptional, but Flamm's argument is open to a much more fundamental objection: whether it was in fact in the town's best interests to exclude foreign traders. Freiburg could be supplied directly with raw materials and produce from the locality without recourse to middlemen, but commodities from further afield—salt, iron, furs and precious stones, paint and spices—clearly had to be imported by merchants. The restrictions upon market access and retailing, therefore, could only have stemmed from the wish to debar foreigners, not from the desire to exclude merchants as such. The measures against foreign traders in salt and iron in 1477 show that quite plainly. The council made no attempt to stop them trading. It merely stated that, since they owed no allegiance to the town and observed none of the duties and burdens of a citizen, their continued right to trade would depend upon their joining a gild and swearing an oath of loyalty (entailing thereby the commitment to pay civic taxes) as did the native craftsmen.[105] In other words, the council's main concern was to keep the necessary commercial life of the town in the hands of Freiburg's own retail merchants, the haberdashers. The closed shop was being used to protect the local gild against unrestricted competition from outsiders, just as in 1468 the council had compelled every artisan working in the town to join his appropriate gild. Moreover, the decree of 1477 stemmed not from a general chorus of complaint throughout the gilds at the activities of foreign merchants,

---

[104] Birkenmeier, 'Fremde Krämer', p. 95. 'Kein fremder man mer feil habe dehendlei gattung in stuckwerk.' 'Stuckwerk' here can only mean piece-work in the sense of finished articles offered for retail sale.
[105] StAFr, B 5 XIIIa, iva, fo. 5ʳ; Flamm, *Niedergang*, p. 63.

but from the sectional lobbying of the haberdashers themselves.

In 1495 the council finally decided to exclude altogether those foreign merchants who still refused to join a gild, and to require the rest to take up residence in Freiburg:[106] some had apparently joined gilds in name only in order to be able to continue trading. In its decrees the council explained quite bluntly that it was acting only on the insistence of the haberdashers who had begged it to ignore the popular fact that the common man—i.e. the townsfolk at large—could buy their goods more cheaply from foreign retailers.[107] Flamm discussed this point himself but failed to see that it destroyed his argument.[108] Far from uniting council and gilds in a campaign against entrepreneurs who were allegedly damaging the craft economy, the measures against foreign retailers heightened political tensions between the two during the 1490s, because they reflected the council's acceptance of protectionist demands from one gild, whose interests conflicted with members of the other eleven gilds as consumers. In yielding to a rich and powerful corporation the council can fairly be accused of abandoning its responsibility towards the community as a whole.[109] As it undoubtedly realized, the council could not reasonably prevent foreign traders from visiting Freiburg, and it clearly made better sense to hinder the export of essential commodities by higher tolls rather than curb imports merely because they were not always supplied and distributed by native retailers.[110]

This detailed examination of retrenchment after 1464 illustrates how far the council was caught between conflicting requirements. It had to reconcile financial and economic priorities, balance the interests of consumer and producer, and weigh eventual benefits against immediate hardship. Its policies, therefore, were bound to involve compromise. It is no surprise that the gilds, whose advocacy of protectionism reflected the interests of particular crafts as producers, and ignored those of the generality as consumers, quite apart from the broader financial implications for the community as a whole, became

---

[106] Birkenmeier, 'Fremde Krämer', pp. 96–7.
[107] Gothein, *Wirtschaftsgeschichte*, p. 466.   [108] Flamm, *Niedergang*, p. 63.
[109] At most the council ensured that the native haberdashers did not forestall or monopolize, and that the various crafts within the gild did not trespass upon one another or upon the activities of outside gilds. Gothein, *Wirtschaftsgeschichte*, p. 466.
[110] Hence the higher export tolls of 1494. In times of shortage there was nothing to stop the council simply banning the export of vital foodstuffs, as in the 1480s when it imposed stiff fines on anyone caught selling wine or corn beyond the town. StAFr, B 5 XIIIa, iv, fo. 53^v.

Economic Decline and Recovery 141

disenchanted with their elected representatives on the council. The political unrest which broke forth in 1490 ultimately led to the council agreeing to undertake a general 'gild reformation' in 1495. Each gild was invited to submit its grievances and recommendations, whereupon a wide-ranging review of gild charters and economic legislation ensued, which went a long way towards adopting protectionism as its guiding principle.[111] Thereafter the council was careful to consult the gilds frequently about economic and commercial affairs: the reformation of 1495 was the prelude to regular inquiries which helped to ease the hostility and misunderstanding between the mass of ordinary craftsmen and the political élite of the community.[112] But before stability and internal peace returned, the community fell victim to a decade of turbulence, during which the latent tensions over financial hardship and economic adversity which had been exacerbated by the council's oligarchic tendencies exploded into popular protest, political faction, and street violence.

IV

The painful retrenchment which the community had to suffer after mid-century helped the town gradually recover its economic and demographic balance, but left at the same time deep scars on the body politic. Despite its careful accommodation to a new gild-oriented economic strategy, the council could not escape widespread distrust of its intentions and even more of its secretive and high-handed methods of government.[113] In theory the gild Eights were meant to act as a check upon the irresponsible conduct of public business, but they appear to have degenerated into self-perpetuating cliques.[114] It is particularly revealing that the gathering storm centred upon the town's finances, for over these the *Achtwer* were supposed to exericse direct supervision if not actual control.

The exact origins of the civic unrest of the early 1490s are hidden in

[111] StAFr, A 1 vi e α 3, 21 Feb. 1472; 14 Apr. 1497; 30 Oct. 1499. 'Reformierung der zunft', n.d. (1495).

[112] Hinderschiedt, 'Zunftordnungen', p. 108. Inquiries were conducted in 1499, 1506, 1511, and 1512.

[113] A revealing minute in the council membership registers for 1479 recorded heartfelt thanks to all those who had served on the council that year 'angesehen der cleinen zitlichen belönung und dz ein yeder, der dem rat mit flyß und ernst dient, unwillen und ungunst uff sich ladet'. StAFr, B 5 I a, 2, fo. 43ʳ.

[114] From 1481 the *Achtwer* were to be appointed each year by their predecessors in office, rather than elected. StAFr, B 5 XIIIa, iv, fo. 48ʳ.

a maze of partial and contradictory sources. It appears, however, that in 1488 the town incurred an unusually large deficit, though whether through mismanagement or the need to advance archduke Sigismund vast sums to prevent the mortgaging of the Outer Austrian lands in 1487 is not clear.[115] The financial disorder led to civil disturbances,[116] during which the commons—disregarding the *Achtwer*—formed a committee of thirty-six to scrutinize the conduct of the town's administration. The committee is first recorded acting as arbitrator between St Märgen and the council in the spring of 1490 over the abbey's attempts to reclaim its estates,[117] but whatever its precise origins it was soon to be transformed into a financial watch-dog by a royal commission which Maximilian sent in midsummer to investigate the town's affairs. The commission, whose despatch was in itself a sign that something was gravely amiss, proposed sweeping changes in the system of public accounting and economic administration. The Exchange was henceforth to be run by five officials, two drawn from the council as before, but with an additional three from the ordinary gildsmen who during their term of office were banned from holding any other public post. Their biannual accounts were to be laid before a new commons' committee reduced in size to twenty-four, drawn equally from all the gilds. The smaller committee, which superseded the previous group of thirty-six, was given the task of nominating the three commons' Exchange officials annually. To shore up the town's finances, the commission suggested halving the amount which Freiburg paid Austria for the mortgaged corn toll, increasing the weights and measures, and turning the sale of salt into a municipal monopoly.[118] The commissioners' report should be seen as the culmination, rather than the inception, of efforts to find a peaceful outcome to Freiburg's difficulties, for in 1488 a delegation of ducal councillors had already reviewed the procedures for council elections. Perhaps bowing to gild pressure, the delegation had recommended that the twelve gildmasters should elect the gild commander (the town's military chief) at the same time as the council was installed.[119] The next year, however, archduke Sigismund overruled the proposal, declaring that the gilds had no right to elect their commander (a point on which the constitution was silent), and that the commander should continue to be appointed by the outgoing council.[120]

[115] Cf. StAFr, E 1 A 1 a 1, no. 2 (1503), fos. 6ʳ, 8ᵛ.
[116] This emerges clearly from *UBStFr* ii. 584, lines 15–17.
[117] StAFr, A 1 VIII a ζ 89, 31 Mar. 1490.   [118] *UBStFr* ii. 582–5.
[119] StAFr, B 5 1 a, 2, fo. 58ʳ⁻ᵛ.   [120] Ibid., fo. 59ʳ.

Economic Decline and Recovery 143

Taken together, these fragments of evidence indicate that trouble was stirring from at least 1488 onwards,[121] with signs of gild pressure for administrative reforms and greater accountability, above all in the Board of the Exchange, the hub of Freiburg's finances. The commission's findings in 1490 should have given the council a breathing-space in which to restore public confidence, but it is not certain whether they were implemented in full. At any rate, encouraged by the provisions preventing a further increase in the public debt, the council began to tackle the question of clerical financial privileges in earnest,[122] perhaps consoling itself in the ensuing uproar with the thought that here, at least, was one issue over which it could count on popular support.

Table C. *Known Participants in the Communal Opposition of the 1490s, Listed by Gilds*

1. *Smiths* Balthasar Seefelder	6. *Cobblers* Caspar Rotenkopf Auberly Louffer
2. *Haberdashers* Hans Götz Niklaus Egkly	7. *Clothmakers* Hans Enderly Jakob Megerich
3. *Butchers* Konrad Walzenmüller Hans Menly Hans Metzger Jakob Strobach ? Jakob Walzenmüller	8. *Tanners* Heinrich Zillig Auberly Meyer (Gerber) 9. *Carpenters* Caspar Has
4. *Tailors* Burkart Müller (Schneider) Jakob Zeller Konrad Rösch (Rost)	10. *Painters* Theodosius Bildhower ? Benedikt Volherpst
5. *Coopers* Klaus Nagel Konrad Helbling	

Source: StAFr, B 5 1 a, 2. No bakers or wine-growers are recorded.

Despite these endeavours the commons were clearly not satisfied that the council was responding swiftly or effectively enough to popular demands, for in 1491 the committee of twenty-four tried to take over

---

[121] Possibly even earlier according to a gloss in the letterbooks of May 1486: 'Die Nun sollen reden von stiefen sach und von ungehorsamen der zunftigen.' StAFr, B 5 XI, v, 3, fo. 80ʳ.

[122] See pp. 133–4.

Table D. *Offices Held by Members of the Communal Opposition, 1487–96*

Year	Gildmaster	Additional councillor	Board of Exchange
1487	Rotenkopf		
1488		Rotenkopf	
1489			
1490	Rotenkopf		
	Seefelder		
1491	Walzenmüller		Rotenkopf
	Müller		
	Zillig		
1492			Walzenmüller (crossed out 'dead')
			Zillig
1493			Rotenkopf
1494			
1495	Zillig		Zillig
1496		Zillig	Zillig

Source: StAFr, B 5 I a, 2. In addition, Rotenkopf sat on the higher court in 1490, and Zillig in 1495/6. Rotenkopf was a bread inspector in 1488, Zillig in 1491, and Müller in 1492. Walzenmüller acted as one of the Hospital superintendents in 1491.

the council.[123] The joint leaders of the protest emerged as Caspar Rotenkopf, a master cobbler who had already served on the council as gildmaster in 1487 and 1490,[124] and who survived to cause further trouble in 1495, and Konrad Walzenmüller, a master butcher and former bailiff of Waltershofen,[125] who was elected gildmaster in 1491 and turned out to be the real instigator of violence.[126] From the subsequent interrogations it is possible to reconstruct much of the sequence and shape of events. In accordance with the composition of the commons' committee, the twenty or so identifiable ringleaders were drawn from across the twelve gilds (with the striking exception of

[123] Nowhere is it explicitly stated that the group which stormed the council was (largely) identical with the committee of twenty-four. The authorities were understandably at pains to brand the agitation as the work of Walzenmüller and his henchmen, bent on personal aggrandizement. Nevertheless, from Zasius's endorsement of the letter of safe conduct for Nikolaus Sattler in July 1492 it is clear that Sattler was under threat because he had offended the commons' committee, rather than simply Walzenmüller's gang. StAFr, B 5 XI, xlix, 29 July 1492. 'Landvogt Niclauß Sattlerß halb, der het etliche wort, die dem usschutz nit gefielen, geredt, in in schutz und gleit dar um ze nemen.'

[124] StAFr, B 5 I a, 2, fos. 55ʳ, 60ᵛ.

[125] GLA 229/80590. He had previously also lived in Freiburg. StAFr, A 1 XIX Wolfenweiler 1, 24 Nov. 1481; 2, 11 Dec. 1481.

[126] StAFr, B 5 I a, 2, fo. 61ᵛ.

Economic Decline and Recovery 145

the wine-growers), though the butchers were particularly prominent (see Table C). Most of those named were mastercraftsmen, and few were noticeably poor (see Table E): together they made up a fraction of disaffected middling gildsmen, the 'outs' of civic politics who saw power increasingly concentrated in the hands of a self-perpetuating oligarchy and who used the commons' committee as the road to office.

Table E. Wealth of Mastercraftsmen who Took Part in the Communal Opposition of the 1490s

Name	Craft	Tallage payment/ Wealth 1491–2
Enderly, Hans	Stonecutter	7s./50 fl.
Götz, Hans	Haberdasher	15s./225 fl.
Has, Caspar	Carpenter	5s./poor
Megerich, Jakob	Clothmaker	5s./poor
Menly, Hans	Butcher	8s./75 fl.
Meyer, Auberly	Tanner	10s./150 fl.
Müller, Burkart	Tailor	20s./400 fl.
Nagel, Klaus	Cooper	10s./125 fl.
Rösch, Konrad	Tailor	5s./poor
Rotenkopf, Caspar	Cobbler	15s./225 fl.
Seefelder, Balthasar	Smith	14s./200 fl.
Strobach, Jakob	Butcher	7s./50 fl.
Walzenmüller, Konrad	Butcher	14s./200 fl.
Zeller, Jakob	Tailor	6s./25 fl.
Zillig, Heinrich	Tanner	13s./175 fl.

Source: StAFr, E 1 A II a 1, 1491/2.

At first the committee was content to use constitutional means. In the 1491 elections three leading dissidents—Walzenmüller, Burkart Müller, a tailor, and Heinrich Zillig, a tanner—were elected as gildmasters, whilst Rotenkopf was listed as one of the five Exchange officials (see Table D). This representation was clearly insufficient to bring about a radical realignment of political interests. What is more, the committee's foothold on the council was effectively crushed the following year, when many of the old and long-serving councillors ousted by the rebels regained their seats. None of the dissidents were returned as supplementary councillors as would normally have been the case, and only by virtue of the revised system of financial administration did Walzenmüller and Zillig succeed in being appointed to the Board of the Exchange as commons' representatives. The most striking reversal was the election of Ytelhug, by far the richest butcher in Freiburg and a pillar of the old order, as gildmaster to replace Walzenmüller. Outmanœuvred by the old guard, the ousted dissidents tried to stage a coup. Thereupon Walzenmüller appears to have led street agitation against the new council until he was killed in mysterious circumstances at the end of June. There seems little doubt that he was assassinated with the council's connivance, if not actually on its direct orders; at any rate the council dragged its feet over investigating the incident.[127]

Meanwhile the public prosecutors interrogated Walzenmüller's supporters and questioned witnesses over the disturbances.[128] The agitators confessed to having stirred up opposition to the new council by seditious and inflammatory talk, especially after Walzenmüller's death. One master butcher in particular, Hans Menly, reportedly declared that the new council had excluded all those who enjoyed the support of the commons in favour of their opponents.[129] Yet the extent of the committee's following is not easy to gauge. Rotenkopf's popularity was certainly sufficient for him to be re-elected to the council after the commotion of 1492, though his wings were finally clipped four years later. Heinrich Zillig survived to be re-elected gildmaster in 1495 and served in several capacities on the town government thereafter. In order to have any chance of seizing the reins of power the faction of middling craftsmen needed to build up a broad following amongst the mass of ordinary citizens, but there is not much sign that they succeeded. On Walzenmüller's death, it is true, one of his humbler adherents, Jakob Megerich, exclaimed, 'People say the king of the Jews is dead!',[130] but this remark must be treated with great caution. Does it refer to Walzenmüller as the champion of the oppressed against the powerful, or is it a satirical jibe against a popular leader who had come to grief? In a town notorious for its anti-Semitism such a remark was more than mildly ambiguous. Certainly there was no shortage of bystanders who were subsequently prepared to denounce Walzenmüller as a knave and a braggart. One witness, on

---

[127] StAFr, A 1 XI e, 6 July 1492; Rowan, 'Guilds', p. 307.
[128] StAFr, A 1 V a 18, n.d. (1492). Hefte A and B. Cf. also B 5 XI, v, 4, fo. 29^r.
[129] StAFr, A 1 V a 18, n.d. (1492). Heft A, fo. 1^r.
[130] Ibid. The remark was also attributed to another of his lowly followers, Caspar Has. Ibid., fo. 1^v. Rowan, 'Guilds', p. 308.

Economic Decline and Recovery 147

overhearing Megerich's boast that there would be trouble in a few weeks' time for a conspiracy was afoot, taunted him, 'Where are his (i.e. Walzenmüller's) seventy-two disciples, then?'[131]

Nevertheless, Walzenmüller's movement had distinct populist overtones, as an incident at the fishmarket during the coup attempt reveals. Nikolaus Sattler, a rich merchant, came upon a knot of Walzenmüller's supporters and exclaimed bitterly, 'The scoundrelly beadles have arrested Hug at the shambles—by now he's probably lying prisoner in the Thieves' Tower. There's no choice now but to chop off a dozen of the fellows' heads.' Thereupon he clapped hands on two of those present, declaring, 'You dare put us rich to the axe and murder us! Anyone who pays 5s. (the poll-tax paid by poor craftsmen in lieu of the tallage) should hang from the gallows outside the gate.'[132] In return Sattler was threatened with bodily violence, and advised by his friends not to show himself out of doors.[133]

The council certainly believed it was faced with widespread opposition, for it acted quickly to imprison or expel any of the demonstrators on whom it could lay its hands.[134] This move, however, backfired, for several of the ringleaders promptly appealed to Maximilian for protection.[135] The council thus found itself by September with an unwelcome public enquiry into the disturbances on its hands, conducted by the Outer Austrian governor.[136] In the end, few of the agitators were severely punished. Some of the lesser fry, such as Caspar Has of the carpenters' and Konrad Rösch of the tailors' gild, were banished for good,[137] but most of the craftmasters involved were too powerful to alienate. Some were temporarily exiled, fined, or simply bound over to keep the peace,[138] but several went entirely

[131] StAFr, A I v a 18, n.d. (1492). Heft A, fo. 1ʳ.

[132] Ibid. Heft B, fo. 4ʳ. The Hug in this passage can hardly refer to Ytelhug, but to an otherwise unidentified Hug who in Caspar Has' quarters had denounced the new councillors as villains. Ibid., Heft A, fo. 2ʳ; Heft B, fo. 3ᵛ.

[133] StAFr, B 5 XI, xlix, 29 July 1492.

[134] StAFr, B 5 I b, 1, fo. 47ᵛ ; A I XI e, 31 July 1492; A I VI a 23, 29 Nov. 1492; TLA, Maximiliana XIV/43, fos. 45ʳ, 46ʳ, 46ᵛ.

[135] StAFr, A I I e 34, 5 Sept. 1492; cf. *UBStFr* ii. 588–9. Cf. also StAFr, A I XI e, 31 July 1492; ibid., 23 Sept. 1492; A I VI a 23, 29 Nov. 1492; 24, 25 Feb. 1493.

[136] StAFr, A I I e 34, 5 Sept. 1495; cf. *UBStFr* ii. 588–9.

[137] Has was not readmitted despite intercession by both Maximilian and the margrave of Baden. StAFr, A I VI a 25, 4 Mar. 1493. Rösch was still exiled at the end of 1492. A I XI f 336, 4 Aug. 1492; A I VI a 23, 29 Nov. 1492. As late as 1496 Maximilian was still trying to persuade the council to take back Balthasar Seefelder, who had been the smith's gildmaster in 1490. TLA, Maximiliana XIV/43, fos. 45ʳ, 46ʳ, 46ᵛ.

[138] Cf. StAFr, A I XI f 333, 17 July 1492; 335, 17 July 1492; 337, 4 Aug. 1492; 344, 23 Aug. 1494; B 5 I b, 1, fo. 47ᵛ.

unscathed. The council even fined Nikolaus Sattler £10 for his outburst at the fishmarket, no doubt to demonstrate its disinterested concern for civic concord and the commonweal.[139]

This mild treatment of the rebels indicates that the council had won a pyrrhic victory. The commons' committee of twenty-four still stood and continued to nominate its men to the Board of the Exchange. Not surprisingly, the council regarded this state of affairs in the long run as intolerable. It complained that confidential business could not be transacted since the Board's deliberations were immediately leaked to the citizenry at large. In 1495 it therefore proposed that the five Board members should in future be drawn once again entirely from the ranks of existing councillors.[140] To achieve this, however, was another matter. After lengthy negotiations with the commons' committee the council agreed on a compromise solution. All five Board members were henceforth to be nominated by the council and committee jointly from the names of returned councillors immediately after the June elections. This arrangement must have proved satisfactory, for it continued to operate until the mid-sixteenth century, with the commons' committee apparently still in active existence.[141]

The broad though fragile consensus between council and commons which was achieved by 1495 found its fullest expression in the 'gild reformation' of that year. But concerted economic action was no guarantee of lasting political harmony between the council and individual gilds. The following year the council was doubly shaken by renewed agitation within the shoemakers' and butchers' corporations. Trouble began with the re-election of Caspar Rotenkopf as gildmaster of the shoemakers. The council promptly quashed the election on the grounds that he had played a leading role in the commons' disturbances four years previously. In his account of the affair Zasius described Rotenkopf as a hothead of little judgment and less sense, who had continued to pass malicious and disparaging comments upon the council when a member of his gild Eight, with the result that some of the senior councillors refused to sit with him. The council took the view that the conduct of public business would not be improved by having Rotenkopf in the chamber, but that, not unnaturally, was not how the shoemakers saw it. The gild protested vigorously at the

[139] StAFr, B 5 XI, v, 4, fo. 7^v.
[140] StAFr, B 5 XIIIa, iva, fo. 20^{r-v}; v, fo. 134^r.
[141] In 1543 the council and XXIV agreed to reduce the Board of the Exchange to three officials in order to save money. StAFr, B 5 XIIIa, xii, fo. 114^v.

council's interference in its election and at first refused to put forward a replacement, even though Rotenkopf's election had been far from unanimous. Eventually the shoemakers did give way and elect an alternative gildmaster, but that was not the end of the story. When the Outer Austrian governor, Kaspar von Mörsberg, arrived in Freiburg a few days later to preside over the council elections, Rotenkopf rushed up to him to complain about his shameful treatment. Mörsberg tried to press his case before the council, but it pointed out that it had reluctantly overruled the gild for the sake of civic concord in order to avoid being saddled with a notorious trouble-maker. Mörsberg, a sworn antagonist of Freiburg, which he suspected of usurping his authority,[142] was not easily placated. He kept the council waiting two days before proceeding with the election, and insisted that it apologize publicly for its behaviour towards Rotenkopf. But the council stood firm; only reluctantly did Mörsberg climb down and confirm the elections, whereupon Rotenkopf, the scent of defeat in his nostrils, slunk away and was not to hold public office again for a decade.[143]

No sooner had the council settled its score with Rotenkopf than it was confronted by an even more serious challenge from the butchers, several of whom had already shown themselves truculent and vicious in 1492. Their anger had been roused by the general reform of the toll-charges in 1494, when a levy of 1s. per £ had been placed upon cattle grazed and fattened in Freiburg's pastures but not slaughtered in the town.[144] When two years later they were required to pay a duty of 8d. a beast on every animal slaughtered in the town as well,[145] their anger erupted into violence. The council tried to argue that the butchers enjoyed an unwarranted tax advantage: they paid no market tolls on the sale or purchase of cattle (unlike the other gilds which paid duty on their raw materials) and made far greater use of the common land than any other gild. The butchers brushed these arguments aside, and amidst ugly scenes[146] threatened to stop slaughtering altogether; in fact they did so, declaring that they would remain on strike unless the council restored the old weights and measures or else revoked the tax. Considering that the butchers were holding the community to ransom by withdrawing the supply of meat, the council decided to interrogate the masters one by one, and gathered the recalcitrant and pliant into two separate groups. Faced with the council's salami tactics the

[142] Cf. StAFr, B 5 III c 10, fos. 5ʳ –6ᵛ.
[143] StAFr, B 1 2, fos. 97ᵛ–99ᵛ.
[144] StAFr, B 5 XIIIa, iva, fos. 1ᵛ–2ʳ.
[145] StAFr, B 1 2, fo. 101ʳ.
[146] Cf. StAFr, A 1 XI e 102, 19 Sept. 1496.

individual butchers naturally displayed much less defiance than the gild collectively. A few declared that they had already decided to abandon their trade, but only one, the gildmaster, Hans Metzger, refused point-blank to comply. With that the butchers' resistance collapsed.[147] When the culprits were brought to book, it emerged that a Swiss drover had played a shadowy role in stirring up trouble.[148] Hans Metzger was expelled from the gild and remained an outcast in the community for years to come.[149]

Even then the council's troubles were not over. The butchers, who were clearly embittered by their humiliating capitulation, tried again in 1502 to have the excise abolished, but were refused on the same grounds as before.[150] Although the gild went back to work after a short strike, several of its members gave the council a nasty fright by threatening to bring their case before Maximilian. To have punished the butchers' heated utterances would only have made matters worse, so the council side-stepped another violent confrontation by declaring that the offenders had not expressed the responsible opinion of the gild.[151] The butchers remained a thorn in the flesh for years to come; in 1520 the entire gild staged a walk-out by retiring *en masse* to Breisach until the council met its demands for an increase in meat prices.[152]

The unrest of the 1490s shows very clearly how difficult it was even for a gild-dominated council to implement policies for economic and financial recovery without antagonizing sectional interest groups among the gilds themselves. Equally, however, it shows that the council, although the victim of financial adversity, compounded its difficulties by arrogance, cliquishness, and secrecy in the conduct of its business. Whatever view one takes of the abilities and motives of the long-established councillors who clung to office for years on end in the later fifteenth century, there can be no doubt that their paternalistic and authoritarian cast of mind made them peculiarly inflexible and unresponsive in the face of popular protest. The council had become

[147] StAFr, B 1 2, fos. 101ʳ–103ʳ.

[148] This is the most likely interpretation of the gloss in the top margin of Michel Disser's testimony. StAFr, A 1 XI e 102, 19 Sept. 1496; cf. B 5 III c 11, fos. 13ʳ, 69ʳ, 85ᵛ; A 1 XI f 358, 26 Sept. 1496.

[149] He was listed amongst the criminals and outcasts in the war-levy list of non-gildsmen in 1500. StAFr, E 1 A II b 4, 26 Mar. 1500.

[150] StAFr, B 5 XIIIa, v, fo. 47ᵛ; cf. B 2 4, p. 255.

[151] Rowan, 'Guilds', pp. 314–15.

[152] StAFr, B 5 XI, x, fos. 268ᵛ, 271ᵛ–272ʳ; xi, 15 June 1520 (draft); Flamm, 'Metzgergewerbe', pp. 46–7.

Economic Decline and Recovery 151

the prisoner of its own dour vision of itself: a small group of men struggling against great odds in the public interest for little reward and no thanks. And yet that vision in the end brought its own grim satisfaction. By the early 1500s the council had succeeded, after many pitfalls and reversals, in laying the foundations of a more stable economy and society. Though not apparent to contemporaries, who only experienced the hardships and deprivations, Freiburg's financial and economic system was well on the way to recovery by the end of the century. What was lacking was a more open and responsive system of government, but here the council learnt its lesson in the 1490s. The 'gild reformation', and the commons' committee were eloquent testimony that the council accepted, however reluctantly, that it must govern by consent. How resilient and real the new-found sense of community and purpose would prove was to be tested most severely during the Peasants' War in 1525.

V

By 1480 the number of craftsmen in Freiburg had stablized at somewhat over 1,000. Though the figure rose to over 1,100 by the turn of the century, it fell back around 1520 on a renewed outbreak of plague, but by mid-century the total was beginning to rise quite fast (see Table F). Rowan believed that this recovery in population was accompanied by a marked redistribution of wealth, as the protectionist economy conferred a modest level of prosperity upon the mass of middling artisans. Attractive though this argument may be, it rests ultimately upon an arbitrary division of the tallage lists into entirely artificial categories of property-holding. Rowan's figures (not always based upon a very reliable reading of the entries) do indeed show the richest gildsmen disappearing and a solid block of moderately wealthy craftsmen emerging,[153] but grouped another way the figures show remarkably little shift until 1550 (see Table G). It lies quite beyond the purpose of the present argument to discuss the technical problems of the tallage lists or the relative merits of particular interpretations,[154] but there is a good case for treating the poor craftsmen who paid the poll-tax as a distinct group, at least (which Rowan does not), since the council itself seems to have done so. Their numbers reached half the

[153] See Tables in Rowan, 'Guilds', pp. 234–6.
[154] Cf. most recently Weißer, 'Verteilung', pp. 14 ff.; Schuler, 'Bevölkerungsstruktur', pp. 167 ff. The Freiburg tallage lists still await thorough investigation.

total of craftmasters by 1490, and only fell back to around one-third by 1550. Whatever evening out of wealth may have occurred, there evidently remained a large pool of very poor craftsmen in Freiburg throughout the period.

Table F. *Total of Craftmasters in each Gild, 1481–1550*

Gild	1481	1490	1500	1508	1520	1530	1540	1550
Smiths	88	98	91	83	68	78	72	82
Haberdashers	82	81	76	78	66	72	77	91
Butchers	91	105	108	90	78	81	80	78
Tailors	94	89	84	80	59	65	76	80
Bakers	53	50	55	48	63	61	57	70
Coopers	88	86	94	90	87	95	101	129
Cobblers	81	73	77	63	64	64	56	58
Clothmakers	78	82	74	68	65	60	65	78
Tanners	36	39	35	34	23	20	21	24
Carpenters	109	115	112	123	128	136	125	152
Painters	67	76	87	83	67	57	61	58
Winegrowers	200	251	244	228	200	269	285	335
TOTAL	1,067	1,145	1,137	1,068	968	1,058	1,076	1,235

Source: StAFr, E 1 A II a 1, 1481–1550.

There is no shortage of evidence, moreover, that the number of shiftless persons outside the gilds, particularly young girls, was on the increase after 1500.[155] The council was seriously worried by the scores of footloose mercenaries, vagabonds, and beggars who roamed the Breisgau, and strove to keep them at arm's length lest they foment unrest.[156] Within the city it strove to isolate the wine-growers' gild as the traditional reservoir of menial labour and kept a close watch on its affairs. Does this mean that Freiburg's economic recovery was a chimera? Too many inferences should not be drawn from the tallage lists which recorded wealth not income. The real criterion of prosperity for the mass of the population remained then, as now, the daily wage or income from sales, rather than accumulated capital. Unfortunately, evidence for wage-rates in Freiburg is very sketchy. The price of basic commodities such as meat[157] and wine[158] was

[155] See pp. 71–2.
[156] Cf. StAFr, B 5 X 1, fo. 12ᵛ; B 2 4, p. 255.
[157] Cf. StAFr, A 1 VI e ε 20, 5 Oct. 1472; 25, 29 Aug. 1505; B 5 XIIIa, xa, fo. 25ʳ (1519).
[158] Cf. StAFr, B 5 XIIIa, iv, fos. 15ᵛ–16ʳ. 'Winslag', 1473–1512.

Table G. Wealth of Craftsmen by Tallage Groups, 1481–1550

Group	Tallage	Wealth	1481	1490	1500	1508	1520	1530	1540	1550
	No Entry		25	20	34	50	52	22	24	12
I	1s.–5s. polltax	under 25 fl.	454 43.6%	553 49.2%	548 49.7%	504 49.5%	412 45.0%	545 52.6%	566 53.8%	394 32.2%
II	6s.–11s.	25 fl.–125 fl.	348 33.4%	341 30.3%	317 28.7%	296 29.1%	278 30.4%	271 26.2%	211 20.1%	410 33.5%
III	11s. 6d.–24s.	135 fl.–500 fl.	154 14.8%	158 14.1%	174 15.8%	147 14.4%	159 17.4%	141 13.6%	172 16.4%	217 17.8%
IV	24s. 9d.–39s.	525 fl.–1,000 fl.	45 4.3%	45 4.0%	37 3.6%	42 4.1%	29 3.2%	46 4.4%	58 5.5%	94 7.7%
V	40s.–119s.	1,050 fl.–5,000 fl.	37 3.6%	26 2.3%	26 2.4%	29 2.9%	38 4.2%	33 3.2%	44 4.2%	106 8.7%
VI	over 120s.	over 5,050 fl.	4 0.4%	2 0.2%	1 0.1%	— —	— —	— —	1 0.1%	2 0.2%

Source: StAFr, E 1 A II a1, 1481–1550. Around 1540 the poll-tax threshold was raised to 6s., so that Group II began at 7s. Around 1500 the lowest point in Group III seems to have corresponded to 150 fl. These adjustments highlight the problems of wealth-grouping, as well as reflecting the impact of inflation.

certainly rising in an age of gathering inflation, but again the sources are too patchy to construct reliable tables. Nevertheless, by the early sixteenth century there is plenty of circumstantial evidence that the fortunes of the city and its inhabitants were on the mend. No longer are the pages of the council minute-books filled with agonized reflections on the repercussions of higher taxes; the letter-books no longer contain despairing enquiries to neighbouring cities on financial and economic affairs; the civic debt no longer makes the headlines. Tangible evidence that the town was recovering its self-esteem is provided by the remarkable spate of renewed public building. In 1498 the corn exchange was erected; between 1525 and 1532 the Exchange was rebuilt in late gothic splendour facing the minster square. After over a century's interruption the minster itself was at long last completed with the construction of the choir in 1513, crowned by the magnificent high altar of Hans Baldung Grien.[159] These public works were complemented by private initiatives: Maximilian's chancellor, Dr Konrad Stürtzel, built the Basler Hof between 1494 and 1515, whilst his treasurer, Dr Jakob Villinger, erected the Haus zum Walfisch, subsequently the residence of Erasmus, around 1516.[160]

The presence of Maximilian's chancellor and treasurer in Freiburg underscores how far the city's fortunes were bound up with its role in Outer Austria. That indispensable connection made Freiburg a bastion of political loyalty and religious orthodoxy throughout the sixteenth century. Yet it is precisely that commitment to the established order which proved fateful for the city in the years of mounting rural unrest across the breadth of South-West Germany culminating in the Peasants' War, when Freiburg reaped the reward for its masterful and ruthless treatment of the peasantry and lesser townsfolk of its Breisgau hinterland.

[159] Cf. Ernst Adam, *Das Freiburger Münster* (Große Bauten Europas, i), 2nd edn. (Stuttgart, 1973), 22 ff.; Wolf Hart, *Die künstlerische Ausstattung des Freiburger Münsters* (Freiburg, 1981).
[160] See p. 30.

V
Conclusion

AT the heart of Freiburg's changing fortunes in the fifteenth century lay an essential paradox: its political centrality waxed as its economic centrality waned. The challenge to the town's socio-political and legal sphere of influence was surmounted, as a loose system of rural clientage gave way to the organized administration of dependent territories. Freiburg's freedom to acquire rural domains in turn underscores the political and strategic importance which it had achieved in Outer Austria. These responsibilities weighed heavily, however, on a town whose domestic economy, already too fragile to be shored up by a landed territory alone, was being further undermined by rural competition.

To what degree were these problems peculiar to Freiburg? The acceptance of rural commoners as burghers was widespread in the towns of southern Germany and Switzerland. In the case of several Swabian cities—notably Augsburg, Isny, Kempten, and Constance—the acquisition of peasant outburghers was clearly intended to compensate for the lack of any substantial landed territory. Though Augsburg's peasant outburghers declined after the middle of the fourteenth century,[1] the numbers of such subjects paying tax to Isny and Kempten ran into several hundreds. On the assumption that they represented heads-of-household, the entire outburgher communities of these two Allgäu cities must have been quite considerable.[2] In Constance their total came to just short of one-tenth of the oppidan population,[3] a figure very similar to Freiburg's. In none of these cities were the outburghers exposed to the harassment which Freiburg's subjects in the Breisgau had to endure, though the town clerk observed on his travels in 1476 that Kempten's peasant burghers were a thorn in

---
[1] Kießling, 'Herrschaft—Markt—Landbesitz', p. 192. The number of noble outburghers rose steadily, however, until the late 15th c.

[2] Scott, *Enquete*.

[3] Bernhard Kirchgässner, *Das Steuerwesen der Reichsstadt Konstanz 1418–1460. Aus der Wirtschafts- und Sozialgeschichte einer oberdeutschen Handelsstadt am Ausgang des Mittelalters* (Konstanzer Geschichts- und Rechtsquellen, x) (Constance, 1960), 161.

the flesh of the local aristocracy. But then all four communities were powerful and privileged free cities of the Empire, in contrast to Freiburg which strove in vain as a territorial town to resist the consolidating policies of the margraves of Baden.

In the northern Swiss cantons, on the other hand, peasant outburghers became pawns in the game of territorial aggrandizement. Since the holding of outburghers was an obstacle to territorialization, the stronger city-states either exchanged their rural dependents wholesale or else elbowed the weaker cantons out of the way. Berne, Basel, and Lucerne all successfully deployed their outburghers as instruments of territorial policy,[4] whereas the smaller and much poorer Solothurn, caught in the pincers of its more powerful neighbours, was forced to abandon its outburghers after 1525.[5]

Whether as a surrogate for a landed territory or as the platform for territorial expansion the acquisiton of outburghers provided a significant demographic, military, and fiscal reservoir for many cities in Upper Germany and Switzerland. Their role was rather different, however, in the one other region of western Europe where they proliferated. In the densely populated countryside of Flanders the already hypertrophic cities, teeming with fifty thousand inhabitants or more, sought desperately to limit further rural–urban migration as the economic climate worsened in the later fourteenth century by granting burgher's rights to peasants on condition that they remained resident in their villages. These *buitenpoorters* (literally 'outburghers') soon became the target of seigneurial hostility, since their urban privileges exempted them from local feudal jurisdiction.[6] In fact the spread of *buitenpoorterij* should be seen as stemming from the rapid disappearance of villeinage in the commercialized countryside of Flanders rather than from any desire on the part of the cities to extend their tutelage to the rural population.[7]

The problems of the overcrowded Flemish cities were utterly remote from the agony of Freiburg's wasting population. If it could not make itself attractive to immigrants, then the town must look elsewhere

---

[4] Ulbrich, *Leibherrschaft*, p. 186 n. 275. Cf. Bruno Amiet, *Die solothurnische Territorialpolitik von 1344–1532* (Solothurn, 1929), 144 ff.

[5] Ulbrich, *Leibherrschaft*, pp. 189–90.

[6] David Nicholas, *Town and Countryside: Social, Economic and Political Tensions in Fourteenth-Century Flanders* (Rijksuniversiteit te Gent: Werken uitgegeven door de Faculteit van de Letteren en Wijsbegeerte, clii) (Bruges, 1971), 220–1, 242.

[7] Ibid., p. 236. Ghent, with a probable population of 60,000 in the mid-14th c., had 5,000 outburghers in 1432, around 10% of the urban total. Ibid., p. 248.

to staunch its demographic haemorrhage. The timing of the first acquisition in the Dreisam valley, however fortuitous St Märgen's bankruptcy, did none the less coincide with the nadir of Freiburg's domestic fortunes. Although the landed territory grew thereafter only in fits and starts, the council must have hoped that its territorial initiative would counteract internal decline as well as restoring a rural sphere of influence. Freiburg was by no means the only territorial town in southern Germany to carve out a landed domain in the later Middle Ages. Aside from Breisach, both Villingen and Bräunlingen in the Black Forest amongst its Outer Austrian neighbours controlled small territories of their own, as did Riedlingen and Ehingen in Danubian Swabia.[8] For the majority of seigneurial towns, however, princely territorial policies usually precluded such independent enterprise. Instead, even where towns served as the administrative headquarters of their surrounding districts (as was the case in Württemberg and Upper Alsace), their constitutional and economic status was commonly reduced to the level of their hinterlands.[9] Freiburg was extremely fortunate, therefore, in building up a territory so large and so late to offset its crumbling network of rural clientage.

The territory which Freiburg accumulated lay chiefly to the east of the town up the Dreisam valley, rather than in the fertile Breisgau plain to the west where the majority of its outburghers was located. This suggests that Freiburg was following the pattern of other late medieval communities, whose expansion aimed more at providing the strategic security of a rural bulwark than towards the maximization of economic return, a point confirmed by the relatively conservative administration of the Valley Bailiwick.[10]

Whilst control of its landed territory helped counteract the damage caused by toll evasion and rival turnpikes, there was very little that Freiburg could do to stifle competition from village markets and country crafts, especially if they flourished beyond its precincts (*Bannmeile*) or in foreign territory. Throughout western Europe in this period the archival record is littered with petitions of grievance and distress against rural usurpers of the traditional economic functions and prerogatives of urban centres. Amongst its Alemannic neighbours a string of Swiss cities—Zürich, Berne, Lucerne, Fribourg—echoed

[8] Scott, 'Territorialpolitik', p. 7.   [9] Ibid, pp. 7–8.
[10] Cf. Raiser, *Städtische Territorialpolitik*, p. 20; Frantisek Graus, 'Tendenzen der Stadt–Land-Beziehungen im ausgehenden Mittelalter', in *Fribourg, ville et territoire*, p. 33.

Freiburg's protests at competition from their hinterlands.[11] The peasantry reacted bitterly to the cities' efforts to suppress the burgeoning economy beyond their walls, be it the planting of new vineyards, the establishment of oil-presses, salt-chests and bath-houses, or the spread of artisan production and informal marketing. Such anger fed the rising of 1489 in canton Zürich, the so-called Waldmann affair, which ended in defeat for burgomaster Waldmann and his cronies, and in far-reaching concessions to the city's dependent peasantry.[12] The challenge to the cities was compounded by the formation of rural gilds; in Lucerne, for instance, an entire canvas of country crafts from cobblers, tailors, smiths, and weavers to fishers, joiners, ropemakers, and mercers was organized into formal associations.[13] The most powerful cities of the northern Confederacy such as Zürich, Basel, and Schaffhausen were able to stamp out rural gilds,[14] but otherwise the only hope lay in their urban counterparts' incorporating them in order to exercise supervision and regulation.

Freiburg fared so badly in the face of rural competition because it was neither a city-state mighty enough to dominate its wider hinterland regardless of political frontiers nor a commercial metropolis which could harness rural labour for proto-industrial production through the putting-out system. Freiburg's *malaise* was quite distinct from the familiar late medieval saga of competition between town and countryside in areas of export-geared textile manufacturing such as Swabia, Franconia, or Flanders, which frequently shook down into a new division of labour advantageous to the former, whereby rural weavers were relegated to the earlier and simpler stages of production or else confined to turning out a range of coarser stuffs—ticking, serges, fustian, and linen—whilst the finishing processes and the manufacture of the more valuable quality woollens and silks were reserved to skilled urban weavers.[15] Rather was it the predicament of a craft town which was being deprived of its *raison d'être* by an increasingly urbanized hinterland.[16]

[11] Peyer, 'Wollgewerbe', pp. 86 ff.; Anne-Marie Dubler, *Handwerk, Gewerbe und Zunft in Stadt und Landschaft Luzern* (Luzerner Historische Veröffentlichungen, xiv) (Lucerne/Stuttgart, 1982), 154–5.
[12] Christian Dietrich, *Die Stadt Zürich und ihre Landgemeinden während der Bauernunruhen von 1489 bis 1525* (Europäische Hochschulschriften, Reihe 3 ccxxix) (Frankfurt am Main/Berne/New York, 1985), 22 ff., 44–5, 49–50, 53 ff., 90.
[13] Dubler, *Handwerk*, pp. 198, 393.   [14] Ibid., pp. 184–5.
[15] Cf. in general Nicholas, *Town and Countryside*, esp. pp. 53–116, 220–1.
[16] Cf. August Skalweit, *Das Dorfhandwerk vor Aufhebung des Städtezwangs* (Abhandlungen des Europäischen Handwerks-Instituts, i) (Frankfurt am Main, 1943), 9.

Conclusion

This transformation was a landmark of the later Middle Ages. Whereas the scattered towns of the High Middle Ages had developed market systems which entrenched commerce and exchange as exclusively urban activities, the fourteenth and fifteenth centuries witnessed the proliferation of local markets predicated upon the social division of labour and consequent exchange of goods within villages.[17] Their foundation was indeed encouraged by the local lords, who espied both additional revenue and a readier flow of cash income from rents through their tenants' market sales.[18] These new local market areas overlapped with and encroached upon the existing borough market franchises, so that their respective boundaries became entirely blurred.[19] The fatal blow dealt by the division of labour to the towns' commercial exclusivity allowed the rural economy to flourish as the urban economy began to falter.[20]

Freiburg and the other Outer Austrian towns on the right bank of the Rhine were at last paying the price for the undue advantage which they had enjoyed as central places in the Breisgau as long as the territories of Baden remained virtually bereft of urban life. Although they had inherited their lands from the dukes of Zähringen, the margraves were notoriously reluctant to follow the Zähringers' example in resting their administration on a network of urban foundations. Instead they preferred to rule their southern lordships from a string of castles—Rötteln, Badenweiler, Hachberg—with the mining community of Sulzburg as the only chartered borough.[21] Whilst their suspicion of urban liberties persisted, the margraves none the less began to confer fair and market rights on many of their villages from the early years of the fifteenth century.[22] Lörrach, Badenweiler, Emmendingen, and Eichstetten were joined at the turn of the century by Britzingen and Malterdingen. The spate of market privileges continued unabated throughout the early modern era in a 'euphoria' of new foundations, in Meinrad Schaab's phrase, which ended in a mass

---

[17] Makoto Terao, 'Rural Small Towns and Market-Towns of *Sachsen*, Central Germany, at the Beginning of the Modern Age', *Keio Economic Studies*, ii (1964), 67–8.

[18] Hilton, 'Towns in Societies', p. 9. In England, he points out, village markets were as common as borough markets in the West Midlands, and much commoner in the East Midlands.

[19] Terao, 'Rural Small Towns', p. 68.

[20] Cf. Karlheinz Blaschke, *Bevölkerungsgeschichte von Sachsen bis zur Industriellen Revolution* (Weimar, 1967), 160–1.

[21] Meinrad Schaab, 'Städtlein, Burg-, Amts- und Marktflecken Südwestdeutschlands in Spätmittelalter und früher Neuzeit', in Meynen, *Zentralität*, p. 232.

[22] Ibid., p. 242.

of mutually paralysing little central places.²³ Several of these local markets petered out, though others, such as Emmendingen, were finally granted full urban charters in the late sixteenth century.

In other words, the Breisgau underwent a classic process of urbanization from the fifteenth century onwards, in which the emergence of artisan villages encouraged a stream of market foundations which in turn gave rise to rural small towns. A similar development occurred in Saxony,²⁴ and has been seen as the genesis of urban growth in Russia.²⁵ The urban system of the Breisgau (to use Rozman's terminology) deprived the ancient centres such as Freiburg of their economic exclusivity by dispersing centrality throughout a regional market network.

Whilst that network may readily be systematized in a hexagonal grid-plan of central places,²⁶ to do so would be to ignore the crucial political factor which crippled Freiburg's central function in the Breisgau: the impact of terrritorial autarky. Just as they had ousted Freiburg's outburghers from their territory, so the margraves of Baden banned their subjects from patronizing markets outside their jurisdiction. No doubt such prohibitions were never entirely effective, but the sixteenth century echoed to the sound of all the Austrian Breisgau towns' bewailing the failure of margravial peasants to visit their long-established borough markets, as well as the competition from rural village markets on Baden soil.

Freiburg, at least, could boast of one compensation for its dwindling economic centrality. The foundation of the university in 1457 created a not insignificant population of professors and students as consumers of urban goods and services. But with Freiburg's rigid adherence to Catholicism the 1520s saw a sharp decline in matriculations, so that the economic benefits of the university's presence were greatly dissipated.²⁷

---

[23] Ibid., p. 265. [24] Terao, 'Rural Small Towns', p. 82.
[25] Cf. R. A. French, 'The Early and Medieval Russian Town', in James H. Bater and R. A. French (eds.), *Studies in Russian Historical Geography* (2 vols., London/New York, 1983), ii. 265.
[26] A central-place system for the Upper Rhine in the 16th c. would, however, differ appreciably from the modern pattern of the Strasbourg region described in Christaller, *Die zentralen Orte*, pp. 217–35. Cf. also the more recent study by H. Gardiner Barnum, *Market Centers and Hinterlands in Baden-Württemberg* (University of Chicago, Department of Geography Research Paper, ciii) (Chicago, 1966).
[27] The lack of reliable sources and a dearth of specialized studies make it very difficult to pursue the other four variables, apart from market function, put forward by Hektor Ammann in determining Freiburg's importance as a central place.

Conclusion

Should Freiburg's experience of decline, therefore, be interpreted as part of a general late medieval urban crisis? Recent research on England has suggested that the period from the fifteenth to the early sixteenth century displayed all the symptoms of such a crisis—falling populations, financial disarray, economic impoverishment, a flight from office, and the rise of rural competition in the production and marketing of goods.[28] Once under way, the process of decay fed upon itself. Since towns were always demographic parasities upon their hinterlands, the fall in inhabitants led to a rapidly ageing population; the capacity of their sluggish economies had shrunk too far to respond to renewed demand: towns, in other words, were without defence against rural by-employments and proto-industrial manufacturing.[29] The evidence for widespread urban decline in England has, none the less, been challenged.[30] Clearly, a fall in population should not automatically be equated with economic retrogression,[31] though rickety municipal budgets and a shortfall of office-holders were commonly enough attested to indicate that all was not well in late medieval council-chambers.[32] In place of a general urban crisis a truer picture may perhaps be gained by examining the demographic and economic fluctuations within a given region. In the case of Coventry, for instance, whose 'desolation' had been so vividly depicted by Charles Phythian-Adams, what stands out is the revival of population in the smaller country towns of surrounding Warwickshire at the same time as the city's was languishing. In general, by the later sixteenth century the lesser market towns seem to have been prospering whilst the county towns and regional centres stagnated or declined.[33]

At first glance these findings might seem to reflect the reality of Freiburg's situation with uncanny accuracy, even though by the

---

[28] Charles Phythian-Adams, *Desolation of a City. Coventry and the Urban Crisis of the Late Middle Ages* (Past and Present Publications) (Cambridge, 1979); idem, 'Urban Decay in Late Medieval England', in Philip Abrams and E. A. Wrigley (eds.), *Towns in Societies: Essays in Economic History and Historical Sociology* (Cambridge, 1978), 159–85; R. B. Dobson, 'Urban Decline in Late Medieval England', *Transactions of the Royal Historical Society*, 5th series xxv (1977), 1–22.

[29] Phythian-Adams, *Desolation of a City*, pp. 281 ff.

[30] Cf. esp. Alan Dyer, 'Growth and Decay in English Towns 1500–1700', *Urban History Yearbook*, 1979, 60–72.

[31] Susan Reynolds, 'Decline and Decay in Late Medieval Towns: A Look at Some of the Concepts and Arguments', *Urban History Yearbook*, 1981, 76.

[32] S. H. Rigby, 'Urban Decline in the Later Middle Ages: The Reliability of the Non-Statistical Evidence', *Urban History Yearbook*, 1984, 45–60.

[33] Dyer, 'Growth and Decay', p. 64.

fifteenth century it had ceased to be a regional commercial centre on the scale of Coventry. Yet neither the advanced political fragmentation nor the diversified, 'Mediterranean' character of the rural economy of the Upper Rhine find any obvious parallel in late medieval England. Despite these structural dissimilarities, however, research on English urban decay underlines the present analysis of Freiburg in two essential respects. On the one hand, it suggests that late medieval towns were often seriously undercapitalized;[34] on the other, it acknowledges that craft gilds were not the invariable authors of urban decline by their unswerving hostility towards economic innovation and investment.[35] For the first, Freiburg had been stripped of its assets after the decline of the silver-mines and the costs of the war of independence; for the second, the carefully managed and cautiously introduced policy of economic protectionism, which was the consequence not the cause of Freiburg's misfortunes, gradually restored the town's economy to an even keel in the face of a contracting market area and much reduced opportunities for profitable commercial enterprise.

[34] Cf. Charles Phythian-Adams, 'Dr Dyer's Urban Undulations', *Urban History Yearbook*, 1979, 75. Dyer concurs in this view.

[35] Cf. Langton and Hoppe, *Town and Country*, p. 39, referring to the economic growth spearheaded by urban gilds in Nottingham and Newcastle.

PART THREE

THE AGE OF PEASANT REVOLT

VI
The Bundschuh Uprisings

I

THROUGHOUT the fifteenth century the Upper Rhine was on permanent alert. The diplomatic turmoil surrounding the Council of Constance infected the whole of South-West Germany, for political rivalries led to the alienation of the western Habsburg lands from duke Frederick of Austria for over a decade after 1415. Even the eventual restoration of Austrian rule in 1427 brought little prospect of calm, since it served only to resurrect the ancient struggle between the Habsburgs and the Swiss for control of the former's territorial bastion in the Aargau. The dukes' campaigns to repulse the Swiss drained the Outer Austrian lands of men and money; moreover, they created a sense of psychological insecurity—the feeling of living in a frontier area which would never see peace. This anxiety was heightened by the incursions of French mercenaries in mid-century, and was borne out by archduke Sigismund's effective abandonment of the Upper Rhine in 1469, when he pawned the bulk of the outer lands to a foreign prince, duke Charles the Bold of Burgundy. Considering the sacrifices which the Austrian military campaigns had imposed upon the population, the Burgundian mortgage must have seemed a bitter betrayal. Though the local lords and cities in the wake of the Burgundian collapse five years later at last formed a league of mutual defence, the Lower Union,[1] it had previously fallen largely to the common people to withstand foreign aggressors and marauders. Many of the leagues of resistance which peasants and burghers formed in desperate emergency threatened subsequently to spill over into

---

[1] Albert Rosenkranz, *Der Bundschuh. Die Erhebungen des südwestdeutschen Bauernstandes in den Jahren 1493–1517* (Schriften des Wissenschaftlichen Instituts der Elsaß-Lothringer im Reich, xii) (2 vols., Heidelberg, 1927), i. 11. Cf. A. W. Matzinger, 'Zur Geschichte der niederen Vereinigung' (Diss. phil. Basel, 1910). The term 'Lower Union' was coined in deliberate contrast to the 'Upper Union' of the Swiss Confederates. Cf. most recently Thomas A. Brady Jr., *Turning Swiss. Cities and Empire, 1450–1550* (Cambridge Studies in Early Modern History) (Cambridge, 1985).

instruments of vengeance against the authorities who had cravenly abandoned their subjects.

Popular unrest in South-West Germany swelled as the fifteenth century wore on, until by the 1490s the Upper Rhine was in a state of perpetual uproar. Amongst the many disturbances certain, whose character, organization, and aims are supposed to embody a new and more radical strand of popular rebellion, have long attracted particular interest—a revolutionary tradition fired by the ideological motive of divine justice which culminated in the Peasants' War of 1524–6. These were the Bundschuh uprisings, named after the peasants' laced boot, which became a charged emblem on the rebels' banners. These revolts were regarded with especial terror by the authorities on account of their drawing-power and tight-knit organization, so that any whisper of a planned Bundschuh sent them into a state of panic.

Long before the fifteenth century the Bundschuh had become a commonplace symbol of popular solidarity and resistance. A familiar legend told of 'duke Bundschuh', count Eckhart of Scheyern, who had carried two red-laced boots to rally the common man on a crusade to Jerusalem in the mid-eleventh century.[2] By the end of the fourteenth century the Bundschuh was being used to describe popular alliances; a chronicler remarked of the defeat of the Rhenish city league in 1398: 'domit nam der grosse buntschuoch ein ende.'[3] On the Upper Rhine the Bundschuh came to epitomize popular resistance to the irruptions of Armagnac mercenaries and the French and Burgundian armies— witness such leagues in Strasbourg in 1439, the Westrich in 1443, and in Schwörstadt by Säckingen in 1444.[4] From the necessity of self-defence the Bundschuh quickly turned against the local feudal authorities, as borne out by revolts in Schliengen in 1443 against the bishop of Basel, and the Hegau west of lake Constance in 1460, where with the aid and encouragement of the Swiss the peasants rounded on their Austrian lords, besieged several towns, and in one village stole the sacrament from the church and cut off the fingers of the priests who tried to prevent them.[5] This incident highlights what were to become leitmotivs of the later Bundschuh rebellions: their attraction towards the Swiss deriving from a vision of alpine communal liberty,

[2] Rosenkranz, *Bundschuh*, i. 15 n. 1.
[3] Günther Franz, 'Zur Geschichte des Bundschuhs', *ZGO* xlvii (1934), 5.
[4] Rosenkranz, *Bundschuh*, i. 14–15; Günther Franz, *Der deutsche Bauernkrieg*, 8th edn. (Darmstadt, 1963), 53–4.
[5] Idem (ed.), *Quellen zur Geschichte des Bauernkrieges* (Darmstadt, 1963), 62; idem, 'Bundschuh', p. 11; idem, *Bauernkrieg*, p. 55.

and the violent anticlericalism which the rebels displayed. In the Alsatian Bundschuh around Sélestat in 1493 one of the principal aims was to enlist the support of the Confederates in Berne and Zürich.[6] During the years of the Burgundian mortgage the Swiss had stood forth as the only force capable of withstanding Charles the Bold, and the potency of this example was tellingly revealed in 1473 when a priest in Basel taunted a messenger from Freiburg that they would all soon become good Swiss, a slur which the Austrian city was quick to reject with outrage.[7]

Günther Franz has demonstrated that the elements of anticlericalism and indeed of anti-Semitism in the Bundschuh hark back to much earlier traditions,[8] but what is so striking is their virulence on the Upper Rhine, particularly in Alsace. There the use of ecclesiastical courts to hear what were effectively civil pleas, above all suits for debt, was a constant source of complaint. These grievances were well known to the authorities. In 1488 the Outer Austrian governor warned the bishop of Basel that prosecutions in his courts were costing the peasants dearly and were driving them off the land. Unless matters improved, he declared, there would be a violent eruption of hatred against the clergy.[9] The issue of ecclesiastical courts was debated before the Outer Austrian diets, and in 1518 the Breisgau towns singled out as a particular abuse the Basel episcopal courts' overstepping their proper jurisdiction.[10]

These features have inspired generations of historians to treat the Bundschuh as especial and distinct from other late medieval German revolts. In the Bundschuh, as Franz and Rosenkranz argued, the tradition of popular self-defence combined with radical anticlericalism under the slogan of the struggle for divine law to forge a potentially revolutionary movement which in contrast to the majority of localized and spontaneous revolts brought together peasants from many separate lordships and the lower orders in the towns in a broad alliance of the oppressed.[11] Rosenkranz saw his argument confirmed by the wave of violent Bundschuh rebellions from 1493 onwards: the Alsatian Bundschuh of that year around Sélestat; the Bundschuh of 1502 in the

---

[6] Rosenkranz, *Bundschuh*, i. 68.
[7] F. J. Mone (ed.), *Quellensammlung der badischen Landesgeschichte*, iii (Karlsruhe, 1863), 426; Brauer-Gramm, *Hagenbach*, p. 276.
[8] Franz. *Bauernkrieg*, p. 43–4.
[9] AAEB, Extradita Wien 42 (new [Basel] 28), ad 27g, 24 Mar. 1488.
[10] StAFr, C 1 Landstände 3, 14 Mar.–4 May 1518.
[11] Franz, *Bauernkrieg*, pp. 41 ff.; Rosenkranz, *Bundschuh*, i. 12 ff.

bishopric of Speyer; the Bundschuh centred upon Lehen in the Breisgau eleven years later; and finally the plan for a general Bundschuh rebellion throughout the Upper Rhine in 1517. All aimed utterly or partly to destroy the feudal order in church and state by force of arms, and all strove consciously to unite both town and country in common rebellion.[12]

A detailed critique of this view lies beyond the bounds of the present argument.[13] What is clear, however, is that until the later fifteenth century the Bundschuh uprisings had little in common except their name. They were too sporadic to constitute a sustained expression of crisis on the south-west frontier of the Empire;[14] too disparate in aims to be subsumed into an unbroken pattern of radical religious protest; and too heterogeneous in composition to be taken as broad alliances of the commons in town and country fighting arm in arm.[15] This mistake is only possible if one divorces the Bundschuh uprisings from the wider context in which they occurred so as to construct an artificially distinct and coherent Bundschuh 'movement'. The later rebellions did indeed hoist the Bundschuh as their emblem because of its familiarity and potency as a symbol of popular resistance, but that tells us very little about why they were radical. Rather than invoking a self-propelling revolutionary tradition which assumes that only revolts fired by an ideology can be radical, and that only an overarching ideology can bridge the gulf between town and country, it must be stressed that whether the later Bundschuh uprisings were revolutionary and whether peasants and burghers were prepared to make common cause depended neither upon the content nor upon the character of their demands but upon the particular and varying circumstances in which they were expressed.

II

The first genuinely radical Bundschuh, conceived as an organized conspiracy, began in a few villages north of the Alsatian imperial city of Sélestat in 1493. The peasants' grievances stemmed less from the weight of feudal dues than from judicial abuses and delays, particularly

---

[12] Ibid., p. 4.   [13] Cf. Scott, 'Relations', pp. 414 ff., with references.
[14] Cf. Hartmut Boockmann, 'Zu den geistigen und religiösen Voraussetzungen des Bauernkrieges', in Bernd Moeller (ed.), *Bauernkriegs-Studien* (Schriften des Vereins für Reformationsgeschichte, clxxxix, vol. 82,2/83) (Gütersloh, 1975), 25–6.
[15] Scott, 'Relations', pp. 427 ff.

citations before the Strasbourg episcopal court and the imperial court of justice in Rottweil.[16] Unlike the towns, who often blocked referrals by invoking their privilege of judicial exclusivity, the peasantry had no means of escaping such summons. The majority of cases arose from debt arrears, as the peasants found themselves unable to repay loans from the scores of money-lenders, sometimes Jews,[17] who preyed upon the Alsatian countryside. Because such complaints were not confined to particular lordships, they furnished the pre-conditions for a broad rebellion, whose programme went well beyond the rectification of specific abuses. This programme was the work of Jakob Hanser, the village magistrate of Blienschwiller, a man of some education and breadth of vision (he could probably read and write), whose standing enabled him to act as a 'broker' or intermediary with the neighbouring towns.[18]

In mid-February Hanser approached a close relative, Hans Ulman,[19] a butcher and former burgomaster of Sélestat, whose influence and support were essential if the revolt was to be militarily successful. Ulman had fallen from grace in Sélestat, having failed to be re-elected to the council in 1492.[20] He seems to have been a rancorous and divisive personality, whose grudge against his home town led him to harbour notions of rebellion. The Bundschuh provided a unique opportunity. Ulman joined on the understanding that he would recruit a following in Sélestat itself whilst Hanser continued to mobilize support in the surrounding villages. On 23 March conspirators from eight villages and Sélestat foregathered on a desolate hill, the Ungersberg, where Hanser insisted that they swear an oath of absolute secrecy. Thereafter, however, Ulman seems to have taken charge of the proceedings, for on his instigation the rebels adopted a list of demands which encompassed the abolition of foreign courts and the expulsion of the Jews, and the cancellation of all existing tolls, excises, and the territorial property tax in favour of a flat rate to be paid by all.

---

[16] Cf. Karl Stenzel, 'Die geistlichen Gerichte Straßburgs im 15. Jahrhundert', *ZGO* NF xxix (1914), 394–418.

[17] Although Dr H. J. Cohn has rightly pointed out that only a minority of suits for debt were brought before the Strasbourg courts by Jews, there can be no questioning the overt hostility towards Jews expressed both in the Bundschuh and the Peasants' War in Alsace. For references to the latter, cf. ADHR, E 658, 659.

[18] Franz, *Bauernkrieg*, p. 58 believed that Hanser was a much travelled man who had visited the Frankfurt fair. In fact he only went there after the Bundschuh had been betrayed. Rosenkranz, *Bundschuh*, ii. 6.

[19] Ibid., pp. 10–11.   [20] Rosenkranz, *Bundschuh*, i. 41–2.

In addition they agreed to raise money from the Alsatian territorial estates in order to regain possession of a town seal (presumably Sélestat's) which had been pawned. Hanser proposed that priests should be limited to one benefice worth no more than 50 fl. per annum, and those clerics who resisted should be slain, but the conspirators apparently refused to endorse such a drastic proposal, and it was dropped.[21] Some of the peasants were reluctant to contemplate armed rebellion at all, but the majority finally agreed upon the programme of demands and drew up a plan of campaign. Captains from four different lordships were nominated to lead the revolt, and if necessary they were to seek the military support of the Swiss Confederacy. Recruitment was to continue until the autumn when the revolt was to start.

On its outbreak Ulman planned to capture one or more leading towns in order to lay hands on a supply of money and weapons and to establish a fortified base of operations. Uppermost was naturally his ambition to capture Sélestat itself and regain power; on the Ungersberg he claimed to have almost five hundred citizens already on his side. Only with Sélestat under their control did the leaders intend to unfurl a Bundschuh flag and march on Dambach, Rosheim, Obernai, and other centres as the entire Alsatian peasantry rallied to their cause. But these schemes came to naught. Four days after the assembly on the Ungersberg the conspiracy had been betrayed. The leaders were caught, tried, and put to death, though Hanser managed to escape.[22]

How far the Bundschuh of 1493 could have succeeded in transforming itself into a mass movement embracing the commons of town and country remains very doubtful. The grievances which inspired the planned revolt were confined to the peasantry, as Franz indeed recognized.[23] Complaints against the use of foreign courts hardly affected burghers, who themselves often deployed such courts against the peasantry.[24] Moreover, the peasants' hostility towards the Jews was unlikely to find much echo in the larger Alsatian towns which had expelled their Israelite communities nearly twenty years before.[25]

---

[21] Rosenkranz, *Bundschuh*, ii. 15–16. [22] Rosenkranz, *Bundschuh*, i. 80 ff.
[23] Franz. *Bauernkrieg*, pp. 58–9.
[24] There is some evidence that the rebels also demanded the abolition of the towns' right of *unverzogenes Recht*, whereby they could force any cases involving burghers to be heard before the civic courts, a weapon which was freely used by townsmen against peasant debtors. Cf. Scott, 'Relations', p. 442 n. 1.
[25] Rosenkranz, *Bundschuh*, i. 33.

Conversely, the plan to regain a town seal was not a very probable rallying-cry for the Alsatian villagers. In other words, the grievances of town and country had very little in common, which accounts for the incongruity of the Bundschuh demands. How far the peasants could have been won over to a more militant attack upon the power of the Church once the revolt was under way is hard to tell, though the deep anticlericalism of the Alsatian countryside was highly evident in the Peasants' War itself.[26] Support in the towns for such an attack was bound to depend in large measure upon their relations with the Church not only as a spiritual but also as a temporal authority: whether, for instance, a town stood under the same ecclesiastical princely jurisdiction as its surrounding countryside, as was the case with Rouffach.

How essential the leadership of a widely known and influential burgher was in recruiting support emerges from the strong reluctance of one participant, Klaus Ziegler from Stotzheim, to join the conspiracy until he was assured that Ulman and others of his stature had already pledged themselves.[27] But Ulman's alliance with the peasants was purely tactical and self-interested; he made little effort to rally support for the Bundschuh's demands within Sélestat itself, preferring merely to boast of a following of five hundred when the town had little over four hundred citizens fit for military service.[28] In fact, no more than five inhabitants were known to have been implicated in the Bundschuh.[29] Ulman's position shows certain parallels with that of Walzenmüller in Freiburg, though he appears more as a lone figure forced to drum up a following outside the town rather than as the leader of a broad commons' movement. Rosenkranz argued that the severity with which Sélestat pursued the conspirators leaves no doubt that it was confronted with widespread opposition within its own walls, but such severity may equally be a sign that, unlike Freiburg, the

---

[26] Nowhere in the confessions of the conspirators is there any indication that the Bundschuh of 1493 was inspired by or embraced the slogan of divine law. The most that can be said is that Ulman confessed that Hanser had approached him for support in the 'godly' task of rectifying their grievances, and that he had agreed that their demands were just and godly. Rosenkranz, *Bundschuh*, ii. 11.

[27] Ibid., p. 14.

[28] Cf. Joseph Gény, *Die Reichsstadt Schlettstadt und ihr Antheil an den social-politischen und religiösen Bewegungen der Jahre 1490–1536* (Erläuterungen und Ergänzungen zur Janssens Geschichte des deutschen Volkes, i) (Freiburg, 1900), 419. His figures for Sélestat's population were revised downwards, however, by Joseph Krischer, *Die Verfassung und Verwaltung der Reichsstadt Schlettstadt im Mittelalter* (Strasbourg, 1909), 71.

[29] Rosenkranz, *Bundschuh*, i. 51.

opposition was too weak and too small to need to be appeased.

What was true of Sélestat as an Imperial Free City, though, was not necessarily applicable to the smaller Alsatian territorial towns whose civic privileges guaranteed them neither independence nor defence against the exactions of their lords. Dambach, for instance, had been granted its civic charter in the mid-fourteenth century, but the town belonged, and was subject, to the bishop of Strasbourg. Its inhabitants were peasant burghers whose status barely differed from that of the surrounding villages. Moreover, as part of the bishop's secular territories it was obliged to grant residence to Jews who had fled from the imperial cities. One Jew in Dambach was apparently notorious throughout the region for his dishonest dealing and maltreatment of the peasantry.[30] No wonder, therefore, that the Bundschuh quickly attracted a sizeable following in Dambach, whose ranks included two men known to have been badly in debt.[31] The same argument applies to Andlau, the home of Ulrich Schütz, one of the four Bundschuh captains, which was no more than a small walled market community in the midst of the lordship of Andlau and subject to the nobles of that ilk.

The fate of Ulrich Schütz provides an interesting sequel which illumines Freiburg's reaction to the growth of agrarian unrest. After the betrayal of the Bundschuh Schütz escaped across the Rhine and took refuge in the household of David von Landeck in Ebnet. Once he was discovered the council made strenuous efforts, including the despatch of an armed posse, to bring Schütz to book, but Landeck refused to hand him over until compelled by the government in Ensisheim.[32] There ensued a complicated legal battle in which the old resentments between Freiburg and the Breisgau nobility surfaced afresh, but finally Schütz was sentenced to have his oath-fingers cut off, a fate far milder than befell either Ulman or Ziegler.[33] Freiburg's own narrative of the proceedings shows plainly how alarmed the council was by the danger of seditious infection on its very doorstep,[34] and how relentlessly it sought to punish Schütz despite Landeck's delaying tatics.[35] The council's behaviour was a foretaste of things to come.

[30] Ibid., pp. 33–4.
[31] Rosenkranz, *Bundschuh*, ii. 58.
[32] Ibid., pp. 50–1.
[33] Rosenkranz, *Bundschuh*, i. 108–10.
[34] At the meeting on the Ungersberg a villager from Blienschwiller who had served in a Black Forest monastery was entrusted with recruiting further support on the right bank of the Rhine. Ibid., p. 69. Whether anything came of this plan is unknown.
[35] StAFr, B 2 4, p. 144; Rosenkranz, *Bundschuh*, ii. 74–5.

Although it was never launched, the Alsatian Bundschuh by its composition and objectives contained the potential for a more deliberate and radical mode of rebellion which was to be taken up again at the beginning of the sixteenth century in the bishopric of Speyer under one of the most remarkable figures in the history of popular rebellion in early modern Germany, Joss Fritz from Untergrombach near Bruchsal.

III

The Bundschuh of 1502 began in the Bruhrain, the area between Bruchsal and Wiesloch. From the outset it displayed a cohesion and determination which surpassed the revolt of 1493. Peasants and townsfolk under the worldly jurisdiction of the bishop of Speyer united in opposition to bishop Ludwig, whose precarious finances had led him to step up taxation and curtail customary rights. From 1482 onwards Ludwig issued a series of forest ordinances whch restricted his subjects' grazing and timber rights and put a limit on the number of beasts they could hold.[36] After 1500 the inhabitants of the small episcopal town of Bruchsal faced a vastly increased excise duty whose collection was stringently enforced by the bishop's officials.[37] Though older charges of extravagance and bad housekeeping levied against the bishop have been questioned by recent scholarship,[38] there is no doubt that Ludwig found himself at the turn of the fifteenth century in a similar financial and administrative predicament to that of many other German princes, and sought to extricate himself by greater impositions on his subjects. Their hardships were compounded by the ravages of a feud against the Swabian League in 1490 and a period of dearth and rising prices after 1500 which caused many peasants to seek help from the bishop in cash or in kind. Bishop Ludwig, who had a reputation for gentleness and charity, gave help where he could, but remained ultimately the prisoner of his chronic indebtedness. The peasantry could hardly be expected to sympathize with his predicament, however, since they had to bear the growing weight of boon-services, tithes, tolls, and taxes from which the clergy were largely exempt.[39]

[36] Rosenkranz, *Bundschuh*, i. 158–9.   [37] Ibid., p. 163–6.
[38] Lawrence Gerald Duggan, *Bishop and Chapter. The Governance of the Bishopric of Speyer to 1552* (Studies presented to the International Commission for the History of Representative and Parliamentary Institutions, lxii) (New Brunswick, NJ, 1978), 176, 179, 263–4. He is particularly critical of Franz, *Bauernkrieg*, pp. 62–8.
[39] Rosenkranz, *Bundschuh*, i. 170, 193.

The grievances of the Speyer subjects did not lead to a spontaneous uprising: the Bundschuh was the work of Joss Fritz alone, an episcopal bondman who emerged as a genuine political revolutionary and went on to organize and direct the wider conspiracies of 1513 and 1517. Very little is known of him, except that he must have been a charismatic figure of extraordinary resourcefulness and conviction. How his revolutionary ideas developed is obscure, though as an episcopal subject he knew the hatred of the clergy at first hand. Yet Fritz contemplated more than simply a savage destruction of the ecclesiastical hierarchy. He aimed to purge and purify the Church in accordance with the tenets of divine justice. This religious inspiration was manifested in the ritual of the Speyer Bundschuh. Those who joined were required to recite five Paternosters and five Ave Marias on their knees; the Bundschuh password ran, 'God greet you, fellow. How fares the world?' with the reply, 'We cannot rid ourselves of the plague of priests.' The Bundschuh flag contained a crucified Christ and the Gregorian man of sorrows, together with the legend 'nothing save the justice of the Lord'.[40]

The demands of the conspirators, articulated at stealthy meetings in the countryside, envisaged abolition of the Church's privileges and power, expropriation of its property, and a return to apostolic poverty. Control of all ecclesiastical foundations was to pass to the peasantry who would strictly limit the number of priests and determine communally their appointment and remuneration. Nor were the secular lords to be spared. The rebels attacked the basis of feudal lordship by demanding free rights of hunting and fishing and unrestricted usufruct of pasture and woodland, to be controlled by the village communities. By the same token the Bundschuh demanded the abolition of all feudal dues, both ecclesiastical and lay: tithes, rents, taxes, and tolls were to be swept away.[41] Unlike the Sélestat Bundschuh the rebels intended from the outset to press their demands by physical force. First they meant to march on the bishop's castle at Obergrombach to secure a stronghold, and then to Bruchsal where they reckoned on the support of four hundred citizens. Thence they planned to capture Udenheim (Philippsburg), the seat of the bishop himself, and afterwards head eastwards through episcopal territory

---

[40] Rosenkranz, *Bundschuh*, ii. 89–90. For an exhaustive discussion of the Bundschuh flags and their imagery cf. Ulrich Steinmann, 'Die Bundschuh-Fahnen des Joss Fritz', *Deutsches Jahrbuch für Volkskunde*, vi (1960), 243–84.

[41] Rosenkranz, *Bundschuh*, ii. 90–2.

towards the margraviate of Baden-Durlach, whilst making overtures to the Swiss.[42]

These plans never materialized, for a delay in launching the revolt (the flag was not ready) allowed a mercenary who had enlisted to betray the conspiracy to the bishop in person.[43] News of the impending revolt was quickly passed to the bishop of Strasbourg who, drawing his lesson from the events of 1493, immediately ordered a full-scale man-hunt on the left bank of the Rhine.[44] The conspirators were rounded up and interrogated; ten were executed and many more banished or fined. But the begetter and commander of the Bundschuh, Joss Fritz, managed to escape.[45]

At the heart of the conspiracy in and around Bruchsal the Bundschuh undoubtedly gained a considerable following. Within the town the figure of four hundred conspirators, mostly adult males, is plausible,[46] whilst in Untergrombach, Fritz's home village, all but eight peasants were supposed to have joined the Bundschuh, and in the nearby villages another five hundred supporters had already been sworn in. The episcopal officials were convinced that the Imperial Free City of Speyer itself harboured numerous sympathizers. There was certainly unrest in the city, directed chiefly at the clergy for amassing property and accumulating rent-charges, which ran parallel with many of the Bundschuh's grievances and was to erupt in the urban revolt of 1512. Joss Fritz's plan of campaign ostensibly ignored Speyer altogether, concentrating instead on the smaller episcopal territorial towns to the south-east. Rosenkranz regarded this as a crass strategic error, evidence of the haphazard and ill-considered nature of Fritz's schemes.[47] But a man who recognized the importance of mercenaries in his campaign, who employed forty agents throughout the whole of

[42] Ibid., pp. 89–92.
[43] Ibid., p. 95.   [44] Ibid., pp. 98–100, 109, 115–16.
[45] Ibid., pp. 95–6. Fritz did not remain idle, for at the end of June reports reached Maximilian that a new Bundschuh was in the making which planned to invade the imperial bailiwick of Haguenau in Alsace. ADHR, E 657. Maximilian to count Wolf [of Fürstenberg], 25 June 1502.
[46] Abbot Johannes Trithemius, upon whose garbled and unreliable account much of our knowledge of the 1502 Bundschuh depends, believed that half Bruchsal's population of around 2,500 had enlisted. The figure of 2,075 given for its population by Kuno Drollinger, *Kleine Städte Südwestdeutschlands* (Veröffentlichungen der Kommission für geschichtliche Landeskunde in Baden-Württemberg, Reihe B xlviii) (Stuttgart, 1968), 11 is probably too low, and is based upon an unsatisfactory analysis of the source in GLA 67/314, fos. 211^r–223^r. It has been accepted unquestioningly by Duggan, *Bishop and Chapter*, p. 175.
[47] Rosenkranz, *Bundschuh*, i. 204.

the south-west to spread the seeds of revolt, and who hoped to raise an army of at least 20,000 and keep it on the move ready for battle, cannot be accused of blustering ineptitude.[48] If the Bundschuh had succeeded, then Speyer would probably have been besieged in due course. The planned march south-eastwards led down an important trade route to the margravial capital, Pforzheim. Its conquest would have given the Bundschuh a bridgehead into foreign territory and a stronghold from which to raise the whole of the Upper Rhine. Moreover, according to one account, the Bundschuh had already gained a sizeable following in and around Pforzheim, though it is far from clear what grievances the inhabitants shared with the Speyer peasants.

What remains mysterious is the striking absence from the catalogue of conspirators of the Palatine peasantry, even though subjects of the Elector were to be found in Speyer villages, indeed in Untergrombach itself.[49] There is no reason in principle to doubt that they would in the end have joined ranks with their neighbours, especially since close contact between subjects of different lords resident in one village could not help but heighten their political awareness by comparison and contrast with the variations and anomalies in their respective rights and obligations.

IV

The wave of unrest in South-West Germany which had left the Breisgau relatively unscathed ebbed in the next decade, but, when the tide turned, a fresh storm of insurrection engulfed the whole of the Upper Rhine with the Breisgau as its epicentre and Freiburg as its principal target. By 1513, when the new Bundschuh was planned, the city was no stranger to protest within and without its walls, but the conspiracy which Joss Fritz launched in Lehen, a mere two miles to the west of Freiburg, far outstripped all previous manifestations of discontent both in radicalism and extent.

After the Speyer Bundschuh Joss Fritz went underground. For ten years no news of him reached the authorities, though there are indications that he may have served in a Swiss mercenary army. The beginning of the second decade of the sixteenth century, however, saw him settled in the Breisgau acting as a field-watch for the village community of Lehen. Gradually he took stock of his surroundings and

[48] Cf. Rosenkranz, *Bundschuh*, ii. 100–1.
[49] Rosenkranz, *Bundschuh*, i. 179 n. 1.

prepared the ground for a fresh uprising. His chief recruitment lay amongst the peasants of the many fragmented, diminutive, and overlapping jurisdictions of the Breisgau country lords. Some were Austrian vassals, others bailiffs of the margraves of Baden, but all were concerned to underpin their rights of lordship by imposing exclusive allegiance on their subjects by means of local bondage. Many of these lesser lords were the victims of rising expenditure set against fixed revenues in an age of gathering inflation. To compensate they sought to retrict the usufruct of common—forest, pasture, water—and to demand higher recognition fees from their serfs. In common with the Alsatian Bundschuh of 1493 rural indebtedness gave rise to frequent complaint. The peasants voiced resentment at the wrongful and oppressive use of church courts and the high rates of interest on loans. Caught between arbitrary lordship and adverse economic pressures the grievances of the Bundschuh rebels can readily be understood.

A particularly telling example of the peasantry's afflictions is provided by the bitter dispute in 1511 between Gabriel von Bollschweil, a noble outburgher and heir to one of the several branches of the old Freiburg patrician dynasty of Snewlin, and his subjects in the villages of Bollschweil and Biezighofen. As well as reciting a whole catalogue of concrete infringements of their rights, the peasants protested at Bollschweil's high-handed and tyrannical behaviour, which even the Outer Austrian estates conceded.[50] He had scoffed at any attempt to appeal to Maximilian and scabrously taunted his serfs that they must do as he say or else be cut to pieces.[51] One of the bondmen called to testify in court was Kilian Meiger, a villager of Lehen who became Joss Fritz's first recruit and chief henchman in the Bundschuh two years later.

During the spring and summer of 1513 under the pretext of helping the cause of divine justice[52] Fritz and his fellow-conspirators succeeded in gaining a foothold in a good number of Breisgau villages—Lehen, Betzenhausen, Munzingen, Haslach, Merzhausen, Au, Leutersberg, Wolfenweiler, Schallstadt, Norsingen, Mengen, Merdingen, and in the Glotter valley. Strikingly enough, only one of these villages—Merdingen—contained any outburghers by 1513. Of all the known conspirators only one was an outburgher, though he was

[50] StAFr, B 5 XI, viii, 2, fo. 184^{r-v}. Cf. A 1 XIV Schnewlin: Bärlapp-Bollschweil 30, 7 Nov. 1511.
[51] GLA 229/8577. Article xxiv.
[52] Cf. Rosenkranz, *Bundschuh*, i. 292.

Hans Schwarz, the village priest of Lehen,[53] who encouraged Fritz to believe that the Bundschuh was a just and godly undertaking. At first glance the absence of outburghers seems surprising: their standing in the villages and their connections with Freiburg made them ideal 'brokers' who could use their position both to attract support amongst their own communities and to recruit townsfolk in a like manner to Jakob Hanser in 1493. As outburghers they bore the brunt of the village lords' harassment, against which Freiburg's protection was visibly faltering. The behaviour of the Merdingen outburghers at the Ebringen church-ale in 1495 and the loud protestations by the Waltershofen community at its abandonment ten years later show plainly that their loyalty to Freiburg was rapidly crumbling. All the same, the outburghers' position within the villages, it has been argued, was too anomalous and ambivalent to make them reliable allies for the rebels.

From the names that are known, it seems that Fritz was concerned to draw his ringleaders from the ranks of country craftsmen[54] and village notables, men whose perceptions and expectations outran the mass of agricultural smallholders. Although the authorities were subsequently unable to identify more than forty participants, recruitment seems to have been eminently successful. Matern Weinman, one of the rebels from Mengen, confessed that a great many peasants in the Kaiserstuhl and the march of Buchheim had sworn allegiance.[55]

Though the demands of the conspirators reflected the tension within rural society, Fritz could not simply take over the programme of the Speyer Bundschuh, which had been so deeply coloured by anti-clericalism within an ecclesiastical principality. Though it denounced clerical corruption and demanded the expropriation of all religious foundations, the Lehen Bundschuh directed its attack just as much against the exactions of the local secular nobility.[56] In his recruitment,

[53] StAFr, B 5 1 f, 2, fo. 16ᵛ.

[54] Fritz's right-hand man was Hieronymus, a journeyman miller from Lehen, who hailed from the Alto Adige (South Tirol).

[55] StAFr, C 1 Militaria 98, no. 12; Rosenkranz, *Bundschuh*, ii. 151–2. The march of Buchheim comprised the villages of Buchheim, Hochdorf, Holzhausen, Betzenhausen, Hugstetten, Oberreute, and Niederreute.

[56] The most concise account is contained in Freiburg's first report compiled between 9 and 15 Oct. from the testimonies of captured conspirators. StAFr, C 1 Militaria 98, no. 57; Rosenkranz, *Bundschuh*, ii. 144–6. Cf. also StAFr, C 1 Militaria 98, no. 6; Rosenkranz, *Bundschuh*, ii. 181–5; ADHR, 1 C 7, pp. 86–9; and the confessions of Simon Strüblin (ADHR, E 658, 18 Oct.–15 Nov. 1513; Rosenkranz, *Bundschuh*, ii. 186–8) and Jakob Huser and Kilian Meiger (AVS, AA 364; StAFr, C 1 Militaria 98, no. 23; Rosenkranz, *Bundschuh*, ii. 190–7).

indeed, Fritz appears somewhat to have played down the religious ritual and symbolism of the earlier conspiracy. Whilst he was at pains to emphasize the just and godly nature of the rebellion which would recognize the sovereignty of Pope and Emperor,[57] those who joined had only to swear an oath of secrecy rather than recite religious litanies. The Bundschuh password, too, lost its explicitly anticlerical tenor and became a general lament at the lot of the common people: 'God greet you, fellow. How fares the world?' 'In all the world the common man can find no comfort.' Nonetheless, the conspirators were encouraged to believe that they were fighting for divine justice based upon the Holy Scriptures and for a moral reform of society.[58] The flag, which was left unfinished in 1502, was completed with a Bundschuh on one side, and on the other Christ crucified, the Virgin Mary, and St John the Baptist with a peasant kneeling before them, along with the insignia of Pope and Emperor and the legend: 'Lord, stand by Thy Divine Justice.'[59]

By the beginning of September the flag was ready,[60] and under cover of darkness Fritz called the conspirators together in a secluded field near Lehen to agree upon the military organization of the revolt and a plan of campaign.[61] At the Biengen church-ale on 9 October, which as many conspirators as possible were to attend, the Bundschuh flag was

[57] Some peasants afterwards declared that they believed Maximilian had instructed that the rebels be neither tortured nor executed. StAFr, B 5 XI, ix, fos. 97^v–98^r; Rosenkranz, *Bundschuh*, ii. 165–6.

[58] One conspirator, Konrad Brun, from Freiburg's village of Betzenhausen, even claimed that the aim of the Bundschuh was ultimately to attain the Holy Sepulchre at Jerusalem. StAFr, C 1 Militaria 98, no. 39; Rosenkranz, *Bundschuh*, ii. 206. Brun was an elder of the church at Betzenhausen, however, and may have been something of a religious simpleton. Cf. StAFr, A 1 VIII a β 16, 14 Nov. 1510.

[59] AVS, AA 364; Rosenkranz, *Bundschuh*, ii. 193; cf. StAFr, C 1 Militaria 98, no. 57; Rosenkranz, *Bundschuh*, ii. 145. Cf. Steinmann, 'Bundschuh-Fahnen', pp. 255–6. Rosenkranz doubted whether the flag contained any slogan at all, since Fritz would otherwise have found it impossible to persuade the attendants at the shrine of the Virgin at Einsiedeln in Switzerland, whither he journeyed, disguised as a pilgrim, after the betrayal of the Bundschuh, to accept the flag as a votive offering. Rosenkranz, *Bundschuh*, i. 349. Steinmann has demonstrated, however, that Fritz put around the story of his proposed pilgrimage on purpose, in order to conceal his secret organization of the Bundschuh in Alsace after the exposure of the conspiracy on the right bank of the Rhine. Steinmann, 'Bundschuh-Fahnen', p. 266.

[60] Ibid., pp. 254–5.

[61] Rosenkranz, *Bundschuh*, i. 318; AVS, AA 364; Rosenkranz, *Bundschuh*, ii. 197. Each sworn member had to pay ½ fl., which Rosenkranz believed was intended to pay for the flag, *Bundschuh*, i. 309; StAFr, C 1 Militaria 98, no. 46; Rosenkranz, *Bundschuh*, ii. 227. In fact, as Steinmann has shown, 'Bundschuh-Fahnen', p. 250, the flag was already made in 1502; all that remained was for it to be painted.

to be unfurled in order to gauge its impact on the bystanders. In that way Fritz hoped to gain as many as two hundred new adherents at a stroke. Within a week the revolt proper was to begin. The Alsatian recruits were to cross the Rhine at Burkheim and join forces with the Breisgau contingent. Having taken Burkheim the rebels planned to march eastwards to besiege Endingen and other small country towns.[62] With these in their grasp they meant to strike southwards in order to link up with the Swiss, with whose support they could then launch a full-scale attack upon the two leading and best-fortified towns in the Breisgau, Freiburg and Breisach. Once they had succumbed, the rebels would be in control of the whole right bank of the Upper Rhine.[63] Thereupon they could hope to sweep all South-West Germany before them—a design far more shrewd and ambitious than any previous Bundschuh rising.

Once again Rosenkranz failed to appreciate the thoroughness and logic of the planned campaign. He imagined that the Bundschuh intended to attack either Freiburg, Breisach, or Endingen, although only Freiburg, he believed, was of real strategic significance. Moreover, he was puzzled why the revolt, which was due to start in mid-October, should spend nearly a month besieging towns of the second rank before attacking Freiburg on 11 November during the Martinmas fair.[64] In fact, the plan demonstrates the thoroughness of Fritz's preparations; the rebels must first make sure of controlling their rural lordships and enlisting Confederate support before embarking upon a major offensive.[65] Even so, that does not entirely account for Fritz's reluctance to attack Freiburg at once, when day by day the threat of massive retaliation was bound to grow. The answer is simple: he had no choice. The Bundschuh, it transpired, had negligible support in what was a heavily fortified and well-guarded city. To capture it, Fritz would either have had to bring up artillery and bombard the town into submission (as the peasants successfully attempted in 1525), or else raise a sufficiently large army to beleaguer the town and starve it into surrender. Neither manœuvre could be undertaken without a preliminary

---

[62] According to the confession of Simon Weber from Montbéliard, the rebels planned to march on Staufen and then on the margravial town of Sulzburg. Staatsbibliothek Munich, Codex germ. 4925, fo. 240 (inserted leaf). This undated document is assigned by Franz, 'Bundschuh', p. 18 n. 2 to 1513. The ascription is plausible, though not entirely compelling: it may refer to the Upper Rhine Bundschuh of 1517.
[63] Cf. Rosenkranz, *Bundschuh*, ii. 145, 185, 191.
[64] Rosenkranz, *Bundschuh*, i. 321–2.
[65] Cf. AVS, AA 364; Rosenkranz, *Bundschuh*, ii. 191.

campaign to win over the more tractable towns, within whose walls the rebels could hope to find arms, equipment, and support. In fact Joss Fritz chose a third course—to take Freiburg by surprise. But that had to wait upon a suitable opportunity such as a fair, when the presence of hundreds of peasants from the surrounding villages would occasion neither comment nor alarm.

To seize Freiburg was not enough; Breisach, as a fortress commanding the Rhine, was strategically vital to the rebels if they were to overrun both the Breisgau and Alsace. But Breisach's capture depended upon an army with cannonry, for it was otherwise impregnable without subversion from within. It is no accident that the Alsatian rebels planned to cross the Rhine at Burkheim and then march inland to Endingen, for they thereby avoided Breisach.

But nothing was to come of these plans. The authorities had already been alerted in the summer to the possibility of another Bundschuh by an artist in Freiburg, to whom Fritz had sent a peasant to enquire whether he would decorate the Bundschuh flag. The painter, Theodosion,[66] promptly reported the incident to the council, but Freiburg could take no action apart from putting its watch on the alert and informing neighbouring lords of impending danger, since it had neither names nor descriptions of the conspirators. Not until 4 October did the authorities receive firm proof, for a conspirator from Schallstadt, Michael Hanser, revealed the names of fellow-members and the entire plan of the Bundschuh to margrave Philipp of Baden at Rötteln.[67] The margrave immediately informed Freiburg, which set about rounding up the rebels. At a hasty gathering Joss Fritz gave his last instructions to the ringleaders. Two of them, Jakob Huser and Kilian Meiger, were to accompany him to Zürich to seek assistance from the Swiss. On the way they were captured,[68] but Fritz once again contrived to escape. Undaunted he began to lay the foundations for another rising in Alsace. In the early months of 1514 there were

---

[66] Cf. AVS, AA 364; Rosenkranz, *Bundschuh*, ii. 195. It is impossible to know whether he was identical with Theodosius Bildhower who had been one of the commons' opposition in 1492.

[67] Rosenkranz, *Bundschuh*, i. 323 ff. The confession of a planned Bundschuh by a peasant to his priest after he had been waylaid by three conspirators belongs not to 1513, as Rosenkranz, ibid., p. 324 believed, but to 1517, when an identical incident was supposed to have occurred. Cf. Friedrich Schaub, 'Der Bundschuh zu Lehen', *ZFrGV* xlii (1929), 147 ff.

[68] AVS, AA 364; Rosenkranz, *Bundschuh*, ii. 193, 197.

stirrings of unrest on both banks of the Rhine,⁶⁹ in middle Baden, and by the summer in the bishop of Strasbourg's territory of the Obermundat around Rouffach as well.⁷⁰

Despite Fritz's ambitious plan of campaign it still remains open how far the Bundschuh really gained a following in the Breisgau towns. Its ringleaders made frequent journeys to Freiburg where they hoped to recruit two or three supporters in each gild who would spread the conspiracy amongst their colleagues.⁷¹ Hans Stüdlin from Lehen, for instance, had a cousin in the town, Kaspar Schwarz a former mercenary, whom the rebels hope to win over. The henchmen met in taverns such as the inn 'zum Sponhart' or visited the gild-halls. In the tailors' hall Fritz told Bernhard Enderlin that the Bundschuh stretched as far as Cologne,⁷² an obvious device to imply that those townsfolk, who were in revolt in several German cities during 1513, would combine with the peasantry in a general struggle of liberation. On his arrest Matern Weinman from Mengen maintained that half the town had joined the Bundschuh, though the council hastily reassured neighbouring authorities that the allegation was quite unfounded.⁷³ Hans Humel, a tailor living in Lehen, too boasted of a large following in Freiburg.⁷⁴ None of these statements carry conviction, least of all Humel's whose utterances were intended to win over a hesitant peasant. The only Freiburgers named in connection with the Bundschuh were Heinrich Spies, a night-watchman, and Martin Tüfel from Adelhausen, both of whom knew of the conspiracy but seem not to have been active members thereof.⁷⁵

⁶⁹ Rosenkranz, *Bundschuh*, i. 389–93. Steinmann argues that the sign of recognition used in the Upper Rhine Bundschuh (see below, n. 92); must have been agreed towards the end of 1513, for a woodcut of 1514 already indicated the thumb of the right hand tucked under the fingers on the Bundschuh ensign. Steinmann, 'Bundschuh-Fahnen', pp. 264–5, 267.
⁷⁰ Cf. HHSA, Maximiliana 32, sheaf 1, fos. 23ʳ–24ᵛ, 159ʳ–159ᵛ, 160; AAEB, Missiven 332, fo. 334ʳ⁻ᵛ. The authorities were naturally inclined to see a connection between the Poor Konrad revolt in Württemberg and the stirrings of rebellion in the Obermundat. ADHR, 1 C 7, pp. 161–8; AVS, Archives du Grand Chapitre, IV/(2), fo. 41ʳ. Cf. Jean Rott, 'Documents inédits sur le "Bundschuh" et la Guerre des Paysans en Alsace', *Revue d'Alsace*, cv (1979) 63. In fact, the disturbances in the Obermundat are more likely to be the aftermath of the known continued Bundschuh agitation in Alsace rather than a distant echo of the quite separate rising in Württemberg.
⁷¹ AVS, AA 364; Rosenkranz, *Bundschuh*, ii. 195.
⁷² StAFr, C 1 Militaria 98, no. 39; Rosenkranz, *Bundschuh*, ii. 205.
⁷³ StAFr, B 5 XI, ix, fos. 83ᵛ–84ʳ, 94ᵛ–95ᵛ, 105ʳ–107ʳ; Rosenkranz, *Bundschuh*, ii. 139, 161, 179.
⁷⁴ StAFr, C 1 Militaria, 98, no. 44a; Rosenkranz, *Bundschuh*, ii. 225.
⁷⁵ StAFr, C 1 Militaria 98, nos. 29, 30; Rosenkranz, *Bundschuh*, ii. 172–3.

The Bundschuh Uprisings

How many inhabitants would have rallied to the Bundschuh during the surprise attack at Martinmas cannot be known; but around midnight on the eve of the fair a carpenter in fact started a fire in the tavern 'zum Kiel' next door to the town hall, but when the alarm was sounded the gilds gathered in orderly fashion on the minster square without a hint of insurrection.[76] When the culprit was finally caught four years later, he admitted feeding information to the conspirators in Lehen which would have helped them to capture the town,[77] but what he can have divulged is not clear. The two groups in Freiburg most likely to be sympathetic to the Bundschuh were the wine-growers and the foreign journeymen. It is all the more remarkable, therefore, that Joss Fritz and his followers did not concentrate upon recruiting these plebeian groupings, but planned instead to win over the gilds as a whole. The explanation is quite straightforward: the Bundschuh had no interest in enlisting the wine-growers or journeymen for their own sake. Fritz had to capture the leading Breisgau towns in order to gain a series of strongholds and to forestall a counter-attack. Above all else he needed followers within Freiburg who would help subvert the inhabitants; how far they shared the grievances and aims of the peasantry was quite secondary. For his purposes the support of the wine-growers was next to useless: they were many but they were powerless. The council had kept them under strict supervision for two decades, and was never slow to expel the more obviously vagabond elements. Moreover, the only gild not to possess its own firearms was scarcely a very credible spearhead of revolt. Similar surveillance applied to the journeymen. Instead Fritz had to try to find confederates across the entire range of craftsmen. But in a town whose economic difficulties stemmed not least from the encroachment of country crafts, village markets, and rival turnpikes through its hinterland, a Bundschuh, which drew its essential support from the peasantry, had small chance of winning over to its cause those very artisans who were exposed to rural competition.

This helps to explain the singular failure of the Bundschuh leaders to draw up a programme of demands which would have united the citizens of Freiburg with the surrounding villagers. Joss Fritz's only hope of support lay in a tactical alliance with a discontented faction within the town, as had happened in the Alsatian Bundschuh of 1493. Here the Lehen Bundschuh fell victim to the mischief of historical

---

[76] StAFr B 5 XI, ix, fos. 103ʳ⁻ᵛ, 105ʳ–107ʳ; Rosenkranz, *Bundschuh*, ii. 175, 180.
[77] StAFr, C 1 Militaria 98, no. 64; Rosenkranz, *Bundschuh*, ii. 305.

accident. Had the conspiracy been launched twenty years earlier, it would have coincided with Walzenmüller's agitation. If Jakob Hanser could join forces with his cousin, Hans Ulman, in Sélestat, then Fritz might well have been able to capitalize upon Walzenmüller's attack on the town council: the situations had many parallels.

The Freiburg authorities, who regarded any sign of agrarian unrest with a mixture of loathing and horror, could not be certain how far the conspiracy had penetrated the gilds. At the first rumours of a new Bundschuh they had issued an exhaustive ordinance detailing additional guard duties and giving instructions in case of emergency.[78] With the support of the *Ächtwer*, the gilds were enjoined to remain loyal to the council and to Austria under direst penalties for transgression.[79] After the arson on the eve of the Martinmas fair the proclamation was renewed.[80] These measures illustrate how nervous the council was, but it would be unwise to interpret them as a sign of widespread ferment in the town.[81] Instead they should be seen as a reaction against the years of economic and social hardship and the decade of disturbances in the 1490s, which made both council and citizenry eager to cling to their hard-won recovery and anxious to suppress any sign of unrest which might upset the precarious balance. The council's roughshod treatment of the plebeian groups amongst the population is not a pretty sight, but there is no reason to think that the mass of Freiburg's craftsmen was fundamentally opposed to the council's policy: what aroused misgivings was not its purpose but its style.

It is characteristic that the Freiburg council took the leading role in tracking down the perpetrators. The energy which it had displayed in 1493 in bringing Ulrich Schütz to justice was now turned to hounding the Breisgau conspirators. A week before the Biengen church-ale the council had already sent scouts into the countryside to see what was afoot,[82] and on the eve of the festival an armed posse rode round the villages in search of Bundschuh members, though by then the ringleaders had sought safety in flight.[83] Freiburg alerted its neighbours in the Black Forest and Alsace[84] and appealed to the Swiss

---

[78] StAFr, C 1 Militaria 98, no. 4; Rosenkranz, *Bundschuh*, ii. 130–1.
[79] StAFr, C 1 Militaria 98, no. 5; Rosenkranz, *Bundschuh*, ii. 131–2.
[80] StAFr, C 1 Militaria 98, no. 31; Rosenkranz, *Bundschuh*, ii. 176.
[81] The older view is uncritically reiterated by Peter Seibert, *Aufstandsbewegungen in Deutschland 1476–1517 in der zeitgenössischen Reimliteratur* (Reihe Siegen. Beiträge zur Literatur- und Sprachwissenschaft, xi) (Heidelberg, 1978), 163–5.
[82] Rosenkranz, *Bundschuh*, i. 325.   [83] Ibid., pp. 332, 350.
[84] Rosenkranz, *Bundschuh*, ii. 134–5, 136, 143–4, 148–9, 150, 153–4.

Confederates for cooperation,[85] whilst a senior councillor, Ulrich Württner, was sent to Ensisheim to co-ordinate countermeasures with the Outer Austrian government.[86] During the work of pacification the council was at pains to emphasize that the rebels had not the slightest cause to revolt; from a town which over the years had expended considerable energy on defending its outburghers against harassment, quite apart from riding roughshod over the peasantry's rights whenever they clashed with the town's, that was a truly remarkable statement. In the years to come Freiburg remained relentless in pursuing conspirators who had slipped through the net.[87]

Whether the other Breisgau towns would have supported the Bundschuh remains a matter for conjecture, though the peasant burgher communities would presumably have sided with the rebels as elsewhere. The indulgence which the Waldkirch council displayed—in telling contrast to Freiburg—towards those rebels who fell into its hands reinforces this assumption. With Breisach, however, the situation is less certain: the town itself owned villages in the western Breisgau, with whom its relations as a feudal overlord were deteriorating in much the same manner as the country nobles over similar issues such as forest rights.[88]

V

The Bundschuh of 1513 had been organized from one centre with its tentacles extending throughout the Breisgau and into Alsace. But the Bundschuh which Joss Fritz began to organize four years later was no longer confined by the need to build up a following gradually amongst the local peasantry from village to village. Fritz recruited simultaneously throughout Upper and Lower Alsace, the Breisgau, Baden, and the Black Forest. From the outset the Upper Rhine Bundschuh concentrated upon gaining a foothold in the towns no less than on winning over the peasantry. Cells of conspirators were discovered in the territorial towns of the bishop of Strasbourg such as Molsheim, Soultz-les-Bains, and Rouffach; in Barr, the municipality of the lordship of Barr;

---

[85] StAFr, B 5 XI, ix, fos. 91ᵛ, 93ᵛ; Rosenkranz, *Bundschuh*, ii. 155–6.
[86] StAFr, B 5 XI, ix, fos. 85ᵛ–86ʳ, 87ᵛ–88ʳ; Rosenkranz, *Bundschuh*, ii. 142, 150.
[87] As in the case of Hans Freuder. StAFr, B 5 XI, x, fos. 157ʳ–158ʳ; C 1 Militaria 98, nos. 68, 70; Rosenkranz, *Bundschuh*, ii. 233–4.
[88] Cf. Ernst-Volker Bärthel, *Der Stadtwald Breisach. 700 Jahre Waldgeschichte in der Aue des Oberrheins* (Schriftenreihe der Landesforstverwaltung Baden-Württemberg, xviii) (Stuttgart, 1965), 53 ff.

and in two of the smaller Imperial Free Cities of Lower Alsace, Rosheim and Obernai. In addition the Bundschuh had infiltrated around fifty villages on both sides of the Rhine. Some lay within the imperial bailiwick of Haguenau; some were the property of cathedral chapters and the bishop of Strasbourg; others belonged to secular lords—the counts of Fürstenberg, the margraves of Baden, the counts of Hanau-Lichtenberg and Bitsch-Zweibrücken, or were owned by cities such as Strasbourg.[89]

This network of recruitment could only be carried through successfully by radically new methods. Fritz had to rely upon those whose occupations did not tie them to a particular locality or the rhythm of the seasons, and who stood outside the established social order. Fritz himself could no longer hope to settle in a town or village for fear of rapid discovery. He therefore chose his agents from the legions of beggars, vagabonds, strolling players, ballad-mongers, hawkers, questionaries (sellers of holy relics), and quacks, and the discharged mercenaries who thronged the highways of the Empire. Chief amongst these agents was a native of Freiburg itself, one Stoffel, who shared the leadership of the conspiracy with Joss Fritz. Both travelled the Upper Rhine recruiting mostly in village taverns, whose landlords frequently belonged to the conspiracy.[90] As four years earlier, the Bundschuh found a marked following amongst village craftsmen and journeymen, but now its organization was different.[91] No more than a sign of mutual recognition was to identify the conspirators;[92] but once the revolt was under way the Bundschuh contingents were to muster with an 'H' emblazoned on their kerchiefs or else three slashes across their right sleeve, and should rally to the slogan of 'St George!'[93] The trappings of religious ceremony, the emphasis on paroles of divine justice, and the evocative imagery of the flag were all but discarded.

This change was equally marked in the progamme of the Bundschuh. The intention of mounting a general uprising of town and country meant that its demands could no longer take account of the local and specific grievances of peasants and townsfolk. Instead the Bundschuh rebels embraced two general aims—cancellation of all

[89] Rosenkranz, *Bundschuh*, i. 453–5.
[90] Rosenkranz, *Bundschuh*, ii. 269, 271 ff., 283 ff.
[91] Ibid., pp. 273 ff., 280 ff.
[92] The thumb of the right hand was to be held under the two forefingers with the password, 'It is good.' AVS, AA 365, fo. 61ʳ; Rosenkranz, *Bundschuh*, ii. 309.
[93] Ibid., p. 284.

debt- and interest-charges, and abolition of all feudal obligations. Together these demands were intended to strike at the heart of all seigneurial authority in city and countryside alike.[94] The call to cancel interest-payments certainly tapped a common strain of anticlerical grievance, which the Bundschuh clearly hoped to turn to its advantage: one old beggar was told to set fire to the houses of the village priests of Teningen and Denzlingen as part of the campaign.[95]

From the outset the capture of towns was given pride of place. In the autumn the Bundschuh was to be launched by capturing Kenzingen under cover of a deliberate blaze;[96] in September the Alsatian rebels were to gather in Rosheim and make it safe;[97] then Mittelbergheim was to be attacked, where they counted upon considerable support.[98] Thence the united forces of townsfolk and peasants would march on Haguenau and Wissembourg, the two larger centres of northern Lower Alsace, one the capital of the Imperial Bailiwick, the other a leading member of the Alsatian Decapolis. Faced with the likelihood that the authorities in these powerful communities would refuse them any assistance—a suspicion amply confirmed in the Peasants' War itself—the rebels for the first time embraced demands which directly challenged civic authority. They certainly intended to topple the town council and judiciary of both cities and may even have planned to put all the magistrates to death.[99]

Meanwhile, the Black Forest and Breisgau contingents were to meet near Freudenstadt on 26 September, so that by the end of the month the two wings could merge into a single force, aided by reinforcements from the Swiss.[100] Under Joss Fritz the Bundschuh would then sweep

---

[94] StAFr, B 5 XI, x, fo. 62ʳ; Rosenkranz, *Bundschuh*, ii. 266. AVS, AA 365, fo. 30ʳ; Rosenkranz, *Bundschuh*, ii. 290.

[95] StAFr, C 1 Militaria 98, no. 60; Rosenkranz, *Bundschuh*, ii. 268.

[96] Ibid., p. 284. Kenzingen was the capital of the mortgaged lordship of Kürnberg, which had already been bought by an Austrian official, Wolf von Hürnheim, from the city of Strasbourg. Cf. GLA D 1160, 18 May 1515; StAFr, L 4 (Stadtarchiv Kenzingen), Urk. 75, 22 Dec. 1515.

[97] Rosenkranz, *Bundschuh*, ii. 283.   [98] Ibid., p. 284.

[99] AVS, AA 365, fo. 61ʳ; Rosenkranz, *Bundschuh*, ii. 308. The testimony of the Wissembourg captive, Klaus Fleckenstein, falls on close reading into two distinct halves. In the first he admitted that the Bundschuh planned to depose the magistracy; in the second that the rebels intended to kill the authorities and all who stood in their way. This division strongly suggests that the second and more bloodthirsty part of the confession was extracted under torture. That is not to say, however, that what Fleckenstein revealed was necessarily untrue or exaggerated. The general tenor of the 1517 Bundschuh was radical and violent enough as it was.

[100] Ibid., pp. 284, 308.

the Upper Rhine, slaying any who resisted its advance.[101] For the fourth time, however, the day of revolt never dawned. Rumours of a new conspiracy were already circulating in May.[102] These were borne out in mid-August when a peasant, who had been entrusted with the task of raising fire in Freiburg, lost courage and confessed to his priest, who promptly alerted the town authorities.[103] Despite immediate and assiduous attempts to track down the rebels, the authorities were unable to lay their hands on any conspirators until the margravial bailiff of Rötteln captured two members of the Bundschuh at the beginning of September. One was Michael von Dinkelsbühl, a leading henchman, who in the course of his lengthy confession, the chief source of our knowledge of the 1517 Bundschuh, gave the names and descriptions of well over one hundred conspirators.[104]

Nevertheless, the lords still found it hard to discover the rebels' lairs. Dinkelsbühl, who slyly admitted that not every detail of his confession was accurate, could not always say for sure whether the conspirators were natives of the places he named or belonged to the shifting population which Fritz successfully used to recruit support. Fritz himself was never captured. Seven years later in the Peasants' War there is a fleeting mention of the Bundschuh leader, by then a grey-bearded veteran, still agitating amongst the peasantry for the victory of the Bundschuh.[105]

Because so few of the conspirators were captured, evidence for the scope and programme of the Bundschuh is necessarily partial, though the main contours of the rebellion can be discerned. As in 1513, the Bundschuh planned to attack the smaller country towns first, whether imperial or territorial communities. The lack of widespread commitment in the larger cities such as Wissembourg[106] and Haguenau[107] is

[101] Again, if Fleckenstein's presumably forced confession is to believed.
[102] Cf. AVS, Archives du Grand Chapitre, III/(1), fo. 65ᵛ; Rott, 'Documents', p. 64.
[103] StAFr, B 5 XI, x, fos. 69ᵛ–70ʳ; Rosenkranz, *Bundschuh*, ii. 303; ibid., p. 299. Cf. Schaub, 'Bundschuh', p. 148. See above, n. 67.
[104] Cf. Rosenkranz, *Bundschuh*, i. 484–6. Dinkelsbühl confessed without torture.
[105] Mone, *Quellensammlung*, ii (Karlsruhe, 1854), 17; Franz. *Bauernkrieg*, p. 79. It has recently been suggested that in 1525 Fritz was serving as a mercenary under Georg von Frundsberg in Italy. Gottfried Ginter, 'Die Vorwehen des Bauernkrieges im Bauland und Kraichgau. Hans Beheim von Niklashausen und Jos Fritz aus Untergrombach', *Badische Heimat*, li (1971), 318. Ginter gives no source for this remarkable assertion.
[106] Active commitment to the rebels in the Peasants' War, it is worth noting, came only from the wine-growers and gardeners. Jean-Laurent Vonau, 'La Guerre des Paysans dans l'Outre-Forêt', in Alphonse Wollbrett (ed.), *La Guerre des Paysans 1525* (Société d'Histoire et d'Archéologie de Saverne et Environs, Études alsatiques, numéro supplémentaire xciii) (Saverne, 1975), 41.

very noticeable, whilst the plan to seize Freiburg would have encountered the same hurdles as in 1513. Even though Stoffel from Freiburg was joint commander of the rebellion, there is no sign whatever that he or anyone else managed to drum up a sizeable following in the town. The Peasants' War was to demonstrate afresh that a broad-based coalition of the common man, whatever general and overarching demands it embraced, was wellnigh powerless to overcome the barriers between craft towns and the peasantry. Genuine solidarity could only develop out of common circumstances—when, for instance, town and country could combine against a common overlord.[108] Otherwise the rebels were reduced to alliances of tactical convenience, but on the Upper Rhine rural rebellion rarely coincided with urban opposition.[109]

In an area of political fragmentation the Bundschuh uprisings thrust much of the responsibility for law and order by default on to the cities. Here Freiburg took a leading part and thus irreversibly identified itself with the governing order. All its efforts to create a sphere of influence in its hinterland, to build up goodwill, to protect its outburghers, to construct a home territory counted for little when the storm broke. The rural opposition of the Bundschuh was to be reinforced by the antagonism of its lesser urban neighbours once Freiburg turned from the suppression of secular unrest to the persecution of the new religious doctrines in the age of the Reformation.

---

[107] In Haguenau, too, support was restricted to the peasant burgher element of the population in 1525. André-Marcel Burg, 'La Guerre des Paysans dans la région de Haguenau', in Wollbrett, *Guerre des Paysans*, p. 50.

[108] Even then there was no guarantee of lasting co-operation. There are indications, for example, that the disturbances of 1514 in the Strasbourg episcopal territory of the Obermundat only temporarily and contingently brought together peasants and the inhabitants of Rouffach.

[109] On this point see the detailed investigation by Tom Scott, 'Reformation and Peasants' War in Waldshut and Environs: A Structural Analysis', *Archiv für Reformationsgeschichte*, lxix (1978), 82–102; lxx (1979), 140–69, and the general remarks in idem, 'The Peasants' War: A Historiographical Review', part II, *Historical Journal*, xxii (1979), 957 ff.

VII

Freiburg and the Peasants' War

I

AT first glance a strange calm descended on the Upper Rhine after the failure of the Bundschuh in 1517. The countryside apparently remained quiet until the torch of rebellion was carried back into the Breisgau in late 1524 by the Black Forest peasants of St Blasien who had been amongst the first to take up arms that midsummer. But appearances were deceptive. Not only did the Bundschuh emblem live on as a potent symbol in popular consciousness; unrest was never far from the surface in town and country, even if it rarely spilt over into open protest for any length of time. Rebelliousness, in other words, was endemic, though revolt was rare. In 1519 there were signs of a new Bundschuh conspiracy at Dangolsheim in Alsace;[1] in 1521 there were disturbances in Kaysersberg;[2] in 1523 riots in Sennheim.[3] More ominous were duke Ulrich of Württemberg's attempts in 1522 to regain his duchy by depicting a Bundschuh on his flag in order to rally support for his cause in Switzerland and around lake Constance.[4] The authorities remained constantly on the alert, well aware of trouble brewing. But in the Breisgau, unlike Alsace or Swabia, there were no outward signs of pent-up discontent. Joss Fritz, it is true was still alive and plotting, though his whereabouts are unknown.[5]

Yet the Breisgau was certainly not at rest, for the commons' sense of

---

[1] Rosenkranz, *Bundschuh*, i. 499; ii. 310; Franz, *Bauernkrieg*, p. 79.
[2] AVKy, BB 10, fo. 57^{r-v}. Bundschuh sympathies had been voiced there eleven years earlier. BB 9, fo. 74^r.
[3] HSA, B 17 1*, fos. 9^v–10^r, 13^r–14^r.
[4] TLA, Oberösterreichische Hofregistratur, Reihe A 12/33; SAZh, A 195/1, nos. 157–8, 160–1; StAA, Literaliensammlung 1522; StAFr, K 1/27 35. Cf. Anna Feyler, 'Die Beziehungen des Hauses Württemberg zur schweizerischen Eidgenossenschaft in der ersten Hälfte des XVI. Jahrhunderts' (Diss. phil. Zürich, 1905) 240–1; Franz, *Bauernkrieg*, p. 79.
[5] In a dispute in 1518 between the shareholders of the silver-mines of Todtnau and the Forest bailiff there was loose talk of fetching the Swiss and beginning another Bundschuh. Rosenkranz, *Bundschuh*, i. 498; ii. 309.

grievance and injustice was fuelled and impelled by the impact of the Reformation. How soon reforming doctrines gained a hold throughout the countryside can only be conjectured, but it is striking how widely they infiltrated the diocese of Constance on the right bank of the Rhine under the nose of the Catholic Austrian authorities. Whether the condition of the Church in the Breisgau particularly conduced to religious disaffection remains doubtful.[6] The usual run of complaints about clerical abuses can be found. In 1496, for instance, the subjects of Triberg protested to Maximilian as their cameral overlord at the appointment of non-resident priests who arbitrarily increased tithe-charges and cited recalcitrants before the church courts.[7] During 1522–3, moreover, on Freiburg's own doorstep Johannes Kuder, the curate of Kappel, was frequently at loggerheads with his parishioners on account of his drunken and unruly behaviour.[8] But such incidents seem to have been uncommon, and bishop Hugo von Hohenlandenberg, the well-intentioned but somewhat ineffectual prelate of the Reformation era, made some attempt to stamp out slackness and corruption.[9] Furthermore, the Breisgau never produced a popular preacher of the calibre of Geiler von Kaysersberg to scourge the evils of the contemporary Church, nor did any of its leading towns become a centre of Protestant resistance on the scale of Strasbourg.

In the countryside, none the less, there is evidence of widespread agitation which successfully exploited the tradition of anticlericalism so prominent in the Bundschuh conspiracies. Even Freiburg, despite what the council chose to maintain, was by no means immune. The most effective agitator was not identified until 1523, although rumours of his activities had reached the authorities long before. He was Hans Murer, a native of Horb in Württemberg, who had studied in Tübingen and later Freiburg, where his stepfather resided. He claimed to be a medico possessed of great skills who had spent much time in Turkey and Bohemia. He let it be known, however, that he had given up quackery for the Gospel and, styling himself Karsthans, the peasant with the two-pronged hoe, after the evangelical peasant popularized in the eponymous satirical tract of 1521,[10] had formed a

[6] Cf. Albert Braun, *Der Klerus des Bistums Konstanz im Ausgang des Mittelalters* (Vorreformationsgeschichtliche Forschungen, xiv) (Münster, 1938), 106–90.

[7] GLA 21/424.

[8] StAFr, C 1 Kirchensachen 1; B 5 XI, xii, fos. 12, 31^{r-v}, 63^r, 92^v.

[9] Cf. Martin Brecht and Hermann Ehmer, *Südwestdeutsche Reformationsgeschichte. Zur Einführung der Reformation im Herzogtum Württemberg 1534* (Stuttgart, 1984), 26.

[10] Cf. Herbert Burckhardt (ed.), 'Karsthans (1521)' in Otto Clemen (ed.), *Flugschriften*

group of twenty-four disciples who went around spreading the new biblical doctrines.[11] From the testimony of a Freiburg councillor, to whom Murer divulged his beliefs, it appears that he was indeed expounding conventional reforming sentiments. But these were larded with threats of violence, for, as he confided to a Freiburg commoner, the leading councillors would shortly be driven out. Understandably, Murer never preached openly in Freiburg, but chose to stir up unrest on clandestine visits. When the council got wind of his intrigues, it took the lead in hunting down the agitators. At the end of January 1523 it sent out a batch of warnings about three journeymen who were scouring the Kaiserstuhl spreading subversive Lutheran doctrines.[12] Murer himself was variously reported to be in Württemberg,[13] in Strasbourg,[14] Wissembourg, or Sélestat—the flurry of correspondence in itself reveals the degree of panic which had gripped the authorities, who were confronted with pullulating opposition but quite unable to lay their hands on the ringleader. The only success came with the capture of a mason by the administration in Ensisheim, who confessed under interrogation that he planned to raise a Bundschuh flag in order to rally the commons to the new doctrines.[15] The government in Innsbruck was deeply worried by the deteriorating situation throughout the whole of Outer Austria, but its main concern was the hold which reforming doctrines had taken in the towns—Waldshut, Neuenburg, and Kenzingen.[16] In reality, the spread of religious dissent was much more serious in the countryside, for there many local priests with reforming convictions helped inculcate often radically egalitarian Christian tenets in their congregations in both Austrian and margravial villages.[17] Several such clerics went on to take an active part in the Peasants' War itself.

As the mood of the rural population grew ever more truculent, Freiburg found itself the target of particular hostility. The council's

aus den ersten Jahren der Reformation, iv (Halle a. d. Saale, 1910; repr. Nieuwkoop, 1967), 1–133.

[11] StAFr, B 5 XI, xii, fos. 74ᵛ–75ʳ, 87ᵛ–89ʳ. Peter Paul Albert, 'Die reformatorische Bewegung zu Freiburg bis zum Jahre 1525', *FDA* xlvi (1919), 44–5.

[12] StAFr, B 5 XI, xii, fo. 67ʳ; K 1/27 35; GLA 46/4546; Albert, 'Bewegung', p. 46.

[13] StAFr, B 5 XI, xii, fos. 74ᵛ–75ʳ.

[14] AVS, AA 374, fo. 31ʳ⁻ᵛ; StAFr, B 5 XI, xii, fo. 87ʳ⁻ᵛ.

[15] StAFr, C 1 Kirchensachen 143; cf. K 1/27 35.

[16] Cf. HSA, B 17 1*, fos. 8ᵛ–9ʳ, 28 Sept. 1523; TLA, An die fürstl. Durchlaucht 1523–5, fo. 123ʳ⁻ᵛ, n.d. (20 Feb. 1524).

[17] On the role of preachers in the Peasants' War cf. Justus Maurer, *Prediger im Bauernkrieg* (Calwer Theologische Monographien, v) (Stuttgart, 1979).

Map 7. Reforming Priests in the Breisgau to 1525

dread of what it regarded as Lutheran subversion earned it the reputation of a grinding oppressor of the common people well before its persecution of the reforming movement in Kenzingen in mid-1524 brought that hatred to a head. Earlier that year the town's preceptor and other clerics were roundly jeered as they toured the neighbouring margravial villages begging for alms.[18] Yet the council's implacable stand could not disguise that reforming sympathies had gained a firm foothold in both Freiburg's territories and the town itself. In the Valley Bailiwick the rector of Kirchzarten, Ulrich Wesiner from Glarus, seems beyond all doubt to have embraced evangelical doctrines, which his later denials of any involvement in the Peasants' War do nothing to mitigate, since the Christian Union of the Black Forest peasants, pledged to defence of the Gospel and the triumph of divine justice, readily gained a following in the Dreisam valley on its march into the Breisgau the following spring.[19]

In the city itself signs of heterodoxy can be discerned as early as 1515 when a bookbinder, Franz Steyndorfer, was arraigned for denying the immaculate conception.[20] Leanings towards religious renewal were, it appears, strongest amongst members of the university and some of the clergy rather than the laity at large. The most ardent advocate of Luther's cause was the professor of poetry, Philipp Engelbrecht, who had come to know Luther personally during his studies in Wittenberg. After his championship of reform in lectures and public proclamations had incurred the wrath of the university authorities, however, he had to lie low, whilst ill health in any case increasingly caused him to withdraw from public life.[21] Another sympathizer, Johann Lonitzer, the professor of Hebrew, had been forced to vacate his chair and leave town early in 1522.[22] In the early years, the former town clerk, Ulrich Zasius, who had succeeded to the chair of law in 1506, was much drawn to Luther since the Wittenberg reformer's attack upon the corrupt practices and texts of the Church

---

[18] StAFr, B 5 XI, xii, fo. 169ᵛ.

[19] StAFr, B 5 XI, xlix, 9 Aug. 1525; Johann Heinrich Schreiber (ed.), *Der deutsche Bauernkrieg. Gleichzeitige Urkunden* (*Urkundenbuch der Stadt Freiburg im Breisgau*, NF), iii (Freiburg, 1866), 80–2, nos. CCCCXI, CCCCXII.

[20] Albert, 'Bewegung', p. 4.

[21] Winfried Hagenmaier, 'Das Verhältnis der Universität Freiburg i. Br. zur Reformation. Untersuchungen über das Verhalten der Universität und die Einstellung einzelner Professoren und Studenten gegenüber der reformatorischen Bewegung in den Jahren 1517–1530' (Diss. phil. Freiburg, 1968), 10–11. 25–8; Albert, 'Bewegung', pp. 6–7, 51–2.

[22] Hagenmaier, 'Universität', pp. 20–1; Albert, 'Bewegung', p. 37.

Freiburg and the Peasants' War

so closely paralleled his own efforts to rescue the original texts of Roman law from the accretions of the glossators. Zasius kept open house for his students, so that a circle of younger scholars was infected by his enthusiasm for Luther, notably Jakob Otter, the reformer of Kenzingen and subsequently Eßlingen.[23] Zasius's admiration for Luther, however, cooled rapidly after 1520, as did that of the two professors of theology, Johann Brisgoicus and Georg Wägelin.[24] For their part, many students only became adherents of Luther after their departure from Freiburg, and though several lecturers, as Zasius alleged, were Lutherans, they had no real following, he claimed, within the body of the university or the town at large.[25]

The university was beyond doubt the hub of reforming activity in Freiburg, in so far as one existed, but its impact was in truth astonishingly slight; it never became a lighthouse of the new learning such as Wittenberg or Tübingen.[26] Its modest effulgence can hardly be attributed to its remoteness from the everyday life of the citizenry: neither Zasius nor Engelbrecht were retiring academics inhabiting an ivory tower but well-known figures in the town. Certainly the social control exercised by the arch-Catholic city fathers and university officers helps account for the swift suppression of heterodox opinions whenever they occurred,[27] but it can scarcely explain the apparent absence from the outset of any wave of support for reform emanating from the university.

Yet there was no love lost between the university and the town. The former's attempts to preserve its privileges and immunities both fiscal and judicial gave rise to frequent conflict with the council and brought upon it exactly the same odium as befell those other endowed and propertied institutions, the monastic houses.[28] Moreover, the often loutish and arrogant behaviour of the students, many the offspring of aristocratic families, did nothing to endear them to the mass of citizens who were humble craftsmen. The council minute-books are full of

[23] Hagenmaier, 'Universität', pp. 10–11; Albert, 'Bewegung', pp. 7 ff.
[24] Hagenmaier, 'Universität', p. 12.   [25] Ibid., p. 23.
[26] Rohde's view that the university exercised a strong reforming influence is not supported by a closer scrutiny of the facts. Hans-Wilhelm Rohde, 'Evangelische Bewegung und katholische Restauration im österreichischen Breisgau unter Ferdinand I. und Ferdinand II. (1521–1595). Studien zur Kirchenpolitik der Habsburger in Vorderösterreich im 16. Jh.' (Diss. phil. Freiburg, 1957), 23–4.
[27] Hagenmaier, 'Universität', pp. 16–17.
[28] Cf. StAFr, B 2 36, fos. 24^r–31^v (1494), 35^r–40^v (1501), 70^r–72^v (1523); TLA, Maximiliana XIV/55, Processe, fo. 66 (1518); and in general StAFr, C 1 Schulsachen—Universität 2 and 3.

incidents of student misdemeanour; even when the university was transferred to Colmar on account of plague in 1502, the students contrived to put the citizens' backs up by horseplay and threatening behaviour.[29] Even if the university's relations with the community were too uneasy to make it a natural focus for reforming activity amongst the citizens, there were certainly clerics in Freiburg who inclined to the new doctrines. Several of the minster chaplains were brought to book by the council for voicing religious dissent. Foremost was Ludwig Öler, who was forced to seek refuge in Strasbourg in 1523, where he subsequently gained notoriety by publishing a tirade against the Freiburg authorities for their suppression of the true faith at the very moment when they were harrying the reforming movement in Kenzingen.[30] Another was Diebold Kempf, who bitterly accused his fellow-clergy of hounding him because of his reforming convictions.[31] The council was also alive to danger from the pulpit. In 1522 it punished Gregorius Frauenfeld for preaching in the parish church against the intercession of saints,[32] and the next year it expelled a Carmelite friar for delivering Lutheran sermons in the priory of All Saints.[33] In general, though, the majority of Freiburg's clerics remained loyal to the Church. Whilst that clearly hindered any concerted dissemination of the new doctrines, it might at the same time have fuelled existing anticlericalism if widespread pressure for reform had already built up amongst the laity.

The first signs of such pressure can be detected early in 1522 when a group of burghers petitioned the bishop of Constance to receive the Eucharist in both kinds. When the request was not surprisingly turned down, a satirical broadsheet appeared in the town mocking the bishop and the avarice of monks and priests. Its anonymous author denied any allegiance to Luther; he was, he claimed, merely seeking to be a good Christian.[34] How far this pamphlet represented popular feeling is hard to tell, but we do know that Lutheran books and tracts were hawked around the town, for in 1523 the council arrested two members of the university on that very charge.[35] How many were in circulation can only

[29] AVC, FF 15, no. 1, 22 Nov. 1502.
[30] Hagenmaier, 'Universität', p. 25; Albert, 'Bewegung', pp. 50, 52–3; cf. StAFr, B 5 XI, xii, fos. 199ᵛ–200ʳ.
[31] Albert, 'Bewegung', pp. 48–9.
[32] StAFr, A 1 xv A a 12, 14 Nov. 1522; Cf. Albert, 'Bewegung', pp. 41–2.
[33] Hagenmaier, 'Universität', p. 17.
[34] Albert, 'Bewegung', pp. 35–6; StAFr, K 1/27 35.
[35] Hagenmaier, 'Universität', p. 17.

Freiburg and the Peasants' War

be guessed; after archduke Ferdinand ordered all heretical books to be burnt in November 1522, the council carried out a house-to-house search, but the story that a bonfire of 2,000 books took place on the minster square is probably apocryphal.[36] Hard evidence of bookburning only comes in 1525 when the council ordered Capito's anticlerical lampoon, *On Three Strasbourg Priests*, to be put to the flames. There survives, however, the curious testimony of an unnamed citizen who admitted to having bought and read the works of eminent late medieval theologians such as Tauler, Gerson, and Geiler, and later those of Luther. From these, he declared, he had derived much profit, for he sought enlightenment not controversy. Indeed, on several points—the venerations of saints and the Virgin Mary, and the practice of fasting—he remained loyal to the traditional teachings of the Church. As a Catholic apologist, Albert sneered at this man as a naïve and self-righteous worthy, unaware of the subtleties upon which he had stumbled.[37] It would be truer to say that the testimony reveals the earnest quest of one pious individual for salvation, who was attracted to the new doctrines but reluctant to embrace them wholesale. Others were more outspoken, though, in their espousal of reforming doctrines. One unnamed burgher was charged with having challenged a preacher over the intercession of saints and justification by works;[38] a woman citizen, Magdalena Thiergarterin, admitted eating meat in Lent;[39] and in 1524 a tawer, Claus Rehar, defied the council's proclamations by engaging in a public disputation over the new learning.[40] Such incidents at least suggest that sympathy for reform did not merely exist underground. Yet although these scraps of evidence may well conceal more than they reveal, there is nothing to indicate that Freiburg witnessed a broad swell of popular support for the Reformation, a genuine reforming movement.

Some of the reasons have already been touched upon: the lack of a charismatic reformer—the most spirited and articulate of the town's preachers was, in fact, the prior of the Carthusians, Gregor Reisch, who threw his energies into denouncing the new doctrines; the ambivalent role of the university, compounded by Zasius's retreat and Engelbrecht's ill health; and, above all, the firm and unrelenting action

---

[36] Albert, 'Bewegung', pp. 38–9; Rohde, 'Evangelische Bewegung', p. 45. According to Hermann Sussann, 'Jakob Otter. Ein Beitrag zur Geschichte der Reformation' (Diss. phil. Freiburg, 1892), 20, the burning took place in 1524.
[37] Albert, 'Bewegung', pp. 38 ff.
[38] StAFr, A I xv A f, (c. 1522). [39] StAFr, A I xI f 469, 24 July 1522.
[40] StAFr, A I xv f 477, 21 Apr. 1524; cf. ibid., 483, 8 Mar. 1525.

of the civic authorities in stamping upon any trace of heterodoxy, not only amongst the citizens but amongst members of the university as well. The council's policy of suppression was no more than the logical outcome of its scrutiny of potential trouble-makers from the 1490s onwards. On the issue of possible sedition the council had no compunction in overriding the university's judicial independence. As early as January 1522 it had sent envoys to the emperor to denounce university members, and at the end of the following year it tried to get rid of a humanist lawyer, Johann Sichard, on the grounds that he was corrupting the youth with Lutheran doctrines.[41] Even more strenuous were its efforts to bring Ludwig Öler to book for his satirical diatribe; as well as persuading the Outer Austrian government to arrest Öler and his printer, and confiscate copies of the pasquil, the council demanded that the university seize and ban the lampoon or any other Lutheran tracts, as well as threatening dire consequences upon anyone caught in possession.[42]

But why were the Freiburg authorities so wedded to the old faith, and how did they succeed in preserving the city as a bastion of Catholicism? For the first, the dictates of foreign policy were paramount. The city's politial power was predicated directly upon its role within Outer Austria, and its fortunes depended largely upon its ability to exploit that position to the full. Archduke Ferdinand's refusal to tolerate any deviation from the Catholic religion robbed Freiburg of any choice: political influence demanded religious orthodoxy, a lesson not so quickly appreciated by lesser communities such as Kenzingen, Waldshut, or Rheinfelden which were not part of the governing order. There were domestic reasons, too, for the authorities' rigid rejection of the Reformation. After more than a century of decline, retrenchment, and upheaval Freiburg had at last achieved a precarious stability. Its population and economy were reviving, albeit gradually, thanks in no small measure to reforms expressly sanctioned by Maximilian as territorial ruler. There was little incentive, therefore, to place its hard-won recovery wantonly and mischievously at risk by embracing doctrines which would not only antagonize the town's lifeline of protection, but also in all likelihood tear the fragile polity asunder.

That, in turn, helps to explain why the council's policies encountered such sporadic and uncoordinated opposition. The community had been restored to an even keel by an increasingly paternalistic and restrictive

[41] Hagenmaier, 'Universität', pp. 16–18.
[42] Ibid., pp. 26–8.

system of social control. Yet that system could not have functioned unless it was founded—however contingently or reluctantly—upon popular acquiescence. And that is exactly what it was. From the days of the 'gild reformation' onwards the council had been able to maintain its authority only by accommodating the wishes of the gilds themselves. The mechanisms of social control could, of course, never be foolproof. There were bound to be voices of dissent during the storm years of religious and secular revolt—but they were lone voices. By then a consensus—however uneasy or contrived—had been established in the city which identified the external interests of the community with the maintenance of the Austrian connection and allegiance to the Catholic church, and its internal interests with policies for survival which saw dissent as a threat to civic unity and accepted a strait-laced and authoritarian magistracy as long as it was seen to uphold the commonweal.

The strength of civic unity was to be severely tested during the Peasants' War when Freiburg stood forth as the champion of oppression. It is all the more significant, therefore, that the only concerted challenge to the prevailing order came not from the body of craft gildsmen but from the one group within Freiburg's society which had been constantly and consciously ostracized and supervised during the preceding half-century—the wine-growers' gild.

II

For Freiburg, the outbreak of rebellion in the south-eastern Black Forest at midsummer 1524, which signalled the onset of the Peasants' War, fulfilled its most sombre prophecy of the subversive consequences of reforming preaching. In responding to the lords' appeals for help, the council ascribed the revolt directly to the spread of Lutheran and Hussite heresy.[43] Already at the Outer Austrian diet at Breisach in early June in the presence of the archduke himself the Freiburg envoy, Ulrich Württner, had launched into a violent denunciation of the three Austrian communities on the Upper Rhine which had openly embraced the new doctrines: Waldshut, Rheinfelden, and Kenzingen. Not only, he proclaimed, were Luther's teachings heretical, they encouraged rebelliousness and would lead to a fresh Bundschuh uprising. He announced Freiburg's willingness to shoulder the burden

[43] StAFr, B 5 XI, xii, fos. 214^r, 214^v–215^r.

of suppression, to which Breisach, Waldkirch, and Endingen added their names.[44]

At first, direct action could only be contemplated against Kenzingen, since both Waldshut and Rheinfelden as border towns were too close to the Protestant Swiss cantons to allow the Austrian authorities a free hand without the risk of military intervention by the Confederacy. The government in Ensisheim accordingly issued an ultimatum to Kenzingen to dismiss its Lutheran preacher, Jakob Otter. An assembly of citizens, however, refused to let him go without explicit instructions from the town's lord, Wolf von Hürnheim, a leading councillor of the Austrian administration in the occupied duchy of Württemberg. Hürnheim had earlier given Otter his backing[45] but now felt that he had no choice but to comply. Freiburg, meanwhile, was already threatening Kenzingen with reprisals if it would not yield.

The town council was in a quandary. Some councillors were willing to discharge Otter but were prevented by an angry crowd of women and journeymen, his most devoted followers. When Kenzingen reported this turn of events to Freiburg, the latter replied in a far from conciliatory tone that the council should not have allowed itself to be swayed by women, whom God had created men's inferiors.[46] Given Kenzingen's impasse, Otter decided for the sake of the community to leave; on 24 June he was escorted out of the town by around two hundred armed citizens who, after camping for several days at Malterdingen in the hope of eliciting the margrave of Baden's intercession,[47] finally made their way to Strasbourg where they were welcomed as refugees persecuted for their faith.[48]

At the next diet in Breisach on 29 June Freiburg promptly offered to send a garrison of 150 men to Kenzingen to guard against disturbances

[44] On this point cf. Sussann, 'Jakob Otter', p. 21. Although its reforming preacher, Otto Brunfels, had left the town by Mar. 1524 Neuenburg held back, doubtless because evangelical preaching was still to the fore there. Erich Sanwald, 'Otto Brunfels, 1488–1534. Ein Beitrag zur Geschichte des Humanismus und der Reformation' (Diss. phil. Munich, 1923), 9.

[45] At the town's annual homage on 22 May Hürnheim had given his broad consent to Otter's remaining, since he preached only the truth, but had forbidden him to administer the Eucharist in both kinds or to celebrate Mass or baptism in German. AVS, Archives du Chapitre de St Thomas, 96, 8, fos. 52^v–53^r. Cf. Sussann, 'Jakob Otter', p. 15.

[46] StAFr, B 5 XI, xii, fos. 187^v–188^r.

[47] StAFr, K 1/27 35. Kenzingen to Freiburg, 25 June 1524; margrave Ernst of Baden to Freiburg, 26 June 1524.

[48] The very second-hand account in the Villingen chronicle states that they were turned away. Cf. Christian Roder (ed.), *Heinrich Hugs Villinger Chronik von 1495 bis 1533* (Bibliothek des Litterarischen Vereins in Stuttgart, clxiv) (Tübingen, 1883), 97.

and prevent the return of the armed escorts. By 2 July its detachment had arrived and was to remain in Kenzingen for the next six weeks.[49] Although under strict instructions to discharge itself honourably and act only on the government's orders, its very presence was bound to cause ill feeling amongst the inhabitants. Incidents of misconduct by the troops, rare at first, had by the end of July become frequent enough for Freiburg to urge Hürnheim to intervene.[50] Such was the backlash of resentment, in fact, that the council reported to Ensisheim on 30 July that its forces would only carry on if backed up by contingents from the other Breisgau towns, so that the odium of occupation would not fall on Freiburg alone.[51] Despite its unpopularity, however, Freiburg was in no mood to show leniency towards Kenzingen, as Wolf von Hürnheim had hoped at least for the innocent.[52] The town clerk had already been beheaded at the beginning of July, whilst a further seven of Otter's supporters were languishing in gaol at Ensisheim.[53] In mid-August, however, the third estate of Outer Austria collectively petitioned the archduke to show some mercy towards the inhabitants: the ringleaders should be punished, but so long as the refugees were prevented from returning 350 children were left orphaned in the town.[54] A month later the *émigrés* were at last readmitted, and a commission of justice was appointed from the Outer Austrian towns to deal with the offenders. The vast majority was pardoned; only ten were sent into exile with their families.[55]

The suppression of the Reformation in Kenzingen left a legacy of hatred towards Freiburg which discharged itself in several rowdy encounters that summer. In the tavern at Malterdingen on 25 July a margravial subject, Mattheus Werkger, nearly came to blows with the landlord of one of Freiburg's inns whom he accused of being one of

---

[49] Sussann, 'Jakob Otter', p. 28. StAFr, B 5 XI, xii, fo. 199ʳ.

[50] StAFr, B 5 XI, xlix, n.d. (10 July 1524?); B 5 XI, xii, fo. 204ᵛ.

[51] Ibid., fo. 295ʳ⁻ᵛ; StAFr, K 1/27 35. The Outer Austrian government to Freiburg, 1 Aug. 1524. The Villingen chronicle states that eleven men from Villingen were sent to supplement the garrison. Roder, *Hug*, p. 97.

[52] StAFr, C 1 Fremde Orte 11 (Kenzingen). Wolf von Hürnheim to Freiburg, 29 July 1524; Schreiber, *Bauernkrieg*, i. (Freiburg, 1863) 9, no. IX.

[53] Sussann, 'Jakob Otter', p. 29; Karl Hartfelder, *Zur Geschichte des Bauernkriegs in Südwestdeutschland* (Stuttgart, 1884), 274. They were still there at the end of August. Cf. StAFr, C 1 Kirchensachen 143. The four Forest Towns to Freiburg, 30 Aug. 1524; cp. K 1/27 35.

[54] StAFr, B 5 XI, xii, fos. 212ᵛ–213ᵛ; cf. Heinrich Schreiber, *Melchior Fattlin, zweiter Stifter des sogenannten Karthäuser-Hauses* (Freiburg, 1832), 25.

[55] Sussann, 'Jakob Otter', p. 38; Roder, *Hug*, p. 98.

the scoundrels who had so brutally attacked Kenzingen;[56] and in a similar incident on 10 August in the inn at Teningen a group of Freiburg gildsmen were taunted with the threat of imminent retaliation which would leave the city a heap of rubble for their shameful treatment of the inhabitants of Kenzingen.[57] Just like the Ebringen church-ale thirty years before, their hostility was directed at the townsmen as a whole, thereby underscoring the gulf between the countryside and even the ordinary craftsmen of Freiburg. The council protested to the margrave,[58] but by the beginning of December it had joined all three estates of Outer Austria in entreating the archduke to show gracious recognition of Kenzingen's restored allegiance.[59] Behind this sudden switch of attitude lay a dramatic change in the situation in the Breisgau. The spectre of mass rebellion was at last transformed into fearful reality as peasants from the Black Forest flocked to arms and threatened to descend upon the abbey of St Trudpert in the Münster valley between the foothills and the plain.

In the autumn of 1524 two peasants from the abbey of St Blasien had laid the groundwork of revolt with villagers from the Breisgau plain at a secret meeting in the inn at Heitersheim.[60] Smouldering anticlericalism provided the clasp for common action, witness the agitation of the nearby peasants of Eschbach who in May had plundered their priest's dwelling, withheld tithes, rents, and renders from both the Church and their lord, Wilhelm von Rappoltstein, the Outer Austrian governor, and threatened to do to death all clergy and nobility alike:[61] memories of the Bundschuh were ominously undimmed.

In early December,[62] with the rural subjects of Villingen already in

---

[56] StAFr, C 1 Fremde Orte 11 (Kenzingen). Margrave Ernst of Baden to Freiburg, 10 Aug. 1524; B 5 XI, xii, fos. 203ʳ–204ʳ.

[57] StAFr, C 1 Militaria 100. Freiburg to margrave Ernst of Baden, 22 Aug. 1524; cf. B 5 XI, xii, fos. 209ʳ–210ᵛ; Karl Hartfelder (ed.) 'Urkundliche Beiträge zur Geschichte des Bauernkrieges im Breisgau', ZGO xxxiv (1882), 395–6.

[58] Schreiber, Bauernkrieg, i. 19, no. XVII.

[59] StAFr, B 5 XI, xii, fos. 256ᵛ–257ʳ; C 1 Militaria 100. The Upper Austrian government to the Outer Austrian goverment, 7 Jan. 1525; cf. HSA, B 17 1*, fos. 45ᵛ–46ʳ, 46ʳ⁻ᵛ; Hartfelder, 'Beiträge', p. 408. Indeed, to prevent further trouble Freiburg tried to stop Hürnheim taking legal action to secure compensation from his subjects. StAFr, B 5 XI, xii, fos. 264ᵛ, 265ʳ.

[60] Schreiberg, Bauernkrieg, i. 170–1, no. CXXXV; Hartfelder, Bauernkrieg, p 276.

[61] GLA 79/1018; Karl Seith, Das Markgräflerland und die Markgräfler im Bauernkrieg des Jahres 1525 betrachtet im Rahmen der Bauernbewegung des 16. Jahrhunderts (Vom Bodensee zum Main, xxviii) (Karlsruhe, 1926), 38. Franz. Quellen, p. 85.

[62] Disturbances in Breisach in mid-Nov. appear to be quite unconnected with the onset of rural rebellion. Cf. StAFr, B 5 XI, xii, fo. 244ʳ⁻ᵛ.

Freiburg and the Peasants' War

revolt and the Foresters' army under the former mercenary, Hans Müller from Bulgenbach, approaching fast, the peasants of St Blasien, Todtnau, and Schönau swept down the Münster valley to combine with St Trudpert's own subjects, whence, ignoring appeals from the steward to remain at peace, they set upon the abbey and sacked it.[63] In the ensuing struggles Freiburg's actions were governed by more than a simple loathing of rebellion. Both St Blasien and St Trudpert were corporate outburghers to whom the town owed loyalty and protection.[64] At the very outbreak of hostilities in June Freiburg had assured St Blasien of its support, and in early September the council agreed to take into custody the abbey's charters, seals, jewellery, and plate.[65] How exposed this solidarity with the leading ecclesiastical landlords of Outer Austria might leave the city had already been demonstrated three years earlier when Freiburg had sided with the abbey of St Peter, yet another outburgher, against its steward, the margrave of Baden, over the collection of an Austrian territorial tax. With dubious legality the abbot had sought to pass the tax directly onto his subjects, who successfully appealed to the margrave for help, so that Freiburg was left in the invidious position of defending its outburgher against both the aggrieved peasants and the margrave, who sent a raiding party to eject the abbot from his convent.[66]

The attack on St Trudpert was doubly worrying to Freiburg because it had already committed a contingent of one hundred men to help guard Villingen against its own subjects' revolt which was spreading rapidly outwards from the Brigach valley.[67] In response to Freiburg's call for aid the government in Ensisheim immediately despatched men across the Rhine to Neuenburg,[68] whilst margrave Ernst, old quarrels

---

[63] Schreiber, *Bauernkrieg*, i. 171–3, no. CXXXVI; Hartfelder, *Bauernkrieg*, pp. 276–7. The Schönau peasants may themselves have nursed grievances against St Trudpert since the abbey had extensive landlord rights there. Seith, *Markgräflerland*, p. 133 n. 118.

[64] Schreiber, *Bauernkrieg*, i. 13, no. XIII; Hartfelder, *Bauernkrieg*, p. 301.

[65] Schreiber, *Bauernkrieg*, i. 40, no. XXX; Arnold Elben, *Vorderösterreich und seine Schutzgebiete im Jahre 1524. Ein Beitrag zur Geschichte des Bauernkriegs* (Stuttgart, 1889), 108.

[66] GLA 14/2. Cf. C. Arnold Snyder, 'Revolution and the Swiss Brethren: The Case of Michael Sattler', *Church History*, l (1981), 281.

[67] Schreiber, *Bauernkrieg*, i. 131, no. LXXXXIV; ibid., pp. 135–6, no. LXXXXVIII. Freiburg excused itself for sending mainly young recruits rather than craftmasters by saying that it had good reasons which it would later reveal. Ibid., p. 136, no. LXXXXIX. The Freiburg sources list 77 men sent from all gilds except the wine-growers. StAFr, B 5 X, 1. Waldkirch and Endingen also sent troops. Schreiber, *Bauernkrieg*, i. 133, no. LXXXXVIa. Cf. Elben, *Vorderösterreich*. p. 129.

[68] Schreiber, *Bauernkrieg*, i. 147–8, no. CXI.

long since buried, promised for his part up to 300 troops to meet the emergency which threatened the Markgräflerland as much as the Austrian lordships.[69] Faced with mysterious assemblies of peasants—up to 1,000 were reported to have gathered near Neuenburg[70]—Freiburg issued peremptory appeals to villages of the Austrian Breisgau—Ebringen, Staufen, Ehrenstetten, Heitersheim, and Krozingen—to remain loyal and at peace.[71] Most complied,[72] but Ehrenstetten and Niederrimsingen (which belonged to Breisach) announced that they would resist any attempt to send Austrian troops into their midst.[73] Meanwhile, peasants from the wider reaches of the Black Forest were pouring into the Breisgau and had been promised support from south of the Rhine by peasants in the Frick valley.[74]

On 17 December troops conscripted from the Austrian towns headed towards St Trudpert under the governor, Wilhelm von Rappoltstein,[75] but at their approach the rebels melted away into the valleys of the Forest without giving battle.[76] What the peasants had left intact, however, the conscripts proceeded to destroy and voices were raised from the ranks urging support for the rebels and vowing death to all monks and nuns.[77] Freiburg itself had considerable trouble in getting its subjects to march against the St Trudpert rebels; one villager from Kirchzarten actively tried to hinder the levy, and many men from the Valley Bailiwick were highly reluctant to go.[78] Three

[69] Ibid., pp. 144–5, no. CVII. Cf. Seith, *Markgräflerland*, p. 40.
[70] Schreiber, *Bauernkrieg*, i. 145–6, no. CIX; Hartfelder, *Bauernkrieg*, p. 278; idem, 'Beiträge', p. 404.
[71] Schreiber, *Bauernkrieg*, i. 146–7, no. CX; Hartfelder, *Bauernkrieg*, pp. 278, 303.
[72] Consenting replies from Heitersheim, Krozingen, and the villages of the *Kirchspiel* on 13 Dec.: Schreiber, *Bauernkrieg*, i. 148–50, nos. CXII–CXIV; Ebringen assented verbally, ibid., p. 151, no. CXVI. Nevertheless, there were apparently many in Heitersheim who supported the attack on St Trudpert and were intending to withhold tithes, rents, and taxes. Ibid., pp. 170–1, no. CXXXV.
[73] Ibid., p. 150, no. CXV; Elben, *Vorderösterreich*, p. 134.
[74] According to Laufenburg's report to Freiburg on 14 Dec. 200 troops had agreed to come. Schreiber, *Bauernkrieg*, i. 152, no. CXVII; cf. Elben, *Vorderösterreich*, p. 134.
[75] Seith, *Markgräflerland*, p. 39.
[76] Schreiber, *Bauernkrieg*, i. 166, no. CXXIX. Hartfelder, *Bauernkrieg*, p. 279, following the account in Franz Ludwig Baumann (ed.), *Quellen zur Geschichte des Bauernkriegs in Oberschwaben* (Bibliothek des Litterarischen Vereins in Stuttgart, cxxix) (Tübingen, 1876; repr. Hildesheim/New York, 1975), 531, believed that battle was joined, but there is no support for this view in the local sources. Schreiber, *Bauernkrieg*, i. 160, no. CXXII. On 17 Dec. Freiburg reported to Villingen that it had heard that the rebels had been beaten, but its letter of 22 Dec. gave a fuller and more informed account. [77] Elben, *Vorderösterreich*, pp. 136–7.
[78] Hartfelder, *Bauernkrieg*, p. 280; idem, 'Beiträge', p. 457. Of the 20 men conscripted from the Dreisam valley 18 refused at first to go. StAFr, B 5 XI, xiii, fos. 42ʳ–43ᵛ.

days later those Münster valley peasants who had not taken to their heels were required humbly to seek pardon and swear new oaths of allegiance.[79] Despite this tame ending to the peasants' first armed assault on the Breisgau, the mood of the country population remained volatile, as the Forest peasants sought to regroup for a renewed campaign.[80] Freiburg was certainly under no illusion that the flames of rebellion had been extinguished, as reports of unrest in Triberg and the Simonswald valley poured in.[81] Throughout the winter peasant couriers were scouring the margravial and Austrian villages preparing more thoroughly for a new uprising the following spring.[82]

After New Year Freiburg's resources were stretched to the limit. As well as sending troops to help repel duke Ulrich of Württemberg's fresh attempts to recapture his duchy,[83] it had committed small contingents to strengthen the garrisons of both Laufenburg[84] and Säckingen[85] on the Upper Rhine. In mid-March the council drew up more stringent ordinances to cope with any emergency, including the review of guard duties and gate watches.[86] By laying in stocks of corn and ammunition, and by digging trenches beyond the walls, the authorities encouraged the inhabitants to believe that all necessary precautions against attack or siege had been taken.[87] More elaborate contingency plans the council could not make, for it knew not whence rebellion would next irrupt. All it could do was to send its spies abroad in the hope of gleaning information in good time. At last on 10 April, it was able to report to Ensisheim that the Black Forest troop under Hans Müller was on the move again and was being urged to march westwards over the mountains into the Breisgau by David von Landeck's subjects in the Dreisam valley[88] who once again had rallied at the Falkenstein pass.[89] In a two-pronged advance the rebels were to

---

[79] Schreiber, *Bauernkrieg*, i. 164–5, no. CXXVII; Seith, *Markgräflerland*, p. 40.
[80] Schreiber, *Bauernkrieg*, i. 163, no. CXXVI.
[81] Ibid., pp. 158–9, no. CXXII; ibid., pp. 167–8, no. CXXXI.
[82] Schreiber, *Bauernkrieg*, iii. 164, no. CCCCLXVIIIb; Seith, *Markgräflerland*, p. 41.
[83] Schreiber, *Bauernkrieg*, ii. (Freiburg, 1864), 10, no. CL.
[84] Cf. ibid., pp. 14–15, no. CLV. These were largely withdrawn at the end of Mar. Ibid., p. 29, no. CLXV; pp. 32–3, no. CLXVIII.
[85] Cf. ibid., pp. 161–2, no. CCLXXXXII. The garrison numbered 20 men. Schreiber, *Bauernkrieg*, iii. 149, no. CCCCLXV.
[86] Schreiber, *Bauernkrieg*, ii. 25–6, no. CLXII.
[87] Ibid., pp. 77–9, no. CCVIII.
[88] Ibid., pp. 36–7, no. CLXXI; pp. 37–8, no. CLXXII; p. 38, no. CLXXIII.
[89] Ibid., pp. 39–40, no. CLXXVI.

strike southwards through the Münster valley yet again and also to the north through the Elz valley down to Waldkirch.[90]

These plans require comment. From Müller's activities around Villingen the previous December it is quite evident that this experienced and resolute mercenary had his sights firmly fixed from the outset on the Upper Rhine valley and Freiburg in particular; his scouts had already reconnoitred the Breisgau during the storming of St Trudpert, when they had camped at Krozingen.[91] Moreover, in early April he deliberately ignored the Christian Union of Upper Swabia's urgent call for help by leading his army away from lake Constance westwards towards Neustadt.[92] Though Freiburg was bound in any case to be a particular target of hatred on account of its stern pursuit of popular agitation, reforming or otherwise, its support for St Blasien and its unrelenting opposition towards Waldshut for harbouring the radical reformer, Balthasar Hubmaier, made it as notorious in the eastern Black Forest as on the Upper Rhine itself. All the same, strategic considerations were probably uppermost in Müller's mind. Just as Freiburg's commercial fortunes had derived not least from its vantage-point on the east–west route over the southern Black Forest, so its capture held the key to linking the revolt in Upper Swabia and the Black Forest uplands with rebellion on the Upper Rhine, the breeding-ground of the Bundschuh. Furthermore, its size and wealth made it the rebels' main prize: if Freiburg capitulated, the whole of South-West Germany was within their grasp. The Outer Austrian government in Ensisheim, by contrast, seems to have weighed little in the rebels' calculations. This subordinate and frequently inept administration delegated much of the task of suppression to Freiburg.[93] Indeed, on 18 April the governor himself appeared in Freiburg to discuss military countermeasures[94] at the very moment when the Alsatian peasants were rising in revolt, so that his staff had urgently to request his return in order to take command of operations there.[95]

By mid-April the entire right bank of the Rhine was up in arms. To

---

[90] Ibid., p. 37, no. CLXXII.   [91] Schreiber, *Bauernkrieg*, i. 160–3, no. CXXIV.
[92] StAFr, C 1 Militaria 100. Laufenburg to Freiburg, 7 Apr. 1525; cf. Johann Heinrich Schreiber, 'Balthasar Hubmaier, Stifter der Wiedertäufer auf dem Schwarzwalde', *Taschenburch für Geschichte und Altertum in Süddeutschland*, ii (1840), 204–5 n. 1. Cf. also Scott, 'Waldshut', part II, pp. 154–5.
[93] Cf. Elben, *Vorderösterreich*, p. 139.
[94] Schreiber, *Bauernkrieg*, ii. 50, no. CLXXXVI; Hartfelder, *Bauernkrieg*, p. 307.
[95] Cf. ADHR, E 659. The Outer Austrian government to Wilhelm von Rappoltstein, 27 Apr. 1525; E 660. Idem to idem, 23 Apr. 1525.

Freiburg and the Peasants' War

the south, the Markgräfler peasants confronted margrave Ernst with demands for acceptance of the Twelve Articles of the Upper Swabia and the establishment of a commons' government for the three lordships of Rötteln-Sausenberg, Badenweiler, and Hochberg.[96] When he declined,[97] the peasants, brushing aside Freiburg's belated attempts at mediation,[98] combined with some of the Austrian Breisgau rebels to sack the commandery of the Knights Hospitaller in Heitersheim on 2 May.[99] Meanwhile, to the north, having taken Endingen and Burkheim with little resistance, the Kaiserstuhl peasants joined forces in Kenzingen with the Hochberg and Ortenau troops,[100] who had just sacked the abbeys of Tennenbach and Ettenheimmünster,[101] and began to lay plans to besiege Freiburg, where margrave Ernst was obliged to seek refuge with his family on 5 May.[102] A week later the Black Foresters under Hans Müller arrived at Kirchzarten.[103] The town was encircled. What made the situation worse was the apparent intention of the Alsatian troops at Bergheim and Cernay to cross over into the Breisgau and form a united peasant army of the Upper Rhine.[104] In extremity, cut off from its neighbours,[105] Freiburg sent a desperate plea to the commander of the Austrian forces in Swabia, Truchseß Georg von Waldburg, but help was not forthcoming.[106]

The Black Forest troop took the lead in presenting the rebels' demands, after a delegation from the town council had gone out to Kirchzarten to treat with the peasants in the field. The commons in town and country, they declared, were weighed down with manifold burdens which their lords forcibly and unlawfully imposed; Freiburg,

---

[96] Cf. Peter Blickle, *The Revolution of 1525. The German Peasants' War from a New Perspective* (Baltimore, Md./London, 1981), 135–7.
[97] Schreiber, *Bauernkrieg*, ii. 85–7, no. CCXVI.
[98] Ibid., pp. 83–4, no. CCXIII.
[99] Ibid., pp. 75–6, no. CCVI; cf. Schreiber, *Bauernkrieg*, iii. 221, no. DIII. On 29 Apr. Freiburg had renewed its appeal to Heitersheim to remain at peace. Schreiber, *Bauernkrieg*, ii. 70, no. CCI.
[100] Cf. Hartfelder, *Bauernkrieg*, pp. 281 ff.
[101] Schreiber, *Bauernkrieg*, ii. 187, no. CCCXIV; Hartfelder, 'Beiträge', pp. 414–5; AVS, AA 394, fos. 19ʳ–24ʳ; Hans Virck (ed.), *Politische Correspondenz der Stadt Straßburg im Zeitalter der Reformation*, i (Strasbourg, 1882), 244–5. Cf. Hans Schadek, 'Das Kloster Ettenheimmünster im Bauernkrieg', in Dieter Weis (ed.), *St Bartholomäus Ettenheim* (Munich/Zürich, 1982), 222.
[102] Schreiber, *Bauernkrieg*, ii. 83–4, no. CCXIII; Hartfelder, *Bauernkrieg*, pp. 308–9.
[103] Cf. Schreiber, *Bauernkrieg*, ii. 100, no. CCXXIX; Hartfelder, *Bauernkrieg*, p. 309.
[104] Schreiber, *Bauernkrieg*, ii. 99–100, no. CCXXVIII.
[105] On 9 May Neuenburg reported that it was under siege and requested 800 fl., but apparently received no answer from Freiburg. Ibid., p. 91, no. CCXX.
[106] The appeal was sent via Villingen on 7 May. Ibid., p. 85, no. CCXV.

moreover, had abetted this grievous oppression of the countryfolk. To right these wrongs they demanded free and unadulterated preaching of the Scriptures, whose divine law should be the sole arbiter of human affairs. The rebels undertook to submit a list of articles detailing their grievances within a few days,[107] but for Freiburg to be spared attack it must join their Evangelic Brotherhood without delay.[108] To buy time the council resorted to a variety of stratagems. It announced that it must first consult the community.[109] Next it declared that the town's allegiance to Austria could not be compromised, though it was ready to assist in rectifying any justified grievances.[110] In response to the Foresters' promise of safe conduct for a delegation of councillors and commoners to enter negotiations, the council declined the prospect of peace on those terms, but offered to use its influence with neighbouring lords, including the margrave, to ensure a peaceful outcome if the peasants would only withdraw.[111] All to no avail: instead, the Foresters linked forces on 17 May with the other Breisgau troops and began their siege of the city.[112]

A flying column of Foresters scaled the Schloßberg and captured the blockhouse beneath the castle. Although two hundred men had been posted in the castle itself, the peasants were thus able to drag up artillery into positions overlooking the town. The bombardment which followed damaged or destroyed several houses, including that of Ulrich Zasius, and created havoc in the Old Town.[113] The peasants, meanwhile, had dammed and diverted the Dreisam, thereby cutting off not only the town's water supply but bringing to a standstill as well the water-driven mills which ground corn for the town's bread. During the six days in which Freiburg held out, the council tried without success to negotiate separately with the individual troops,[114] but eventually on 23 May the gates were opened to admit a contingent of around 250

[107] Ibid., pp. 104–5, no. CCXXXIII. The delay was presumably due to the need to discuss the details of the programme with the other troops first. By 21 May Freiburg had apparently received the articles. Ibid., p. 120, no. CCLI.
[108] Ibid., pp. 100–1, no. CCXXIX.
[109] Ibid., p. 102, no. CCXXXI.   [110] Ibid., p. 103 no. CCXXXII.
[111] Ibid., pp. 109–10, nos. CCXXXVIII–CCXXXIX.
[112] Ibid., p. 113, no. CCXXXXIII.
[113] Cf. AVS, AA 396, fo. 125^r. The size of the peasant armies has been greatly exaggerated. Zasius's estimate of 12,000 (Hartfelder, *Bauernkrieg*, p. 328) has been much quoted in the secondary literature. In fact, it is unlikely that they totalled more than 4,000–5,000. Cf. AVS, AA 396, fo. 125^r.
[114] Schreiber, *Bauernkrieg*, ii. 116–8, 120–3, nos. CCXXXVI, CCXXXVIII–CCXXXIX, CCLI–CCLIII.

peasants to call a truce. The next day after negotiations with the combined armies the town formally surrendered.[115]

Freiburg agreed to join the Evangelic Brotherhood without prejudice to its allegiance to Austria, and promised to pay a ransom of 3,000 fl. to be levied on the prelates and nobles gathered within its walls in recognition of their previous exactions, whilst the dissolution of the town's religious houses was reserved for future execution.[116] Thereupon the peasants withdrew, leaving four companies of infantry in occupation, and marched upon Breisach, which they forced to submit on 26 May.[117] The conquest of the Breisgau was complete. Hans Müller and the Foresters headed back across the mountains to resume their campaign around the western fringes of lake Constance, whilst the local Breisgau forces remained under arms, apparently uncertain what to do next.

The fall of Freiburg was a bitter humiliation for the city fathers who had striven so hard to ward off attack, but what of the populace at large? Did the rebels' programme find a ready echo in the town and its dependent territories? Could they hope to make common cause with the mass of inhabitants, and from which groups could they expect the most support? In the Valley Bailiwick Freiburg's subjects flocked to the peasants' cause.[118] Though the surviving depositions give little detail of their particular grievances, apart from damage to crops from the lords' hunting,[119] they evidently shared the Foresters' radical demands, for one of the ringleaders, Jakob Ziler from Zarten, revealed that if Freiburg had refused to join the Evangelic Brotherhood they would have killed all prelates, priests, nobles, and the town magistrates as well.[120] The assault on David von Landeck's castle at Wiesneck and the sacking of the Carthusian priory near Ebnet show that these were far from empty threats.[121] These intentions echo the earlier Bundschuh

---

[115] Hartfelder, *Bauernkrieg*, pp. 313 ff.; Friedrich Schaub, 'Der Bauernkrieg um Freiburg 1525', *ZFrGV* xlvi (1935), 97 ff. Cf. Siegfried Hoyer, *Das Militärwesen im deutschen Bauernkrieg 1524–1526* (Militärhistorische Studien, NF xvi) (Berlin, 1975), 165–8.

[116] Schreiber, *Bauernkrieg*, ii. 131–3, no. CCLX.

[117] Ibid., pp. 145–7, no. CCLXXIII. Waldkirch had surrendered to a detachment of Hochbergers on the same day as Freiburg. Ibid., pp. 133–5, no. CCLXI; Hartfelder, *Bauernkrieg*, pp. 267–8.

[118] Weber, 'Kirchzarten', pp. 302 ff. maintains that the Valley Bailiwick stayed quiet, but this view is quite erroneous.

[119] StAFr, A 1 VI a 37, 1520–7. Confession of Peter Fry the younger from Kirchzarten, 6 July 1526.

[120] Hartfelder, 'Beiträge', p. 457.   [121] Idem, *Bauernkrieg*, pp. 310, 312–13.

programmes and may have been revived by reforming preaching in the Dreisam valley. Certainly, the priest of Kirchzarten, Ulrich Wesiner, not only challenged Catholic doctrines (despite his assertions to the contrary), but also acted as secretary to the Foresters once they had combined with the valley peasants.[122] The testimony of Blesy Krieg from Oberried, moreover, neatly illustrates how long-standing anti-clericalism towards the Church as a temporal landlord had begun to fuse with rejection of Catholic doctrines as such. At the height of hostilities Krieg and a handful of others had broken into the priory of Oberried where, not content with looting anything of value including the church bells, he had smashed a monstrance, handed out portions of the sacrament, then donned priest's vestments to recite mass in which he mocked the host before consuming it.[123]

Striking though such incidents are, they cannot disguise that the overriding aim of the bailiwick peasants was to avenge themselves upon Freiburg. The council afterwards conceded that its own subjects had been chiefly responsible for ensuring Freiburg's swift capitulation by their counsel at discussions with the Foresters in Kirchzarten.[124] But why should their antagonism towards the city authorities have been so virulent? Freiburg's lordship of the territories which it had purchased from St Märgen and others was, it has been argued, at first highly conservative; in contrast to Herdern, the council made few innovations in administration or justice, nor did it raise taxes.[125] During the sixteenth century, it is true, the town created a closed territory by imposing uniform dependence upon its Dreisam subjects and by excluding foreign serfs, but this process had hardly begun by 1525.[126] Protests against the infringement of communal liberties or the intensification of serfdom, therefore, which underlay the peasants' articles in many areas of revolt, never occurred in the Valley Bailiwick. At a less obvious level, however, Freiburg's rural subjects were the victims of discrimination, even though some were peasant outburghers. They enjoyed no advantages over against foreign subjects such as

---

[122] StAFr, B 5 XI, xlix. Ulrich Wesiner to Freiburg, 9 Aug. 1525. Cf. Schreiber, *Bauernkrieg*, iii. 80–2, nos. CCCCXI–CCCCXII. Wesiner had already been brought before the bishop of Constance charged with denying the real presence. Although he claimed to have been forced to join the rebels' camp, Wesiner was subsequently named as one of their leaders by Burckart Sigrist, the sexton of Kirchzarten. StAFr, C 1 Criminalia 7, 22 Aug. 1526.

[123] Ibid., 28 Aug. 1527.

[124] Schreiber, *Bauernkrieg*, iii. 61, no. CCCLXXXXV.

[125] Cf. pp. 99–101. [126] Cf. Ulbrich, *Leibherrschaft*, p. 208.

greater market access or reduced tolls, though they were admitted to the civic gilds. This may well have lain behind their seizure during the campaign of the town butchers' cattle grazing on the Dreisam meadows,[127] to judge by an incident forty years later when the Kirchzarten butchers complained that they were denied the same market rights as their civic counterparts, despite their being bound by the same craft regulation.[128] Such grievances were not negligible, but the real cause of the Dreisam peasants' hostility was undoubtedly indirect rather than direct: Freiburg's identification with the ruling order though its network of rural clientage amongst the ecclesiastical and secular nobility, its severity towards any stirring of popular unrest, its persecution of reform and, not least, its disdain and distrust of the peasantry in general.

Support for the rebels in the Valley Bailiwick was widespread. In Kirchzarten the leading villagers were deeply implicated and several took commanding posts in the rebel army: Ulrich Kindhans from nearby Burg was one of Hans Müller's lieutenants; the innkeeper, Peter Fry, was quartermaster; Hans Walch a sergeant, the sexton a scout, whilst Hans Mentz from Birken captained a column which attacked the estates of two local noblemen, Jopp von Reischach and Christoph von Landeck.[129] Altogether, the names of over twenty rebels survive from all parts of the Valley Bailiwick and Oberried, amongst them several women, but these were mainly the ringleaders. The broad following can only be gauged from Freiburg's reprisals against Kirchzarten in mid-August, when it sent a sortie to punish those who had taken part in the rebellion. In that village alone the homesteads of fifty-three named peasants and cottagers were sacked and burnt.[130] That is a sizeable total, though property seized by the rebels from non-participants is also recorded, which suggests that some of the support was probably coerced. About Freiburg's other subjects—the villagers of Betzenhausen, and the remaining outburgher communities in the Buchheim march, the *Kirchspiel*, and Gallenweiler, who were included in the subsequent Austrian reparations[131]—no information survives. Their names do not crop up amongst the known ringleaders,

---

[127] StAFr, F A III 3/4 (1525).   [128] StAFr, F B 27/21, 13 June 1567.
[129] Cf. Schreiber, *Bauernkrieg*, ii. 147–8, no. CCLXXV; iii. 57–9, nos. CCCLXXXVIIa–CCCLXXXXIII; ibid., 157, no. CCCCLXVIII; Hartfelder, 'Beiträge', pp. 456–7. StAFr, A I XI f 485, 28 July 1525; ibid., 500, 18 Oct. 1526; ibid., 502, 14 June 1527; B 5 XI, xiii, fos. 42ʳ–43ᵛ; C I Criminalia 7, 22 Aug. 1526 and 28 Aug. 1527; C I Militaria 100; A I VI a 37, 1520–7, 6 July 1526.
[130] StAFr, F A III 3/4 (1525).   [131] Cf. HKA, Reichsakten 9, fo. 177ʳ.

but that cannot rule out their enlisting as ordinary recruits.[132] By contrast, the copious records for Freiburg itself disclose only the most contingent and partial support for the peasants' cause.

At the time of the first invasion of the Breisgau the previous winter several gildsmen had protested against the use of civic troops against Kenzingen and the St Trudpert rebels. One, Claus Rehar, had, it will be recalled, already been bound over that summer for spreading reforming doctrines.[133] Together, he and two colleagues conspired to incite the gilds against the council over imprisonment in civil cases, presumably for debt. But the conspiracy must have petered out since any commotion would have made its mark long before those three were finally uncovered and bound over on 8 March.[134] Thereafter there is not a trace of disaffection in Freiburg until the fresh assault on the Breisgau at the beginning of May.[135]

Once the town was under siege, however, the mood changed. Reports reaching Strasbourg on 25 May after Freiburg's surrender indicated that the council had been hard put to keep the commons in check. When the terms of the truce were announced, the commons had apparently clamoured for the peasants to be admitted, declaring that they were their brothers. After the surrender, in fact, the peasants had led three hundred inhabitants away to accompany them on the march to Breisach, having first extracted a large ransom from the religious houses.[136] Valuable though this previously overlooked account is, it survives only as an entry in the Strasbourg city minute-books;[137] certain details, moreover, are simply wrong (that the bombardment had only dislodged three or four tiles, for instance), which must detract from its general reliability. Above all, the report must be set against the eyewitness account of Peter Beck zur Muschel, a Freiburg baker who had fled to Strasbourg. In mid-October he petitioned the council for a

---

[132] Hans Fischer from Buchheim joined in the attack on the abbey of Tennenbach, but he was not an outburgher. StAFr, C I Militaria 100, 27 Jan. 1526; Hartfelder, 'Beiträge', p. 448.

[133] StAFr, A I XI f 477, 21 Apr. 1524 (correct: 30 June); cf. Albert, 'Bewegung', pp. 42–3.

[134] StAFr, A I XI f 483, 8 Mar. 1525. Affidavit of Claus Rehar; ibid., 482, 8 Mar. 1525. Affidavit of Rudolf Deck; A I IV b 25, 8 Mar. 1525. Affidavit of Martin Sutter; cf. Schreiber, *Bauernkrieg*, ii. 22–4, no. CLX.

[135] Though the town council minute-books do not survive, the letter-books, a crucial source of evidence, survive more or less intact for the period of the Peasants' War.

[136] AVS, AA 396, fo. 125ʳ.

[137] The reports reached Strasbourg from margrave Ernst, who had arrived there on 17 May and was presumably receiving his information second-hand, and an unnamed burgher's son who had left Freiburg.

safe conduct either to return permanently to Freiburg or else to fetch his wife and children.[138] In his supplication he described events in Freiburg during the siege. By his own testimony Beck had played a leading role in voicing criticism of the council, but although he was obviously seeking to exonerate himself from any suspicion of sedition, the graphic detail of his account makes it fairly easy to tell when he is fudging. Because Beck's account has been ignored, even in the local literature, the situation in Freiburg during the Peasants' War has been misrepresented by generations of historians up to the present day. Far from there being a 'faction' itching to ally with the peasants, as Blickle believes,[139] Beck describes a community fearful of the peasants' intentions, dithering and confused, but anxious to make peace at almost any price.

On 22 May, according to Beck, the council called the commons together to debate the peasants' ultimatum for negotiations to begin immediately with a delegation drawn from both councillors and commons. The discussion was led by the town clerk, Johannes Armbruster, who uttered the unpleasant truth that the town had lost control of the Schloßberg and had been without water for five days. Since relief was not in sight and because the council was mindful of its duty to preserve life and property, the town had no alternative but to come to terms with the peasants. He suggested that a delegation of three councillors, three from the Eight, and three from the commons be sent to treat with the peasants at their headquarters in St Georgen. At that point Beck, wishing, as he said, neither a dishonourable treaty nor a blood-bath, interrupted to demand that the commons' representation be increased from three to six. The town clerk thereupon instructed the gilds to foregather at the Franciscan churchyard by the town hall, where each gild nominated one man to step forth; from these twelve the six commoners were to be chosen, but since no gild was willing to give way, it was proposed that all twelve nominees be sent, unless the council insisted on only six.

At the peasants' camp the town clerk enquired what their purpose was. To conclude a treaty of general peace, they replied, with much elaboration. Armbruster then tried to postpone a decision until the next morning, but the peasants would have none of it. Then Beck raised his voice again to protest that the town clerk had spoken only for the council; he would speak on behalf of the commons, of whom there were more present. With that he declared that the commons were

[138] StAFr, A 1 VI a 37, 1520–7, 14 Oct. 1525.
[139] Blickle, *Revolution*, pp. 119–20.

eager to sign a treaty there and then for good or ill (which he had done, be averred, only because the council had failed to consult the commons). After the delegation had returned home, the peasants sent a letter of articles which was read out to the commons in front of the town hall. On these, Beck claimed, he had expressed no opinion, for they were not sealed or validated by any prince or magistrate! The town clerk stated that the articles were not unacceptable, but that in the discussions at St Georgen various threats had also been uttered. Beck rejoined that what he had said there was not meant as disloyalty: neither he nor the commons wished to forsake the council for, as he sententiously observed, once the ancient Romans had disavowed their elders they never again enjoyed victory or fortune! If he forsook the council, might God forsake him! Enjoining obedience upon them, Armbruster then instructed the gilds to meet in their parlours, where the twelve commons' representatives would collect their decisions. Two groups of six commoners each went round the gilds; Beck claimed to have canvassed no decision except from his own gild, the bakers, who replied unanimously that what the council deemed best they would accept. Thereupon council and commons rode out to the peasants to conclude the treaty. There the gild commander enquired of each man his opinion individually, but the next morning the commons as a whole, Beck complained, were never asked about the terms which had been agreed.

From this narrative there can be little doubt that Beck himself pressed for an active alliance of solidarity with the peasants, not merely a league of convenience. Equally, however, the council emerges as an astute judge of the public mood. Rather than one of its own number it put foward as its spokesman the town clerk, an honest broker less obviously identified with the ruling order. His concern for the safety and welfare of his own family in warning of the danger of pointless defiance Beck movingly and persuasively conveys. By 1525 Armbruster was an old and experienced public servant, town clerk since 1504, with only weeks to live,[140] who comes across as a crusty but respected mediator. The council was shrewd enough, moreover, to realize that in such straits it could not carry the commons with it unless they were party to the negotiations, and it wisely chose not to stand out against their much augmented presence on the delegation. Beck nearly succeeded in turning the commons' majority at St Georgen to his

[140] Cf. Folkmar Thiele, *Die Freiburger Stadtschreiber im Mittelalter* (Veröffentlichungen aus dem Archiv der Stadt Freiburg im Breisgau, xiii) (Freiburg, 1973), 129–30.

advantage, but he was thwarted once the envoys had returned home. Deftly the council deflected the implicit challenge to its authority which the commons acting *en bloc* would have posed, by instructing the gilds to deliberate individually. Thereby the hierarchy of membership ensured that the older and more cautious craftsmen's voiced prevailed. Whether the baker's unanimity (no doubt artificial) was echoed by the other gilds cannot be known, but the community appears, however reluctantly, to have closed ranks with the council. Beck's plaintive comment that the commons as a whole were not consulted the next day shows that he knew only too well that he had been outmanœuvred.

Beck, however, can hardly have stood alone. The council itself later admitted that certain seditious knaves had tried to stir up trouble, but had been summarily executed,[141] whilst the Strasbourg reports speak of 300 inhabitants who accompanied the peasants on their march to Breisach. But the only citizens who were put to death were those who took part in the quite separate revolt of the wine-growers, whilst those who joined the rebels' march are expressly described as having been led out of the city—hostages to act as a token of the town's submission and good faith. The relatively complete archival records identify a mere five active supporters, all of whom were released on affidavit (unless they had defected like Beck himself): scarcely proof of particularly heinous behaviour. A miller, Jörg Bechstein, was accused of having urged support for the peasants;[142] a cobbler, Alexander Bomer, encouraged one of the peasant captains to attack Freiburg which, he claimed, was easy prey since the commons had no wish to see their city destroyed and the council's unrelenting stance would soon crumble under pressure.[143] Bernhard Rottel admitted having joined Hans Müller's Foresters at Neustadt, amongst whom he spread the rumour that the commons were on their side.[144] The most active was the wife of the wine-growers' gildmaster, Agatha Haimlichin, who repeatedly insisted on being let through the gates to visit the rebels' camp, and on her return clamoured for the commons to support them, saying that the peasants were so well equipped that none could withstand them. Since they wished to avenge themselves only on the

---

[141] StAFr, C 1 Militaria 100.
[142] StAFr, A 1 IV b 34, 15 Sept. 1525. Partially printed in Schreiber, *Bauernkrieg*, iii. 133, no. CCCCLVI. Bechstein was also accused of having evaded the tolls.
[143] StAFr, A 1 XI f 496, 12 Mar. 1526. Like Beck, he had apparently first fled to Strasbourg. Cf. StAFr, C 1 Militaria 100.
[144] StAFr, A 1 IV b 33, 12 Sept. 1525; Schreiber, *Bauernkrieg*, iii. 127–8, no. CCCCLII.

nobility and religious houses the commons should not hesitate to join their Evangelic Brotherhood; if they refused, the peasants would tear up the vineyards and take the town by storm—a less than subtle threat to coerce the wine-growers.[145] Behind the activists there may, of course, have been many passive sympathizers,[146] but given the council's constant surveillance and the very detailed record of the wine-growers' rebellion, the chances of their having escaped detection cannot be high. These few testimonies, in fact, confirm the tenor of Beck's account: an uneasy mixture of fear and sympathy amongst the citizens at large, little desire to withstand the peasants, but no broad enthusiasm or commitment either.

Though the peasants succeeded in capturing Freiburg, they derived remarkably little advantage from it. Apart from the ransom they extracted,[147] they compelled the council to provide artillery—four rusty old falconets, as it later pleaded in mitigation—to defend the Rhine crossing at Limburg,[148] but thereafter the council steadfastly rejected all requests for reinforcements of men or arms.[149] Freiburg, in fact, remained neutral rather than an active ally at the very moment when the tide was turning against the peasantry. Already on 12 May the Swabian League had defeated the Württemberg peasants at Böblingen, and five days later duke Anthony of Lorraine crushed the main Alsatian peasants' army at Saverne, followed by the mid-Alsatian rebels at Scherwiller and Châtenois. The fall of Freiburg, the key to the right bank of the Rhine, came too late to matter.

Gradually their predicament came home to the Breisgau armies. At the beginning of June both the commander of the Austrian Breisgau troop, Gregorius Müller from Staufen,[150] and the Hochberg commander, Clewi Rudi,[151] made approaches to Freiburg, once their greatest bogy, to mediate an honourable peace. After lengthy

[145] StAFr, A 1 XI f 495, 12 Mar. 1526.
[146] The three supporters mentioned in Ulrich Kindhans's confession—the cobbler next door to the Sponhart inn, Jörg from Ulm, and Bernhard Büchsenschmied (i.e. tinsmith)—are beyond doubt identical with Alexander Bomer, Jörg Bechstein and Bernhard Rottel respectively. Schreiber, *Bauernkrieg*, iii. 58, no. CCCLXXXXIIa.
[147] They also demanded 2 kreuzers per hearth from the inhabitants as members of the Evangelic Brotherhood, but there is no evidence that the sum was ever collected. Schreiber, *Bauernkrieg*, ii. 141, no. CCLXVIII; Hartfelder, *Bauernkrieg*, pp. 316-17.
[148] Schreiber, *Bauernkrieg*, iii. 51, no. CCCLXXXVI; 152, no. CCCCLXV.
[149] Schreiber, *Bauernkrieg*, ii. 189, 198-9, 203-4, 210-11, nos. CCCXVII, CCCXXV, CCCXXX, CCCXXXV; Hartfelder, *Bauernkrieg*, p. 321.
[150] Ibid., pp. 169-70, no. CCLXXXXIX; Hartfelder, *Bauernkrieg*, p. 319.
[151] Schreiber, *Bauernkrieg*, ii. 173-4, nos. CCCIII-CCCIV; Hartfelder, *Bauernkrieg*, p. 335.

negotiations at Offenburg between the margravial and Austrian Breisgau peasants and their lords, with the assistance of Strasbourg and Basel, though not of Freiburg, a preliminary settlement was reached on 13 June, which was accepted by margrave Ernst but not by the Austrian authorites which had to refer back to archduke Ferdinand.[152] Further negotiations to restore calm to the countryside were arranged for 17 June in Freiburg, where two of the peasant commanders had taken up temporary quarters the better to monitor events and the council's activities.[153]

It was only then, when the moment of crisis seemed to have passed, that there occurred by far the most serious unrest in the city which, if it had coincided with the siege, would certainly have driven a large section of the population straight into the arms of the peasants. This was the uprising of the wine-growers. Trouble began at the annual gathering of the gild a week before midsummer to elect a new gildmaster.[154] The old gildmaster, Ulrich Haimlich,[155] asked each man for his nomination, reminding them that the serfs of foreign lords were not eligible to stand. One of the wine-growers, Blasi Bomer, put forward the name of Michel Günter, even though he was a margravial bondman. On being ruled out of order, Bomer defiantly countered that the wine-growers should acknowledge no lord but God and the emperor: why should a serf be held inferior to a free man? For that he was reported to the council, who arrested him on Corpus Christi.[156]

Immediately there was uproar in the gild. The wine-growers in the suburbs were summoned by the bailiff of Adelhausen to the gild parlour in town where a crowd of angry gildsmen was already gathering. The gildmaster was sent for, but could not be found—he was no doubt in hiding. In his absence tempers flared, and it was decided to free Bomer, by force if necessary; one man bragged that two hundred margravial peasants from Vörstetten and Gundelfingen just north of the town would rally to their cause. Some older voices,

[152] Schreiber, *Bauernkrieg*, ii. 205–8, no. CCCXXXII; Hartfelder, *Bauernkrieg*, p. 338.
[153] Ibid., p. 332.
[154] According to Bomer the meeting was supposed to have taken place on the Sunday before midsummer (18 June), but from his own account and the testimony of others, it must have taken place on, or just before, Corpus Christi (15 June).
[155] Ulrich Haimlich was the husband of Agatha Haimlichin who tried actively during the siege to bring about an alliance between the peasants and the commons. Haimlich must have died shortly afterwards, for when she was interrogated in Mar. 1526 she was described as his widow. From the various accounts there is no evidence that Ulrich Haimlich sympathized with the rebels: if anything, the contrary.
[156] StAFr, A 1 XI f 484, 16 June and 7 Aug. 1525. Affidavits of Blasi Bomer.

however, prevailed upon the hotheads that they should first send a delegation to the town hall to demand Bomer's release. When they arrived, they were fobbed off by the mayor who told them to come back in the morning if they had any grievances to express. When they reported this to the gild, some very blunt talking took place. Some were for forcibly freeing Bomer without delay; others demanded that the entire gild march upon the town hall the next morning. Eventually it was agreed to send a delegation thirty or forty strong, which presented itself in the morning before the council. At first the latter refused to set Bomer free unless the wine-growers agreed to stand surety for him to answer for his conduct in court. Reluctantly the wine-growers acquiesced [157] and retired to a nearby inn to await his release, but not before the bailiff of Adelhausen had delivered a rabble-rousing speech in the Prediger suburb urging defiance of the council at all costs.[158]

When some days later Bomer and his warrantors appeared to face charges of riotous assembly, the council was swift to dispense drastic punishment. Bomer, who had taken no part in the disturbances because of his incarceration, was sent into exile from which, despite repeated pleas, he was not allowed to return.[159] Four of the ringleaders were executed,[160] whilst another two dozen men, including the bailiff of Adelhausen, received stiff fines.[161] Altogether, after thorough investigation the council elicited the names of forty men who had joined in the uprising. Although the emergency quickly passed, the savage reaction of the authorities marks the gravity with which they viewed the threat to the town's security and social order.

Several features of the revolt deserve particular attention. The speed and anger of the reaction to Bomer's imprisonment testify to the depth of disaffection amongst the members of Freiburg's lowliest and least regarded gild. Yet there is no indication that its protest found any allies amongst the other gilds; from the lists of participants it appears

[157] Bomer subsequently claimed that he had successfully demanded to be released without conditions, but the presence of warrantors at the court-hearing makes this implausible.
[158] StAFr, A 1 XI f 488, 9 Oct. 1525. Affidavit of Hans Heinricher, bailiff of Adelhausen. C 1 Diener und Dienste (Ratsbesatzung, 1520–1702). Supplication of Blasi Bomer to (margrave Ernst of Baden), n.d. (1525), copy. Schreiber, *Bauernkrieg*, iii. 105–7, no. CCCCXXXV. Testimonies of Hans Wyler and Hans Muntzinger, 25 Aug. 1525.
[159] StAFr, A 1 VI a 37, 1520–7, 9 Nov. 1526; 23 Apr. 1526; 31 Aug. 1526; C 1 Criminalia 7, 22 Dec. 1525.
[160] StAFr, C 1 Militaria 100; Schreiber, *Bauernkrieg*, iii. 107, no. CCCCXXXV.
[161] StAFr, A 1 XI f 487, 4 Oct. 1525; ibid., 488, 9 Oct. 1525.

that support was confined to the wine-growers themselves, especially those living in the suburbs such as Adelhausen.[162] How close the ties were between the motley of carters, labourers, and smallholders—some of them unfree—who made up the gild and the surrounding country-dwellers, the plan to summon help from the margravial villages tellingly underscores. Here was the one group of inhabitants in Freiburg, detached from and despised by the remainder, who turned instinctively to the peasants, with whom they had so much in common, for allies. No wonder the council was aghast. Its fear of the wine-growers' gild as a sump of deprivation and discontent had led it to pursue a conscious policy of isolation and containment: and now the policy lay in ruins, the victim of its own success. With the Breisgau peasants still under arms the wine-growers, by far the largest gild in Freiburg, were revealed as a fifth column. For the council it was the merest luck that the revolt had not occurred the month before.

The storm had been weathered; slowly the town recovered its composure. By 17 July the council felt confident enough to forswear its alliance with the Evangelic Brotherhood.[163] The work of pacification could at last begin.

III

The ratification of the first treaty of Offenburg which had made substantial concessions to the margravial peasants encouraged the Austrian subjects in the Breisgau to hold out for similiar terms. Already on 8 July the elders and villagers of Kirchzarten pressed Freiburg to begin negotiations on that basis, since they were being pulled in two directions at once: they had received the much more onerous articles of submission which the Swabian League had sent to the Black Foresters,[164] whilst at the same time being exhorted by Hans Müller and the Christian Union to hurry eastwards to Radolfzell, where their besieging troops were in imminent danger from the relieving forces of the Swabian League.[165] This tentative was evidently brushed aside, for the next week the council repudiated its alliance

---

[162] Of the 24 participants identifiable as craftmasters in the tallage lists of 1523, 11 were residents in the Wiehre or Adelhausen, and 13 elsewhere. Cf. StAFr, E 1 A II a 1.
[163] Schreiber, *Bauernkrieg*, iii. 50, no. CCCLXXXV.
[164] Cf. ibid., pp. 3–4, no. CCCLXXIII.
[165] Ibid., p. 7, no. CCCLXXVII. Radolfzell was relieved on 26–7 June, and Hans Müller was finally captured near Laufenburg on 9 July. Cf. Scott, 'Waldshut', part II, pp. 159–60; StAFr, A 1 IV b 28, 10 July 1525.

with the peasants and announced its intention of launching reprisals.[166] In a swoop on the market it arrested four suspected rebels from the Valley Bailiwick who had been incautious enough to set foot in the town.[167] Three it was persuaded to release—against a huge surety of 1,200 fl.—only after intervention by the envoys of Basel, Offenburg, Breisach, and Strasbourg who were gathered in Basel to resume peace negotiations with the peasants.[168] They doubtless feared that unilateral reprisals by Freiburg, which was not a party to the Basel talks, could only jeopardize their chances of success. In reluctantly complying, the Freiburg council tartly reminded the envoys that without the active help and information given by the Kirchzarteners the Forest troop and its allies would not have captured the town so readily.[169]

Instead, Freiburg initiated its own talks with the Dreisam peasants. On 26 July it proudly informed the government in Ensisheim that agreement had been reached on all but four points, though on reflection the outstanding issues—the restitution of property, the retention of weapons, the punishment of the ringleaders, and the renewal of oaths—were so crucial to any settlement that it amounted to no agreement at all.[170] Though the peasants were given to the following Sunday to consider their position, Freiburg's unilateral efforts at pacification were unlikely to get it very far, since, as the Outer Austrian government pointed out, the Dreisam rebels had attacked many lordships, not just Freiburg, so that they would have to submit to a general treaty of surrender such as that which archduke Ferdinand had already imposed upon the Hegau rebels in Swabia.[171] The outcome of the peasants' deliberations cannot have satisfied the council, for on 16 August it despatched a mounted expedition up the Dreisam to punish those it believed guilty of rebellion.[172] The homes of over fifty peasants and cottagers were set upon and burnt, their cattle driven off, some men even put to death.[173] Cowed by such brutality, the Kirchzarteners had little option but to sue for peace.[174]

---

[166] Schreiber, *Bauernkrieg*, iii. 55–6, no. CCCLXXXXI.
[167] Ibid., p. 57–9, nos. CCCLXXXXIIa–CCCLXXXXIII. Ulrich Kindhans from Burg was not released, but tortured to extract a confession and then executed on 12 Aug.
[168] Ibid., pp. 60–1, no. CCCLXXXXIIII.
[169] Ibid., pp. 61–2, no. CCCLXXXXV.
[170] Ibid., pp. 69–70, no. CCCLXXXXVII.
[171] Ibid., p. 70, no. CCCLXXXXVIII.
[172] Ibid., pp. 83–4, nos. CCCCXIV–CCCCXV.   [173] StAFr, F A III 3/4 (1525).
[174] Schreiber, *Bauernkrieg*, iii. 84, no. CCCCXVI.

But not all the Dreisam peasants were prepared to give in so readily. Some sought refuge in the Black Forest hills, where they tried to rally resistance. Believing that the riders were in hot pursuit, the peasants around Todtnau and Schönau rushed to arms.[175] The agitation must, however, have soon died down,[176] for on 25 August Freiburg was able to report to the archduke that the Valley Bailiwick had accepted unconditionally its articles of submission, which it requested Ferdinand to ratify.[177]

Freiburg's operations were not confined to its own territories. Even before it had forsworn membership of the Evangelic Brotherhood the council had arrested and executed Hans Wirth from Bahlingen for his part in sacking the abbey of Tennenbach.[178] Such reprisals unleashed a new wave of vituperation against Freiburg. Satirical verses circulated in Staufen excoriating its sanguinary treatment of the peasants,[179] whilst a villager from Heitersheim had his two oath fingers chopped off for denouncing the council's violation of its treaty with the peasants.[180] Ugly rumours abounded that Freiburg was about to take revenge upon Kirchhofen under cover of darkness.[181]

Such uncertainty was bound to persist so long as the Austrian authorities failed to reach a general settlement with their Breisgau subjects, but by then archduke Ferdinand was bent upon military reprisals rather than a negotiated peace. Only through the mediation of margrave Philipp of Baden were these averted and fresh talks set in train at Offenburg in mid-September. Yet the second treaty of Offenburg, concluded on 18 September, imposed conditions upon the Austrian peasants far more humiliating than those earlier agreed for the margravial territories.[182] Apart from unconditional surrender and a ransom of 6 fl. upon every homestead, the peasants were not offered any rectification of their grievances and had to witness the complete

[175] Ibid., p. 90, no. CCCCXX.
[176] As a sequel to the raid a Kirchzartener, Hans Althans, was arrested in Freiburg for gambling in the gild parlours and passing himself off as a Freiburg mercenary by sewing a red cross to his breeches. StAFr, A 1 XI f 486, 21 Aug. 1525.
[177] Schreiber, *Bauernkrieg*, iii. 101–2, no. CCCCXXXI. The same day David von Landeck's subjects in the Dreisam valley submitted and swore renewed allegiance. Ibid., pp. 104–5, no. CCCCXXXIV.
[178] Schreiber, *Bauernkrieg*, ii. 187, no. CCCXIV, 9 June 1525; Hartfelder, *Bauernkrieg*, p. 321.
[179] Schreiber, *Bauernkrieg*, iii. 75–7, nos. CCCCV–CCCCVI.
[180] Ibid., pp. 97–9, nos. CCCCXXXVI–CCCCXXXVII. Jakob Hotz was executed despite intercession by Basel. Cf. ibid., p. 86, no. CCCCXVIII; p. 91, no. CCCCXXI.
[181] Cf. ibid., pp. 78, 85, nos. CCCCVIII, CCCCXVII.
[182] Ibid., pp. 133–41, no. CCCCLVII.

restoration of Catholic doctrines and observance. Such terms Freiburg was more than willing to inflict upon its own subjects,[183] but there are signs that they provoked renewed unrest in the Valley Bailiwick, for the council informed the archduke in some alarm that suspicious assemblies of Dreisam peasants and Foresters had occurred where violent talk of death to all monks and priests was heard.[184]

The second treaty of Offenburg formally brought to an end the armed rebellion in the Austrian Breisgau, but it left one anomaly unresolved: the position of Freiburg itself. Although the town was in the vanguard of repression both before and after the revolt, it had, nevertheless, capitulated to the peasants and joined the Evangelic Brotherhood. That caused the council acute embarrassment as it strove to explain and defend its actions to the Austrian government in Innsbruck and to the archduke himself. Shortly after its surrender, in fact, Freiburg and representatives of the Breisgau estates, who had taken refuge in the town, sent a collective report to Ferdinand setting out what had befallen them and why.[185] Emissaries were sent to Innsbruck, where on 17 June they described the terrible predicament of the town during and after the siege. This submission seems to have had a suitable effect, for the Upper Austrian government was moved to commiserate with the town and the prelates and nobles who had been cooped up there during the dark days of beleaguerment.[186]

As soon as it had forsworn the Evangelic Brotherhood Freiburg hastened to inform the archduke, stressing that it had vouchsafed the rebels no assistance in men or arms during the alliance, except for the rusty falconets sent to Limburg.[187] That was clearly not sufficient in itself, for the town then drew up a much more elaborate justification of its actions towards the end of August. The details are familiar enough, but the council went out of its way to recite the costs which it had incurred through the rebellion, especially in hiring six hundred mercenaries after the surrender to help guard against a renewed attack and save it from forced contributions. So enfeebled was it by these exertions and by the continuing burden of debt that it had then been obliged to dismiss the mercenary garrison, but pleaded in mitigation that it had meanwhile embarked upon its own pacification of the

---

[183] Ibid., p. 144, no. CCCCLXI.
[184] Ibid., pp. 155–7, no. CCCCLXVII; Hartfelder, *Bauernkrieg*, pp. 361–2.
[185] Schreiber, *Bauernkrieg*, ii. 175–9, no. CCCVI, 6 June 1525.
[186] Ibid., pp. 219–21, no. CCCXXXIX.
[187] Schreiber, *Bauernkrieg*, iii. 51, no. CCCLXXXVI.

Dreisam valley.¹⁸⁸ The matter was evidently delegated by Ferdinand to a commission of inquiry which arrived in Freiburg on 4 October charged with examining the council on two central issues: who had attacked Freiburg and how had they succeeded; and what undertakings Freiburg had given the peasants, and for what reasons. In reply, the council composed a formal statement of justification which was essentially an expanded reworking of its August account. It was at pains to insist that it had only agreed to join the Evangelic Brotherhood without prejudice to its oath of allegiance to the house of Austria and the territorial ruler.¹⁸⁹ This statement was then entrusted to an Outer Austrian official, Dr Jakob Stürtzel, for submission to the archduke.¹⁹⁰ And there, for the time being, the matter rested, as Freiburg resumed its efforts to track down those rebels who had dispersed and disappeared.

Freiburg was anxious to see a standing patrol of two to three hundred horse set up which would scour the countryside the coming winter¹⁹¹ and, despite its previous protestations, it took on more mercenaries to stiffen the town's defences.¹⁹² Gradually the ringleaders were rounded up and brought to justice, though the final arrests were not made until 1527. Several rebels from the Valley Bailiwick eluded the authorities for well over a year. Peter Fry from Kirchzarten, who had jumped bail at the end of July 1525, was recaptured twelve months later but not finally released on affidavit until June 1527.¹⁹³ The sexton of Kirchzarten was only brought to book in October 1526,¹⁹⁴ whilst Blesy Krieg from Oberried was not executed until August 1527.¹⁹⁵ But Freiburg pursued not only its own rebellious peasants, or those who had laid siege to the city, but any subject near or far who had taken part in the revolt.¹⁹⁶ Just as before, it confidently assumed the role of

---

¹⁸⁸ StAFr, C 1 Militaria 99, fos. 37ʳ–42ᵛ, 23 Aug. 1525. The account survives in German only as a draft, a truncated version of which was certainly sent out on 25 Aug. Schreiber, *Bauernkrieg*, iii. 101–2, no. CCCCXXXI. A Latin copy and draft in Zasius's hand are to be found in StAFr, C 1 Militaria 101.
¹⁸⁹ Schreiber, *Bauernkrieg*, iii. 148–54, no. CCCCLXV.
¹⁹⁰ Ibid., p. 154, no. CCCCLXVI.
¹⁹¹ Ibid., p. 156, no. CCCCLXVII.
¹⁹² Ibid., pp. 146–8, no. CCCCLXIV, 5 Oct. 1525 (correct: 10 Oct.).
¹⁹³ StAFr, A 1 VI a 37, 1520–7, 6 July 1526; B 5 XI, xiii, fos. 42ʳ–43ᵛ; A 1 XI f 502, 14 June 1527.
¹⁹⁴ StAFr, C 1 Criminalia 7, 22 Aug. 1526; A 1 XI f 500, 18 Oct. 1526.
¹⁹⁵ Cf. StAFr, C 1 Criminalia 7, 28 Aug. 1527.
¹⁹⁶ StAFr, A 1 XI f 491, 20 Nov. 1525. Affidavit of Claus Pfister, the miller of Dachswangen. C 1 Kirchensachen 143, 13 Dec. 1525. Confession of Ulrich Weber from Hergsheim (Alsace). A 1 IV b 38, 27 Jan. 1526. Affidavit of Hans Fischer from

guardian of order and stability on the right bank of the Rhine.[197]

What Freiburg and the other lords feared above all was the recrudescence of mass revolt; no one could be certain that the embers of rebellion were not still aglow. Their fears were amply confirmed at the beginning of 1527 when a well-organized conspircy was uncovered in the Ortenau[198] whose tentacles extended down into the Markgräfler land and over into Lower Alsace.[199] This continuing subersiveness is scarcely surprising given the heavyhanded attempts at pacification and the lords' demands for reparations. Freiburg calculated its own expenditure during the Peasants' War at £5,350 (8,560 fl.),[200] but claimed damages amounting to 20,000 fl.[201] A special assembly met at Villingen in April 1526 to consider compensation, but the haggling continued well into the next year, largely because of the complications of lords pressing claims against each other's subjects.[202]

By 1528 Freiburg must have thought that at long last it was out of the wood, but it had not reckoned with the slow but inexorable workings of the Austrian bureaucracy. The government in Ensisheim, never Freiburg's greatest admirer, had been invited to draw up proposals to penalize the town and ensure that it would never again fall into the hands of recalcitrants. From its findings the Upper Austrian government in Innsbruck then submitted a set of lengthy and lucid recommendations to king Ferdinand which reveal how anxious the authorities were not to upset the delicate balance between Freiburg's hard-won internal recovery and its wider political power within Outer

Buchheim (cf. C 1 Militaria 100, draft). A 1 IV b 42, 7 July 1526. Affidavit of Jakob Zimmermann from Gottenheim. B 5 XI, xiii, fos. 39ᵛ–42ʳ, 8 May 1527; A 1 VI a 37, 1520–7, 5 June 1526. Safe conduct petition of Martin Ziegler from Uffhausen.

[197] On occasion this was taken to ridiculous lengths. As late as 1529 Freiburg protested to Basel that it had accepted as burgher Ulrich Kindhans from Burg's father, whose homestead Freiburg had laid waste even though he may well have been innocent. StAFr, A 1 XIX Basel, 27 Sept. 1529; A 1 VII d 21, 18 Oct. 1529; cf. SABs, Missiven A 30, fos. 31ᵛ–32ʳ. All the same, Freiburg was prepared to speak up for rebels who had obviously repented. Cf. SABs, Politisches M 4,1. Freiburg to Basel, 4 Apr. 1533.

[198] Cf. StAFr, C 1 Fremde Orte 24 (Zabern). The bishop of Strasbourg to Freiburg, 6 Jan. 1527, enclosing the confession of Batholome from Oberkirch.

[199] StAFr, B 5 XI, xiii, fo. 10ʳ⁻ᵛ. Freiburg to Wolf von Hürnheim, 25 Jan. 1527. Cf. Karl Hartfelder (ed.), 'Akten zur Geschichte des Bauernkriegs in Süddeutschland', *ZGO* xxxix (1885), 430.

[200] StAFr, C 1 Militaria 101.

[201] Hartfelder, *Bauernkrieg*, pp. 364–5.

[202] Cf. idem, 'Beiträge', pp. 442–3, 448–9. As late as 1531 Freiburg and the other Breisgau estates took Niederrimsingen before the imperial court of justice at Rottweil for refusing to pay its reparations fixed at Villingen. StAFr, C 1 Militaria 141, 1 July 1531.

Austria.²⁰³ They rejected the idea of fiscal penalties on account of the town's precarious finances and pointed out that the university had already lost many of its wealthier members and only had half as many students on its roll as in recent years. They expressed reservations about the feasibility of punishing rebels within the town after such a lapse of time, since many would have long since disappeared or else settled down to lead a new and law-abiding existence; capital sentences would certainly cause disquiet amongst council and commons alike.

They partly concurred with the Outer Austrian government that there was some scope for altering the appointment of office-holders and the election of councillors, but urged Ferdinand to tread most cautiously. The magistracy, after all, had long been pawned to the town and customarily vested in a nobleman, so that any change would be undesirable unless the pawn were ever redeemed. Similarly, they shrank from suggesting any substantial changes in the procedure for electing the council. The annual elections, which were provided for in the founding statutes (!), were already supervised by the Outer Austrian governor and his councillors, in whose presence the appointment of the mayor and gild commander had to take place. Some councillors, they added, were always drawn from the nobility, not least the mayor himself. If improvements were to be devised, they concluded, the government in Ensisheim should be able to advise on details.

On the question of gild representation, however, the Innsbruck authorities felt the need for some change, but expressly rejected the Outer Austrian administration's proposal that gildmasters no longer be elected to the council directly by the gilds. They explained that at present the craftmasters met in advance to elect their gildmasters, whose names were then presented for admission to the council. Lest it be assumed that their adoption could not be challenged, they recalled the case of the cobbler Rotenkampf (*sic*)²⁰⁴ who had been barred from the town council thirty years earlier on account of his subversive activities. Unless Ferdinand wished to suspend the gild constitution, from which they strongly urged him to refrain, they suggested that the gildmasters first be vetted by the governor and his deputies on the day

---

²⁰³ TLA, Oberösterreichische Hofregistratur, Reihe A 12/33. The Upper Austrian government to king Ferdinand, 24 Sept. 1528.
²⁰⁴ i.e. Caspar Rotenkopf. Cf. pp. 148 ff.

of the elections, when, in consultation with the other town council members if necessary, nominees might be required to stand down in favour of a more suitable candidate to be chosen by the gild. In that way the liberties of the gilds would not be infringed. They did not discount the suggestion that, in order to reduce the preponderance of gildmasters on the council, their number might be reduced from twelve to eight by means of amalgamating several gilds, but they felt that this was a subject best left to the council itself. They advocated no change in the composition or appointment of the lords of the Exchange in view of the sensitive nature of their office, and emphasized that any interference in the management of Freiburg's considerable debt-charge and domestic accounting might be construed as proof of negligence, which might in turn drive away the wealthy, and lead ultimately to a decline in revenue and hence in the town's ability to meet territorial taxation.

To redeem its fall from grace and to give visible expression to its thankfulness for Ferdinand's clemency, however, the Innsbruck government recommended the undertaking of some suitable public work: improvements to the town's defences, for instance, or, even better, the construction of a princely residence, since the territorial ruler had nowhere to stay on his visits except cramped and draughty quarters in the Dominican friary.[205]

These proposals show quite clearly the drift of the government's thinking. To prevent the recurrence of popular unrest it wished to realign the pattern of Freiburg's administration more closely to that of an aristocratic bureaucracy which was emerging in the Austrian dynastic lands by strengthening the patrician or noble element on the council, but not at the expense of overthrowing the gild-based constitution. In that the Innsbruck authorities displayed much greater insight into the foundations of Freiburg's polity than their Outer Austrian subordinates in Ensisheim. Their recommendations amount to nothing less than a triumphant vindication of Freiburg's policies over the preceding seventy years. The town had achieved recovery by embracing reforms which recognized the established and legitimate interests of the gilds, the organized mass of artisans, in all aspects of public life. What it had sacrificed in spendour, it had gained in stability. Of course, that stability had only been earned at a price, as the tribulations of the 1490s had demonstrated. Thereafter the town was

[205] Cf. p. 28 n. 45.

not immune from hardship, adversity, or strife,[206] but it was able to ride out its difficulties in a way that had never been possible throughout most of the fifteenth century. It succeeded because it could depend upon an underlying consensus within the community which the pursuit of gild-oriented policies had gradually created. It failed only where it mistakenly excluded from that consensus one sizeable section of the population, the wine-growers, whose natural affinity with the peasantry made them the only group within the town which could readily bridge the gulf that existed between town and country. That grievous miscalculation brought Freiburg to the brink of calamity during the Peasants' War and left deep scars upon the body politic.[207]

IV

On 13 April 1529 Erasmus, driven out of Basel by the onset of the Reformation, arrived in the safe Catholic haven of Freiburg,[208] shortly to be followed by the city's cathedral chapter.[209] Although he received a warm reception from the town council and was granted handsome quarters in the mansion of Maximilian's imperial treasurer, Jakob Villinger, the eminent humanist was soon passing tart comments on his new home. Several passages in his voluminous correspondence applaud the harmony between council, commons, clergy, and university,[210] but Erasmus found Freiburg remote, provincial, and expensive after the more cosmopolitan Basel.[211] The former, he averred, was better suited as a seat of learning than as a hub of commerce.[212] For a scholar with his sights fixed firmly on the wider fortunes of Christendom, it was perhaps too much to expect Erasmus to lower his gaze in careful scrutiny of Freiburg's more mundane affairs. And yet in his judgment on the town, despite its casual tone, there lies an important truth. Civic unity had been restored sufficiently to weather

---

[206] Cf. the conflict between council and community in 1546. StAFr, B 5 xiiia, xii, fos. 337ʳ–341ᵛ, 10 Feb. 1546.

[207] Cf. the instructions to its envoys at a diet in Ensisheim in 1546 to prevent Freiburg's troops being sent to garrison other towns, lest it be left defenceless as in the Peasant' War. StAFr, B 5 xiiia, xii, fo. 386ʳ, 4 Aug. 1546.

[208] Cf. Karl-Heinz Oelrich, *Der späte Erasmus und die Reformation* (Reformationsgeschichtliche Studien und Texte, lxxxvi) (Münster, 1961), 18–19.

[209] Franz Josef Gemmert, 'Das Basler Domkapitel in Freiburg', *Schau-ins-Land*, lxxxiv/lxxv (1966/7), 128.

[210] P. S. Allen *et al.* (eds.), *Opus Epistolarum Des. Erasmi Roterodami*, viii (Oxford, 1934), 222.

[211] Ibid., p. 456.   [212] Cf. ibid., p. 497.

the crisis of the Reformation and the Peasants' War. Relations between laity and clergy, though never entirely smooth, were no longer marred by the vituperation of the 1490s. No popular movement fired by anticlericalism emerged to challenge the old Church and fracture the fragile policy. With its commercial splendour vanished Freiburg had indeed reverted to a somewhat stuffy and provincial community of artisans and shopkeepers. But what escaped Erasmus was that its civic consciousness and self-perception, however narrow and complacent, were forged in a long but successful struggle for survival. That struggle was not without its price: years of affliction and unrest which had left the citizenry suspicious of new ideas and hostile towards the outside world.

Freiburg's polity, the gild community, survived and flourished until the substantial changes wrought by emperor Ferdinand in the middle of the sixteenth century which enabled greater interference in, and control over, municipal affairs.[213] It was not the ascendancy of a gild economy and society but the rigidity of the new regime, born of the spirit of Habsburg early absolutism in the Catholic Reformation, which consigned Freiburg, as so many middling German towns, to stagnation and inertia until the nineteenth century.

---

[213] Cf. Franz Laubenberger, 'Die Freiburger Stadtverwaltung im 17. und 18. Jahrhundert und ihre gesellschaftliche Struktur', in Erich Maschke and Jürgen Sydow (eds.), *Verwaltung und Gesellschaft in der südwestdeutschen Stadt des 17. und 18. Jahrhunderts* (Veröffentlichungen der Kommission für geschichtliche Landeskunde in Baden-Württemberg, Reihe B lviii) (Stuttgart, 1969), 47–8.

Conclusion

THE foregoing analysis of Freiburg's relations with the Breisgau runs counter to the current interpretation of the Peasants' War as a 'revolution of the common man', advanced by Peter Blickle.[1] Although his thesis has been criticized in general terms, notably by Hans Rosenberg, who has questioned whether revolution is a proper label to attach to a system-conflict within pre-industrial agrarian society,[2] there has been no sustained effort to test Blickle's argument by means of a detailed regional case-study. The revolutionary character of the peasants' struggle derives in his view from three features: adherence to an overriding ideology (a religious vision of Christian liberty expressed in radical communalism); the mass basis of the revolt which transcended local allegiances and class interests to embrace the common man in town and country; and a deliberate recourse to violence in order to overthrow the existing social order.[3] Yet the chronic failure of the rural population to gain any significant bridgehead in Freiburg, either during the Bundschuh uprisings of 1513 and 1517 or in the Peasants' War itself, must cast serious doubt not only upon the relevance of the epithet 'common man' to comprehend let alone elide the real divisions between peasantry and townsfolk,[4] but also upon the capacity of an ideological programme to forge a bond of solidarity between town and country which surmounted those divisions.[5]

In two respects at least, may come the retort, Freiburg's situation

---

[1] Blickle, *Revolution*, p. 11.   [2] Ibid., pp. 11–12.

[3] Cf. in précis Peter Blickle, 'contribution to discussion', in idem (ed.), *Revolte und Revolution in Europa. Referate und Protokolle des Internationalen Symposiums zur Erinnerung an den Bauernkrieg 1525 (Memmingen, 24.–27. März 1975)* (*Historische Zeitschrift*, Beiheft 4 NF) (Munich, 1975), 332.

[4] That the term was current in the 15th and 16th c. to describe the mass of ruled over against their rulers is not in doubt. Cf. Robert H. Lutz, *Wer war der gemeine Mann? Der dritte Stand in der Krise des Spätmittelalters* (Munich/Vienna, 1979). What is at stake is whether its nominal inclusiveness betokens a real affinity.

[5] For a general critique cf. Scott, 'Historiographical Review', *passim*.

should not be regarded as typical. For one, the structural tensions between a middling craft town in difficulties and a thriving hinterland were unusually severe; elsewhere alliances were effortlessly achieved. For another, no reforming movement of any consequence arose within the town which could have created a groundswell of support for the peasants' cause under the banner of evangelical brotherhood. Throughout the Upper Rhine, however, a region at the centre of violent mass rebellion in 1525, the reluctance of the craft communities, be they territorial towns or free cities of the Empire, to join the peasants' struggle cannot be overlooked. Their magistracies were of course vigilant in their efforts to suppress any stirrings of internal protest which threatened their authority, and those councils rent by reforming sympathies or politically less astute were often at a loss to prevent their citizens' attacking ecclesiastical foundations both within and without the walls in outbursts of anticlerical fury, as occurred in Sélestat, Wissembourg, and Colmar. But such actions neither presaged nor presumed a broad alliance between the populace at large and the mass of rural rebels. Where such alliances came about, it was either in the smaller peasant burgher towns (*Ackerbürgestädte*), often little more than walled villages, which shared the same aspirations and identity, situation and mentality as their surrounding countryside, or else amongst the overtly rural element within the larger craft towns—the gardeners, carters, fishers, millers, wine-growers, and labourers—that is, the plebeian groupings separated socially and economically from the bulk of artisan handiworkers both by skills and frequently by residence, but at the same time linked to the peasantry not only by occupation but also by the common obligation to pay tithes, whose administration the rebels in their articles of grievance repeatedly demanded be recast.[6]

This was the case in Wissembourg, whose wine-growers provided the backbone of Cleebourg troop of Lower Alsace, but which otherwise remained aloof.[7] A similar pattern can be discerned in Haguenau,[8] Sélestat,[9] and Colmar,[10] whilst in the commercially more

---

[6] Cf. Philippe Dollinger, 'Un aspect de la Guerre des Paysans en Alsace: l'organisation du soulèvement', in *Paysans d'Alsace* (Publications de la Société Savante d'Alsace et des Régions de l'Est, grandes publications vii) (Strasbourg, 1959), 71.

[7] Vonau, 'L'Outre-Forêt', p. 41; Hans Georg Rott, 'Der Bauernkrieg und die Stadt Weißenburg im Elsaß. Bemerkungen zur Quellenlage und Versuch einer genaueren Chronologie', in Peter Blickle (ed.), *Bauer, Reich und Reformation. Festschrift für Günther Franz zum 80. Geburtstag am 23. Mai 1982* (Stuttgart, 1982), 253.

[8] Burg, 'Haguenau', p. 50.

[9] Lina Baillet, 'Deux villes de la Moyenne Alsace: Sélestat et Colmar, face aux

advanced Strasbourg, the craft gilds were too absorbed in economic and social rivalry brought about by the division and specialization of production to pay much heed to the simple homilies of the gardeners' leader, Clement Ziegler, who attacked tithing and advocated the justice of the peasants' cause.[11] By contrast, the common ties which had prompted the peasant burgher towns of Alsace to join their rural neighbours in the Bundschuh conspiracies once more led lesser communities, regardless of their constitutional status—the imperial cities of Rosheim and Obernai, the seigneurial towns of Riquewihr and Ribeauvillé, for example—to throw in their lot with the rebels. On the right bank of the Rhine and in the Black Forest the territorial towns of Outer Austria as a whole—Villingen, Bräunlingen, Waldkirch, Neuenburg, and Breisach as well as Freiburg—remained remarkably deaf to the peasants' blandishments, and a few of the small seigneurial towns even stood aside.[12]

Beyond the Upper Rhine the picture is no different. Of the Imperial Free Cities of Swabia and Franconia investigated by Sea not a single one entered voluntarily into an alliance with the peasants. In some of the smaller cities with an articulate reforming movement—Schwäbisch Gmünd, Memmingen, Nördlingen—the council kept only a shaky hold on its inhabitants, whilst others tried to temporize or buy the rebels off with arms and provisions. Under attack three cities—Heilbronn, Dinkelsbühl, and Rothenburg ob der Tauber—were obliged to sign treaties of co-operation with their besiegers. But capitulation not consent was the father of these alliances, which were repudiated as soon as the coast was clear. The signs of active sympathy were extraordinarily few; the commons' opposition saw the peasants as

conflits religieux et sociaux', in Wollbrett, *Guerre des Paysans*, pp. 93–102.

[10] Georges Bischoff, 'Colmar et la crise révolutionnaire de 1524–1525', *Annuaire de la Société d'Histoire et d'Archéologie de Colmar*, 1975/6, 43–54.

[11] Jean Rott, 'Artisanat et mouvements sociaux à Strasbourg autour de 1525', in *Artisans et ouvriers d'Alsace* (Publications de la Société Savante d'Alsace et des Régions de l'Est, grandes publications ix) (Strasbourg, 1965), 146–9. In this context note the point made by Bücking that the more socially differentiated and technically progressive the larger towns—he instances Constance, Salzburg, and Freiburg—the more aggressive and antagonistic they were towards the peasants. Jürgen Bücking, 'Der "Bauernkrieg" in den habsburgischen Ländern als sozialer Systemkonflikt, 1524–1526', in Hans-Ulrich Wehler (ed.), *Der Deutsche Bauernkrieg 1524–1526 (Geschichte und Gesellschaft. Zeitschrift für Historische Sozialwissenschaft*, Sonderheft 1) (Göttingen, 1975), 173.

[12] Kenzingen, of course, had been cowed by the military action launched against it the previous year.

useful idiots whose rebellion could be harnessed to the cause of overthrowing civic governments.[13] Even in Saxony, the northern heartland of revolt, where the religious radical Thomas Müntzer strove to bring about a thoroughgoing people's Reformation (*Volksreformation*) by means of Christian leagues uniting town and country, his support amongst peasants and miners, it has recently been argued, melted away at the moment of truth, leaving a rump of plebeian followers from the Saxon towns to fight for Müntzer's essentially amorphous apocalyptic vision.[14]

It is vital, therefore, to distinguish between alliances of convenience and alliances of interest. The former, born of external dangers, were no more than leagues of mutual aid between parties whose situation and interests diverged; the latter presupposed active commitment to a common cause between allies whose circumstances and aims converged.[15] In this light only the self-evident co-operation between country-dwellers and peasant burghers or between rural and urban subjects of the same lord reflect a genuine solidarity and common purpose spanning town and country; elsewhere alliances were at best contingent, temporary, and friable. The notion of extensive co-operation between peasants and burghers during the Peasants' War, which has found its way into the wider literature on popular rebellion in early modern Europe,[16] is a chimera.

This typological distinction between alliances of convenience and of interest provides the key to understanding Freiburg's relations with the Breisgau during the Peasants' War. If the commons' opposition of the 1490s led by Walzenmüller had occurred in May 1525, he would certainly have solicited support from the besieging peasants in a league of tactical convenience, the more so since Walzenmüller himself had close connections with the countryside as a butcher and former steward of Waltershofen. By the same token, if the wine-growers' agitation in June and July had broken out a month earlier, the combined peasant troops under Hans Müller would have been presented with a sizeable fifth column eager to link arms with its brothers in the field: the villagers of Gundelfingen and Zähringen,

[13] Thomas F. Sea, 'Imperial Cities and the Peasants' War in Germany', *Central European History*, xii (1979), 3–4.
[14] Tom Scott, 'The *Volksreformation* of Thomas Müntzer in Allstedt and Mühlhausen', *Journal of Ecclesiastical History*, xxxiv (1983), 194–213, esp. 211 ff.
[15] Idem, 'Reformation and Peasants' War in Waldshut', part II, p. 166.
[16] Cf. Perez Zagorin, *Rebels and Rulers, 1500–1660*, i: *Society, States, and Early Modern Revolution. Agrarian and Urban Rebellions* (Cambridge, 1982), 198.

after all, were said to be ready to rally to the gild's side. Only the mischief of historical accident, therefore, prevented a genuine alliance between wine-growers and the peasant armies or else mutual co-operation between urban dissidents and rural rebels. But could not a broader bond of solidarity between town and country as a whole have been forged by a common commitment to a radical recasting of society in conformity with the reformers' interpretation of the Gospel?

In Freiburg there appears to have been neither a reforming faction on the council in sympathy with, nor a radical religious movement amongst the commons eager to embrace the peasants' slogans of divine justice and evangelical liberty.[17] The reasons have already been discussed. Quite apart from the council's political resolve and constant vigilance, the new legitimacy and consensus after years of hardship and unrest, expressed in the gild reformation of 1495 and the permanent commons' watch-dog committee, created an elaborate system of social control,[18] which identified innovation with instability and opposition with sedition. Even anticlericalism in Freiburg, which elsewhere so often formed the bridge between urban and rural protest,[19] despite the turmoil of the 1490s seems to have lost its sting by 1525, even though it remained virulent amongst the rural population of the Upper Rhine.

Freiburg's experience, therefore, was certainly not typical, but why should the lack of an articulated reforming movement within the town be regarded as decisive when the peasants' own conception of reforming principles seems so curiously ambivalent? It is a most remarkable irony, passed over without comment by most historians of the Peasants' War, that the treaty of capitulation signed by Freiburg in May 1525 with the massed armies of the Black Forest and Breisgau peasantry under the leadership of Hans Müller of Bulgenbach, the one commander unquestionably beholden to violent revolutionary insurrection in the name of egalitarian Christian radicalism, concluded its provisions with an oath explicitly invoking both God and *the saints*![20]

---

[17] Cf. Sea, 'Imperial Cities', pp. 8–9, 14–15, 20–21.

[18] Cf. R. W. Scribner, 'Sozialkontrolle und die Möglichkeit einer städtischen Reformation', in Bernd Moeller (ed.), *Stadt und Kirche im 16. Jahrhundert* (Schriften des Vereins für Reformationsgeschichte, cxc) (Gütersloh, 1978), 57 ff.

[19] Cf. Henry J. Cohn, 'Anticlericalism in the German Peasants' War 1525', *Past and Present*, lxxxiii (1979), 3–31.

[20] Schreiber, *Bauernkrieg*, ii. 131–3, no. CCLX, here p. 132. For comparison' sake it is unfortunate that neither the subsequent treaty with Waldkirch nor that with Breisach are so phrased as to conclude with an oath. Cf. ibid., pp. 133–5, no. CCLXI; pp. 145–7, no. CCLXXIII. The invocation of the saints has been recognized by Torsten Bergsten, *Balthasar Hubmaier. Anabaptist Theologian and Martyr*, ed. W. R. Estep Jr. (Valley Forge,

That is not to deny the incontrovertible evidence for the spread of reforming doctrines throughout the Upper Rhine,[21] but it is to wonder whether the peasants' understanding of those doctrines may not have been as much instrumental—serving the subjective aims of communal defence—as idealistic—committed to objective truths valid for all Christians everywhere. In that case the significance of reforming beliefs as an ideological clasp between town and country is somewhat diminished; that in turn casts doubt on the role of ideology *tout court* as the necessary motor and legitimator in transforming rebellion into war.[22] Even on a common programme of material demands it is not easy to find any substantial agreement between craftsmen and peasants amidst the welter of articles of grievance which 1525 brought forth.[23]

To argue that the gulf between Freiburg and the Breisgau was too wide to be spanned by an ideological bridge is not to perpetuate the fallacy that 'town' and 'country' are distinct and separate historical categories, when in point of fact they are artificial constructs, not *explanans* but *explanandum*.[24] On the contrary, it is to argue that conflict was caused precisely by the intermingling and overlapping of 'urban' and 'rural' qualities and functions, in other words the blurring of previous autonomies. As its economic centrality contracted in the face of rural competition, Freiburg's hostility towards its hinterland increased:[25] as its political centrality expanded with the acquisition of a

Pa., 1978), 200. He is followed by Lionel Rothkrug, 'Icon and Ideology in Religion and Rebellion 1300–1600: *Bauernfreiheit* and *religion royale*', in János M. Bak and Gerhard Benecke (eds.), *Religion and Rural Revolt. Papers presented to the Fourth Interdisciplinary Workshop on Peasant Studies, University of British Columbia, 1982* (Manchester/Dover, NH, 1984) 31–61, who remarks, p. 33: '. . . to apostrophize divine law and scripture in the midst of a rebellion was one thing; but it was clearly quite another to abandon deeply rooted religious practices.'

[21] For the diocese of Constance cf. most recently Hans-Christoph Rublack, 'Die Reformation in Vorderösterreich und Konstanz', in *Luther und die Reformation am Oberrhein* (Ausstellungskatalog, ed. Badische Landesbibliothek) (Karlsruhe, 1983), 103–27.

[22] Cf. Scott, 'Historiographical Review', pp. 953–4, where the character of the revolt and the radicalization of the peasants' aims are ascribed to the organization and internal dynamic of rebellion as it unfolded through successive phases. In this context cf. also Hans-Martin Maurer, 'Der Bauernkrieg als Massenerhebung. Dynamik einer revolutionären Bewegung', in *Bausteine zur geschichtlichen Landeskunde von Baden-Württemberg* (Stuttgart, 1979), 255–95.

[23] An example of partial agreement is provided by the 28 Erfurt Articles. Cf. R. W. Scribner, 'Civic Unity and the Reformation in Erfurt', *Past and Present*, lxvi (1975), 45–6.

[24] Langton and Hoppe, *Town and Country*, p. 39.

[25] Cf. Ulf Dirlmeier, 'Stadt und Bürgertum. Zur Steuerpolitik und zum Stadt–Land–

feudal landed territory the countryside's antagonism towards the town grew deeper.[26] Their battleground was the Breisgau, the region which embraced them both.

Verhältnis', in Horst Buszello, Peter Blickle, and Rudolf Endres (eds.), *Der deutsche Bauernkrieg* (Paderborn/Munich/Vienna/Zürich, 1984), 275 ff.

[26] Graus, 'Tendenzen', pp. 39–40.

Bibliography

I. UNPUBLISHED SOURCES

A: Archives in the Federal Republic of Germany

1: *Stadtarchiv Freiburg im Breisgau (StAFr)*

A1 Städtische Urkunden
    I: Recht und Verfassung
      I d   Privilegia medii aevi
      I e   Ordnungen von Österreich
      I k   Erhaltene Rechte
    IV: Kriegs- und Landessachen
      IV b Neuere Kriegssachen
    V: Rat und Beamte
      V a   Ratsbesatzung
    VI: Verkehr, Handel, und Gewerbe
      VI a Geleit
      VI b Straßen
      VI d Zoll
      VI e: Zünfte
          α Allgemeines
          ε Metzgerzunft
          ν Malerzunft
    VII: Finanzwesen
      VII b Steuer und Schatzung
      VII d Frei- und Abzug
      VII f Gemeindevermögen
    VIII: Städtisches Gut und seine Verwaltung
      VIII a α Adelhausen
              β Betzenhausen
              γ Herdern
              ζ Talvogtei
              θ Zähringen
    X: Öffentliche Wohlfahrt
      X a   Allgemeine und Sicherheitspolizei
    XI: Gerichtswesen
      XI e Criminalia
      XI f Urfehden
      XI g Prozesse der Stadt
    XII: Bevölkerungswesen
      XII c Juden
      XII d Ausbürger
    XIV: Fürsten und Herren
      XIV a Allgemeines
              Blumeneck
              Schnewlin: Bärlapp-Bollschweil
              Schnewlin: Landeck
              Staufen
    XV: Kirchen- und Schulsachen
      XV A Kirchensachen
          a Allgemeines
          f Münster
    XVI: Klostersachen
      XVI A Klöster
          a Adelhausen
          e Augustiner
          k Karthaus
          o Oberried
          p Prediger
    XIX: Auswärtige Herrschaften, Städte und Orte
      Basel

Unpublished Sources

    Ebringen
    Marchdörfer
    Wolfenweiler

B Bücher
  1 Handschriften
     2
     255
  2 Urkundenabschriften
     2
     3
     4
     12
     36
  3 Ordnungen und Statuten
     11
     18
  4 Beraine
     10
  5 Protokolle
    I a Ratsbesatzungs-
         bücher
       b Richterbücher
       f Bürgerbücher
    III c Gerichtsprotokolle
         9
         10
         11
         12 δ ββ
    VIII a Kontraktenproto-
         kolle der Stadt
    X Militärprotokolle
    XI Missiven
        vols. II, III, IV, V, VII,
        VIII, IX, X, XI, XII,
        XIII, XIV, XIX, XLIX
    XIIIa Ratsprotokolle und
         Ratsbücher
        vols. IV, IVa, V, VI,
        VII, IX, X, Xa, XI, XII

C1 Akten der städtischen Hauptverwaltung bis etwa 1860
    Criminalia 7
    Kirchensachen 1, 80, 129, 143
    Landstände 1, 3
    Militaria 98, 99, 100, 101, 180
    Schulsachen—Universität 2, 3
    Straßenbau 23
    Waidgang 4
    Fremde Orte
      11 Kenzingen
      24 Zabern

E1 Rechnungen
  A Städtische Rechnungen
    I Rentamt
      a 1
      b 1
    II Steuer und Schatzung
      a 1
        4
      b 4
    III Zoll und Handel
      1
    IV Zins- und Gefällbücher
      i
    V Städtisches Gut und
       Vororte
      b 2
        9
  F Talvogtei
    A Generalia
      III 3
      VI 15
    B Specialia
      27
  K Nachlässe
    1/27 Nachlaß Schreiber
  L Deposita

1 **Stadtarchiv Breisach**
    Urk. I 143

4 Stadtarchiv Kenzingen
   Urk. 75
M Sammlungen
   53/1
   ungeordnete Bestände
   to: B 5 XIIIa, vol. IIa
        B 5 XIIIa, vol. IV
        C 1 Gemeindevermögen
        12
        C 1 Gemeindevermögen
        14

2: Generallandesarchiv Karlsruhe (GLA)
D 1160
13/8
14/2
21/424
21/5814
21/5815
21/5816
36/69
36/73
46/4546
67/124
67/206
67/314
79/1018
79/1657
102/316
229/8577
229/80590

3: Hauptstaatsarchiv Stuttgart (HSA)
B 17 1*

4: Stadtarchiv Augsburg (StAA)
Literaliensammlung 1522

5: Stadtarchiv Villingen (StAVl)
N 16 (No. 2014)

6: Bayerische Staatsbibliothek, Munich: Handschriftensammlung
Codex germ. 4925

B: Archives in Austria

1: Haus-, Hof- und Staatsarchiv, Vienna (HHSA)
Maximiliana 2
          23
          32
          33

2: Hofkammerarchiv, Vienna (HKA)
Reichsakten 9

3: Tiroler Landesarchiv, Innsbruck (TLA)
Schatzarchiv
   Urk. I 2340
        2342
Oberösterreichische Hofregistratur
   Reihe A 12/33
Kanzleibücher, ältere Reihe
   Lit. D
        H
Kopialbücher
   An die fürstliche Durchlaucht
   1523–5
Maximiliana
   XIV/43, 44, 55

4: Stiftsarchiv St Paul im Lavanttal, Carinthia
Handschriften 93/2

C: Archives in Switzerland

1: Staatsarchiv des Kantons Basel-Stadt (SABs)
Missiven A 30
Politisches M 4, 1

2: Staatsarchiv des Kantons Zürich (SAZh)
A 195/1

3: Archives de l'Ancien Évêché de Bâle, Porrentruy (AAEB)

Missiven 332
Extradita Wien 42 (neu [Basel] 28)

D: Archives in France

1: Archives Départementales du Haut-Rhin, Colmar (ADHR)

1 C 7
E 657
E 658
E 659
E 660

2: Archives de la Ville de Colmar (AVC)

FF 15, 1

3: Archives de la Ville de Strasbourg (AVS)

AA 364
AA 365
AA 374
AA 394
AA 396
Archives du Grand Chapitre
III/(1)
IV/(2)
Archives du Chapitre de St Thomas
96/8

4: Archives de la Ville de Kaysersberg (AVKy)

BB 9
BB 10

5: Bibliothèque Nationale et Universitaire de Strasbourg (BNUS)

MS 845

II. PRINTED PRIMARY MATERIALS

Allen, P. S., et al. (eds.), *Opus Epistolarum Des. Erasmi Roterodami*, vol. viii (Oxford, 1934).
Baumann, Franz Ludwig (ed.), *Quellen zur Geschichte des Bauernkriegs in Oberschwaben* (Bibliothek des Litterarischen Vereins in Stutttgart, cxxix) (Tübingen, 1876; reprint Hildesheim/New York, 1975).
—— and Tumbült, Georg (eds.), *Mitteilungen aus dem fürstlich fürstenbergischen Archive*, vol. i (Tübingen, 1894).
Burckhardt, Herbert (ed.), 'Karsthans (1521)', in Otto Clemen (ed.), *Flugschriften aus den ersten Jahren der Reformation*, vol. iv (Halle a. d. Saale, 1910; reprint Nieuwkoop, 1967).
Deutsche Reichstagsakten, ältere Reihe, vol. ix, ed. Dietrich Kerler (Gotha, 1887).
Deutsche Reichstagsakten, mittlere Reihe, vol. v, ed. Heinz Angermeier (Göttingen, 1981).
Franz, Günther (ed.), *Quellen zur Geschichte des Bauernkriegs* (Darmstadt, 1963).
Hartfelder, Karl (ed.), 'Akten zur Geschichte des Bauernkriegs in Süddeutschland', *ZGO* xxxix (1885).

—— (ed.), 'Urkundliche Beiträge zur Geschichte des Bauernkrieges im Breisgau', *ZGO* xxxiv (1882).

Hefele, Friedrich (ed.), *Freiburger Urkundenbuch*, vol. iii (Freiburg, 1957).

Krieger, Albert (ed.), *Regesten der Markgrafen von Baden und Hachberg, 1050–1515*, vol. iv: 1453–1475 (Innsbruck, 1915).

Lahusen, Johannes, 'Die Urkunden über Freiburgs i. Br. Übergang an Österreich 1368', *Mitteilungen des Instituts für österreichische Geschichtsforschung*, xxxiv (1913).

Mone, Franz Joseph (ed.), *Quellensammlung der badischen Landesgeschichte*, vols. ii and iii (Karlsruhe, 1845–63).

Monumenta Germaniae Historica. Legum sectio IV: Constitutiones et acta publica imperatorum et regum, vol. ii, ed. Ludwig Weiland (Hanover, 1896).

—— *Staatsschriften des späteren Mittelalters*, vol. vi: *Reformation Kaiser Siegmunds*, ed. Heinrich Koller (Stuttgart, 1964).

Reizler, Siegmund (ed.), *Fürstenbergisches Urkundenbuch*, vol. iii (Tübingen, 1878).

Roder, Christian (ed.), *Heinrich Hugs Villinger Chronik von 1495 bis 1533* (Bibliothek des Litterarischen Vereins in Stuttgart, clxiv) (Tübingen, 1883).

Rott, Jean (ed.), 'Documents inédits sur le "Bundschuh" et la Guerre des Paysans en Alsace', *Revue d'Alsace*, cv (1979).

Rowan, Steven W. (ed.), 'Die Jahresrechnungen eines Freiburger Kaufmanns 1487/88. Ein Beitrag zur Handelsgeschichte des Oberrheins', mit einem Nachwort von Berent Schwineköper, in Erich Maschke and Jürgen Sydow (eds.), *Stadt und Umland* (Veröffentlichungen der Kommission für geschichtliche Landeskunde in Baden-Württemberg, Reihe B lxxxii) (Stuttgart, 1974).

Schreiber, Johann Heinrich (ed.), *Urkundenbuch der Stadt Freiburg in Breisgau*, (2 vols., Freiburg, 1828–9).

—— (ed.), *Der deutsche Bauernkrieg. Gleichzeitige Urkunden* (Urkundenbuch der Stadt Freiburg im Breisgau, NF), (3 vols., Freiburg, 1863–6).

Scott, Tom (ed.), *Die Freiburger Enquete von 1476. Quellen zur Wirtschafts- und Verwaltungsgeschichte der Stadt Freiburg im Breisgau im fünfzehnten Jahrhundert* (Veröffentlichungen aus dem Archiv der Stadt Freiburg im Breisgau, xx) (Freiburg, 1986).

Virck, Hans (ed.), *Politische Correspondenz der Stadt Straßburg im Zeitalter der Reformation*, vol. i (Strasbourg, 1882).

Zasius, Ulrich, *Nüwe Stattrechten und Statuten der löblichen Statt Fryburg im Pryszgow gelegen* (Basel, 1520).

III. PRINTED SECONDARY MATERIALS

Adam, Ernst, *Das Freiburger Münster* (Große Bauten Europas, vol. i), 2nd edn. (Stuttgart, 1973).

Albert, Peter Paul, *Freiburg im Urteil der Jahrhunderte* (Freiburg, 1924).

Printed Secondary Materials 241

—— 'Die reformatorische Bewegung zu Freiburg bis zum Jahre 1525', *FDA* xlvi (1919).

Amiet, Bruno, *Die solothurnische Territorialpolitik von 1344–1532* (Solothurn, 1929).

Ammann, Hektor, 'Vom Lebensraum der mittelalterlichen Stadt. Eine Untersuchung an schwäbischen Beispielen', in Karl Heinz Schröder (ed.), *Studien zur südwestdeutschen Landeskunde. Festschrift zu Ehren von Friedrich Huttenlocher anläßlich seines 70. Geburtstages* (Bad Godesberg, 1963).

—— *Schaffhauser Wirtschaft im Mittelalter* (Thayngen, 1948).

—— *Wirtschaft und Lebensraum der mittelalterlichen Kleinstadt*, vol. i: *Rheinfelden* (Frick, 1950).

—— *Die wirtschaftliche Stellung der Reichsstadt Nürnberg im Spätmittelalter* (Nürnberger Forschungen, xiii) (Nuremberg, 1970).

Armbruster, Fritz, 'Die Freiburger Talvogtei im Dreisamtal. Studien zur Entwicklung und zur Verfassungsgeschichte bis zum Jahre 1661' (Diss. jur. Freiburg, 1950).

—— 'Die Freiburger Talvogtei im Dreisamtal', in Friedrich Metz (ed.), *Vorderösterreich. Eine geschichtliche Landeskunde*, 2nd edn. (Freiburg, 1967).

Bader, Karl Siegfried, *Der deutsche Südwesten in seiner territorialstaatlichen Entwicklung* (Stuttgart, 1950).

—— *Studien zur Rechtsgeschichte des mittelalterlichen Dorfes*, vol i: *Das mittelalterliche Dorf als Friedens- und Rechtsbereich* (Weimar, 1957).

Baillet, Lina, 'Deux villes de la Moyenne Alsace: Sélestat et Colmar, face aux conflits religieux et sociaux', in Alphonse Wollbrett (ed.), *La Guerre des Paysans 1525* (Société d'Histoire et d'Archéologie de Saverne et Environs. Études Alsatiques, numéro supplémentaire xciii) (Saverne, 1975).

Barnum, H. Gardiner, *Market Centers and Hinterlands in Baden-Württemberg* (University of Chicago, Department of Geography, Research Paper ciii) (Chicago, 1966).

Bärthel, Ernst-Volker, *Der Stadtwald Breisach. 700 Jahre Waldgeschichte in der Aue des Oberrheins* (Schriftenreihe der Landesforstverwaltung Baden-Württemberg, xviii) (Stuttgart, 1965).

Bastian, Johanna, *Der Freiburger Oberhof* (Veröffentlichungen des Alemannischen Instituts Freiburg im Breisgau, ii) (Freiburg, 1934).

Bauer, Clemens, 'Jakob Villinger, Großschatzmeister Kaiser Maximilians. Ein Umriß', in idem, *Gesammelte Aufsätze zur Wirtschafts- und Sozialgeschichte* (Freiburg/Basel/Vienna, 1965).

—— 'Die wirtschaftliche Ausstattung der Freiburger Universität in ihrer Gründungsperiode', in idem, *Gesammelte Aufsätze*.

Beemelmans, Wilhelm, 'Die Organisation der vorderösterreichischen Behörden in Ensisheim im 16. Jahrhundert', *ZGO* NF xxii (1907).

Bergier, Jean-François, 'Les rapports économiques et sociaux entre les villes et la campagne en Suisse au cours du temps moderne', in Gaston Gaudard, Carl Pfaff, and Roland Ruffieux (eds.), *Fribourg, ville et territoire. Aspects politiques, sociaux et culturels de la relation ville–campagne depuis le bas Moyen Age* (Fribourg, 1981).

Bergsten, Torsten, *Balthasar Hubmaier. Anabaptist Theologian and Martyr*, ed. W. R. Estep Jr. (Valley Forge, Pa., 1978).

Birkenmeier, Adolf, 'Die fremden Krämer zu Freiburg im Breisgau und Zürich im Mittelalter bis zum Ausgang des 16. Jahrhunderts', *ZGGFr* xxix (1913).

Bischoff, Georges, 'Colmar et la crise révolutionnaire de 1524–1525', *Annuaire de la Société d'Histoire et d'Archéologie de Colmar*, 1975/6.

Blaschke, Karlheinz, *Bevölkerungsgeschichte von Sachsen bis zur Industriellen Revolution* (Weimar, 1967).

Blickle, Peter, 'contribution to discussion', in idem (ed.), *Revolte und Revolution in Europa. Referate und Protokolle des Internationalen Symposiums zur Erinnerung an den Bauernkrieg 1525 (Memmingen, 24.–27. März 1975) (Historische Zeitschrift*, Beiheft 4 NF) (Munich, 1975).

—— *Landschaften im Alten Reich.Die staatliche Funktion des gemeinen Mannes in Oberdeutschland* (Munich, 1973).

—— *The Revolution of 1525. The German Peasants' War from a New Perspective* (Baltimore, Md./London, 1981).

Boockmann, Hartmut, 'Zu den geistigen und religiösen Voraussetzungen des Bauernkrieges', in Bernd Moeller (ed.), *Bauernkriegs-Studien* (Schriften des Vereins für Reformationsgeschichte, clxxxix, vol. 82,2/83) (Gütersloh, 1975).

Brady, Thomas A., Jr., *Turning Swiss. Cities and Empire, 1450–1550* (Cambridge Studies in Early Modern History) (Cambridge, 1985).

Brandl, Helmut, *Der Stadtwald von Freiburg. Eine forst- und wirtschaftsgeschichtliche Untersuchung über die Beziehung zwischen Waldnutzung und wirtschaflicher Entwicklung der Stadt Freiburg vom Mittelalter bis zur Gegenwart* (Veröffentlichungen aus dem Archiv der Stadt Freiburg in Breisgau, xii) (Freiburg, 1970).

Brauer-Gramm, Hildburg, *Der Landvogt Peter von Hagenbach. Die burgundische Herrschaft am Oberrhein 1469–1474* (Göttinger Bausteine zur Geschichtswissenschaft, xxvii) (Göttingen, 1957).

Braun, Albert, *Der Klerus des Bistums Konstanz im Ausgang des Mittelalters* (Vorreformationsgeschichtliche Forschungen, xiv) (Münster, 1938).

Brecht, Martin, and Ehmer, Hermann, *Südwestdeutsche Reformationsgeschichte. Zur Einführung der Reformation im Herzogtum Württemberg 1534* (Stuttgart, 1984).

Brenner, Robert, 'Agrarian Class Structure and Economic Development in Pre-Industrial Europe', *Past and Present*, lxx (1976).

—— 'The Agrarian Roots of European Capitalism', *Past and Present*, xcvii (1982).

Bücking, Jürgen, 'Der "Bauernkrieg" in den habsburgischen Ländern als sozialer Systemkonflikt, 1524–1526', in Hans-Ulrich Wehler (ed.), *Der Deutsche Bauernkrieg 1524–1526 (Geschichte und Gesellschaft. Zeitschrift für Historische Sozialwissenschaft*, Sonderheft 1) (Göttingen, 1975).

Burg, André-Marcel, 'La Guerre des Paysans dans la région de Haguenau', in Alphonse Wollbrett (ed.), *La Guerre des Paysans 1525* (Société d'Histoire et d'Archéologie de Saverne et Environs, Études alsatiques, numéro supplémentaire xciii) (Saverne, 1975).

Carol, Hans, 'Sozialräumliche Gliederung und planerische Gestaltung des Großstadtbereiches. Dargestellt am Beispiel Zürich (1956)', in Peter Schöller (ed.), *Zentralitätsforschung* (Wege der Forschung, ccci) (Darmstadt, 1972).

Christaller, Walter, *Central Places in Southern Germany* (Englewood Cliffs, NJ, 1966).

——*Die zentralen Orte in Süddeutschland. Eine ökonomisch-geographische Untersuchung über die Gesetzmäßigkeit der Verbreitung und Entwicklung der Siedlungen mit städtischer Funktion* (Jena, 1933; repr. Darmstadt, 1968).

Cohn, Henry J., 'Anticlericalism in the German Peasants' War 1525', *Past and Present*, lxxxiii (1979).

Dietrich, Christian, *Die Stadt Zürich und ihre Landgemeinden während der Bauernunruhen von 1489 bis 1525* (Europäische Hochschulschriften, Reihe 3 ccxxix) (Frankfurt am Main/Berne/New York, 1985).

Dirlmeier, Ulf, 'Stadt und Bürgertum. Zur Steuerpolitik und zum Stadt–Land–Verhältnis', in Horst Buszello, Peter Blickle, and Rudolf Endres (eds.), *Der deutsche Bauernkrieg* (Paderborn/Munich/Vienna/Zürich, 1984).

Dobson, R. B., 'Urban Decline in Late Medieval England', *Transactions of the Royal Historical Society*, 5th series xxv (1977).

Dold, Augustin, 'Zur Wirtschaftsgeschichte des ehemaligen Dominikanerklosters zu Freiburg i. Br.', *ZGGFr* xxvi (1910).

Dollinger, Philippe, 'Un aspect de la Guerre des Paysans en Alsace: l'organisation du soulèvement', in *Paysans d'Alsace* (Publications de la Société Savante d'Alsace et des Régions de l'Est, grandes publications vii) (Strasbourg, 1959).

Domsta, Hans J., *Die Kölner Außenbürger. Untersuchungen zur Politik und Verfassung der Stadt Köln von der Mitte des 13. bis zur Mitte des 16. Jahrhunderts* (Rheinisches Archiv, lxxxiv) (Bonn, 1973).

Drollinger, Kuno, *Kleine Städte Südwestdeutschlands. Studien zur Sozial- und Wirtschaftsgeschichte der Städte im rechtsrheinischen Teil des Hochstifts Speyer bis zur Mitte des 17. Jahrhunderts* (Veröffentlichungen der Kommission für geschichtliche Landeskunde in Baden-Württemberg, Reihe B xlviii) (Stuttgart, 1968).

Dubled, Henri, 'La bourgeoisie foraine en Alsace, principalement à Strasbourg: "Pfalburger" et "Ausburger"', *Cahiers d'Archéologie et d'Histoire d'Alsace*, cxxxiii (1953).

Dubler, Anne-Marie, *Handwerk, Gewerbe und Zunft in Stadt und Landschaft Luzern* (Luzerner Historische Veröffentlichungen, xiv) (Lucerne/Stuttgart, 1982).

Duggan, Lawrence Gerald, *Bishop and Chapter. The Governance of the Bishopric of Speyer to 1552* (Studies presented to the International Commission for the History of Representative and Parliamentary Institutions, lxii) (New Brunswick, NJ, 1978).

Dyer, Alan, 'Growth and Decay in English Towns 1500–1700', *Urban History Yearbook*, 1979.

Ehrler, Joseph, 'Stadtverfassung und Zünfte Freiburgs im Breisgau. Ein Beitrag zur oberrheinischen Wirtschaftsgeschichte', *Jahrbücher für National-ökonomie und Statistik*, xli (1911); xliv (1912).

Elben, Arnold, *Vorderösterreich und seine Schutzgebiete im Jahre 1524. Ein Beitrag zur Geschichte des Bauernkriegs* (Stuttgart, 1889).

Elm, Kaspar, *Beiträge zur Geschichte des Wilhelmiterordens* (Münstersche Forschungen, xiv) (Cologne/Graz, 1962).

Engel, Evamaria, 'Zu einigen Aspekten spätmittelalterlicher Stadt–Land-Beziehungen vornehmlich im Bereich von Hansestädten', *Jahrbuch für Geschichte des Feudalismus*, iv (1980).

Everitt, Alan, 'The Marketing of Agricultural Produce', in Joan Thirsk (ed.), *The Agrarian History of England and Wales*, vol. iv (Cambridge, 1967).

Fehn, Klaus, 'Die Bedeutung der zentralörtlichen Funktionen für die früh- und hochmittelalterlichen Zentren Altbayerns', in *Stadt–Land-Beziehungen und Zentralität als Problem der historischen Raumforschung* (Forschungs- und Sitzungsberichte der Akademie für Raumforschung und Landesplanung, lxxxviii: Historische Raumforschung, xi) (Hanover, 1974).

—— *Die zentralörtlichen Funktionen früher Zentren in Altbayern. Raumbindende Umlandbeziehungen im bayerisch-österreichischen Altsiedelland von der Spät-latènezeit bis zum Ende des Hochmittelalters* (Wiesbaden, 1970).

Feine, Hans Erich, 'Die Territorialbildung der Habsburger im deutschen Südwesten vornehmlich im späten Mittelalter', *Zeitschrift der Savigny-Stiftung für Rechtsgeschichte, Germanistiche Abteilung*, lxvii (1950).

Fester, Richard, 'Markgraf Bernhard I. und die Anfänge des badischen Territorialstaates', *Neujahrsblätter der Badischen Historischen Kommission*, vi (1896).

Feyler, Anna, 'Die Beziehungen des Hauses Württemberg zur schweizerischen Eidgenossenschaft in der ersten Hälfte des XVI. Jahrhunderts' (Diss. phil. Zürich, 1905).

Fischer, Thomas, *Städtische Armut und Armenfürsorge im 15. und 16. Jahrhundert. Sozialgeschichtliche Untersuchungen am Beispiel der Städte Basel, Freiburg i. Br. und Straßburg* (Göttinger Beiträge zur Wirtschafts- und Sozialgeschichte, iv) (Göttingen, 1979).

Flamm, Hermann, 'Das Bruderschaftsbuch der Küfergesellen in Freiburg im Breisgau, 1475–1552 bzw. 1584', *Freiburger Adresskalender*, 1907.

—— 'Die Einwohnerzahl Freiburgs im Jahre 1459', *Schau-ins-Land*, xxxix (1912).

—— 'Die Geschichte des Metzgergewerbes in Freiburg im Breisgau seit Gründung der Stadt bis zur Gegenwart', in *Festschrift zum 28. Deutschen Fleischerverbandstag in Freiburg* (Freiburg, 1905).

—— *Der wirtschaftliche Niedergang Freiburgs i. Br. und die Lage des städtischen Grundeigentums im 14. und 15. Jahrhundert. Ein Beitrag zur Geschichte der geschlossenen Stadtwirtschaft* (Volkswirtschaftliche Abhandlungen der badischen Hochschulen, viii supplementary vol. 3) (Karlsruhe, 1905).

Fleckenstein, Josef, 'Bürgertum und Rittertum in der Geschichte des mittelalterlichen Breisgaus', in Wolfgang Müller (ed.), *Freiburg im Mittelalter. Vorträge zum Stadtjubiläum 1970* (Veröffentlichungen des Alemannischen Instituts, xxix) (Bühl, 1970).

Frank, Theophil, 'Das Textilgewerbe der Stadt Freiburg i. Br. bis zum Ausgang des 16. Jahrhunderts' (Diss. phil. Freiburg, 1912).

Franz, Günther, *Der deutsche Bauernkrieg*, 8th edn. (Darmstadt, 1963).

—— 'Zur Geschichte des Bundschuhs', *ZGO* NF xlvii (1934).

French, R. A., 'The Early and Medieval Russian Town', in James H. Bater and R. A. French (eds.), *Studies in Russian Historical Geography* (2 vols., London/New York, 1983), vol. ii.

Fritze, Konrad, *Bürger und Bauern zur Hansezeit. Studien zu den Stadt–Land-Beziehungen an der südwestlichen Ostseeküste vom 13. bis zum 16. Jahrhundert* (Abhandlungen zur Handels- und Sozialgeschichte, xvi) (Weimar, 1976).

—— 'Probleme der Stadt–Land-Beziehungen im Bereich der Wendischen Hansestädte nach 1370', *Hansische Geschichtsblätter*, lxxxv (1967).

Fryde, E. B. and M. M., 'Public Credit, with Special Reference to North-Western Europe', in *Cambridge Economic History of Europe*, vol. iii, ed. M. M. Postan, E. E. Rich, and Edward Miller (Cambridge, 1963).

Geiges, Fritz, *Der mittelalterliche Fensterschmuck des Freiburger Münsters* (Freiburg, 1931).

Gemmert, Franz Josef, 'Das Basler Domkapitel in Freiburg', *Schau-ins-Land*, lxxxiv/lxxxv (1966/7).

Gény, Joseph, *Die Reichsstadt Schlettstadt und ihr Antheil an den social-politischen und religiösen Bewegungen der Jahre 1490–1536* (Erläuterungen und Ergänzungen zur Janssens Geschichte des deutschen Volkes, i) (Freiburg, 1900).

Germer, Heinz, *Die Landgebietspolitik der Stadt Braunschweig bis zum Ausgang des 15. Jahrhunderts* (Studien und Vorarbeiten zum historischen Atlas Niedersachsens, xvi) (Göttingen, 1937).

Gießler, Ferdinand, *Die Geschichte des Wilhelmitenklosters in Oberried bei Freiburg im Breisgau* (Freiburg, 1911).

Ginter, Gottfried, 'Die Vorwehen des Bauernkrieges im Bauland und Kraichgau. Hans Beheim von Niklashausen und Jos Fritz aus Untergrombach', *Badische Heimat*, li (1971).

Gönnenwein, Otto, 'Marktrecht und Städtewesen im alemannischen Gebiet', *ZGO* NF lix (1950).

Gothein, Eberhard, *Wirtschaftsgeschichte des Schwarzwaldes und der angrenzenden Landschaften*, vol. i: *Städte- und Gewerbegeschichte* (Strasbourg, 1892).

Graus, Frantisek, 'Tendenzen der Stadt–Land-Beziehungen im ausgehenden Mittelalter', in Gaston Gaudard, Carl Pfaff, and Roland Ruffieux (eds.), *Fribourg, ville et territoire. Aspects politiques, sociaux et culturels de la relation ville–campagne depuis le bas Moyen Age* (Fribourg, 1981).

Grüneisen, Henny, 'Herzog Sigmund von Tirol, der Kaiser und die Ächtung der Eidgenossen 1469', in *Aus Reichstagen des 15. und 16. Jahrhunderts* (Schriftenreihe der Historischen Kommission bei der Bayerischen Akademie der Wissenschaften, v) (Göttingen, 1958).

Gutzwiller, Hellmut, 'Die Zünfte in Freiburg im Üchtland, 1460–1650', *Freiburger Geschichtsblätter*, xli/xlii (1949).

Hagenmaier, Winfried, 'Das Verhältnis der Universität Freiburg i. Br. zur Reformation. Untersuchungen über das Verhalten der Universität und die Einstellung einzelner Professoren und Studenten gegenüber der reformatorischen Bewegung in den Jahren 1517–1530' (Diss. phil. Freiburg, 1968).

Hart, Wolf, *Die künstlerische Ausstattung des Freiburger Münsters* (Freiburg, 1981).

Hartfelder, Karl, *Die alten Zunftordnungen der Stadt Freiburg im Breisgau*, part I (Beilage zum Programm des Gymnasiums zu Freiburg im Breisgau) (Freiburg, 1879).

—— *Zur Geschichte des Bauernkriegs in Südwestdeutschland* (Stuttgart, 1884).

Hefele, Friedrich, 'Freiburg als vorderösterreichische Stadt', in Friedrich Metz (ed.), *Vorderösterreich. Eine geschichtliche Landeskunde*, 2nd edn. (Freiburg, 1967).

Hilton, Rodney, Review of Alan Macfarlane, *The Origins of English Individualism* (Oxford, 1978), *New Left Review*, CXX (1980).

—— 'Towns in Societies—Medieval England', *Urban History Yearbook*, 1982.

Hinderschiedt, Gustav, 'Die Freiburger Zunftordnungen des 15. und des 16. Jahrhunderts' (Diss. phil. Freiburg, 1953).

Hoskins, W. G. 'An Elizabethan Provincial Town, Leicester', in J. H. Plumb (ed.), *Studies in Social History* (London, 1955).

Hoyer, Siegfried, *Das Militärwesen im deutschen Bauernkrieg 1524–1526* (Militärhistorische Studien, NF xvi) (Berlin, 1975).

Hugard, Rudolf, 'Die Beziehungen der Herren von Staufen zur Stadt Freiburg', *Schau-ins-Land*, xiv (1887).

Huter, Franz, 'Vorderösterreich und Österreich: Von ihren mittelalterlichen Beziehungen', in Friedrich Metz (ed.), *Vorderösterreich. Eine geschichtliche Landeskunde*, 2nd edn. (Freiburg, 1967).

Irsigler, Franz, 'Stadt und Umland in der historischen Forschung: Theorien und Konzepte', in Neithard Bulst, Jochen Hoock, and Franz Irsigler (eds.),

Bevölkerung, Wirtschaft und Gesellschaft. Stadt–Land-Beziehungen in Deutschland und Frankreich 14. bis 19. Jahrhundert (Trier, 1983).
—— 'Stadt und Umland im Spätmittelalter. Zur zentralitätsfördernden Kraft von Fernhandel und Exportgewerbe', in Emil Meynen (ed.), *Zentralität als Problem der mittelalterlichen Stadtgeschichtsforschung* (Städteforschung: Veröffentlichungen des Instituts für vergleichende Städtegeschichte in Münster, Reihe A viii) (Cologne/Vienna, 1979).
Juillard, Etienne, 'Paysans d'Alsace, paysans rhénans', in *Paysans d'Alsace* (Publications de la Société Savante d'Alsace et des Régions de l'Est, grandes publications vii) (Strasbourg, 1959).
Joachim, Hermann, 'Gilde und Stadtgemeinde in Freiburg i. Br. Zugleich ein Beitrag zur Rechts- und Verfassungsgeschichte dieser Stadt', in *Festgabe zum 21. Juli 1905 Anton Hagedorn . . . gewidmet* (Hamburg/Leipzig, 1906).
Kartels, Josef, *Herdern bei Freiburg i. Br.* (Freiburg, 1905).
Kellenbenz, Hermann, 'Rural Industries in the West from the End of the Middle Ages to the Eighteenth Century', in Peter Earle (ed.), *Essays in European Economic History 1500–1800* (Oxford, 1974).
Keßner, Ute, 'Albrecht VI. von Österreich und das Freiburger Zunftverbot 1454' (Wissenschaftliche Prüfungsarbeit, University of Freiburg, 1976).
Kießling, Rolf, 'Bürgerlicher Besitz auf dem Land—ein Schlüssel zu den Stadt–Land-Beziehungen im Spätmittelalter, aufgezeigt am Beispiel Augsburgs und anderer oberschwäbischer Städte', *Augsburger Beiträge zur Landesgeschichte Bayerisch-Schwabens*, i (1979).
—— 'Herrschaft — Markt — Landbesitz. Aspekte der Zentralität und der Stadt–Land-Beziehungen spätmittelalterlicher Städte an ostschwäbischen Beispielen', in Emil Meynen (ed.), *Zentralität als Problem der mittelalterlichen Stadtgeschichtsforschung* (Städteforschung: Veröffentlichungen des Instituts für vergleichende Städtegeschichte in Münster, Reihe A viii) (Cologne/Vienna, 1979).
—— 'Stadt–Land–Beziehungen im Spätmittelalter. Überlegungen zur Problemstellung und Methode anhand neuerer Arbeiten vorwiegend zu süddeutschen Beispielen', *Zeitschrift für bayerische Landesgeschichte*, xl (1977).
—— 'Stadt und Land im Textilgewerbe Ostschwabens vom 14. bis zur Mitte des 16. Jahrhunderts', in Neithard Bulst, Jochen Hoock, and Franz Irsigler (eds.), *Bevölkerung, Wirtschaft und Gesellschaft. Stadt–Land-Beziehungen in Deutschland und Frankreich 14. bis. 19. Jahrhundert* (Trier, 1983).
Kirchgässner, Bernhard, *Das Steuerwesen der Reichsstadt Konstanz 1418–1460. Aus der Wirtschafts- und Sozialgeschichte einer oberdeutschen Handelsstadt am Ausgang des Mittelalters* (Konstanzer Geschichts- und Rechtsquellen, x) (Constance, 1960).
Körner, Martin H., *Solidarités financières suisses au XVIe siècle* (Bibliothèque Historique Vaudoise, lxvi) (Lausanne, 1980).

Kreutter, Franz, *Geschichte der k. k. Vorderösterreichischen Staaten*, vol. i (St Blasien, 1790).

Kriedte, Peter, Medick, Hans, and Schlumbohm, Jürgen, *Industrialization before Industrialization. Rural Industry in the Genesis of Capitalism* (Cambridge/Paris, 1981).

Krimm, Konrad, *Baden und Habsburg um die Mitte des 15. Jahrhunderts. Fürstlicher Dienst und Reichsgewalt im späten Mittelalter* (Veröffentlichungen der Kommission für geschichtliche Landeskunde in Baden-Württemberg, Reihe B lxxxix) (Stuttgart, 1976).

Krischer, Joseph, *Die Verfassung und Verwaltung der Reichsstadt Schlettstadt im Mittelalter* (Strasbourg, 1909).

Langton, John and Hoppe, Göran, *Town and Country in the Development of Early Modern Western Europe* (Historical Geography Research Series, xi) (Norwich, 1983).

Laubenberger, Franz, 'Die Freiburger Stadtverwaltung im 17. und 18. Jahrhundert und ihre gesellschaftliche Struktur', in Erich Maschke and Jürgen Sydow (eds.), *Verwaltung und Gesellschaft in der südwestdeutschen Stadt des 17. und 18. Jahrhunderts* (Veröffentlichungen der Kommission für geschichtliche Landeskunde in Baden-Württemberg, Reihe B lviii) (Stuttgart, 1969).

Leiser, Wolfgang, *'Sie dienen auch jetzt noch aber fremden Göttern.' Der Freiburger Herrschaftswechsel 1368* (Veröffentlichungen des Alemannischen Instituts, xxv) (Bühl, 1968).

Lösch, August, *The Economics of Location* (New Haven/London, 1954).

Lutz, Robert H., *Wer war der gemeine Mann? Der dritte Stand in der Krise des Spätmittelalters* (Munich/Vienna, 1979).

Macfarlane, Alan, *The Origins of English Individualism* (Oxford, 1978).

Machalka-Felser, Rautgundis, 'Stadt und Umland in Herrschafts- und Wirtschaftsgefüge des Spätmittelalters', *Die Alte Stadt. Zeitschrift für Stadtgeschichte und Denkmalpflege*, vi (1979).

Martin, Karl, 'Die Einwanderung aus Savoyen nach Südbaden. Ein Beitrag zur Erforschung der blutmäßigen Zusammensetzung unserer Bevölkerung', *Schau-ins-Land*, lxv/lxvi (1938–9).

Martini, Eduard Christian, 'Sulzburg: Eine Stadt-, Bergwerks- und Waldgeschichte', *ZGGFr* v (1879–82).

Matzinger, A. W., 'Zur Geschichte der niederen Vereinigung' (Diss. phil. Basel, 1910).

Maurer, Hans-Martin, 'Der Bauernkrieg als Massenerhebung. Dynamik einer revolutionären Bewegung', in *Bausteine zur geschichtlichen Landeskunde von Baden-Württemberg* (Stuttgart, 1979).

Maurer, Justus, *Prediger im Bauernkrieg* (Calwer Theologische Monographien, v) (Stuttgart, 1979).

Mayer, Hermann, 'Zur Geschichte der Pest im 15. und 16. Jahrhundert', *Schau-ins-Land*, xxviii (1901).

Mayer, Theodor, 'Die Habsburger am Oberrhein im Mittelalter', in idem, *Mittelalterliche Studien. Gesammelte Aufsätze* (Lindau/Constance, 1959).
—— 'Der Staat der Herzöge von Zähringen', in idem, *Mittelalterliche Studien*.
—— 'Die Zähringer und Freiburg im Breisgau', in idem, *Mittelalterliche Studien*.
Merrington, John, 'Town and Country in the Transition to Capitalism', in Rodney Hilton *et al.*, *The Transition from Feudalism to Capitalism* (London, 1976).
Metz, Rudolf, 'Bergbau und Hüttenwesen in den Vorlanden', in Friedrich Metz (ed.), *Vorderösterreich. Eine geschichtliche Landeskunde*, 2nd edn. (Freiburg, 1967).
Morard, Nicolas, 'Les investissements bourgeois dans le plat pays autour de Fribourg de 1250 à 1350', in Gaston Gaudard, Carl Pfaff, and Roland Ruffieux (eds.), *Fribourg, ville et territoire. Aspects politiques, sociaux et culturels de la relation ville–campagne depuis le bas Moyen Age* (Fribourg, 1981).
Müller, Karl Friedrich, *Geschichte der Getreidehandelspolitik, des Bäcker- und Müllergewerbes der Stadt Freiburg i. Br. im 14., 15. und 16. Jahrhundert*. ZGGFr Beiheft II (Freiburg, 1926).
Müller, Wolfgang, 'Studien zur Geschichte der Klöster St. Märgen und Allerheiligen, Freiburg im Breisgau', *FDA* lxxxix (1969).
Nauck, Ernst Theodor, *Aus der Geschichte der Freiburger Wundärzte und verwandter Berufe* (Veröffentlichungen aus dem Archiv der Stadt Freiburg im Breisgau, viii) (Freiburg, 1965).
Naujoks, Eberhard, 'Obrigkeit und Zunftverfassung in den süddeutschen Reichsstädten', *Zeitschrift für württembergische Landesgeschichte*, xxxiii (1974).
Neef, Ernst, 'Das Problem der zentralen Orte', in Peter Schöller (ed.), *Zentralitätsforschung* (Wege der Forschung, ccci) (Darmstadt, 1972).
Nehlsen, Hermann, *Die Freiburger Familie Snewlin. Rechts- und sozialgeschichtliche Studien zur Entwicklung des mittelalterlichen Bürgertums* (Veröffentlichungen aus dem Archiv der Stadt Freiburg im Breisgau, ix) (Freiburg, 1967).
Nicholas, David, *Town and Countryside: Social, Economic and Political Tensions in Fourteenth-Century Flanders* (Rijksuniversiteit te Gent: Werken uitgegeven door de Faculteit van de Letteren en Wijsbegeerte, clii) (Bruges, 1971).
Notheisen, Emil, 'Stadtgemeinde: Außenbesitzungen', in *AmtKrB* vol. i. 2.
—— 'Die Vororte', in *AmtKrB*, vol. i. 2.
Oelrich, Karl-Heinz, *Der späte Erasmus und die Reformation* (Reformationsgeschichtliche Studien und Texte, lxxxvi) (Münster, 1961).
Ohler, Norbert, 'Freiburg i. Br. im 16. und 17. Jahrhundert. Kreditaufnahme und Geldanlage der Stadt', in Hans Fenske, Wolfgang Reinhard, and Ernst Schulin (eds.), *Historia Integra. Festschrift für Erich Hassinger zum 70. Geburtstag* (Berlin, 1977).
—— 'Zum Haushalt der Stadt Freiburg im Breisgau im 16. und 17. Jahrhundert', *Zeitschrift des Breisgau-Geschichtsvereins ('Schau-ins-Land')*, xciv/xcv (1976/7).

—— 'Strukturen des Finanzhaushalts der Stadt Freiburg i. Br. in der frühen Neuzeit', *ZGO* cxxv (1977).

Peyer, Hans Conrad, 'Wollgewerbe, Viehzucht, Solddienst und Bevölkerungsentwicklung in Stadt und Landschaft Freiburg i. Ue. vom 14. bis 16. Jahrhundert', in Hermann Kellenbenz (ed.), *Agrarisches Nebengewerbe und Formen der Reagrarisierung im Spätmittelalter und 19./20. Jahrhundert* (Forschungen zur Sozial- und Wirtschaftsgeschichte, xxi) (Stuttgart, 1975).

Phythian-Adams, Charles, *Desolation of a City. Coventry and the Urban Crisis of the Late Middle Ages* (Past and Present Publications) (Cambridge, 1979).

—— 'Dr Dyer's Urban Undulations', *Urban History Yearbook*, 1979.

—— 'Urban Decay in Late Medieval England', in Philip Abrams and E. A. Wrigley (eds.), *Towns in Societies: Essays in Economic History and Historical Sociology* (Cambridge, 1978).

Poinsignon, Adalbert, *Geschichtliche Ortsbeschreibung der Stadt Freiburg i. Br.*, vol. i (Veröffentlichungen aus dem Archiv der Stadt Freiburg im Breisgau, ii) (Freiburg, 1891).

Pollard, Sidney, *Peaceful Conquest. The Industrialization of Europe, 1760–1970* (Oxford, 1981).

Portmann, Urs, 'Die Datenbank "Freiburger Bürgerbuch 1341–1416" als Forschungsinstrument: Herkunft der Bewohner Freiburgs im XIV. Jahrhundert', in Gaston Gaudard, Carl Pfaff, and Roland Ruffieux (eds.), *Fribourg, ville et territoire. Aspects politiques, sociaux et culturels de la relation ville–campagne depuis le bas Moyen Age* (Fribourg, 1981).

Raiser, Elisabeth, *Städtische Territorialpolitik im Mittelalter. Eine vergleichende Untersuchung über verschiedene Formen am Beispiel Lübecks und Zürichs* (Historische Studien, cdvi) (Lübeck/Hamburg, 1969).

Reynolds, Susan, 'Decline and Decay in Late Medieval Towns: A Look at Some of the Concepts and Arguments', *Urban History Yearbook*, 1981.

Riezler, Siegmund, *Geschichte des fürstlichen Hauses Fürstenberg und seiner Ahnen bis zum Jahre 1509* (Tübingen, 1883).

Rigby, S. H., 'Urban Decline in the Later Middle Ages: The Reliability of the Non-Statistical Evidence', *Urban History Yearbook*, 1984.

Rohde, Hans-Wilhelm, 'Evangelische Bewegung und katholische Restauration im österreichischen Breisgau unter Ferdinand I. und Ferdinand II. (1521–1595). Studien zur Kirchenpolitik der Habsburger in Vorderösterreich im 16. Jh.' (Diss. phil. Freiburg, 1957).

Rösch, Josef, 'Die Straßenanlagen und Zollrechte der Städte Freiburg und Villingen', *Freiburger Adresskalender*, 1853.

Rosen, Josef, 'Der Staatshaushalt Basels von 1360 bis 1535', in Hermann Kellenbenz (ed.), *Öffentliche Finanzen und privates Kapital im späten Mittelalter und in der ersten Hälfte des 19. Jahrhunderts* (Forschungen zur Sozial- und Wirtschaftsgeschichte, xvi) (Stuttgart, 1971).

Rosenkranz, Albert, *Der Bundschuh. Die Erhebungen des südwestdeutschen*

Bauernstandes in den Jahren 1493–1517 (Schriften des Wissenschaftlichen Instituts der Elsaß-Lothringer im Reich, xii) (2 vols., Heidelberg, 1927).

van Rossum, Thea, 'Studien zur Politik Freiburgs als Reichsstadt' (Diss. phil. Freiburg, 1950).

Rothkrug, Lionel, 'Icon and Ideology in Religion and Rebellion 1300–1600: *Bauernfreiheit* and *religion royale*', in János M. Bak and Gerhard Benecke (eds.), *Religion and Rural Revolt. Papers presented to the Fourth Interdisciplinary Workshop on Peasant Studies, University of British Columbia, 1982* (Manchester/Dover, NH, 1984).

Rott, Hans-Georg, 'Der Bauernkrieg und die Stadt Weißenburg im Elsaß. Bemerkungen zur Quellenlage und Versuch einer genaueren Chronologie', in Peter Blickle (ed.), *Bauer, Reich und Reformation. Festschrift für Günther Franz zum 80. Geburtstag am 23. Mai 1982* (Stuttgart, 1982).

Rott, Jean, 'Artisanat et mouvements sociaux à Strasbourg autour de 1525', in *Artisans et Ouvriers d'Alsace* (Publications de la Société Savante d'Alsace et des Régions de l'Est, grandes publications ix) (Strasbourg, 1965).

Rowan, Steven W., 'The Common Penny (1495–99) as a Source of German Social and Demographic History', *Central European History*, x (1977).

—— 'Community Survival. Freiburg im Breisgau from the Black Death to the Reformation' (unpublished MS).

—— 'The Guilds of Freiburg im Breisgau in the Later Middle Ages as Social and Political Entities' (Ph.D. Dissertation, Harvard University, 1970).

—— 'A Reichstag in the Reform Era: Freiburg im Breisgau, 1497–98', in idem and James A. Vann (eds.), *The Old Reich. Essays on German Political Institutions 1495–1806* (Studies presented to the International Commission for the History of Representative and Parliamentary Institutions, xlviii) (Brussels, 1974).

Rozman, Gilbert, 'Urban Networks and Historical Stages', *Journal of Interdisciplinary History*, ix (1978).

—— *Urban Networks in Russia, 1750–1800, and Pre-Modern Periodization* (Princeton, NJ, 1976).

Rublack, Hans-Christoph, 'Die Reformation in Vorderösterreich und Konstanz', in *Luther und die Reformation am Oberrhein* (Ausstellungskatalog, ed. Badische Landesbibliothek) (Karlsruhe, 1983).

Russell, J. C., *Medieval Regions and their Cities* (Studies in Historical Geography) (Newton Abbot, 1972).

Rüthing, Heinrich, 'Bürgerlicher Landbesitz in Höxter um 1500', in Neithard Bulst, Jochen Hoock, and Franz Irsigler (eds.), *Bevölkerung, Wirtschaft und Gesellschaft. Stadt–Land-Beziehungen in Deutschland und Frankreich 14. bis 19. Jahrhundert* (Trier, 1983).

Sanwald, Erich, 'Otto Brunfels, 1488–1534. Ein Beitrag zur Geschichte des Humanismus und Der reformation' (Diss. phil. Munich, 1932).

Schaab, Meinrad, 'Städtlein, Burg-, Amts- und Marktflecken Südwest deutschlands in Spätmittelalter und früher Neuzeit', in Emil Meynen (ed.), *Zentralität als Problem der mittelalterlichen Stadtgeschichtsforschung* (Städteforschung: Veröffentlichungen des Instituts für vergleichende Städtegeschichte in Münster, Reihe A viii) (Cologne/Vienna, 1979).

Schadek, Hans, 'Das Kloster Ettenheimmünster im Bauernkrieg', in Dieter Weis (ed.), *St Bartholomäus Ettenheim* (Munich/Zürich, 1982).

—— 'Wurde das Haus "Zum Walfisch" in Freiburg als Stadtresidenz und Alterssitz Kaiser Maximilians I. erbaut?', *Zeitschrift des Breisgau-Geschichtsvereins* (*'Schau-ins-Land'*), xcviii (1979).

Schäfer, Alfons, 'Die Höllentalstraße. Ihre Erschließung und ihre Bedeutung für den Handelsverkehr vom Mittelalter bis ins 19. Jahrhundert', in Erich Hassinger, H. J. Müller, and Hugo Ott (eds.), *Geschichte, Wirtschaft, Gesellschaft. Festschrift für Clemens Bauer zum 75. Geburtstag* (Berlin, 1974).

Schaub, Friedrich, 'Der Bauernkrieg um Freiburg 1525', *ZFrGV* xlvi (1935).

—— 'Der Bundschuh zu Lehen', *ZFrGV* xlii (1929).

—— 'Die Freiburger Universität und der Gemeine Pfennig von 1497', in Johannes Vincke (ed.), *Zur Geschichte der Universität Freiburg i. Br.* (Beiträge zur Freiburger Wissenschafts- und Universitätsgeschichte, xxxiii) (Freiburg, 1966).

—— 'Die vorderösterreichische Universität Freiburg', in Friedrich Metz (ed.), *Vorderösterreich. Eine geschichtliche Landeskunde*, 2nd edn. (Freiburg, 1967).

Schib, Karl, 'Die vier Waldstädte', in Friedrich Metz (ed.), *Vorderösterreich. Eine geschichtliche Landeskunde*, 2nd edn. (Freiburg, 1967).

Schlageter, Albrecht, 'Der mittelalterliche Bergbau im Schauinslandrevier', *Schau-ins-Land*, lxxxviii (1970).

Schmidt, Max Georg, 'Die Pfalbürger', *Zeitschrift für Kulturgeschichte*, ix (1902).

Schöller, Peter, 'Aufgaben und Probleme der Stadtgeographie', *Erdkunde*, vii (1953).

—— 'Der Markt als Zentralisationsphänomen. Das Grundprinzip und seine Wandlungen in Zeit und Raum', *Westfälische Forschungen*, xv (1962).

—— 'Stadt und Einzugsgebiet. Ein geographisches Forschungsproblem und seine Bedeutung für Landeskunde, Geschichte und Kulturraumforschung', in idem (ed.), *Zentralitätsforschung* (Wege der Forschung, ccci) (Darmstadt, 1972).

Schragmüller, Elsbeth, *Die Bruderschaft der Borer und Balierer von Freiburg und Waldkirch. Beitrag zur Gewerbegeschichte* (Volkswirtschaftliche Abhandlungen der badischen Hochschulen, NF xxx) (Karlsruhe, 1914).

Schreiber, Johann Heinrich, 'Balthasar Hubmaier, Stifter der Wiedertäufer auf dem Schwarzwalde', *Taschenbuch für Geschichte und Altertum in Süddeutschland*, ii (1840).

—— *Geschichte der Stadt und Universität Freiburg im Breisgau* (3 vols., Freiburg, 1857–8).

—— 'Melchior Fattlin, zweiter Stifter des sogenannten Karthäuser-Hauses.' Vortrag bei der Gedächtnisfeier der Stifter an der Albert-Ludwigs-Hochschule, den 30. Juni 1832 (Freiburg, 1832).

Schuler, Peter Johannes, 'Die Bevölkerungsstruktur der Stadt Freiburg im Breisgau im Spätmittelalter—Möglichkeiten und Grenzen einer quantitativen Quellenanalyse', in Wilfried Ehbrecht (ed.), *Voraussetzungen und Methoden geschichtlicher Städteforschung* (Städteforschung: Veröffentlichungen des Instituts für vergleichende Städtegeschichte in Münster, Reihe A vii) (Cologne/Vienna, 1979).

Schulte, Aloys, 'Die Einwohnerzahl von Freiburg im Jahre 1247', *ZGO* NF i (1886).

Schwarzweber, Hermann J., 'Die Landstände Vorderösterreichs im 15. Jahrhundert', *Forschungen und Mitteilungen zur Geschichte Tirols und Vorarlbergs*, v (1908).

Schwineköper, Berent, 'Bemerkungen zum Problem der städtischen Unterschichten aus Freiburger Sicht', in Erich Maschke and Jürgen Sydow (eds.), *Gesellschaftliche Unterschichten in den südwestdeutschen Städten* (Veröffentlichungen der Kommission für geschichtliche Landeskunde in Baden-Württemberg, Reihe B xli) (Stuttgart, 1967).

—— 'Beobachtungen zum Lebensraum südwestdeutscher Städte im Mittelalter, insbesondere zum engeren und weiteren Einzugsbereich der Freiburger Jahrmärkte in der zweiten Hälfte des 16. Jahrhunderts', in Erich Maschke and Jürgen Sydow (eds.), *Stadt und Umland* (Veröffentlichungen der Kommission für geschichtliche Landeskunde in Baden-Württemberg, Reihe B lxxxii) (Stuttgart, 1974).

—— 'Bonn, Köln und Freiburg im Breisgau. Bemerkungen zu den mittelalterlichen Beziehungen der Städte', in Werner Besch, Kalus Fehn, Dietrich Höroldt, Franz Irsigler, and Matthias Zender (eds.), *Die Stadt in der europäischen Geschichte. Festschrift Edith Ennen* (Bonn, 1972).

—— 'Das "Große Fest" zu Freiburg (3.–8. Juli 1454)', in Erich Hassinger, H. J. Müller, and Hugo Ott (eds.), *Geschichte, Wirtschaft, Gesellschaft. Festschrift für Clemens Bauer zum 75. Geburtstag* (Berlin, 1974).

—— 'Die Vorstädte von Freiburg im Breisgau während des Mittelalters', in Erich Maschke und Jürgen Sydow (eds.), *Stadterweiterung und Vorstadt* (Veröffentlichungen der Kommission für geschichtliche Landeskunde in Baden-Württemberg, Reihe B li) (Stuttgart, 1969).

—— and Laubenberger, Franz, *Geschichte und Schicksal der Freiburger Juden. Aus Anlaß des 100jährigen Bestehens der israelitischen Gemeinde in Freiburg* (Freiburger Stadthefte, vi) (Freiburg, 1963).

Scott, Tom, 'Economic Conflict and Co-operation on the Upper Rhine, 1450–1600', in idem and E. I. Kouri (eds.), *Politics and Society in Reformation Europe* (London/Munich, 1987).

—— 'The Peasants' War: A Historiographical Review', parts I and II, *Historical Journal*, xxii (1979).

—— 'Zum Problem der Rechts- und Besitzverhältnisse eines Freiburger Vorortes: Das Dorf Adelhausen im 15. Jahrhundert', *Zeitschrift des Breisgau-Geschichtsvereins ('Schau-ins-Land')*, ci (1982).

—— 'Reformation and Peasants' War in Waldshut and Environs: A Structural Analysis', parts I and II, *Archiv für Reformationsgeschichte*, lxix (1978); lxx (1979).

—— 'Relations between Freiburg im Breisgau and the surrounding countryside in the age of South-West German agrarian unrest before the Peasants' War, circa 1450–1520' (Ph.D. diss. Univ. of Cambridge, 1973).

—— 'Die Territorialpolitik der Stadt Freiburg im Breisgau im ausgehenden Mittelalter', *Zeitschrift des Breisgau-Geschichtsvereins ('Schau-ins-Land')*, cii (1983).

—— 'The *Volksreformation* of Thomas Müntzer in Allstedt and Mühlhausen', *Journal of Ecclesiastical History*, xxxiv (1983).

Scribner, R. W., 'Civic Unity and the Reformation in Erfurt', *Past and Present*, lxvi (1975).

—— 'Sozialkontrolle und die Möglichkeit einer städtischen Reformation', in Bernd Moeller (ed.), *Stadt und Kirche im 16. Jahrhundert* (Schriften des Vereins für Reformationsgeschichte, cxc) (Gütersloh, 1978).

Sea, Thomas F., 'Imperial Cities and the Peasants' War in Germany', *Central European History*, xii (1979).

Seibert, Peter, *Aufstandsbewegungen in Deutschland 1476–1517 in der zeitgenössischen Reimliteratur* (Reihe Siegen. Beiträge zur Literatur-und Sprachwissenschaft, xi) (Heidelberg, 1978).

Seith, Karl, *Das Markgräflerland und die Markgräfler im Bauernkrieg des Jahres 1525 betrachtet im Rahmen der Bauernbewegung des 16. Jahrhunderts* (Vom Bodensee zum Main, xxviii) (Karlsruhe, 1926).

Skalweit, August, *Das Dorfhandwerk vor Aufhebung des Städtezwangs* (Abhandlungen des Europäischen Handwerks-Instituts, i) (Frankfurt am Main, 1943).

Skinner, G. William, 'Marketing and Social Structure in Rural China', *Journal of Asian Studies*, xxiv (1964–5).

Snyder, C. Arnold, 'Revolution and the Swiss Brethren: The Case of Michael Sattler', *Church History*, l (1981).

Steinmann, Ulrich, 'Die Bundschuh-Fahnen des Joss Fritz', *Deutsches Jahrbuch für Volkskunde*, vi (1960).

Stenzel, Karl, 'Die geistlichen Gerichte Straßburgs im 15. Jahrhundert', *ZGO* NF xxix (1914).

Stolz, Otto, *Geschichtliche Beschreibung der ober- und vorderösterreichischen Lande* (Quellen und Forschungen zur Siedlungs- und Volkstumsgeschichte der Oberrheinlande, iv) (Karlsruhe, 1943).

Strobel, Albrecht, *Agrarverfassung im Übergang. Studien zur Agrargeschichte des badischen Breisgaus vom Beginn des 16. bis zum Ausgang des 18. Jahrhunderts* (Forschungen zur oberrheinischen Landesgeschichte, xxiii) (Freiburg/Munich, 1972).

Stülpnagel, Wolfgang, 'Die Herren von Staufen im Breisgau', *Schau-ins-Land*, lxxvi (1958).

—— 'Herrschaft und Stadt', in *AmtKrB* vol. i. 1.

—— 'Merdingen: Frühere Herrschafts- und Besitzverhältnisse', in *AmtKrB* vol. ii. 2.

—— 'Oberried: Frühere Herrschafts- und Besitzverhältnisse', in *AmtKrB*, vol. ii. 2.

Süss, Rolf, *Heimat am Tuniberg: Opfingen gestern und heute, 1006–1976* (Opfingen, 1976).

Sussann, Hermann, 'Jakob Otter. Ein Beitrag zur Geschichte der Reformation' (Diss. phil. Freiburg, 1892).

Sütterlin, Berthold, *Geschichte Badens*, vol. i, 2nd edn. (Karlsruhe, 1968).

Symposium on Agrarian Class Structure and Economic Development in Pre-Industrial Europe', *Past and Present*, lxxviii (1978); lxxix (1978); lxxx (1978); lxxxv (1979).

Terao, Makoto, 'Rural Small Towns and Market-Towns of *Sachsen*, Central Germany, at the Beginning of the Modern Age', *Keio Economic Studies*, ii (1964).

Thiele, Folkmar, *Die Freiburger Stadtschreiber im Mittelalter* (Veröffentlichungen aus dem Archiv der Stadt Freiburg im Breisgau, xiii) (Freiburg, 1973).

von Thünen, J. H., *Der isolierte Staat in Beziehung auf Landwirtschaft und Nationalökonomie* (Hamburg, 1826).

Ulbrich, Claudia, 'Bäuerlicher Widerstand in Triberg', in Peter Blickle (ed.), *Aufruhr und Empörung? Studien zum bäuerlichen Widerstand im Alten Reich* (Munich, 1980).

—— *Leibherrschaft am Oberrhein im Spätmittelalter* (Veröffentlichungen des Max-Planck-Instituts für Geschichte, lviii) (Göttingen, 1979).

Vogel, Karl, *Geschichte des Zollwesens der Stadt Freiburg i. Br. bis zum Ende des 16. Jahrhunderts* (Abhandlungen zur mittleren und neueren Geschichte, xxxiv) (Berlin/Leipzig, 1911).

Vonau, Jean-Laurent, 'La Guerre des Paysans dans l'Outre-Forêt', in Alphonse Wollbrett (ed.), *La Guerre des Paysans 1525* (Société d'Histoire et d'Archéologie de Saverne et Environs, Études alsatiques, numéro supplémentaire xciii) (Saverne, 1975).

de Vries, Jan, *European Urbanization 1500–1800* (London, 1984).

Weber, Max, 'Die Kirchzartner Geschichte', in Günther Haselier (ed.), *Kirchzarten: Geographie — Geschichte — Gegenwart* (Kirchzarten, 1966).

Weißer, Hubert, 'Verteilung und politischer Einfluß des Vermögens bei den Freiburger Zünften in der ersten Hälfte des 16. Jahrhunderts' (Staatsexamensarbeit, Univ. of Freiburg, 1972).

Wellmer, Martin, *Zur Entstehungsgeschichte der Markgenossenschaften. Der Vierdörferwald bei Emmendingen* (Veröffentlichungen des Oberrheinischen Instituts für geschichtliche Landeskunde Freiburg im Breisgau, iv) (Freiburg, 1938).

—— 'Der vorderösterreichische Breisgau', in Friedrich Metz (ed.), *Vorderösterreich. Eine geschichtliche Landeskunde*, 2nd edn. (Freiburg, 1967).

Wiesflecker, Hermann, *Kaiser Maximilian I. Das Reich, Österreich und Europa an der Wende zur Neuzeit*, vol. i (Munich, 1971).

Williams, Raymond, *The Country and the City* (London, 1973).

Witte, Heinrich, *Die Armagnaken im Elsaß* (Beiträge zur Landes- und Volkskunde von Elsaß-Lothringen, iii. 11) (Strasbourg, 1892).

Wohleb, Joseph Ludolph, 'Bauernkriegsluft um Freiburg. Die Ebringer Kirchweihe von 1495', *Badische Heimat*, xxxix (1959).

Wunder, Heide, 'Serfdom in Later Medieval and Early Modern Germany', in T. H. Aston, P. R. Coss, Christopher Dyer, and Joan Thirsk (eds.), *Social Relations and Ideas. Essays in Honour of R. H. Hilton* (Cambridge, 1983).

Zagorin, Perez, *Rebels and Rulers, 1500–1660*, vol. i: *Society, States, and Early Modern Revolution. Agrarian and Urban Rebellions* (Cambridge, 1982).

Zeumer, Karl, *Die Goldene Bulle Kaiser Karls IV. Entstehung und Bedeutung der Goldenen Bulle* (Quellen und Studien zur Verfassungsgeschichte des Deutschen Reiches in Mittelalter und Neuzeit, ii. 1) (Weimar, 1908).

Index

The Austrian (arch)dukes are listed under the Habsburg dynasty. *Von* precedes the name in the case of noble families, and follows the name as a designation of place of origin.

Aargau, 19, 165
Adelhausen, 38–9, 182, 217 ff., 219 n. 162
Albert, Peter Paul, 197
Allgäu, 155
Allgower, Hans, 107
Allgower, Paule, 107–8
All Saints priory, *see* Freiburg im Breisgau: religious houses, Austin canons
Alsace, 15, 16, 18, 19, 23, 24, 25 n. 33, 26, 61, 62 n. 54, 157, 167, 175 n. 45, 179 n. 59, 181, 182 n. 70, 184, 185, 187, 190, 206, 207, 224, 230–1; *see also* Bundschuh rebellions: Alsatian Bundschuh
Althans, Hans, 221 n. 176
Alto Adige, 178 n. 54
Ambringen, *see Kirchspiel*
Ammann, Hektor, 8–9, 160 n. 27
Andlau, 172
Armagnacs, 31, 166
Armbruster, Fritz, 100 n. 113
Armbruster, Johannes, 213–14
Atten valley, 44, 45 n. 123
Au, 177
Augsburg, 9, 155
Austria, house of, *see* Habsburg dynasty
Austria (territory), 30

Baden, house of, 11, 20, 27–8, 32, 36–7, 40–1, 81, 109 n. 183, 118, 156, 159–60, 177, 186, 217
  margrave Bernhard I, 23, 27, 36
  margrave Christoph, 25 n. 32, 109, 147 n. 137
  margrave Ernst (of Baden-Durlach), 200, 202, 203, 207, 208, 212, 217
  margrave Jakob, 105
  margrave Karl, 24, 29, 33, 34 n. 72, 42 n. 113
  margrave Philipp I (of Baden-Baden), 181, 221

Baden (territory), 18, 26, 36–7, 90, 159–60, 182, 185
Baden-Durlach (territory), 175
Badenweiler, 18–19, 37 n. 86, 90, 91, 115, 159, 207
Bahlingen, 221
Barr, 185
Basel, 10, 11, 17, 18, 64, 115, 126, 156, 158, 167, 217, 220, 227
Basel, bishops of, 166, 167
Bavaria, dukes and duchy of, 20, 24
Bechstein, Jörg, 215, 216 n. 146
Beck zur Muschel, Peter, 212–15, 216
Bergheim, 207
Berne, 156, 157, 167
Betzenhausen, 39–40, 107 n. 165, 177, 178 n. 55, 179 n. 58, 211
Biengen, 118 n. 11, 179, 184
Biezighofen, 177
Bildhower, Theodosius, 181 n. 66
Birken (Dreisam), 211
Birkenreute, 44 n. 114, 45 n. 123
Bitsch-Zweibrücken, counts of, 186
Black Death, 118
Black Forest, 11, 16–18, 20, 25 n. 33, 29 n. 52, 32, 39, 41, 61, 63, 78, 102–5, 115, 118, 157, 172 n. 34, 184, 185, 187, 190, 199, 202, 204, 206, 221, 231, 233
Blickle, Peter, 213, 229
Blienschwiller, 169, 172 n. 34
von Blumeneck family, 90, 92, 93
  Balthasar, 77 n. 1
  Dietrich, 44, 46 n. 124
  Engelhart, 78 n. 2
  Kaspar, 88, 90, 96
  Ludwig, 90, 93
  Martin, 44
  Rudolf, 41 n. 107, 88, 90, 92, 93, 95–6, 98 n. 102
Böblingen, 216
Bohemia, 20, 63, 191

Bohrer, 62
Bollschweil, 177
von Bollschweil, Gabriel, *see* Snewlin: Bärlapp-Bollschweil
Bomer, Alexander, 215, 216 n. 146
Bomer, Blasi, 217–18; *see also* Freiburg im Breisgau: civic unrest, winegrowers
bondage, *see* serfdom
Bräunlingen, 16, 20, 30 n. 52, 157, 231
Bregenz, 20
Breisach, 17, 23, 26, 34, 36, 80 n. 14, 86, 87 n. 34, 92 n. 62, 95, 96, 107, 109, 118, 157, 180–1, 185, 199, 200, 202 n. 62, 204, 209, 212, 215, 220, 231, 233 n. 20
Breisgau, 11, 16–26, 27 ff., 31 ff., 36 ff., 42, 46, 61, 62, 63, 72, 77 ff., 82, 84 ff., 94 ff., 99 n. 106, 102, 107, 110, 113, 116, 125 n. 46, 126, 131, 137, 155, 157, 159–60, 167, 168, 176 ff., 180 ff., 187, 190 ff., 194, 201, 202, 204 ff., 208 ff., 212, 216, 219, 221, 222, 233–5
landgraviate of, 18–19, 78–9
Brenner, Robert, 2, 3 n. 14
Brigach valley, 203
Brisgoicus, Johann, 195
Briswerch, Pauly, 110–11
Britzingen, 159
Bruchsal, 173–5
Bruhrain, 173
Brun, Konrad, 179 n. 58
Brunfels, Otto, 200 n. 44
Brunswick, 42 n. 110
Bücher, Karl, 129 n. 56
Buchheim, 82, 84, 97 n. 97, 178, 211, 212 n. 132; *see also* March villages
Bücking, Jürgen, 231 n. 11
Buitenpoortes, 156; *see also* Flanders
Bulgenbach, 203, 233
Bundschuh rebellions, 95, 96, 98, 166, 167–8, 190, 191, 192, 199, 202, 206, 209–10, 229, 231
Alsatian Bundschuh, 167, 168–73, 174, 177, 183
Lehen Bundschuh, 96, 168, 176–85
Speyer Bundschuh, 167–8, 173–6, 178
Upper Rhine Bundschuh, 168, 180 n. 62, 185–9
Burg (Kirchzarten), 211, 220 n. 167, 224 n. 197
Burgau, 20 n. 17

Burgundy, house of, 26
duke Charles the Bold, 23, 25, 165, 167
Maria (married emperor Maximilian I), 25
occupation of the Upper Rhine, 23–4, 26, 28, 29, 31, 34, 165, 167
Burgundy (territory), 20, 30, 62, 115, 127, 136, 138, 166
Burkheim, 25 n. 33, 34 n. 75, 180, 207

Capito, Wolfgang, 197
central place theory, 4–7, 8–9, 160; *see also* regional studies; urban systems
Cernay, 62 n. 54, 207
Charles IV, emperor, 35, 84
Charles V, emperor, 58 n. 36, 104
Châtenois, 216
China, 6
Christaller, Walter, 4–5; *see also* central place theory
Christian Union of the Black Forest, 194, 205, 207–9, 210, 215, 219, 232–3
Christian Union of Upper Swabia, 206
Cleebourg troop, 230
Cohn, H. J., 167 n. 17
Colmar, 196, 220
Cologne, 6, 9, 64, 94, 130, 182
Common Penny, 70, 115, 124
Confederacy, -ates, *see* Switzerland, Swiss
Constance, bishops of, 109
Hugo von Hohenlandenberg, 191, 196, 210 n. 122
Constance, city, 155, 231 n. 11
Constance, Council of, 19, 165
Constance, diocese of, 191, 234 n. 21
Constance, lake, 16, 69, 166, 190, 206, 209
Counts palatine, *see* Rhineland Palatinate
Coventry, 161–2

Dambach, 170, 172
Dangolsheim, 190
Danube river, 17, 19
Danubian Swabia, *see* Swabia
Decapolis, Alsatian, 187
Denzlingen, 187
Diesbach-Watt merchant company, 114
Disser, Michel, 150 n. 148
Dinkelsbühl, 231
Dinkelsbühl, Michael von, 188
Donaueschingen, 41
Dreisam river and valley, 11, 38, 41–5,

Index

48, 61, 68, 77, 82, 98, 99–102, 103, 105, 157, 194, 204 n. 78, 205, 208, 210–11, 220, 221 n. 77, 223; *see also* Freiburg im Breisgau: Valley Bailiwick
Dryhod, Hans, 107–10

East Germany, *see* Germany, Democratic Republic of
East Midlands, 159 n. 18
Ebnet, 78, 172, 209
Ebringen, 110–13, 178, 202, 204
Ehingen, 20, 157
Ehrenstetten, *see Kirchspiel*
Eichstetten, 159
Einsiedeln, 179 n. 59
Elbe river, 25
Electors palatine, *see* Rhineland Palatinate
Elz valley, 104, 118, 206
Elzach, 34 n. 75, 103 n. 132
Elzach, Hans von, 94
Emmendingen, 107, 118, 159–60
Enderlin, Bernhard, 182
Endingen, 18, 34, 36, 116, 180–1, 200, 203 n. 67, 207
Engelbrecht, Philipp, 194, 195, 197
England, 2, 6, 159 n. 18, 161–2
Ensisheim, 20–3, 25, 28, 29, 108, 112, 172, 185, 192, 200, 201, 203, 205, 220, 224, 225, 226, 227 n. 207
Erasmus of Rotterdam, Desiderius, 30 n. 55, 154, 227–8
Erfurt, 234 n. 23
Eschbach (Breisgau), 202
Eßlingen, 114, 195
Ettenheimmünster, 207
Everitt, Alan, 6
Evil Penny, 24, 29, 115

Falkenstein, 41, 78, 102–3, 119, 205
von Falkenstein, Kaspar, 86
von Falkenstein, Melchior, 99
Fischer, Hans, 212 n. 132
Flamm, Hermann, 124 n. 39, n. 42, 129, 135, 136, 139–40; *see also* Freiburg im Breisgau: protectionism
Flanders, 156, 158
Fleckenstein, Klaus, 187 n. 99, 188 n. 101
Forest Towns, 16, 20, 23, 26, 29 n. 52; *see also* Laufenburg; Rheinfelden; Säckingen; Waldshut
France, 6, 115, 165–6
Franconia, 10, 158, 231

Frankfurt am Main, 62, 64, 107
Franz, Günther, 167, 170
Frauenfeld, Gregorius, 196
Frederick II, emperor, 35 n. 76
Frederick III, emperor, 24, 64 n. 63
Freiburg im Breisgau,
 as capital of the Breisgau, 29
 as Imperial Free City, 27
 as venue for imperial diets, 30
 administration, 27, 32, 48–56, 141 ff.
 Board of the Exchange, 49, 51 n. 13, 53, 55, 63, 100, 142–3, 145–6, 148, 226
 civic unrest, 141–50, 212–19, 232–3; (*see also* gild revolution; wine-growers; Peasants' War)
 competition from countryside, 116–18, 119, 137, 157–60, 183; (*see also* relations with the Breisgau)
 economy, 57, 60–7, 114–41
 economic decline, 58–9, 114–28
 economic recovery, 58, 128–41, 152–4
 gild revolution, 27, 32, 48–50, 129
 gilds, 47 ff., 56–60, 65–6, 67–73, 128 ff., 138 ff., 184, 199, 214–15, 225–7; (*see also* wine growers)
 Old Town, 38, 120, 121, 208
 outburghers, 27, 31–2, 34–8, 50 n. 10, 70, 78–98, 101, 105, 112–13, 131, 155–6, 177–8, 185, 203, 211
 population, 69–72, 116, 123–5, 127–8
 protectionism, 129–31, 135–41, 151–3, 162
 public debt, 27, 52, 56, 115, 125–7, 130, 131, 154, 226
 relations with the Breisgau, 7, 10–12, 31 ff., 61–3, 77 ff., 102–13, 131, 155 ff., 229–30, 232–3
 religious houses, 116, 121–3, 131, 133–5, 195, 202
  Austin canons, 134, 196
  Carthusians, 133–4, 197
  Dominicans, 28 n. 45, 133–4, 226
  Franciscans, 134
 suburbs, 38–9, 68; (*see also* Adelhausen; Lehen suburb; Neuburg suburb; Prediger suburb; Schnecken suburb; Wiehre)
 territorial expansion, 31, 39–46, 98–102, 126, 210
 town council, *see* administration
 Valley Bailiwick, 44–5, 61, 82, 100–1, 131, 137, 157, 194, 204, 209,

Freiburg im Breisgau (*cont.*)
210–11, 220–2, 223; (*see also* Dreisam river and valley)
wine-growers, 48, 57, 59, 67–8, 145, 152, 183, 199, 203 n. 67, 216, 217–19, 227, 232–3; (*see also* civic unrest; Peasants' War)
Freiburg castle, 18, 28 n. 45, 208, 213
Freiburg, counts of, 17–19, 32, 34, 35, 39
count Egon, 18, 19, 26–7, 32, 36, 78, 115
count Konrad, 19
Freiburg university, 28, 71, 124, 128, 135, 160, 194–6, 198
Freiburg im Uchtland, *see* Fribourg
French Revolution, 7
Freudenstadt, 187
Fribourg, 137 n. 92, 157
Frick valley, 204
Fritz, Joss, 173–88; *see also* Bundschuh rebellions
von Frundsberg, Georg, 188 n. 105
Fry, Peter, 211, 223
Fürstenberg, house of, 22, 40, 44, 99, 186
count Heinrich, 98
Furtwangen, 103, 104, 118

Gallenweiler, 37 n. 86, 82, 97, 211
Geiler von Kaysersberg, Johann, 191, 197
Geneva, 64
German Peasants' War, *see* Peasants' War
Germany, Democratic Republic of, 7
Germany, Federal Republic of, 7
Geroldstal, 45
Gerson, Jean, 197
geschichtliche Landeskunde, *see* regional studies
Gesellschaft zum Gauch, 71
Gesellschaft zum Ritter, 32, 70
Ghent, 156 n. 7
Glarus, 194
Glotter valley, 17, 105, 177
Golden Bull, 35, 84, 85
Grien, Hans Baldung, 154
Gundelfingen, 106–7, 217, 232
Günter, Michel, 217
Günterstal, 62
Günzburg, 20 n. 17
Gutach river, 104

Habsburg dynasty, 11, 15–20, 23, 25, 27, 28, 35, 37, 38 n. 92, 39, 40, 49, 85, 115, 165, 217

archduke Albrecht of Tirol, 28, 37 n. 87, 38 n. 92, 52–4, 58, 67
archduke Ferdinand, later king and emperor, 197, 198, 199, 217, 220–1, 222–3, 224–6, 228
archduke Frederick, *see* Frederick III, emperor
duke Frederick IV of Tirol, 19, 21 n. 19, 23, 51, 165
duke Leopold, 49, 50
archduke Maximilian, *see* Maximilian I, emperor
duke Rudolf, German king, 15, 17
archduke Sigismund, 23–6, 29, 30, 33–4, 38 n. 92, 54, 87 n. 34, 92, 103, 108, 121, 125 n. 46, 132 n. 61, 142, 165
see also Outer Austria
Hachberg, 105, 159, 207, 209 n. 117, 216
Hachberg, margraves of, 17–19
margrave Otto, 18
Haguenau, 187, 188, 189 n. 107, 230
Haguenau, imperial bailiwick of, 175 n. 45, 186, 187
Haimlich, Ulrich, 217
Haimlichin, Agatha, 215, 217 n. 155
von Halfingen, Konrad, 44, 45 n. 123, 46 n. 124
von Hallwil, Thüring, 34 n. 72
Han, Hans, 134
Hanau-Lichtenberg, counts of, 186
Hanseatic League, 9
Hanser, Jakob, 169–70, 171 n. 26, 178, 184
Hanser, Michael, 181
Has, Caspar, 147
Haslach (Freiburg), 37 n. 86, 40, 177
Hauenstein, 16, 20, 25 n. 33
Hegau, 166, 220
Heilbronn, 231
Heitersheim, 62, 89, 139, 202, 204, 207, 221
Henry VII, German king, *see* Hohenstaufen, dukes and duchy of
Herdern, 40, 42, 98–9, 210
Hieronymus, 178 n. 54
Himmelreich, 44, 45 n. 123
Hintersassen, 78–9, 84–8, 92–3, 96, 101–2
Hochberg, *see* Hachberg
Hochdorf, 178 n. 55
Hoff, Marx, 64
Hofsgrund, 45, 114
Hohenberg, 20 n. 17

Hohenstaufen, dukes and duchy of, 15
Henry VII, German king, 35 n. 76
Höllental, 41, 44, 102
Holzhausen, 178 n. 55
Hoppe, Göran, *see* Langton, John
Horb, 191
Hornberg, 104
Hoskins, W. G., 6
Hospitallers, *see* Knights of St John
Hubmaier, Balthasar, 206
Hug, 147
Hugstetten, 178 n. 55
Humel, Hans, 182
von Hürnheim, Wolf, 187 n. 96, 200–1, 202 n. 59; *see also* Kenzingen
Huser, Jakob, 181
Hussite doctrines, 199

Ihringen, 90
Innocent IV, pope, 124 n. 40
Innsbruck, 20, 92, 103, 192, 222, 224
Isny, 155
Italy, 64, 188 n. 105

Japan, 6
Jerusalem, 166, 179 n. 58
John XXIII, antipope, 19

Kaiserstuhl, 82, 178, 192, 207
Kappel valley, 44, 191
Karsthans, 191
Kastelberg, 17
Kaysersberg, 190, 191
Kempf, Diebold, 196
Kempten, 155
Kenzingen, 17, 34 n. 75, 187, 192, 194 ff., 199–202, 207, 212, 231 n. 12
Kindhans, Ulrich, 211, 216 n. 146, 220 n. 167, 224 n. 197
Kinzig river and valley, 104, 114
Kirchhofen, *see* Kirchspiel
Kirchspiel, 82, 91, 97, 112, 204, 211, 221
Kirchzarten, 42, 44–5, 46 n. 124, 100, 194, 204, 207, 210, 211, 219, 220, 221 n. 176, 223
Knights of St John, 62, 89, 91, 92, 93–4, 207
Köndringen, 107–9
von Kranznau, Konrad, 92, 94
Krieg, Blesy, 210, 223
Krozingen, 82 n. 19, 89, 92, 94, 204, 206
Kuder, Johannes, 191

Kürnberg, 17, 187 n. 96

von Landeck, for entries under this name *see* Snewlin-Landeck
Langton, John, and Hoppe, Göran, 1–4
Laufenburg, 16, 204 n. 74, 205, 219 n. 165
Lehen suburb, 68, 120
Lehen (Breisgau), 96, 107 n. 165, 176–9, 182, 183
Leutersberg, 37 n. 86, 177
von Lichtenfels, Hans, 97
von Lichtenfels, Wilhelm, 81, 88–9, 97
Liège, 62
Limburg (Sasbach), 16 n. 5, 216, 222
von Lindau, Ulrich, 93
Lombardy, 63
London, 62
Lonitzer, Johann, 194
Lorraine, duke Anthony of, 216
Lösch, August, 4
Lower Alsace, *see* Alsace
Lower Union, 165
Lucerne, 48, 137 n. 92, 156, 157–8
Luther, Martin, 194, 195, 196, 197
Lutheran doctrines, 192, 194, 196, 198, 199
Luxemburg dynasty, 20

Mainz, 130 n. 57
Malines, 62
Malterdingen, 102 n. 126, 118, 159, 200, 201
March villages, 88, 178, 211; *see also* Buchheim
Markgräflerland, 204, 207, 224
Marx, Karl, 1
Maximilian I, emperor, 24–5, 29 n. 52, 30, 37, 40–1, 45–6, 56, 64, 70, 89 n. 40, 94, 95, 97, 103 n. 139, 120 n. 27, 125 n. 46, 133–4, 142, 147, 150, 154, 175 n. 45, 177, 179 n. 57, 191, 198, 227; *see also* Habsburg dynasty
Megerich, Jakob, 146–7
Meiger, Kilian, 177, 181
Memmingen, 231
Mengen, 177, 178, 182
Menly, Hans, 146
Mentz, Hans, 211
Merano, 24, 29 n. 49
Merdingen, 82, 88, 90, 92, 93, 95–6, 112, 113, 177, 178
Merzhausen, 177

Metzger, Hans, 150
Mittelbergheim, 187
Molsheim, 185
Montbéliard, 180 n. 62
von Mörsberg, Kaspar, 94, 149
Mühlburg, treaty of, 27, 36, 86
Mulhouse, 33
Müller, Burkart, 145
Müller, Gregorius, 216
Müller, Hans, 203, 205–6, 207, 209, 215, 219, 232–3
Münster valley, 17, 202–3, 205, 206
Müntzer, Thomas, 232
Munzingen, 177
Murer, Hans, 191–2

Napoleonic Wars, 15
Naujoks, Eberhard, 56
Nellenburg, 20 n. 17
Neuburg suburb, 38, 68, 120
Neuenburg, 17, 29, 34, 36, 192, 200 n. 44, 203, 204, 207 n. 105, 231
von Neuenfels, Christoph, 89
von Neuenfels, Hansmichael, 90, 92, 94
Neuershausen, 81, 88, 89 n. 38, 95, 97
Neustadt (Black Forest), 41, 103 n. 132, 206, 215
Newcastle, 162 n. 35
Niederreute, 178 n. 55
Niederrimsingen, 92 n. 62, 204, 224 n. 202
Nördlingen, 231
Norsingen, 177
Nottingham, 162 n. 35
Nuremberg, 8, 9, 10, 63

Obergrombach, 174
Obermundat, 182, 189 n. 108
Obernai, 170, 186, 231
Obernheim, Konrad, 132 n. 62
Oberreute, 178 n. 55
Oberried, 44–5, 100 n. 113, 210, 211, 223
Oberschaffhausen, 82, 92, 94
Offenburg, 114, 217, 219, 220, 221–2
Öhlinsweiler, 86 n. 30
Öler, Ludwig, 196, 198
Opfingen, 40
Ortenau, 207, 224
Otter, Jakob, 195, 200–1; *see also* Kenzingen
Outer Austria, 11, 20–6, 27–30, 31, 46, 92, 95, 142, 155, 159, 165, 192, 198, 203, 224–5, 231; *see also* Breisgau; Habsburg dynasty
Outer lands, *see* Outer Austria

Peasants' War, 7, 11–12, 34, 98, 110, 113, 151, 166, 169 n. 17, 171, 187, 188, 189, 192, 194, 199–224, 227, 228, 229–35
    as 'revolution of the common man', 25, 229–35
Pfaffenweiler, 86 n. 30
von Pfirt, Ludwig, 90
Pforzheim, 176
Philippsburg, *see* Udenheim
Phythian-Adams, Charles, 161
Pirenne, Henri, 1
Poor Konrad revolt, 182 n. 70
Postan, M. M., 1
Prech valley, 103, 105 n. 147
Prediger suburb, 68, 120
proto-industrialization, 3–4, 158, 161
putting-out system, 7, 9, 10, 137, 158

Radolfzell, 219
Raiser, Elisabeth, 100
Rapp, Konrad, 99
Rapp, Peter, 99
von Rappoltstein, Wilhelm, junior, 202, 204, 206
von Rappoltstein, Wilhelm, senior, 108–9
Reformatio Sigismundi, 84 n. 23
Reformation, 34, 189, 191 ff., 199 ff., 228, 232–3
regional studies, 6–11; *see also* central place theory; urban systems
Rehar, Claus, 197, 262
Reisch, Gregor, 197
von Reischach, Jopp, 211
Rheinfelden, 16, 29 n. 52, 198 ff.
Rhine river, 17, 19, 20, 26, 29, 39, 41, 172, 175, 179 n. 59, 180, 182, 186, 203, 204, 206, 216, 224, 231
Rhineland, 6
Rhineland Palatinate, 63, 176
    count Frederick, 42 n. 113
    electors, 23, 27, 34 n. 72, 42, 176
Ribeauvillé, 231
Riedlingen, 157
Riquewihr, 231
Rohde, Hans-Wilhelm, 195 n. 26
Rohr valley, 105 n. 150
Rome, 134
Rösch, Konrad, 147